Making Policy in Europe

second edition

edited by

Svein S. Andersen and Kjell A. Eliassen

SAGE Publications

London • Thousand Oaks • New Delhi

Editorial arrangement and material, Chapter 1, Chapter 3 and
Chapter 12 © Svein S. Andersen and Kjell A. Eliassen 2001
Chapter 2 © Svein S. Andersen, Kjell A. Eliassen and
Nick Sitter 2001
Chapter 4 © Frank Dobbin 2001
Chapter 5 © Kjell A. Eliassen and Marit S. Marino 2001
Chapter 6 © Svein S. Andersen 2001
Chapter 7 © Erik Beukel 2001
Chapter 8 © Ellen Ahnfelt and Johan From 2001
Chapter 9 © Miriam L. Campanella 2001
Chapter 10 © Helene Sjursen 2001
Chapter 11 © Finn Laursen 2001

First published 1993
Reprinted 1994, 1998
Second edition 2001

SAGE Publications Ltd
6 Bonhill Street
London EC2A 4PU

SAGE Publications Inc
2455 Teller Road
Thousand Oaks, California 91320

SAGE Publications India Pvt Ltd
32, M-Block Market
Greater Kailash – I
New Delhi 110 048

British Library Cataloguing in Publication Data

A catalogue record for this book is
available from the British Library

ISBN 0 7619 6750 8
ISBN 0 7619 6751 6 (pbk)

Library of Congress catalog card number 00 135055

Typeset by Keystroke, Jacaranda Lodge, Wolverhampton.
Printed in Great Britain by The Cromwell Press Ltd, Trowbridge, Wiltshire

Making Policy in Europe

CONTENTS

3 The Future of the EU and European Integration

NOTES ON THE CONTRIBUTORS

Professor Svein S. Andersen is director of ARENA (Advanced Research on the Europeanization of the Nation-State), University of Oslo, and also a professor at the Norwegian School of Management. He holds a Ph.D. in sociology from Stanford University. He has published 10 books and numerous articles. Working within the area of comparative institutions and institutional theory his empirical studies have focused on issues relating to energy and the EU. He also has an interest in research method. His last book was about the possibilities of generalizing from case-studies. He has been a visiting professor at several European and American universities, among them Centre des Hautes Etudes in Paris, UC Berkeley and UC Santa Barbara.

Kjell A. Eliassen is a professor of Public Management and director of the Centre for European and Asian Studies at the Norwegian School of Management – BI in Oslo – and professor of European Studies at The Free University in Brussels. He has published 12 books and several articles on European and Asian Affairs. His latest book is *European Telecom Liberalisation* (1999). He has been a visiting professor at several European, American and Asian universities. During the last three years he has built up a part-time Master of Management programme in Infocom in Asia, in co-operation with leading Asian universities, representing the Norwegian School of Management. He has been working closely with the Fudan University in Shanghai and the Chulalongkorn University in Thailand both within research and the development of management training programmes.

Ellen Ahnfelt, is a senior advisor on international police co-operation in the Norwegian Ministry of Justice. She worked as a researcher at the Center for European and Asian Studies at the Norwegian School of Management, Oslo during the period 1990–95. She has published several articles and a book on European police co-operation and EU integration. She is Cand. Polit. from the University of Oslo, 1986.

Erik Beukel is dr. scient. pol. and Associate Professor in the Department of Political Science and Public Management at the University of Southern Denmark, Odense, where he also holds the Jean Monnet Chair in European Political Integration. He has written on issues concerning global environmental protection as a collective good, European integration, the evolving regimes in post-cold-war Europe, and the political economy of the trade and environment nexus. Previous research was in the area of arms control and American and Soviet nuclear policies. He has been a Visiting Scholar at the Center for Strategic and International Studies, Georgetown University, the Center for International Affairs, Harvard University, and Institute of International Relations, The University of British Columbia.

Miriam L. Campanella is a lecturer in International Political Economy at the Faculty of Political Science, University of Turin and holds a Jean Monnet 'Permanent Course' on 'EMU: Policies and Institutions'. She has studied at the Centre for International Studies, at MIT (1980–86) and has taught as Fulbright Professor at the Department of Political Science, University of Pittsburgh. Centring on the consequences of globalization for nation-states, her research field has shifted towards regional integration in Europe. Since 1994, her research programme has focused on the potential of neo-institutionalism in EMU policies and institutions. Her publications include: 'Getting the core. A neo-institutionalist approach to EMU' (1995); 'Central Eastern European enlargement and the EU budget policy. A strategic agenda-setter for joint (Pareto-improving) gains' (1998).

Frank Dobbin is Professor of Sociology at Princeton University. His *Forging Industrial Policy: The United States, Britain and France in the Railway Age* (Cambridge University Press, 1994), which explores the origins of national industrial strategies, won the Max Weber Award from the Organizations, Occupations, and Work section of the American Sociological Association. He has been exploring how antitrust law shaped American business strategy (most recently with Timothy Dowd in 'The market that antitrust built', *American Sociological Review*, 2000, and how national institutions shape the workplace (most recently with Terry Boychuk in 'Job autonomy and national employment systems', *Organization Studies*, 1999).

Johan From is Head of Department, Department of Public Governance at the Norwegian School of Management – BI in Oslo. He holds a Ph.D. from the University of Sussex, Sussex European Institute in Contemporary European Studies. He has published books on EU competition policy and public monopolies, police co-operation and European integration, and the impact of EU policy-making on local governments.

Finn Laursen holds a Ph.D. (Political Science) from the University of Pennsylvania (1980) and cand. scient. pol. from Aarhus University (1974). Currently Professor of International Politics at the University of Southern Denmark, Odense, he has also held positions at the London School of Economics (1985–88), the European Institute of Public Administration, Maastricht (1988–95). His current research is focused upon various aspects of European integration and EU external relations. Major works include *The Ratification of the Maastricht Treaty* (Nijhoff, 1994), both co-edited with Sophie Vanhoonacker.

Nick Sitter is an Associate Professor in the Department of International Relations and European Studies at the Central European University in Budapest, where he teaches EU politics and comparative West European politics. He holds a Ph.D. from the London School of Economics and Political Science, and worked for five years as a political consultant in London.

Marit S. Marino is a Ph.D. student at the London School of Economics. She has a Master of Science degree from the Norwegian School of Management and a B.Sc. in Natural Sciences from the University of Oslo, Norway, and Université de Caen, France. Her main research interests include regulation, European telecommunications policy, comparative public policy, French and German politics, and security policy. Her latest publications are *European Telecommunications Liberalisation* (as a co-editor with Kjell A. Eliassen, 1999).

Helene Sjursen is a Senior Researcher at ARENA (Advanced Research on the Europeanization of the Nation-State), University of Oslo. She has previously been a lecturer in Politics at University College Dublin and at Glasgow University. She holds a Ph.D. in international relations from the London School of Economics. Her main research interests are in the Europeanization of foreign policies and EU enlargement. Previous publications include *A Common Foreign Policy for Europe? Competing Visions of the CFSP*, co-edited with John Peterson (Routledge, 1998).

PREFACE

This volume is a new edition of a book published seven years ago on policy-making in Europe, focusing on the Europeanization of national policy-making. Our approach differed from the foreign policy and formal legal perspectives in emphasizing the totality of the European Union's institutions and the political system. Today, this perspective is more widely used, and the focus on Europeanization of member states' policy-making process is common to most studies.

In this book we have tried to asses the functioning and the present policy-making process of the EU, at a time when the Union has accomplished many of its last decennium goals, and when even a common foreign and security policy could become more than a vision. At the same time, we find ourselves at a point when the EU is confronted by the challenge of a far-reaching expansion to the east which may ultimately increase the number of member states to around thirty. Thus, this volume reflects both the present state of affairs and the different dimensions of the internal and external tasks ahead.

The book contains both completely revised versions of the majority of the chapters in the previous edition and a couple of new chapters reflecting the new developments within the Union, the establishment of the European Monetary Union and the revitalization of the Common Foreign and Security Policy.

We would like to thank a number of people for their help in the development of this second edition. They include Yansong Wen and Grete Haug, both employed at the Centre for European and Asian Studies at the Norwegian School of Management – BI in Oslo.

However, the book project would not have been possible at all without the help and continuous encouragement of Maria Andredaki. She has both assisted the editors in all aspects of the editing and has been the most demanding editor of our own contributions. We express our heartfelt thanks.

Svein S. Andersen   Kjell A. Eliassen

LIST OF ABBREVIATIONS

ACP	Africa, the Caribbean and the Pacific
APT	Advanced Passenger Transport (British rail project)
ARENA	Advanced Research on the Europeanization of the Nation State
BEUC	European Bureau of Consumers' Unions
BR	British Rail
CAP	Common Agricultural Policy
CEECs	central and eastern European countries
CEPT	European Conference of Postal and Telecommunications Administrations
CFSP	Common Foreign and Security Policy
CJTF	Combined Joint Task Forces
COMETT	Community Programme for Education and Training in Technology
COREPER	Committee of Permanent Representatives
CPE	customer premises equipment (telecommunications)
DG	Directorate General
EC	European Community
ECB	European Central Bank
ECJ	European Court of Justice
ECMT	European Conference of Ministers of Transport
ECOFIN	European Council of Finance Ministers
ECSC	European Coal and Steel Community
Ecu	European Currency Unit
EDC	European Defence Community
EDIU	European Drugs Intelligence Unit
EDU	Europol Drugs Unit
EEA	European Economic Area
EEB	European Environmental Bureau
EFTA	European Free Trade Association
EIB	European Investment Bank
EMU	Economic and Monetary Union / European Monetary Union
EP	European Parliament
EPC	European Political Co-operation
ERASMUS	European Community Action Scheme for the Mobility of University Students
ERM	Exchange Rate Mechanism
ESC	Economic and Social Council
ESDI	European Security and Defence Identity
ESPRIT	European Strategic Programme for Research and Development in Information Technology

ETUC	European Trade Union Confederation
EU	European Union
GATT	General Agreement on Tariffs and Trade
GSM	Global Systems for Mobile Communications
IGC	Intergovernmental Conference
IR	international relations
ITU	International Telecommunications Union
LINGUA	Language and Training Programme
OECD	Organization for Economic Co-operation and Development
ONP	Open Network Provision
PHARE	Poland and Hungary: Aid for the Restructuring of Economies
PTT	Post, Telegraph and Telephone administration
QMV	Qualified Majority Voting
RACE	Research and Development in Advanced Communications
SEA	Single European Act
SNCF	Société Nationale des Chemins de Fer (French rail administration)
SOEC	Statistical Office of the European Communities
TAIEX	Technical Assistance Information Exchange Office
TEU	Treaty on European Union
TGV	Train à Grande Vitesse (French high-speed train)
TREVI	Terrorisme, Radicalisme, Extrémisme, Violence, Information (Agreement on Police Co-operation)
UCLAF	Unit for the Co-ordination of Fraud Prevention
UIC	Union Internationale des Chemins de fer (international rail administration)
VANS	value added network services
WEU	West European Union
WTO	World Trade Organization

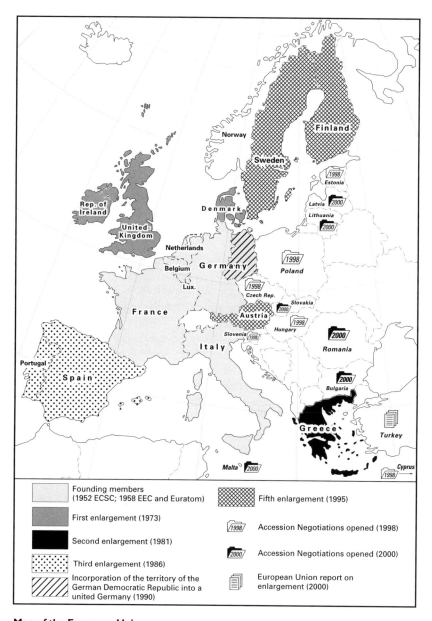

Founding members
(1952 ECSC; 1958 EEC and Euratom)

First enlargement (1973)

Second enlargement (1981)

Third enlargement (1986)

Incorporation of the territory of the
German Democratic Republic into a
united Germany (1990)

Fifth enlargement (1995)

Accession Negotiations opened (1998)

Accession Negotiations opened (2000)

European Union report on
enlargement (2000)

Map of the European Union

PART I

POLICY-MAKING IN THE EUROPEAN UNION

CHAPTER I

INTRODUCTION:
THE EU AS A NEW POLITICAL SYSTEM

Svein S. Andersen and Kjell A. Eliassen

Towards an Ever Closer Union

This book does *not* try to answer the questions of why and how the European Union (EU) develops in a certain direction. We will mainly focus upon decisions on policy-making and legislation in important sectors within the EU system. The book is a contribution to the under-standing of the unique character of EU policy-making. Within general perspectives on comparative politics and political organization the EU represents a new type of complex, multi-level and loosely coupled decision-making and implementation where processes often have strong elements of informal influence. It might be regarded as an experiment with new types of political structure (Laffan et al. 1999). During the 1990s, EU decision-making has increased in scope, depth and volume. The introduction of the Euro, the revitalization of the Common Foreign and Security Policy (CFSP), the new dynamics of the enlargement process, and the increased importance of EU citizen-rights and values have created new challenges for the study of EU policy-making. This is reflected in a growing number of contributions that have been pursuing such ideas in various ways (Richardson 1996, Wallace and Wallace 2000, Hix 1999, Peterson and Bomberg 1999).

Since the mid-1980s the EU has gone through radical changes. There has been a persistent development towards deepening of integration and expansion of the scope of EU-level policy-making (Middlemas 1995). We can roughly distinguish three major stages, as follows.

The first stage was the realization of the single European market and the Maastricht agreement. The Single European Act marked a definite change in the pace of European integration (Hix 1999: 211–40). It introduced two key elements: a common market and majority voting. In addition it increased the influence of the European Parliament and established a European Political Co-operation (EPC) linked to the EU. The implementation of the internal market from the 1980s was an unprecedented success. The Euro-optimism created by this success led to the next step in the process of integration, namely the Maastricht Treaty revision.

The second stage was characterized by increased scepticism to the Maastricht ideas. Several factors, including a slowdown in the economies of the member states, in the following years lead to economic stagnation and considerable pessimism concerning the implementation of the revisions of the Maastricht Treaty. This was particularly true for the two main achievements in the Maastricht accord, namely the plans for the realization of European Monetary Union (EMU) (Gros and Thygesen 1998, Notermans 1998) and the establishment of the CFSP (Peterson and Sjursen 1998, Eliassen 1998).

The third stage was the renewed dynamism of the late 1990s. In 1997 (for the EMU) and 1998 (for the CFSP) the aims of the Maastricht accord were accomplished. On the other hand, the Amsterdam Treaty revision, which was planned for in the Maastricht Treaty, failed to solve the institutional problems relating to future enlargement: i.e. the size and composition of the Commission, the role and composition of the Presidency, and distributions of votes and voting rules in the Council (Laurent and Maresceau 1998). The big challenge is how to deal with enlargement and how this will influence EU's architecture.

The basic question after the fall of the Berlin Wall was whether it was possible to have deepening together with widening of the membership base (Wessels 1996). Since Greece was admitted in 1981 and after the accession of Spain and Portugal in 1986, three new members had joined (in 1995; Austria, Finland and Sweden). The entrance of these members coincided with a new period of EU dynamics – even in the area of the CFSP, which was considered to be problematic for these former neutral countries. Presently more than a dozen countries are in a dialogue with the EU with a view to acquiring membership in two planned rounds of enlargement. The first five or six countries may join within a few years time (Laursen 1997, Maresceau 1997). This may induce the remaining European Free Trade Association (EFTA) countries to reconsider membership.

The time frame for the next rounds of enlargement is somewhat uncertain. The first new members may join between 2003 and 2005 but the timetable is not fixed. The Kosovo war has opened the way for a more active EU policy on the Balkans, and this may lead to a more rapid inclusion of these countries in the European family. It is not unlikely that the EU in 10 years may have 25–30 member states (Andersen 1999).

The enlargement to the east differs from earlier expansions of the EU in three ways. First, previous candidate countries had to fulfil certain pre-entry requirements concerning economic and political development (possibly with the exception of Greece). The present enlargement is motivated by the wish to create such conditions in future member countries. Second, earlier expansions had the character of adding to a core set of member states, whereas the present process aims at doubling the number and redefining the concept of Europe. Third, in earlier rounds the problem was often that the new members were reluctant to accept new commitments. In the ongoing enlargement the present member states are reluctant to extend all commitments to new members in the short term. It was considered necessary to have institutional reform in place before the accession of the first group of new entrants, but this was postponed in Amsterdam. The EU has, however, decided to try to solve the institutional problems well ahead of the entry of the first new members, by a mini institutional conference before the end of the year 2000.

A prime motivation for the creation of the original EU (the EEC in 1957) was to prevent war in Europe, by binding together Germany and France. The EEC consisted of three treaties. The Coal and Steel Community aimed at controlling the basic and contested resources. The Atomic Energy Community was to transform the potentially deadly technology into a means used for peaceful civil purposes. And finally, the European Economic Community emphasized economic co-operation as a way to prevent war. This process was also linked to the efforts through the Marshall Plan to rebuild Europe after the war. Behind it there was a vision of a united Europe, and this made the establishment of supranational institutions a necessity. The Cold War limited the scope of European integration to western Europe.

After a period of stagnation and a so-called Eurosclerosis in the EEC, the 1980s witnessed a revitalization of the integration process. A strong need was felt to make European industry competitive in global markets. The internal market was regarded as a precondition for the European multinational companies to be able to compete with American and Japanese firms. The success of the internal market made it possible to return to historical ambitions for a deepening of the integration in western Europe. From the early 1990s the EU integration has been dominated by two major concerns. The first is to deepen and widen the scope of the internal EU-integration. The second is to strengthen the role of the EU as an international economic and political actor. This was symbolized by the Maastricht Treaty

The Maastricht Treaty was mainly a product of optimism among politicians and industry leaders (Duff et al. 1994). Nevertheless, the concept of a union was, at first, well received by a large majority of the voters. After the Treaty was signed by the Heads of States and Governments in December 1991, political leaders, to their surprise, experienced considerable scepticism among the public. The total lack of parliamentary debate at the national level, prior to the negotiation on the plans for a European Union, caused a great deal of uncertainty in the member countries. The problems were manifested in the narrow Danish rejection of the Maastricht Treaty in the June 1992 referendum. Nevertheless, it was accepted later with a few reservations.

The implementation of the European Union involved two types of

change. Traditional EC co-operation would become wider and deeper.
The widening meant that the EC would get involved in several new areas
of policy-making, and the deepening meant increased power in existing
areas as well as a strengthening of the competence of the EC institutions
in relation to national governments. These changes would also affect
the distribution of power and tasks among the central EC institutions.
One of the most important elements of supranational authority in the
Treaty was the increased importance of majority voting in the Council
of Ministers. At the same time, the competence and role of the European
Parliament were to be strengthened in the decision-making process,
including the introduction of a right of veto in several areas (Nugent
1999b).

The European Union after the Maastricht Treaty established a
so-called three-pillar structure and introduced several new policy areas.
The first pillar was built around the traditional EEC economic
co-operation with supranational EU institutions involved. The two new
pillars were based on intergovernmental decision-making. Among
the new areas introduced, three were more important in terms of
institutional implications, as follows.

The first was Economic and Monetary Union (EMU) which was
included in the first pillar, but with a high degree of autonomy. It
established a strong element of supranationality and a new EC institution, a common Central European Bank. These factors would reduce
the role and influence of both the EC Commission and the member states
in these matters.

The second area was the EPC, which was now included in the formal
EU structure as the 'second pillar' under a new name, the Common
Foreign and Security Policy. In this area the Council not only made
decisions on the basis of unanimity, but also played a more dominant
role in preparing decisions. The weak institutional basis created
problems when the EU faced serious foreign and security issues.

The third area was co-operation in the spheres of justice, police and
home affairs. This co-operation was established as the third pillar on
the same institutional basis as the second. This policy was considered
necessary as a consequence of the full implementation of the four
freedoms in the internal market. Again, it turned out that a weak
institutional structure created problems of realizing intended policies.

All these three new key policy areas created problems for Denmark,
and two of them for Britain. In Britain there seemed to exist a general
scepticism towards a stronger supranational authority in the EU. The
most controversial issue was the EMU.

Furthermore, the Treaty incorporated a protocol on the 'Social
Community', which regulated the co-operation between eleven member
states, not including the United Kingdom. Both on the EMU issue and
on that of the Social Community, the British opted out during the

Maastricht negotiations. The Social protocol was initially meant as a deepening of the traditional EC co-operation, but because of resistance from Britain the Community had to make special arrangements. The protocol incorporating the Social Charter was an intergovernmental agreement, but it would be operational within the Community bodies.

The Maastricht treaty was negotiated in a period of 'Euro-optimism' after the success of the Single Market. The implementation in the first years of the 1990s took place in a period with the European economies in recession and with a growing popular scepticism towards the European project in most of the member states. This was also reflected in the problems of ratification, with a rejection at the first referendum in Denmark, a slim majority in the referendum in France and a divided population in Germany and Britain.

The uncertainty regarding the implementation of the Treaty had three major aspects:

1 Would all member states commit themselves to the Treaty?
2 To what extent and how fast would the Treaty be implemented?
3 What would be the next step on the road towards a United Europe?

The first question was settled by October 1993. The Treaty was finally ratified, with the United Kingdom and Denmark being granted the opt-outs that they required, a thin majority in France, and Germany, one of the main promoters, being the last to ratify it.

The prevailing Euro-pessimism in the beginning of the 1990s reduced the room for EU activism and put constraints on efforts to realize the intention of the Maastricht treaty. Rather than focusing on deepening, the discussion of subsidiarity directed attention towards possible limitation to solve problems at the EU level. Instead of vigorous attempts at further deepening, the first half of the decade was dominated by the completion of the European Economic Area agreement bringing the EFTA countries (apart from Switzerland) into the Internal Market and later the inclusion of three EFTA countries as full EU members on 1 January 1995.

The realization of all the three main new areas in the Maastricht Treaty was plagued by uncertainty and serious implementation problems. The CFSP arrangement was unable to handle the foreign and security policy challenges confronting the EU. This general inability of action co-ordinated through the EU became particularly clear in relation to the developments in the former Yugoslavia. The third pillar had some similar problems of efficiency. In addition, the Europeanization of these functions was not followed by European-level parliamentary super-vision and the control of the European High Court of Justice.

The successful implementation of the EMU was questioned for two reasons. The first had to do with the willingness of the countries to support a reform of this nature, and the second had to do with the ability of the individual countries to fulfil the economic performance criteria for membership. However, all member states except Greece were finally able to fulfil these criteria at the second deadline on 1 January 1999. This was due to a combination of tight financial discipline, new accounting methods providing certain flexibility, and an upswing in the business circle (Sverdrup 1998). Still, not all the countries that qualified wanted to join the EMU at this stage. Britain and Denmark held reservations, and Sweden, when becoming a member of the EU, had deliberately not joined the European Exchange Rate Mechanism, fulfilling only one of the criteria for being granted membership.

The last few years of the 1990s presented several challenges, some due to the problems of the Maastricht Treaty, and some due to the foreseen problems of expansion to the east, i.e. the need for budgetary and institutional reform.

Already in 1991 it had become evident that the fall of the Berlin Wall and the gradual introduction of democracy and market economy in central and eastern Europe would open the way for 15 to 20 countries qualified for and very interested in joining the European Union. The institutional structure of the EU created in 1957 for six member countries had basically been kept unchanged even with the extension to 12 members. There existed, however, no possibility to develop the new structures in the early 1990s and article N of the Maastricht Treaty had already provided for another intergovernmental conference in 1996.

The new Intergovernmental Conference in 1996–97, resulting in the Amsterdam Treaty, did not solve these problems either. Again it was proven that institutional reform of the EU is extremely troublesome. There was, however, agreement on a few changes. The maximum number of members of the European Parliament was fixed and there was a limited extension to qualified majority voting in the Council. On the two most important, but also most difficult, issues – the size of the College of Commissioners and the voting strength in the council – a small new Intergovernmental Conference (IGC) will take place in 2000 aimed at resolving them. A new governing structure has to be found before several new members are allowed to enter the Union. Other issues that could come on the table at the IGC are: extension of majority voting, the strengthening of the CFSP, integrating the West European Union into the EU, and the extension of citizen rights.

In addition to the revisions required under the Amsterdam Treaty, there are several other challenges that have to be resolved before the first wave of enlargement. One of the most difficult concerns the EU budget. This has been a problem for some time and will be even more difficult after enlargement. A key controversy involves the Common Agricultural Policy (CAP) and structural policies. The Agenda 2000 programme agreed in March 1999 in Berlin only partly resolved the budgetary issues. Especially, the changes to agricultural policies were less radical than the Commission thought necessary to meet the challenges of enlargement.

The next main challenge for the EU is the expansion of the Union in several phases over the next 10 years or more, with perhaps 10 to 15 new members. For the moment, 10 central and east European countries and three Mediterranean countries have applied for membership. The preparations for the enlargement are already well underway in Brussels and in the new potential member countries, but many challenges have still to be overcome before this enlargement is completed, and new applications will also be made.

At the same time the EU would like not only to widen its membership base, but also to deepen the level of co-operation among members. First of all they would like to increase the economic integration among the present member countries to address the new requirements for further policy co-ordination arising from monetary integration. In addition, they aim at increased political integration in foreign and security policy. This issue has been put on the agenda partly to try to match the high degree of economic integration in the EU with a high degree of political integration. The present drive in this area can be regarded as a result of the problems arising from the tensions and conflicts in the Balkan region and the war over Kosovo. The radical change in the character and scope of European economic and political co-operation in the 1990s has also been reflected in academic thinking and theorizing about European regional integration.

Approaches to Europeanization

During the latter half of the 1990s, several major contributions have emphasized and developed the idea of the EU as a complex multi-level political system. An important distinction has been made between two types of EU decision. One is the few but very important history-making decisions, leading to treaty revisions. This is a key element in the revitalization of intergovernmentalism with a stronger theoretical and empirical emphasis on the processes leading up to such decisions (Moravcsik 1993, 1998a, 2000). The other type is the large number of policy-making and legislative decisions in different policy sectors (Peterson 1995, Wallace and Wallace 1996b, Peterson and Bomberg 1999, Richardson 1996). There is a dynamic relationship between these two types of decisions. Treaty revisions not only change the rules of the game for everyday decisions. Even in a rational intergovernmental perspective, it can be argued that treaty revisions contain elements that may turn out to produce unintended consequences later (Pierson 1996). The large number of decisions taken within the EU system substantiate and elaborate the historical compromises in a way which allows for future treaty revisions. In this book, however, we are not trying to answer the questions of why and how the EU develops in a certain direction. We will mainly focus on decisions on policy-making and legislation in important sectors within the EU system. The intention is to refine our understanding of the unique character of EU decision-making and implementation *processes*.

Until the beginning of the 1990s the EU system of policy-making was mainly studied from three perspectives. Two were comprehensive theoretical perspectives. The first, intergovernmentalism, represents an international politics perspective in which the EU is viewed as a special type of regime, an extension of national policy, and the important political processes are mainly intergovernmental negotiations. This perspective has been revitalized in the 1990s, particularly through the work of Moravcsik (1993, 1998a, 1999). The second theoretical perspective, neo-functionalism, is an institutional approach emphasizing functional relationships, where political processes have a role to play too. The idea of political spillover is partly in line with a pluralist perspective on the role of interest groups, but it also emphasizes the role of supranational institutions and in particular the Commission. This perspective experienced a temporary revival in the late 1980s and early 1990s (Keohane and Hoffmann 1991, Taylor 1996). A third perspective is mainly empirically descriptive, it is a formal legal-politico-administrative perspective whose exponents sometimes go into great detail about the relationship between the EU legal-administrative system and the various national systems (Mathijsen 1990).

These perspectives only to a limited degree captured how policy was made and implemented in an interplay between the national political system and the EU system with a logic of its own. To address such issues we tried, in the previous edition of this volume, to combine two alternative approaches to the study of policy-making and applied them to the EU: the EU as a complex political system and characterized by multi-level decision-making. Studies of policy-making had preserved a national comparative perspective, in the comparative politics tradition where national systems were the unit of analysis. To the degree that the EU was brought into the analysis, it was regarded as a context for predominantly national processes. This perspective was probably not fully capturing the EU dimension of national politics even before the revitalization of the EU in the mid-1980s.

After the introduction of the Single Act and the Internal Market, there was a need for a more comprehensive approach to the study of EU policy-making and implementation. Alternatively, we emphasized three aspects of the EU. The first was to view the EU as the unit of analysis, a political system in its own right. The second was to emphasize the interplay between the EU and the national level. The third was the role of central EU institutions, characterized by competition and conflict. The result was a new type of political system characterized by a high degree of complexity, and where national policy-making increasingly became Europeanized.

However, even in a confederal model the EU is a new form of transnational system, and the link to the EU of each member state comprises much more than the mere extension of foreign policy. This creates new challenges and new solutions, in a situation where the logic of economic and social integration continuously demonstrates the need for an increasingly tighter political unity in the EU system. There is a need for an open system approach that also takes into account the complexity embedded in national histories (Andersen and Eliassen 1991, Olsen 1992, Van Schendelen 1993).

Formal institutions and legislation provide a framework for policy-making, but there is considerable room for variation in outcomes. All formal systems have some degree of freedom in this sense. However the loose structure, combined with complexity and heterogeneity, generates a variety of sub-systems. In addition, actors bring with them national styles, strategies and tactics. Consequently, we will emphasize actor strategies, coalitions and dependencies; in short the complexity of policy-making and lobbying. This system, typically comprising loosely coupled processes, has been characterized as 'an emerging garbage can' (Richardson 1996).

We will distinguish between three aspects of complexity.

- One aspect concerns the linking of national traditions through a system of transnational policy-making. This widens the scope of the national policy-making process, as well as the number and type of actors to be taken into consideration. A key dimension is the relation between the national and transnational levels of authority. National traditions may vary a lot in terms of the order and predictability of the policy-making process, but at least they represent familiar settings for the actors.
- The second aspect concerns the fact that the EU is not only trans-national, but also represents new and changing forms of transnational authority. It experiments with new kinds of political authority and new ways of regulating the economy and society. Harmonization and the principle of subsidiarity, for example, open up a number of possibilities which, to a large extent, have to be clarified through international market and political processes respectively.
- The third aspect of complexity stems from the broadening of the EU. For a long time, EU policy was restricted to a few specific areas of economic and social life. The Single European Act and subsequent Treaty revisions have broadened the scope and variety of policy issues that will be influenced by the EU.

These developments towards increased complexity of the European policy context require a Europeanization of the policy-making process, which extends deep into the national systems. The Europeanization of EU policy-making has three aspects: the policy context, the policy-making processes, and the policy outcomes.

Most studies of policy-making have retained a national bias, and this is true even in the case of comparative studies. The national system has been taken as the unit of analysis, and the EU has mainly been regarded as external to the national system, almost as a disturbance. Europeanization of policy-making implies a need for a new way of delineating the policy context, where the European political system becomes the unit of analysis. The scope of national policy-making has to be widened, to include the central EU institutions, the European network of national political institutions and the actors operating at both levels.

Such a definition of a European political system raises the question of how it relates to the wider international context. It is important to see that there are global regimes, principles and institutions, which serve to legitimize and support the general development of the EU. Some of them relate directly to the core areas in the EU, such as the principles of the free market and trade, which are supported by international institutions like the World Trade Organization (WTO). Other regimes support environmental protection or human rights. They produce both a general ideology and specific institutional decisions that influence European and national policy-making.

A widening of the policy-making context also has implications for the analysis of policy-making processes and their outcomes too. A key dimension is the interaction between the national and the EU level. This may be conceptualized in three stages, which are not necessarily separated in time (see Figure 1.1).

Two aspects of this figure are important. Firstly, it looks like a model describing different phases in a policy-making process where a time dimension is implicit. To us, however, the figure serves more as an illustration of the focus on important actors, processes and policy outcomes.

Furthermore, the model illustrates the fact that, in the book, we do not claim a fully-fledged 'Europeanization' of the system. At its most extreme, this would imply a European decision-making system without any national segmentation. As demonstrated in the following chapters, this is not possible in reality.

The concept of Europeanization differs, in several ways, from the traditional concept of 'integration' employed in EU studies. For instance, we do not assume that a higher degree of Europeanization leads to more efficient policy-making. Secondly, the theoretical background for the concept is based more on organizational theory than on neo-functionalism and, as a result, it focuses more on actors and processes

Figure 1.1 Europeanization of national policy-making in a global context

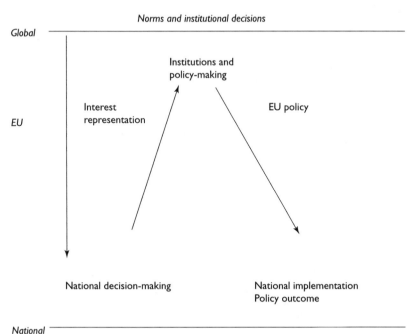

Norms and institutional decisions

Global

Institutions and
policy-making

Interest
representation

EU policy

EU

National decision-making

National implementation
Policy outcome

National

than on system properties. Finally, the concept implies a comparative approach across member countries and between states and the European Union.

The concept of Europeanization also implies that areas like foreign policy and relations between the EU and eastern Europe should be addressed from an angle different from that which we usually find: namely, as a process of integration, incorporating a move from planned to market economies and long-term, sustainable growth.

From our perspective, the key question to be asked is how policy-making is affected; or more specifically, questions of national interests, resources, legitimacy, influence at the EU level and organizational alternatives in the restructuring of the European architecture. This is related to issues like the widening and deepening of the EU. In the case of eastern Europe, the association agreements may also be viewed as part of the Europeanization of the policy context in the associated countries.

The Europeanization of EU policy-making leads to increased complexity. A system's complexity is generally thought to be a function of the number of elements, their heterogeneity, the number and variations of linkages and the degree to which the system is in transformation. In this sense, the trend towards Europeanization is also producing more complexity. The central and national-level institutions, interest associations, corporations, regions, etc. are being brought together. However, the pattern is not fixed. On the contrary, effective participation in the policy-making process stimulates actors to operate 'wearing different hats', in different political channels and in changing coalitions (see Figure 1.2). At the same time, the EU system is undergoing continuous changes regarding the role of the central institutions, the forms of authority and the areas affected by EU policies.

Figure 1.2 Complex policy-making

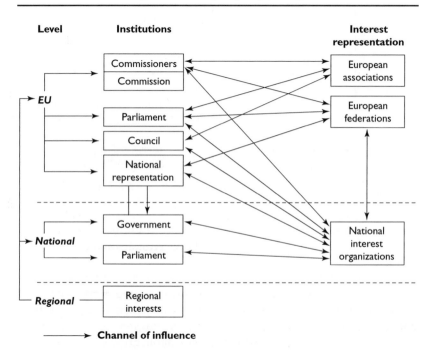

Governance and Decision-making

There are several competing attempts to conceptualize the EU system. One extreme is the traditional view of the EU as a special form of international co-operation. Another extreme is to view the EU almost as a 'normal' national-state-like political system. However, there exists an important difference, namely that the EU as a political system does not reproduce dominant national cleavage systems (Hix 1999). Our approach to the EU as a political system has many similarities, but is perhaps more in accordance with the 'governance' perspective on the EU. The EU development has produced a remarkable regional system of rules, which is often referred to by the notion of 'governance'. The notion of governance is neither new nor original to the EU, although this concept has increasingly become the focus of effort to describe and explain EU institutions and decision-making, as discussed by Wind (1997: 1–3).

As Wind points out, although 'governance' is used in various and somewhat ambiguous ways, it seems to emphasize three major points. First, it implies change: change away from a traditional state-centred conceptualization of political systems with one centre of authority. Matlary (1997b) writes about new 'forms of governance', and Kohler-Koch (1996) about the 'transformation of governance'. Secondly, referring to Jachtenfuchs (1995), it is emphasized that the idea of 'governance beyond the state' does not simply mean governance above the state, thus reconstituting the state on a higher (international) level. Thirdly, the idea of 'governance beyond the state' has to stop relying on the state as the institutional form and hierarchical centre of society.

The governance perspective emphasizes multi-level, competing and overlapping central EU institutions, lack of clear authority centre, and complex networks. Some scholars focus on the institutional aspects of governance (Kohler-Koch 1996, Kohler-Koch and Eising 1999). Others focus more on the importance of policy networks and decision-making processes (Richardson 1996, Forster 1998). This is close to the perspective in this book, with its emphasis on multi-level and complex decision-making. Much in accordance with this, Peterson (1995) and Peterson and Bomberg (1999) underline the need to develop a coherent, general theoretical framework for understanding the EU as a multi-level system of policy-making. What is proposed is a three-level model of decision-making (Peterson 1995: 72–5).

1 History-making decisions are taken at a 'super-system' level, or one that transcends the day-to-day EU policy process. Such decisions alter the Union's legislative procedures, rebalance the relative powers of institutions or change the EU remit. They can be treaty revisions, which have been the focus for new intergovernmental analysis (Moravcsik 1993, 1998a). In addition, they might be broad strategic decisions taken by the European Council or legal decisions by the European Court of Justice (ECJ) that can make history by setting out the limits of the powers of the EU.

2 Policy-setting decisions are taken at the 'systematic' level where choices are made between alternative courses of action according to one of several versions of the 'Community method' of decision-making. Power to set policy is shared between institutions, but the Council often has a dominating role. However, often COREPER will make important decisions. The Commission can play a crucial role in deciding what to do, particularly in relation to competition policy, but it rarely dominates at this level of analysis.

3 Policy-shaping takes place at the meso-level of individual policy

sectors. Often key actors are formally 'non-political', like the Commission's DGs, national civil servants and private actors who bargain with each other in various types of committees or Council working groups. Technocratic rationality based on specialized or technical knowledge often dominates at this level. Private parties frequently provide expertise that is otherwise not available. However, 'technocratic' does not necessarily mean 'apolitical'. The Commission often indirectly reflects various political concerns: 'A widely held view in the services is that "Intergovernmentalism starts in the cabinets. They are mini-Councils within the Commission"' (Peterson 1995: 74).

This multi-level model occupies a unique position located at the interface of IR and comparative politics approaches. It underlines three different types of logic, and the importance of policy networks. However, as Peterson and Bomberg (1999: 272) themselves point out, this perspective has been criticized for not making the distinctions between levels clear enough, for being too eclectic and for not having a proper theoretical foundation. It might be that as they have the ambition to link both different levels of analysis and different intellectual traditions it becomes problematic to develop a comprehensive and thorough analysis of the decision-making process.

Here the ambition is more modest. We employ the analytical tools of comparative politics, focusing mostly on meso-level policy-making: i.e. sector studies and detailed processes of interest articulation as part of policy-formulation. In a complex and loosely coupled system like the EU, there is considerable room for processes to impact outcomes. Also, we assume that there may be substantial differences between policy sectors in the way policies are formulated and implemented and we would like to develop some assumptions about this in the context of rather detailed empirical studies.

Dimensions of Europeanization

When looking at specific policy-making areas, it is important to keep the following questions in mind:

1 What are the factors stimulating or blocking Europeanization? What are the implications for complexity?
2 To what degree are policies institutionalized at the EU level and at the national level? In some areas, like energy, there is a high degree of institutionalization at the national level, but policies are weak at the EU level. Immigration policy is also weak at the EU level.
3 What characterizes the distribution of interests? To what extent can we identify segmented and polarized conflicts between member

states, or member states and central EU institutions? To what extent are interests overlapping or complementary? What kinds of alliances are possible and through which channels?

4 At what decision-making level do we find the driving forces? Is it a bottom-up process driven by initiatives and alliances at the national level or is it a top-down process reflecting central EU initiatives, perhaps supported by fundamental changes at the global level, as we have seen in the case of environmental policies? To what extent is policy development driven by the need to relate to other political areas?

The result is that the policy context can vary considerably in terms of Europeanization. In most cases the result will be increased complexity: lobbyfication at the central EU level, while, at the same time, a higher degree of co-ordination will be necessary at the national level if the national systems are to survive as key actors. The alternative is that various interests in the member states are articulated independently of, and even in conflict with, those of national authorities. It follows that the nature of the EU policy-making processes may vary considerably, from a relatively high degree of order and rationality, due to control by the member states, to processes that may be somewhat disorderly.

Actors are most likely to pursue rational strategies in areas where there are only a few others with similar attitudes. This normally means that the subject matter limits the type of decisions that can be made, from detailed questions of distribution, to general technical rules. When the number of actors is high and the issue allows for complicated politics, the result may be a lack of oversight and co-ordination. The latter may be described as organized anarchy – or the Garbage Can process (Cohen et al. 1972).

A real implementation of Directives involves not only the incorporation of EU law through national politic-administrative systems and a top-down process. Numerous studies of implementation show that successful implementation also depends, to a large extent, on how the upstream process of legislation has been handled (Philip 1987, Siedentopf and Ziller 1988a, Dehousse 1992). As a result, we will emphasize the interplay between legislation and implementation, in order to try and understand why the speed and quality of implementation differs among the member states.

A second issue about implementation is that national adaptation depends on the level of embeddedness of existing national structures (Knill 1998). A key to understanding efficient implementation is the degree to which EU policies challenge the national institutional core. Moderate adaptation pressures refer to cases where EU legislation is interpreted as demanding changes within the core of national administrative traditions, but does not challenge core factors themselves. Radical pressure refers to cases that imply changes in the core itself. In the first case Europeanization is compatible with the reproduction of existing cores. Therefore adaptation may take place, in an efficient way. In the latter case implementation becomes problematic.

In the next section we briefly present the structure of the book, focusing on Europeanization and the complexity of EU decision-making in different policy areas.

Contents of the Book

So far, we have discussed the development towards the European Union, and presented some conceptual tools for the analysis of policy-making. Part I of the book develops the conceptual framework for policy analysis in more detail. The focus is on the role and structure of central EU institutions and the rivalry that exists between them and between member states as part of the tendencies towards Europeanization and lobbyfication of EU policy-making.

The development of the EU over the last twenty years has been characterized by continuous rivalry between the key institutions, resulting in a substantial shift of balance in two directions. First, there has been an increase in the importance of transnational authority through majority decisions in the Council of Ministers. Second, there has been a growth in the importance of the only institution that is based on direct popular legitimacy, namely the European Parliament.

The strengthening of transnational decision-making has not eliminated cross-national competition and conflict. However, the increased importance of the central EU institutions has mobilized a wide variety of interests that are seeking to influence the decision-making process through direct contacts. This, in turn, has further strengthened the role of central EU institutions in relation to member states, and stimulated the growth of complex game-playing centred on the policy-making process.

In Part II we show the way in which EU policy-making and implementation actually work in selected policy areas. There are considerable differences with respect to the interests and loyalties of member states. Moreover, the nature of the policy area plays an important role in shaping the nature of EU policy-making.

The different studies show how policy development depends upon the ongoing changes in the EU. For example, political integration in the EU has implications for infrastructure that cut across national boundaries, involving, for instance, railroads, telecommunications and gas transmission lines. Institutional development has also had consequences for harmonization and integration within central policy areas such as labour market policy, immigration, police, etc.

Central questions concerning the relationship between EU institutions and national systems include the question: when do attempts to structure policy sectors from above actually succeed, creating one dominant institutional form? Under what conditions do certain institutional forms spread through imitation of success – when do national traditions prevail?

In Part III we explore some of the possibilities for the future of the EU and European integration, including the relationship with central and eastern Europe. The European Union is not finalized. There is a continuing struggle over the future shape that it should take. The number of countries which should be included, and which ones, are of the greatest strategic importance in this respect. Central and eastern European countries are more eager to join than EFTA countries, but the European Union gives greater preference to the latter group. A central question is how the new European architecture alters the environment for EU development.

The democratic deficit in the EU has been of increasing importance for the political agenda of the EU, especially after the signing of the Maastricht Treaty. The main problem is often perceived as a conflict between the federalists who wish for an integrated Europe with strong supranational authorities and the confederalists who wish for the creation of a Europe where the national governments have a strong influence. Even if there exist minor differences in this picture, it reflects the main dimensions of the political debate.

CHAPTER 2

FORMAL PROCESSES: EU INSTITUTIONS AND ACTORS

Svein S. Andersen, Kjell A. Eliassen and Nick Sitter

Do institutions matter? March and Olsen's (1984) question has been answered in the affirmative as institutions have drawn increasing academic attention over the last decade. This has generated a considerable literature that analyses the European Union's institutions as more than merely a framework or arena for negotiation between member states. The classical approach to EU institutions, focusing on their functions, competencies and relationships with each other and the member states, has been supplemented by focus on the organization of the EU institutions, their internal differentiation and specialization, the dynamics of institutional change, and co-operation, control and competition between them.

This development has entailed increased use of comparative politics in analyses of EU decision making, generating a body of literature where the EU emerges as a new type of political system. In Helen Wallace's (1996a) analysis, the EU institutions are (i) based on and similar to state institutions, but also (ii) contain some unique features, and (iii) are evolving through a series of intergovernmental conferences and changing patterns of policy making. A more explicit comparative politics approach can be found in Hix's book-length analysis of the Union as 'a political system but not a state' (1999: 2). Though the EU is analysed in comparative terms, its direct comparison with member states can be problematic because it does not feature a clearly defined 'government'. Hence Bulmer's (1998) call for a focus on governance, which encourages focus on the political character of the Union. This also warrants analysis of the evolution of the EU institutions (Pierson 1996), or even their metamorphosis (Wilks 1992), and the plethora of different rules for decision-making, which has resulted in a degree of fragmentation (Peterson 1997).

This book focuses on both the formal and informal arenas of policy-making, from agenda-setting and articulation and representation of interests to implementation of policy, based on investigations of the formal decision-making processes. We will focus on the institutions, the actors involved, their relative power and importance, and the variations in procedures. This chapter will not give a detailed picture of the

EU's institutions as covered in standard textbooks, e.g. Nugent (1999b), but will cover the role of the institutions in the policy process, their significance, the key questions raised in the literatures on institutions, and the implications for the accessibility of the policy-making process in the EU.

The Institutions

There exists a classical summary of the EU policy process – the Commission proposes, the European Parliament advises, and the Council of Ministers decides. Up to the mid-1980s this was a valid statement for all policy areas under the (then) EC, which today is included in the first pillar of the EU. The Single European Act and the Maastricht Treaty established both the Common Foreign Security Policy within a second pillar and the Justice and Home Affairs in a third pillar since the Treaty of Amsterdam (police and judicial co-operation). Parallel to this, there has been a radical change in the roles and authority base of central EU institutions making decisions.

In the first pillar, there has been a movement towards a higher degree of supranational authority with majority voting in the Council and a stronger role for the European Parliament. With the establishment of the second and third pillars the EU extended the scope of co-operation. However, in these areas the countries have been reluctant to accept supranational authority. In fact here the Council has been given a more dominant role in the decision-making process. The Commission's role is weak even if it tries to expand its influence, and the Parliament has a very limited role, if any at all (see Figure 2.1).

Within the EC pillar the new rule-of-thumb is more along the lines of: the Commission proposes and the Council and Parliament jointly decide. Before the Single European Act (1987), Parliament's legislative powers were limited to issuing an opinion under the *consultation procedure* (which conferred some delaying power on it), though it enjoyed the power to reject the budget. The SEA introduced the *assent* procedure, requiring that the EP approves certain decisions (first related to accession and association agreements, but expanded somewhat with the 1992 Maastricht and 1997 Amsterdam Treaties). More significantly, the SEA expanded Parliaments' powers in areas related to implementation of the Single European Market through the *co-operation procedure*, a two-reading legislative procedure that grants Parliament the right to propose amendments (subject to Commission approval), which the Council may adopt by Qualified Majority Voting (QMV) but can only over-ride unanimously. In other words, the Council needs Parliament's approval if it adopts legislation by QMV, but may ignore the Parliament if there is unanimity.

Figure 2.1 The EU Policy Process

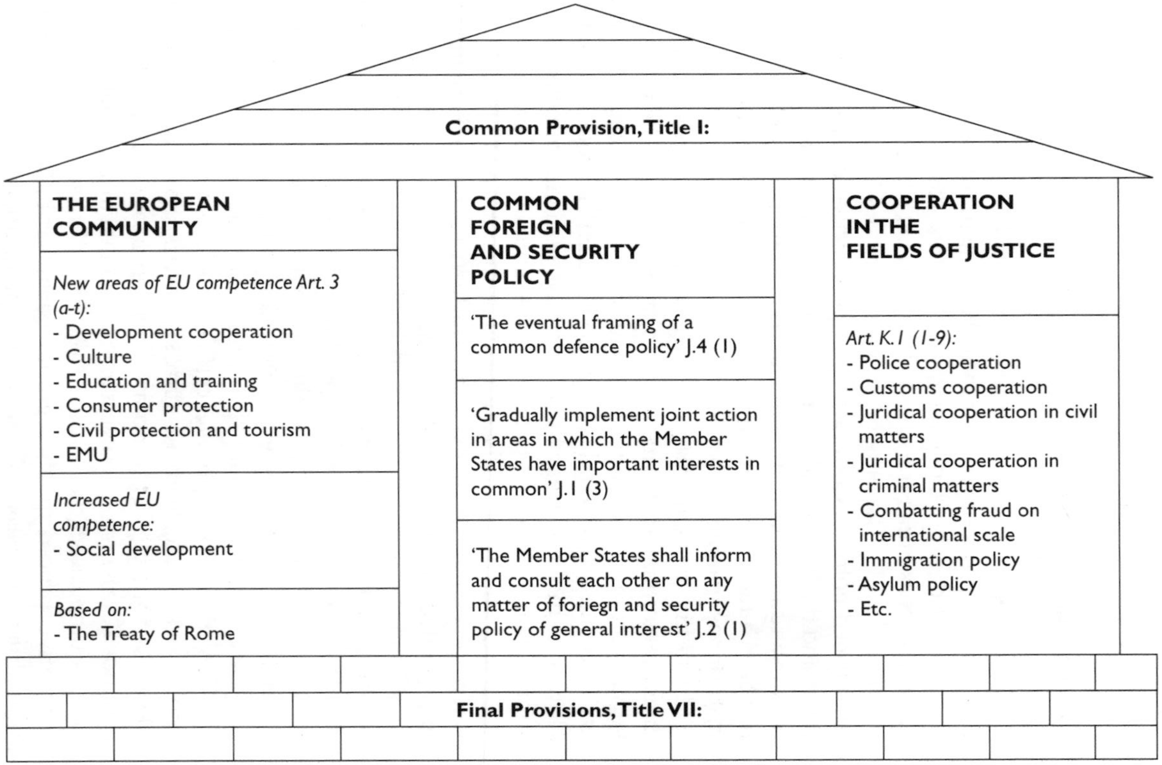

THE EUROPEAN COMMUNITY	COMMON FOREIGN AND SECURITY POLICY	COOPERATION IN THE FIELDS OF JUSTICE
New areas of EU competence Art. 3 (a-t): - Development cooperation - Culture - Education and training - Consumer protection - Civil protection and tourism - EMU *Increased EU competence:* - Social development *Based on:* - The Treaty of Rome	'The eventual framing of a common defence policy' J.4 (1) 'Gradually implement joint action in areas in which the Member States have important interests in common' J.1 (3) 'The Member States shall inform and consult each other on any matter of foriegn and security policy of general interest' J.2 (1)	*Art. K.1 (1-9):* - Police cooperation - Customs cooperation - Juridical cooperation in civil matters - Juridical cooperation in criminal matters - Combatting fraud on international scale - Immigration policy - Asylum policy - Etc.

Common Provision, Title I:

Final Provisions, Title VII:

The Maastricht Treaty extended the scope of this procedure within the EC pillar, while for legislation on completing the Single Market a new, three-reading, *co-decision procedure* was introduced, granting Parliament a veto and nearly-equal status to the Council. The 1999 Amsterdam Treaty subsequently removed some of the imbalances that favoured the Council in the co-decision procedure and extended its scope to most legislation in the EC pillar (with the notable exception of fiscal matters), to the extent that the 1996/97 Inter-Governmental Conference has been described as 'a *major step towards a system based on bicameral parliamentary democracy at the EC level*' (Nentwich and Falkner 1997: 1).

The Commission

In comparative politics terms, the Commission enjoys a dual role as the EU's executive and bureaucracy. Its political head, the twenty-strong *College of Commissioners* headed by the President, is appointed by the member states, but Treaty-bound to foreswear any national loyalties. Exercising powers granted to him in the Amsterdam Treaty, President Prodi told Parliament that he would restructure the Commissioners' portfolios and link them closer to the 25 Directorates General into which the bulk of the Commission's administrative personnel (the 'bureaucracy') is organized (*Financial Times* 3 June 1999). Prodi also suggested a clearer demarcation between the political College of Commissioners and the *Cabinets* that support each Commissioner on one hand, and the Directorates General in charge of implementation on the other, thus seeking to separate its political and bureaucratic functions more clearly. The Commission's roles (in the EC pillar) may be summed up as:

- an executive role, which includes presenting proposals for legislation and defending (and amending) them before the Council and Parliament and arbitrating between the two institutions or the member states; but which also includes management of the EU's finances and programmes, discretionary rule-making, supervision of implementation, and external representation of the EU;
- a bureaucratic role, which includes drawing up proposed legislation;
- a regulatory role, because the Competition Directorate General is acting increasingly like an independent 'federal' agency (Wilks 1992).

Finally, the Commission acts as the 'guardian of the legal framework', and is often seen as a driving force behind pressure for further integration. However, the Commission is in fact less cohesive than the picture that is painted in the classical model (Cram 1994, Ross 1995). Disputes between the several Directorates General often involved in a single proposal are not uncommon, particularly if the more independent

Competition Directorate is opposed by DGs of more *dirigiste* leanings (Nugent 1997). The same holds for differences between the more interventionist and free-market Commissioners (Christiansen 1996).

In the EU framework, the Commission functions as a repository of technocratic legitimacy that is sometimes ignored in the comparative politics literature (Rometch and Wessels 1997). Through its expertise and independence, it provides a type of legitimacy that may be compared to that enjoyed by independent regulatory institutions or central banks. In other words, its legitimacy is based on policy *output* rather than on democratic *input* (Scharpf 1999).

The Parliament

Continuing to draw parallels with the democratic institutions in the member states, the Parliament aspires to the role of the general representative body of the European people (in the singular). However, the role of this representative institution is presently limited mainly to the first pillar. Elected by proportional electoral systems in the fifteen member states every five years, the 626-member Parliament has staked a claim to representing the EU's main repository of democratic legitimacy because of its directly elected status. However, the parallel is more problematic in the light of the limited development of the EU-level party system and the suggestion that the EU features a collection of peoples, not a single people (the Maastricht Treaty's introduction of EU citizenship notwithstanding). Yet, as the only directly elected EU-level body, it is increasingly taking on three functions that are closely associated with Parliaments in the member states:

- Traditionally, the EP's decision-making was limited to the power to reject the budget (the classical parliamentary 'power of the purse').
- The introduction and extension of the co-decision procedure has granted it something close to co-legislator status with the Council.
- In precipitating the resignation of the Santer Commission in March 1999 the EP increased its role in holding the executive (the Commission) to account.

Though the Parliament continues to explore its powers in the last two of these areas, its claim to power has been limited by its nascent party system and the technical (as opposed to left vs right) nature of much EU legislation. Commission President Santer's confirmation vote in 1994 saw a socialist majority approve a centre-right candidate, which was explained in terms of some centre-left parties' reluctance to reject a compromise accepted by their national leaders in government (*Financial Times* 22 May 1994, Hix and Lord 1996). It is therefore no surprise to find that its first exercise of the veto came over an issue that reflected the institution's power (committee procedures in voice telephony, Docksey and Williams 1997: 149).

The Court of Justice

The European Court of Justice is perhaps the closest equivalent to its counterparts in federal states like Germany or the USA. Judges are appointed by the member states for six-year terms, and make their rulings by majority vote (though, in contrast to the US Supreme Court, 'dissenting opinions' are not published). In rational actor terms, the court is considered an 'agent', created by the principals (member states) to monitor their compliance with EU law. If the effort to create a common market is seen as a 'prisoners' dilemma' game, the ECJ is the institution charged with overcoming such collective action problems (Hix 1999: 99–101). To the extent that the Treaties can be considered the functional equivalent of a constitution, the Court's formal roles therefore reflect those of federal constitutional courts:

- interpreting the treaties, including ruling on the applicability of EU law and the competencies of the institutions;
- ruling on conflicts between the institutions or between institutions and member states (e.g. over the Treaty articles used as basis for legislative proposals, which can be significant given the different articles provisions for use of QMV);
- ruling on implementation of EU legislation (cases may be brought by the Commission, member state governments, firms, interest groups or individuals).

Through the use of its formal powers, the Court has drawn some criticism for alleged pursuit of integration. Significant land-mark rulings include establishing the direct effect of EU law in 1963 (*Van Gend*, Case 26/62) and its supremacy in 1964 (*Costa*, Case 6/64), free movement of goods (*Dassonville*, Case 8/74; *Cassis de Dijon*, 120/78) in the 1970s, and rulings that strengthened the Commission's competencies in merger policy (*Continental Can*, Case 6/72; *Philip Morris*, Cases 142/84 and 156/84; see Wincott 1996). However, though the Court is sometimes considered to be pro-integration overall, this does not by any means guarantee pro-integration judgements. Wincott's analysis concludes that the Court has played a considerable role in shaping the EU legal system and the balance of power in the policy-making process, but not in the development of substantive policies (1996: 183).

The Council of Ministers

In the rule-of-thumb summary set out above, the Council of Ministers is comparable to a second chamber in a federal decision-making process. However, this understates the role of the Council of Ministers, both as a decision-maker and as a repository of EU legitimacy. If the Parliament may claim direct legitimacy from the *people* of the EU, the Council represents its *peoples* indirectly through the member state parliaments and national governments. The Council's role is therefore far more than a second chamber:

- The legislative role of the Council is increasingly shared with the Parliament, as co-decision is becoming the norm in the EC pillar; however, this is complemented by:
- its role in negotiating compromises (Parliament has explicitly refrained from amending fragile compromises negotiated in the Council); and
- its role as an inter-governmental forum, i.e. the institution that protects the interests of the member states through consensual decision-making.

Despite the provision for majority voting votes are rarely taken in the Council, and some 85 per cent of decisions are agreed at the Committee of Permanent Representatives (COREPER) or working group level (Hayes-Renshaw and Wallace 1997: 78). The Luxembourg Compromise has long protected member states by providing an informal veto (to be invoked only in cases of 'vital national interest')[1] that renders the Council of Ministers a consensual rather than confrontational body. Game theory analysis suggests that increased use of majority voting would strengthen the Commission and Parliament because they could exploit differences within the Council (Tsebelis 1994). However, this threat could also reinforce the Council's focus on collegiality. In fact, even the Commission has been wary of exploiting the potential for use of QMV in matters of 'vital national interest' such as liberalization of electricity markets. Moreover, the rules of the Council, including the rotating Presidency (held by each member state for six months), are comparable to those set out in the literature on power-sharing in plural societies (Lijphart 1977, Taylor 1996). Its operation is compared to the *executive* 'grand coalitions' found in consociational democracies, featuring mutual veto rights (even if they are only informal) and avoiding adversary politics, thereby guarding the segments'/states' autonomy. This interpretation is supported by analyses of operations at COREPER and working group level, where most agreements are thrashed out, which indicate co-operation rather than hard bargaining (see below).

The European Council

The European Council is more problematic in comparative politics terms, given its similarity to more traditional intergovernmental bodies. What began as informal gatherings of heads of state during the 1960s and 1970s, was formalized in 1974, given legal recognition with the SEA, and established as a formal EU institution at Maastricht. The European Council currently meets at the end of each six-month Presidency, but has increasingly been convened for mid-term summits if and when special issues have to be dealt with (e.g. employment during the Austrian Presidency in autumn 1998, EU finances and nominating Santer's successor during the German presidency in spring 1999). Composed of two representatives from each member state (usually prime minister and foreign minister) and two from the Commission, it has developed into a system of 'institutionalized summitry' which has detracted from the power of the three institutions discussed above, whilst strengthening the member states' position (Nugent 1994: 171–3). Its main roles reflect this. Its main role is political and does not include legislation. The types of decisions made by the European Council are:

- provision of broad guidelines and policy initiatives, often inviting (or mandating) the Commission to propose legislation;
- review of the economic situation in the Union;
- an external relations dimension, especially in matters that involve both politics and trade, and co-ordinating member state positions in international fora;
- negotiation of constitutional reform, and directing the evolution of the Union.

By its very nature the European Council operates in a close relationship with the Council of Ministers, and may act as an appellate body on matters that ministers are 'unable or unwilling' to decide (Hayes-Renshaw and Wallace 1997: 167), i.e. as 'with, but not of, the council hierarchy' (Hayes-Renshaw and Wallace 1997: 162). This has led to heads of states' involvement in mandating the Commission to seek specific types of solutions, which may be of particular significance in matters that require unanimity in the Council of Ministers, such as fiscal policy.

How and When do Institutions Matter?

How and when do institutions matter? Two sets of answers to this question shape our analyses and interpretations of policy-making in the European Union. Though the gap between institutionalist and rational choice analyses has narrowed considerably as both approaches have been refined and applied to EU politics, significant differences remain. While rational-choice-based institutionalist analysis considers institutions as constraints on actors' freedom of action, the new or historical institutionalists suggest that institutions play a greater role in shaping both actors' preferences and the policy-making processes (e.g. in a shift toward co-operative rather than competitive games).

Rational choice and 'thin' institutionalism

Drawing on the realist paradigm that casts the state as the central actor on the international stage, intergovernmentalist approaches to the EU interpret the institutions as agents of the member states that are designed to overcome some of the problems inherent in international co-operation. Accordingly, Pollack suggests that the powers delegated by the states to the Commission and the ECJ can be interpreted in rational-choice terms of principals and agents. The tasks of the supranational institutions can therefore be summarized as (i) monitoring compliance by the member states to the agreed rules; (ii) solving problems of incomplete contracting (no legislation can foresee all potential scenarios; discretionary power is therefore lodged with the Commission); (iii) acting as independent regulators; (iv) engaging in impartial agenda-setting (thereby avoiding biased or rotating agendas) and (v) external representation (Pollack 1996, 1997). Consequently, a rational-choice explanation of delegation and pooling of sovereignty is offered. In this analysis, the institutions matter inasmuch as they escape member state control and deviate from their instructions. Ex-post and ex-ante mechanisms for oversight exist, but are not completely effective because the cost of monitoring limits the scope for efficient oversight. However, the role of the EP represents a problem for this type of analysis: as Pollack (1999) points out, its power cannot be explained by intergovernmental bargaining and the principal-agent approach. Even the co-operation procedure provided this institution with considerable power, examined in Tsebelis' (1994) analysis based on game theory. Though Tsebelis' analysis may underestimate the consensual practices in the Council, it seems clear that Parliament's power has been increased considerably at the expense of the member states. This can be explained in terms of efforts to render the EU decision-making process more democratic and 'plug' the gap in democratic control referred to as the democratic deficit, but not in pure 'principal-agent' terms.

Rational choice analyses are increasingly complemented by a focus on the role institutions play in constraining rational choice. Hence the *rational choice institutionalists'* focus on the autonomous role that institutions may play. This is explained in wider terms than mere incomplete supervision of principals by agents, though the institutions are seen as 'intervening rather than independent variables' (Pollack 1996: 454). The scope for institutions to play an autonomous role depends on uncertainty and the difficulty of reforming institutions. Past institutional choices therefore shape trajectories of future change (March and Olsen 1989), or even limit the possibility of change (Scharpf 1988). Perhaps more significantly, this approach relaxes some of the rational-choice assumptions about actors' fixed (exogenous) preferences, and therefore allows for change in and development of preferences (which may even be 'discovered' through negotiation processes). It therefore shares much with Moravcsik's 'liberal intergovernmentalism' (1991, 1993) inasmuch as the main focus on the states is complemented by focus on how domestic politics affect states' preferences and how these develop and change (Stavridis and Hill 1996).

In this analysis the key focus remains on the member state governments as actors and on the predictability of their positions (Moravcsik and Nicolaidis 1999), though institutions matter under three main sets of circumstances:

- if they provide a degree of stability; or
- if they shape the trajectories of future changes or limit the scope for policy reform; or
- if they deprive the member states of complete control of policy-making or the supranational bodies.

Historical institutionalism

Historical institutionalism differs from rational-choice institutionalism in its broader focus, which includes informal institutions: sometimes described as 'thick' institutionalism (Bulmer 1993, 1998). In this view, 'institutions play a much greater role in shaping politics, and political history more generally, than suggested by a narrow rational choice model' (Thelen and Steinmo 1992: 7). Therefore, it 'is implicit but crucial in this and most other conceptions of historical institutionalism that institutions constrain and refract politics but they are never the sole "cause" of outcomes' (Thelen and Steinmo 1992: 3). Moreover, institutions do not necessarily evolve from a historically efficient process, but may develop beyond the intention of the member states, thereby creating gaps between the states' preferences and the actual operation of institutions (Pierson 1996). This is explained by the states' short-term preferences, which are subject to change, and the unanticipated consequences of their actions, as well as the autonomy of institutions that is emphasized in the rational-choice literature. This approach also moves further away from the rational approach by focusing on preference *satisfaction* rather than on *maximization*. Finally it emphasizes the role of ideas and norms, i.e. the 'embedded values' written into the institutional set-up, in addition to the formal rules of the game. However, it is important to note that these values may change, as evident in the shift to free-market orientation in the Single Market programme (Bulmer 1998), and to avoid a 'political culture trap' of deriving current political culture from past beliefs (political culture) that are in turn derived from that period's political practices (McAuley 1984).

In its 'thicker' form, this kind of analysis readily forms the basis for arguing that the Union is a unique or *sui generis* system due to its specific ideas and institutions, and that this has implications for the nature of decision-making and democracy (Jachtenfuchs 1995). Institutions are therefore considered more significant than in the rational choice institutionalist approach.

- A 'community method', or 'way of doing business' shapes policy-making at the EU-level, and includes a normative element (Jachtenfuchs 1995).
- Institutions matter because there is a 'temporal lag' between member states' short-term-oriented decisions and their longer-term, unanticipated consequences, and this allows institutions to develop beyond states' intentions (Pierson 1996).
- Institutional reform therefore becomes more problematic than in the rational institutionalist approaches, and though it can be effected the consequences may be less than predictable (March and Olsen 1989).
- Member state government preferences are considered potentially endogamous, i.e. subject to influence by e.g. Commission expert arguments and persuasion (Smyrl 1998).
- This less than fixed nature of preferences has prompted focus on the fora in which preferences may be developed or changed, such as informal policy networks, and to the practices involved in agenda-setting and policy development, generating a literature on learning and 'co-operative governance' as well as the changing role of the state (Kohler-Koch 1996).
- Finally, differences in member states' 'thick' institutions (i.e. including ideas and norms) mean that uniform 'Europeanization' cannot be expected across the policy sectors (Lodge 2000).

Institutions and Policy-making: Technocratic Politics and a 'Community Method'?

The debate between rational-choice and historical institutionalists about the role of institutions, their autonomy and the nature of the EU system shapes our interpretation of the decision-making process and its

openness to interest representation. Questions about the extent of the
EU's uniqueness as a political system have been answered by suggestions
that it is 'less than a federation but more than a regime' (W. Wallace 1983).
A decade later, this suggestion of linear progress was modified to
a system of 'over-lapping circles of governance' (H. Wallace 1996a: 41).
Other characterizations that see the EU as a joint effort between member
states that has produced a new system of governance feature 'co-
operative federalism' (Kirchner 1992, 1994), 'multi-level governance'
(Marks 1993, Marks et al. 1996, Kohler-Koch 1996), and a process
of 'fusion' that is linked to the development of the states (Wessels
1997). Taylor's analysis of the EU as a consociational democracy (1991,
1996) suggests that if it can be thought of as a nascent state the EU is
comparable to power-sharing in plural societies.[2]

Though the EU's institutional structure shares several of the attributes
of a consociational state, it differs in two key respects: the extent of
fragmentation and its susceptibility to change. While the integrity of
Europe's consociational states and the political predominance of the
centre were established prior to democratization, the EU has developed
from co-operation between sovereign liberal democracies with established national centres of political power. Moreover, most member states
featured well-developed national 'policy styles', which, as a rule, they
have attempted to project onto the EU level. The EU system has therefore
been described as a compromise between the policy regimes of the
member states, particularly France and Germany (e.g. George 1996,
Nugent 1994). The result has been a fragmented system, in which
procedures differ not only between the pillars, but also within the EC
pillar. The actors (member states, EU institutions, interest groups) play
different roles in different policy areas, and a range of formal decision-
making procedures apply in different sectors. Even the philosophy
behind the policies differs according to sector, usually more free-market
oriented in the case of 'negative integration' (removal of barriers to trade)
and more interventionist in matters of 'positive integration' (economic
regulation) (Scharpf 1999). Moreover, both policy competencies and the
underlying principles have developed and changed considerably over
time, with some, such as competition policy, becoming far more
supranational than others (McGowan and Wilks 1995).

The unsurprising result is that the EU's institutions have been less
stable than most of their member state counterparts. The powers and
competencies of the Commission, Court and Parliament have not only
developed and changed considerably from the original set-up, but also
developed to different extents in different policy areas. The same holds
for the member states' control over the policy-making process and
oversight over supranational institutions. This in turn raises questions
about the cohesiveness of the institutions, some of which have been
alluded to above and are touched upon in the paragraphs below.

The literature of the 1990s has therefore addressed broader aspects of the institutions, including: the role of leadership; the role of expertise and technocratic politics; the differentiation and fragmentation of policy-making and the role of policy networks that focus on specific issues or policy areas; the relationship between the institutions in terms of control and oversight; and finally, the question of whether the European Union has developed a unique policy-making style or 'Community method'. These issues, in turn, have broader implications for our understanding of both decision-making in the EU and its democratic legitimacy.

Leadership

The literature on EU institutions has focused increasingly on the role of *leadership*. Though institutions (thick or thin) may maintain a degree of stability, their evolution prompts focus on institutional change (both formal and informal) and the scope for leadership to explore the boundaries of power. Perhaps the most significant change in both 'thin' (rules) and 'thick' (ideas and norms) institutions came with the ascendance of free-market ideas leading up to the SEA agreement, replacing the *dirigisme* and interventionism more characteristic of the two preceding decades. Despite the free-market bias inherent in international co-operation (because protectionism can easily be achieved at national level), the role of free-market ideas in European integration has fluctuated substantially (Moravcsik 1998b; Scharpf 1999). Building a single market has involved collective-action problems at the EU level, which the Commission has attempted to overcome through provision of political leadership (Sandholz 1993).

Commission President Delors' high profile in the 1980s prompted a surge in studies focusing on leadership at EU level (Grant 1994, Ross 1995, Cini 1996). Yet the variation in the role played by the Commission President has prompted questions as to whether strong leadership is exceptional. Peterson (1999) finds that it is. The Commission President is charged with mediating between his colleagues, a task that Delors and Hallstein performed more efficiently than most other Presidents. However, this pattern of one strong President followed by several weaker ones is questionable given the choice of Prodi as new Commission President in March 1999. In fact, Prodi received a considerable degree of support from member state governments when he indicated his intention to embark on reforms that stand to enhance the President's control over the College of Commissioners. Moreover, as Peterson points out, Santer had started to tackle some problems of fragmentation and disunity within the Commission, e.g. through increased use of cabinet committee-type meetings in the College of Commissioners and among the Directors General.

The classical idea of the Council of Ministers as the defender of member state interests has been challenged by analyses of the leadership role played by the Presidency and the Council of Europe (Kirchner 1992, Hayes-Renshaw and Wallace 1997). Both draw attention to the importance of mediation and efforts to find compromise and upgrade the common interest rather than focus on 'lowest common denominator' deals. Though most Council deals are brokered at the COREPER or working group levels, both the Presidency and the European Council have proved central to efforts to break deadlocks and broker compromises over politically salient questions. This has been the case particularly where one or more member states are concerned about the impact on their industries or when liberalization involves rendering different economic policy regimes compatible, e.g. in confrontations between interventionist and free-market approaches to utilities regulation or monetary policy-making.

Even within the European Parliament the role of leadership, in this case partisan leadership, has increased as parties attempt to build more-cohesive blocs. The 1994 hearings on Santer's appointment, the subsequent hearings of his new Commissioners, and the 1998/99 winter's events that precipitated the Commission's resignation all helped the leaders of the transnational parties emerge with a higher public profile. However, the effect of transnational party leadership and bloc unity should not be exaggerated, as the above-cited Santer confirmation vote illustrated.

Expertise and consensus politics

Despite the increasing focus on leadership at the EU level, the reality is that much of the policy-making in the EU is done at the levels below the Council of Ministers or College of Commissioners. The sheer volume of business and the technocratic (as opposed to politically divisive 'left vs right') nature of much legislation means that the permanent Brussels staff in the Commission and the Council are responsible for much of the drafting and decision-making, and the process is largely consensual. This should hardly be surprising in the case of the Commission, given its mandate of impartiality. If anything, the Commission is becoming increasingly fragmented along sectoral (not national) lines, as the DGs develop 'administrative cultures' that range from 'neo-liberal' in the DG IV (competition) to DG XI's (environment) more interventionist focus on high standards of environment protection (Cini 1997).

Analyses of COREPER indicate that its members are subject to dual (implicit) instructions and loyalties, i.e. that the loyalty to their governments is supplemented by a disposition to achieving results, and that this generates consensual politics rather than 'hard bargaining'

(Hayes-Renshaw and Wallace 1997, Lewis 1998). In other words, there is evidence of a 'Community method' that entails more power-sharing than the formal rules suggest. This includes the permanent representatives' shared goals and values, and their commitment to making the system work. Lewis (1998) argues that this overcomes Scharpf's (1988) 'joint decision trap', which is found in federal systems when it is easier to make rules than to modify them and decision makers are therefore 'locked-in' to previous decisions (see also Peters 1997). To be sure, this has changed over time, prompting Helen Wallace (1996a) to suggest that a 'co-option method' has replaced Monnet's partnership model (pre-1966) and De Gaulle's negotiation model (after 1966).

Since the SEA, decision-making on matters subject to majority voting has been based on persuading and accommodating reluctant states (but with the implicit threat of qualified majority voting ever present). Edwards (1996) makes a similar point, concluding that the Council is working as a 'network' rather than through intergovernmental bargaining. In other words, European integration reflects the adaptation of the state. The oft-cited German permanent representative's 'semi-joke' about being known in Bonn as the 'ständiger Verräter' (permanent traitor) rather than 'ständiger Vertreder' sums up this dual pressure (*Financial Times* 11/12 March 1996, cited in Edwards 1996: 137). And it is worth noting that some 85–90 per cent of all Council decisions are reached as 'A-points', i.e. settled at COREPER or working group level and adopted as a formality by the Council of Ministers. Even some of the remaining 'B-points' (i.e. for ministers' decision) are 'false' inasmuch as their 'discussion' at ministerial level is for domestic consumption only (Hayes-Renshaw and Wallace 1997; Lewis 1998).

Specialization and differentiation: policy communities, networks and 'social partners'

The complexity of EU legislation has brought about a high degree of specialization and differentiation, evident in the plethora of working groups in the Council of Ministers, *Rapporteurs* and Committees in the Parliament, and in the Directorates General. This, in turn, has prompted focus on the importance of policy networks ranging from close and stable 'policy communities' to looser 'policy networks' (Richardson 1996). Briefly, this suggests that informal relationship may be more significant than formal rules (Richardson and Jordan 1979), and implies that actors' shared views and their positions in a network or membership of a policy community may matter more than resources or preferences. Again this suggests the potential for differences among the policy sectors or stages of decision-making exceeding differences in formal rules of the game. This characteristic of the Union is enhanced both by the Commission's need for external input and its commitment to consultation. The most institutionalized case is its 'negotiate or we will legislate' approach to social policy, with provisions for agreements between the 'social partners' (the EU federations of unions and private and public sector employers) to form the basis for legislative proposals.

Inter-institutional relationships: comitology and oversight

Though policy-making in the EU may be characterized as technocratic and fragmented, the international nature of the system is reflected in the member states' quest for oversight. If the states are considered principals that assign and delegate tasks to the agents, they would be expected to seek to control the agents' operation. For this purpose, a series of committees were established to oversee the work of the Commission (by a Council decision of 13 July 1987), their workings hidden behind the term 'comitology'. Their key function is oversight of the Commission, both in drafting policy and in management of programmes (H. Wallace 1996a: 47). Pollack interprets this as 'police-patrol' supervision by principals (member states) over agents (the Commission), and though only one per cent of cases are refered to Council by committees it is the anticipation of potential referral that shapes Commission action (Pollack 1996, 1997). Though the system may be compared to the procedures used for delegated legislation in member states such as the UK, the powers of the EU committees vary considerably (Docksey and Williams 1997: 139). The system takes the form of three types of committees, and four different degrees of power (for a more detailed breakdown and analysis, see Dogan 1997: 33–6):

- advisory committees – the Commission must consult national experts, but do not need to heed their advice;
- management committees – the Commission may enact measures unless opposed by the committee;
- regulatory committees – the Commission must secure the approval of the committee;
- safeguard procedure – any member state may refer a Commission decision to the Council.

Though the Commission proposes the type of procedure and committee, the decisions are made according to the relevant legislative procedures. In other words, the Council retains considerable influence over which procedure is invoked and may even retain the right to implement legislation itself, a threat that may be used to gain Commission acceptance of the desired procedures (Docksey and Williams 1997). Nevertheless, analysis of the operation of the committee system has led to some counter-intuitive findings inasmuch as the institutions appear to attach more weight to achieving results than to increasing or defending their own power. Both the member states and the Commission appear more concerned with policy-making than sovereignty, and the type of issue or policy sector rather than formal decision-making power accounts for variations in type of committee used (Dogan 1997). However, 'comitology' remains mainly a matter of relations between the Council of Ministers and the Commission. To be sure, the European Parliament has attempted to gain more powers of oversight, notably through efforts to secure further involvement in the comitology procedures, but with only moderate success, e.g. getting access to information at the same time as committees (Hix 1999: 44–5).

Finally, the EU system leaves a considerable degree of implementation up to the member states, as directives are transposed into national legislation. Though the Commission monitors member state implementation, and, with the help of the Court, may seek to redress failures through sanctions and fines, the member states retain considerable freedom to manoeuvre. Temporary derogations and more permanent opt-outs have allowed states exemptions from EU legislation, from free movement of persons to protection of monopolies. Moreover, the EU regime faces potential legitimacy problems: 'when firms choose to ignore, evade or defy European regulatory requirements, they do so with a stronger moral justification and with more public (and official?) sympathy than when they flout national regulations' (Wilks 1992: 553). Strict regulation e.g. in environment policy, may therefore be difficult inasmuch as 'the price of imposing uniform rules on non-uniform economic constellations is then paid in terms of non-uniform implementation . . .]' (Scharpf 1999: 173). Hence the need for acceptable policy outcomes, and the emphasis on consensual policy making, which means that outcomes are more likely to 'represent genuine efforts to reach the Pareto-frontier', partly because of the comitology procedures and potential problems of implementation (Scharpf 1999: 190).

A 'community method'?

EU decision-making is dependent upon a complex negotiation process, where decisions are reached after long and tortuous dialogues. Already the neo-functionalists recognized one form of cumulative and solidarity-inducing negotiation as the characteristic '*community method*' (H. Wallace 1996a: 32); typically represented by the common agricultural policy, with a form of supranational and common policy and a dense relationship between Commission, Council, member states and extensive interest groups in Brussels.

Can we, then, speak of a 'community method'? Does the institutional set-up and policy-making style add up to a distinct way of 'doing politics'? If so, is the Union being run by elites on the basis of Lindberg and Scheingold's 'permissive consensus' (1970)? The points set out above reveal not so much a *sui generis* 'community method', as a 'consensual politics' approach that has also characterized decision-making in some member states. Paradoxically, consociational theory may be more relevant to the EU than to the states for which it was originally developed. Not only are Lijphart's power-sharing mechanisms found at the EU level (Taylor 1996, Gabel 1998), Pappalardo's (1981) require-ments in terms of stable segmentation, compromise-oriented leadership and leaders in control over their own segments are also met (if the states are considered as 'segments'). This reflects the primacy of member states' interests as well as an effort to reach agreement (and to avoid the potential sclerosis and immobility that accompany veto-rights). Therefore, like most states, the EU system of governance features some 'peculiar' characteristics, but whether these are sufficient to warrant the *sui generis* label is debatable. That the EU features a somewhat distinct style of policy-making is not.

However, in recent years additional modes of policy-making have been identified. Helen Wallace (1999: 1–2) describes four types:

- The *regulatory mode* developed in the single market, competition policy and regulatory approaches in domains such as social policy and the environment. In this form the European Parliament is a co-legislator, there are powerful influences from the EU legal system and courts and much interaction with national regulatory agencies.
- The *'multi-level distributional'* mode has developed in domains where financial resources are allocated with a very pluralist pattern of adaptation. The latter includes local and regional authorities and a wide array of socio-economic actors.
- The *policy co-ordination and 'benchmarking'* mode has emerged in areas of policy development and it is beginning to invade established areas. In a way, this is importing OECD-techniques into the EU, like spreading best practice.
- *'Intensive tranationalism'* is the term H. Wallace (1999) uses for the last type of policy-making mode. She argues that this is fast emerging to create strong collective regimes in traditionally sensitive domains of 'high politics', typically illustrated by the cases of EMU and CFSP.

The notion of a 'community method' or policy style has implications for a broader question: is there a democratic deficit in the EU? If the 'permissive consensus' has in fact come to an end (Norris 1997), the 'democratic deficit' argument implies that the problem can be solved by increasing the Parliament's role. The problem is the lack of a single demos (Chryssochoou 1997), which arguably makes majoritarian solutions problematic at the EU level (Dehousse 1995, Scharpf 1999).

However, this debate is complicated by the existence of at least three sources of legitimacy in the EU – direct, indirect and technocratic – that can be re-shuffled but not resolved (Höerth 1999). Hence the effort to find new bases for legitimacy, and suggestions that the EU's 'community method' or consensual politics provides a non-parliamentarian form of legitimacy. Jachtenfuchs (1995) argues that legitimacy is historically contingent, a question of support for the EU political system which reflects the transformation of the European states (which have lost some problem-solving capacity due to globalization). Wessels' 'fusion thesis' sees the EU as 'a new exercise in indirect democracy' (1997: 291), where legitimacy is vested in both the Commission and the member states. In this new 'transnational state', the involvement of non-state actors through policy networks and lobbying on the input-side strengthens legitimacy. Dehousse points to a 'real political deficit [that] super-imposes itself on the democratic deficit' (1995: 125), hinting at the need for more politicized and transparent policy-making. Common to these cases is a focus on consensual politics, where the EU system of governance is legitimized partly by its output and the wide scope for interest representation (see also Andersen and Eliassen 1996). This is accompanied by a somewhat legalistic approach to policy-making and implementation in the EU, which Wilks (1996) accounts for by the EU's limited resources and legitimacy (in the classical, state, sense of the concept).

EU Institutions in the Legislative Process

There are many different types of EU decision-making. We will focus on the legislative process, where the Council plays a key role. Legislation is a core element in the EU integration. It is also the most interesting area for a study of the relationship between national and supranational decision-making. At the same time, it presents opportunities to study various sources of external influence (Andersen and Eliassen 1992). Community legislation is the result of a complex and often lengthy process of consultation and negotiation. The policy-making process in the EU is more open and pluralist than in most member states, in terms of points of access as well as fragmentation and plurality of both government and industry actors.

The EU policy-making regime features a wider range of opportunities for influence at all three stages: (1) agenda-setting, (2) formulation of proposals and (3) inter-institutional decision-making. An examination of the different phases in the EU decision-making process is necessary in order to identify the possibilities for influencing this process. We will present the main elements of the EU decision-making process and highlight, in particular, the various patterns of institutional rivalry.

Despite the increased power of the Parliament, the Commission is still recognized as the most important starting point, i.e. *agenda-setting*. Still, the process of agenda-setting reflects the multiple levels of political leadership and multiple access points (Peters 1996). Most initiatives come from the Commission or other central EU institutions, but they often reflect input from national governments, citizens, firms or organizations.

Where the Council or the Parliament wants action taken, they may request that the Commission undertakes studies and submits appropriate proposals. However, requests for action may also come from other actors without a formal role in the decision-making prosess. Events during 1997 and 1998 illustrated the importance of meetings of the heads of national parties, especially the meetings of centre-left prime ministers and heads of parties of the EU's then 11 centre-left governments.

Interest groups may influence the agenda not only through these institutions, but also through taking cases to the Court. Moreover, the 1995 Brent Spar affair, when a Greenpeace campaign prevented disposal of the eponymous oil platform at sea, illustrated the potential effect of public campaigns. The Commissioner of environment threatened to propose EU laws banning disposal at sea (which could be adopted by QMV) unless a satisfactory agreement could be reached at the Oslo and Paris Convention (a non-EU body, whose majority decisions are not binding on dissenting states).

Thus, a wide range of actors can approach the Commission and ask them to undertake a new initiative. The Commissioners and the officials determine which cases should be pursued. Such agenda-setting power is of decisive importance, particularly in a system such as the EU that has limited decision-making capacity.

The Commission remains the key point of *influence when proposals are formulated*. Once the decision has been made to pursue an initiative, it is then made more specific by the officials of the Directors General. These officials formulate a preliminary proposal, using analysis carried out by independent experts from the member states. This process often involves more than one DG and therefore competition between two or more DGs and Commissioners. Organizations and firms also have the opportunity to be heard at this stage, particularly major European federations or large multinational companies. After discussions in the various offices of the Commission, the case is presented to the Directors General who, on behalf of the Commissioners, attempt to reach an agreement on the substance of a proposition.

During this internal Commission process, national experts are consulted in an attempt to consider the likely consequences of the proposals. Calculations are made and arguments are considered. The Commissioner responsible for the proposal formulates the proposition and puts it on the agenda for one of the two weekly meetings of the

Commission. The cabinets of the Commissioners have an important role to play in the decision-making process. They are not only involved in the sectors for which 'their' Commissioner is responsible, but like the Commissioner they are involved in all areas of the EU policy-making.

If the Directors General have reached a consensus previous to these meetings, the decision is of a merely formal nature. If this is not the case, the subject is discussed before the final vote is taken. When Commissioners decide to propose a new piece of legislation on the issue in question, the proposal is then sent to the Parliament and the Council for its first reading as part of the inter-institutional decision-making process. These two institutions are partly dealing with the proposals in a parellel process, but the Parliamentary recommendation is required as part of the input for the Council decisions.

The work of the Parliament is prepared in different expert committees, each responsible for certain areas (for example, the Committee of Transport). When the Parliament receives a proposition from the Commission, it channels this directly to the respective committee, without any preliminary parliamentary process. In each case, the committees choose a chairman who prepares the recommendation. The recommendation is presented to the different parties, and the Parliament makes a preliminary comment on the case.

Parallel to the parliamentary process, a hearing is run in the Economic and Social Council (ESC) and the Committee of the Regions. The nine committees of the ESC prepare the propositions. The three constituent elements of the ESC are employers, employees and 'others', which includes consumer councils and national organizations for agriculture. The ESC has only an advisory status and is not regarded as an important part of *the EU decision-making process*.

After the first hearing in Parliament, the Council makes a temporary statement on the proposition. The daily work of the Council is taken care of by one permanent representative and one deputy permanent representative from each state, in addition to the national attachés. The fifteen permanent representatives constitute COREPER (abbreviation for the French *Comité des Représentantes Permanentes*). It is within this body that the final discussions, coordination and mediation between the different countries take place (Kirchner 1992, Nugent 1999b).

The 15 national attachés within the relevant field form a working group. The country that holds the chairmanship decides which of the Commission's proposals should be put on the agenda during the following six months and how they should be dealt with. There are three categories here: (1) the leading issues of the presidency; (2) mere formalities; and (3) 'left-overs' from the previous presidency.

After considering the issue, the working group hands over a recommendation to the COREPER. While considering the case, the national attachés stay informally in touch with national interest groups and firms, but at this stage there are no formal hearing procedures.

The deputy permanent representatives meet in COREPER I, which fulfils a kind of secretarial function in relation to COREPER II. Here the proposition is discussed and a decision is made as to whether the temporary recommendation from the Council should be passed or rejected. In the next phase, the more controversial propositions are dealt with by the permanent representatives in the meetings of COREPER II, usually after having caused serious disagreement in COREPER I.

If the permanent representatives cannot produce a qualified majority, the proposition is taken to the Council of Ministers. At this stage, it is dealt with by the national ministers who are in charge of the particular area congruent to the issue on the agenda. In order for a final decision to be passed, either unanimity or a qualified majority is required, depending on the case under consideration. In the instance of serious, continued disagreement or a simple majority, the Council advises the Commission to withdraw the proposition or to make sure that necessary alterations are made to get it through. If COREPER reaches a consensus, the Council merely gives the formal clearance – the proposition is decided upon as an A point.

During the second parliamentary hearing the preliminary recommendation of the Council is again subjected to a hearing in Parliament and is dealt with according to one of the different procedures laid down in the Treaty, which include both co-operation and co-decision procedures. The outcome, according to the different procedures used, determines the future treatment of the proposal.

The ultimate phase in the decision-making procedure is the final settlement agreed in the Council. After the second hearing in Parliament and possibly also in the Commission, the Council reaches its final decision. If the Parliament has passed the proposition without any objections, it will be sent to the deputy permanent representatives at COREPER I. In the case of conflict with the Council, the proposition is subject to the same procedure as was employed during its first Council hearing.

One thing that should be noted is the power of the Commission. Not only does it, in most cases, have the exclusive right to propose a motion, it is often also able to heavily influence the deliberation stage that takes place in the Parliament and in the Council, as well as the administration and enforcement of the legislation.

Because legislation and decisions are put into effect at the national level, it is most often the case that the national authorities are responsible for the implementation of the legislation. The Commission ensures that this is carried out in a satisfactory manner in the various countries (From 1998, Knill 1998).

Based on the fact that the co-decision procedure means increased use of majority voting, and that the Commission and the Parliament are the most supranational or European institutions, two hypotheses can be formulated, as follows.

The first hypothesis is that both institutions will make an effort to maximize the possibilities of both the co-operation and the co-decision procedures, in order to drive the EU forward by ensuring that the new propositions will be adopted. This implies that the Parliament will be careful in its right to veto. The second hypothesis is that the Commission, when making initial proposals, will take into consideration the view of important coalitions in the Parliament. This means that inter-institutional alliances will be more important than before. Experiences gained through the practice of the co-operation procedure indicate that qualified majority voting encourages the Commission and the Parliament to exploit differences between member states, in order to build coalitions in favour of their propositions.

Increased majority voting means that the Council, on behalf of the member states, delegates power to supranational institutions. On the other hand, the competence and control of the Council with regard to the new pillars of the EU are increased. However, as mentioned earlier, in spite of the three-pillar structure, one could argue that increasing the Council's power in new areas will also strengthen the powers of the other EU institutions (especially the Commission). It could be concluded that the Maastricht Treaty strengthens all of the three main EU institutions, in relation to the member states.

The principle of subsidiarity and the ongoing debate concerning openness might balance out this conclusion. However, it may be the case that the most realistic way to increase member state influence and reduce the 'democratic deficit' is to be found at the national level and not in Brussels. This means that the national parliaments must increase their effort to control their governments, and make sure that they become more 'national' than European.

What about the overall picture of the inter-institutional balance and the balance between member states and the EU institutions? As argued earlier in this chapter, the Single European Act increased the role of both the Commission and the Parliament. The new cooperation procedure made it possible for the Commission to propose legislation that did not have to take into consideration all the member countries or the need to make compromises in order to finally get the proposition adopted in the Council.

However, the increased legislative influence of the Parliament under the cooperation procedure has still been very much dependent on support from the Commission. Changes proposed by the Parliament can only be adopted by qualified majority voting in the Council if the changes have support of the Commission. The co-decision procedure that is detailed in the Maastricht treaty[3], gives the Parliament the right to veto legislation independently of the Commission. After the Amsterdam treaty this is the dominant procedure for majority decision-making. This 'negative legislative power' has been widely discussed, and the way that the Parliament will make use of it, still remains to be seen.

This chapter has provided a general overview of the Union's institutions and formal decision-making processes, as well as the debate on the role of wider, informal, institutions. EU legislation is the result of a complex and often lengthy process of consultation and negotiation. The pluralist nature of the institutions and policy-process leaves considerable room for external influence – and some of the opportunities for this have been suggested here. The analysis of policy-making will be developed further in the following chapters, taking into account the openness and pluralism of the EU system as well as the significance of and scope for informal influence.

Notes

1 This is the usual expression; in fact the actual term is 'very important national interests' (Hayes-Renshaw and Wallace 1997: 14).

2 Lijphart's term (1969) has, of course been the subject of considerable debate, centred on the 'fuzziness' of the theory as well as its application to the Netherlands, Belgium, Austria and Switzerland (see e.g. Barry 1975, Halpern 1986). Here, however, we are mainly concerned with the argument that democracy in a plural society *may* require power sharing, and thus differs from more adversarial models of liberal democracy. Hence Taylor's (1991) suggestion that the model encapsulates the pressure against neo-functionalist integration, in defence of member states interests not merely *qua* states, but also *qua* 'segments' in a plural society.

3 Along with new powers, e.g. requirements that give the Parliament 'assent' to agreements concerning the objectives of the Structural Funds, rights of European citizenship, harmonization of electoral systems for European elections and increased influence concerning international agreements.

CHAPTER 3

INFORMAL PROCESSES: LOBBYING, ACTOR STRATEGIES, COALITIONS AND DEPENDENCIES

Svein S. Andersen and Kjell A. Eliassen

The focus of this chapter is the increased role of lobbying in decision-making at the European Community level. The new emerging forms of EU lobbying are part of a broader process of institutionalization that contributes to shaping a new political system in the EU. The most important EU institution is still the Council, which basically acts as an arena for national interest representation. Direct lobbying of EU institutions constitutes an important part of the decision-making process within the Union, increasing EU autonomy over the interests of the member states. Such activities have mushroomed over the last decade. As a result, we can talk about the Europeanization and lobbyfication of EU decision-making. This has attracted a considerable attention and a number of studies have been produced in recent years (Andersen and Eliassen 1991, Mazey and Richardson 1993, Greenwood 1997, Greenwood and Aspinwall 1998, Claeys et al. 1998).

One major perspective on lobbying in the EU is to regard it as a form of transnational collective action, motivated by rational self interests or broader social identities, values and norms (Greenwood and Aspinwall 1998: 7). Another major volume on EU lobbying emphasizes the way it supplements and legitimizes the role of EU institutions (Mazey and Richardson 1993, Andersen and Eliassen 1996). These contributions investigate the role of lobbying both in relation to the EU political system as a whole and in relation to sectoral decision-making that may vary considerably. While the first perspective focuses on the input for lobbying activities, i.e. what motivates action and activities, the second perspective targets the way that lobbying contributes to and is integrated into the EU decision-making process. The latter is also our focus bearing in mind both the systemic and sectoral aspect of lobbying. An overview of various interests and their role in EU decision-making is found in Nugent (1999a: 302–16). In contrast to such attempts to provide a more comprehensive perspective, the largest number of EU studies is descriptive and case- or issue-oriented. A large number focus on industry regulation.

Originally lobbying meant the informal influencing of parliamentarians. However, we define the concept of lobbying by contrasting it with the integrated corporatist participation in public decision-making. Representative associations may engage in lobbying but, in principle, anyone can become involved in lobbying directed at one or more of the EU institutions. Unlike in Washington, where a system of lobbying is well established, the system in Brussels is still in the making. For this reason, EU lobbying includes activities aimed at gathering information and establishing oneself as an actor. These are the preconditions for influencing decision-shaping and decision-making.

Prior to 1987, the European Union decision-making process was mainly a Commission–Council relationship. Lobbying directed towards the main EU institutions did exist. Mostly it was carried out by representatives of national organizations that were also involved in the representation of special interest groups within a specific country. Relatively few associations and companies were involved in systematic attempts to influence directly institutions of the EU, independently of the national channels of influence. The situation before lobbying in Brussels really took off is described in a few articles (Kirchner 1981, Sidjanski 1982, Philip 1983, Buksti and Martens 1984). Over the last years our knowledge has increased considerably but few comprehensive analyses exist (Van Schendelen 1993, Greenwood 1997, Andersen and Eliassen 1998).

The passing of the Single European Act represented a revitalization of the decision-making system in Brussels. The intention was to pass 279 Directives before 1992 and this suddenly made the EU common policy-making an important political arena. In addition to the traditional lobbying through channels that stem from national systems, an enormous growth in the direct lobbying of the EU Institutions has taken place. One important reason for this was the need for European businesses to obtain information concerning new EU legislation and policies in the internal market programme. Such activities contributed to the development of a European political system that is independent of the member states (Sandholz and Zysman 1989, McLaughlin and Maloney 1999).

Before the Single European Act part of traditional lobbying was directed to the Council, and the Council continues to be an important target of direct influence. However, a major political part of the new and direct lobbying is directed towards the Commission and the Parliament. This strengthens the legitimacy of the EU policy across national borders. The emerging multi-level and multi-channel system is increasingly characterized by the use of elaborate strategies that enable the participants to play across the whole system. Moreover, actors who come from the national channels of influence, have to take part in lobbying at the EU level (Andersen and Eliassen 1991, Mazey and Richardson 1993, Van Schendelen, 1993).

This chapter will describe the overall picture and the way the lobbying growth relates to ongoing changes in the EU decision-making system. The focus will be on three major questions:

1 In what way does the explosion of lobbying influence the decision-making system in Brussels?
2 Where can influence be exercised in the EU decision-making process?
3 What characterizes lobbying in different policy areas?

The answers to these questions are of great practical and theoretical interest. In the final section, we will briefly discuss the way that trends in the EU decision-making relate to the dynamic relationships that exist between different EU institutions. However, before we enter into these discussions, we will take a closer look at the kind of lobbying that takes place in Brussels.

The Growth of EU Lobbying

The EU institutions have always been the object of lobbying. However, the degree and nature of lobbying have changed dramatically, particularly during the 1980s. No exact numbers exist but all estimates indicate that the number of lobbyists increased ten-fold between the early 1970s and mid-1980s and again four-fold between 1985 and 1992 (Van Schendelen 1993, Greenwood 1997). This growth reflected mainly the increased mobilization of special interests from the national level. It was due to the invasion of professional lobbyists, accounting firms, legal advisers and representatives of individual companies, counties and cities. The growth in the EU-level interest associations was limited. This means that the relative proportion of European associations among those lobbying in Brussels has dropped. After 1992 the number of specialized interests trying to influence in Brussels seems to have been more or less stable.

Below we will describe the changes in the EU lobbying in more detail. However, it is also necessary to look at this phenomenon in the context of the changing relations between the EU institutions engaged in decision-making. The EU system may be described as a quasi-parliamentary system. We will distinguish between three major stages in the development of the overall pattern of EU institutions. The first stage is the period of the EC's stagnation in the 1970s and early 1980s. The second stage is that of the revitalized EC, starting in the mid-1980s. The third stage is from the mid-1990s to the present.

Lobbying is as old as the EU. In the years after 1975, Europe-wide pressure groups were established within the various areas of Community policy. By 1970, it was possible to identify more than 300 Euro-groups

(Philip 1987: 75). In 1980, Community officials created a register of all the formally recognized Euro-groups and these were found to amount to 439 at that time (Economic and Social Committee 1980). In addition, there were some unrecognized Euro-groups and other lobbies active in Brussels (Philip 1987: 76). The limited number reflects the fact that the EC was suffering from a period of stagnation, but also that the EC decision-making was organized around inputs from the national channels of influence.

During the 1970s and early 1980s, the relationship that existed between the major EC institutions could be described as follows: the Commission's role was supposed to be the initiation and preparation of proposals, much in the same way as a government in a parliamentary system. However, it was not able to fulfil this role in the same way as it had done during the preceding years. The Commission's task became mainly one of administering the EC system. The EC decision-making was mainly an arena for processing input from national governments based on unanimous agreements, as there was little room for autonomous EC decision-making (Mazey and Richardson 1993).

As a result, the major institution in this period was the Council. It acted not only as a parliament but, in many ways, it also took the role of a government. New proposals had to be sounded out here before it was worthwhile starting a formal process. The Commission tried to strengthen its position through coalition-building with European associations in an advisory and corporatist fashion (Philip 1987: 75). More than two hundred 'Euroquangos', advisory and consultative bodies with representatives of both interest organizations and EU institutions, have been established (Sargent 1985: 241). Most of these bodies have only an advisory status and the European Union has not been very successful in establishing a corporatist structure. One exception to this fact is the Economic and Social Committee of the European Union and its sub-committees. However, the influence of this body has been limited.

From the mid-1980s it was clear that the role of lobbying would be increasingly important for the European Union. This was reflected in the growth of the number of associations and lobbyists pursuing interests in Brussels. A survey from 1985/86 registered 659 federations at the European level, represented in Brussels, and about six thousand lobbyists and national interest associations in member countries, deemed to be of relevance to the policy-making process in Brussels (Morris et al. 1986). Parallel to this growth, there developed a shift towards the Commission as the target of influence, and eventually towards the Parliament as well. This change reflected the fact that the majority decision-making procedure in the Council had also introduced a bargaining relationship between central EU institutions.

For 1992, there are no exact figures detailing the total number of lobbyists, but all estimates indicate that lobbying has exploded since

1987. Attempts to count the total number of interest groups or lobbyists result in general in a figure of three to ten thousand depending on how lobbyists are defined. The highest number includes everyone trying to get access to and influence key actors at the EU decision-making level. This includes those who come to Brussels in order to pursue particular issues, as well as those who are more permanently positioned in the European capital. However, because there is no formal registration of lobbyists in Brussels, it is hard to find exact numbers. The tendency in the mid-1980s was that the industry interests lobbied the Commission and a weaker environmental, consumer, social and women's rights interest tried to influence through the Parliament. From the mid-1990s, both types of interests were increasingly active in relation to both institutions.

From the mid-1990s the EU experienced a new dynamic period: strengthening the political union, fully implementing the internal market and launching the Euro. There was also a shift in policy instruments, from a heavy emphasis on legislation towards other instruments like agenda setting, green papers, white papers, discussion groups, etc. Estimates are uncertain, but indications are that the number of lobbyists in Brussels has levelled off. However, the degree of structure appears to have increased (Greenwood 1997). Still, the lobbying patterns are by no means fixed. There are tendencies towards more stable policy-making, through the formation of networks and alliances, at least on a case-by-case basis, but few tendencies towards corporatist arrangements can be found. The exceptions to this are primarily the social dialogue and the agricultural sector, which has always had this nature.

The actors involved in interest representation and lobbying at the EU level are the same as we find at the national level, but their relative importance differs considerably. First and foremost, there are interest associations, either national organizations or European federations, or both. Back in 1980, national interest associations and European federations for agriculture, the labour market, industry, business, commerce and finance had by far the strongest representation in Brussels, as they also have on the national scene today. They cover the traditional areas of EU policies. However, over the last 10 years there has been a considerable growth in the number of 'weak' non-economic interests lobbying in Brussels. This development has even been encouraged and partly sponsored by the EU Commission. The Commission has had an increased interest for legitimacy concerning the representativity and balance of interests involved (Holmes and McGowan 1997).

Of the interest associations recognized by the Community in 1980, 40 per cent represented industrial employer interests and one third was from the food and agriculture sectors, totalling 71 per cent from these two sectors (Philip 1987: 76). In 1985/6, 55 per cent of the European organizations were from industry and agriculture (Morris et al. 1986).

Our own interviews indicate that the relative proportion of industry, labour and agriculture was dramatically reduced during the rapid expansion of lobbying in the following years. In 1990, we estimated that only about 30 per cent of the interest groups lobbying in Brussels came from industry and agriculture (Andersen and Eliassen 1991).

One type of lobbying in Brussels is the representatives of individual firms. To a larger extent than in the member countries, business firms have established offices with the purpose of influencing the EU policies. All major European firms and also several American and Japanese firms are present in Brussels.

Another type of actor is the professional lobbyist such as lobbying firms, law firms and consulting firms. They operate on behalf of associations, firms, regional or local councils in member countries and other institutions. An interesting development is that an increasing number of top civil servants in the Commission take up positions as lobbyists for associations or industry, after leaving their EU position.

A third type of lobbying is that exercised by representatives of various regional and local public councils including county councils, cities and regional development organizations. At the national level, their activities are directed towards the national ministries, parliament and government. On the European scene we find much the same pattern as in Washington, where local and regional lobby organizations have chosen to establish offices in order to try to influence the legislative process. Important issues are the regional distribution of the EU subsidies and the location of certain EU institutions and projects. The number of these associations is rapidly increasing.

Finally, a group that is actively involved in lobbying in Brussels is constituted by the representatives of the non-EU nations. In 1990, more than 130 countries were represented by ambassadors to the EU. Both the number of embassies and in particular the total number of employees has increased during recent years. Together with groups from the member states they lobby the appropriate Directorate Generals, the Commissioners, the Parliament and the European Court.

So far, we have described the growth and changing composition of lobbyists in Brussels. What is special, though, about this system if we compare it with national systems of interest representation? How does it relate to theories about interest articulation and mediation versus parliamentary representation?

What is New: Europeanization and Lobbyfication

Why has lobbying become so important in contrast to national systems of parliamentary government and interest articulation? The Single European Act represented a revitalization of the decision-making system in Brussels. The 279 directives that were to be passed before 1992 suddenly turned the EU common policy formulation into an important political arena. The growth of direct lobbying of the EU institutions has also contributed towards developing a European political system independent of the member states. All the important actors in European politics, e.g. businesses, trade unions and other interest groups, local and national authorities, have become more and more focused on the EU system. This increased interest in the EU central institutions is closely linked to the establishment of the internal market and the general expansion of the EU spheres of competence. The new forms of participation in the EU decision-making system and the development of direct interest representation are characterized by a high degree of specialization and fragmentation.

Definitions of corporatism tend to emphasize structural variables in relation to interest groups. EU lobbying is even more specialized and fragmented than traditional systems of interest representation. Professional expert knowledge is also a central matter. Highly specialized skills are an important part of lobbying in Brussels, where the Commission works on proposals for detailed laws and regulations. An executive officer in Brussels thus seeks contact with persons who have knowledge on the relevant problem area. There are only approximately 3500 higher administrative positions in the EU institutions (Greenwood et al. 1992: 24), and that makes contacts between the economic and other interest organizations and the EU bureaucrats particularly important.

Most studies of EU lobbying are descriptive and case- or issue-oriented. A majority of the research has focused on the lobbying of business regulation (Greenwood *et al.* 1992, Calingaert 1993). There exist, however, studies on 'softer' EU policy areas too, e.g. consumer policy (Helenius 1994) and environment (Monfort 1994).

One reason why business lobbyists have paid little attention to the European Parliament until quite recently is that it was considered less influential than the Commission. When business interests want to influence the Council they do it mostly through national governments. This pattern may change as a result of institutional reforms strengthening the role of the Parliament and the new priority given to unemployment and social issues in which national parliaments used to have a strong interest.

An important reason why lobbying plays a central role in the EU is the EU institutional system itself. It is different from those we are accustomed to from the representative democracies of both western Europe and the USA in the following ways:

- The EU is based on a *new form of supranational authority*. It is not a state in the traditional European sense. At the same time, the EU is also quite different from the federal state in the United States. The

EU is based on strong national systems, the formally independent EU Court has little sanctioning power.

- *The Commission plays a key role with the right to initiate legislation.* In this sense it has the function of a government. The Parliament is still politically weak.
- *Since direct democratic representativity and legitimacy have a weak position* in the EU, functional representativity linked to expertise in the Commission plays a central role.

Compared with the national traditions, the EU stands out through a number of unique features of interest articulation:

- *New types of actors* have easy access. For instance, European consumer interests, individual firms and cities have all established themselves as lobbyists.
- *There are very few procedures regulating participation.* Unlike the United States, it is not required that interest associations and lobbyists register, and lobbying is not professionalized.
- *Interest articulation takes place on many levels*: regional, national and supranational. These levels can operate simultaneously or actors can have another try at a different level if their first attempt fails.
- *The system is still in the formative stage.* This means that outcomes of particular decisions are important for the further elaboration of the system. The strategic implications of decisions are great.

The Commission and other EU institutions are, in many cases, dependent upon information from outside interests. It is therefore important to be aware of matters under discussion in Brussels that may be relevant to one's company, region, town, organization, etc. At the same time, it is important to know how to send one's information through the EU system.

The EU is a special form of political system within the liberal Western tradition. However, if we compare it with other political systems it differs not only in terms of its institutional set up, but also in terms of the functions it fulfils. Normally, political systems legislate, make decisions, implement, control results and sanction violations. The central EU decision-making process is primarily directed towards one of these functions, namely legislating, and to some extent decision-making.

In only a few cases does the central EU decision-making process lead directly to new legally binding EU legislation. Such decisions, called Regulations, are automatically integrated into the body of national law. Most of the time, however, the EU Council decides on directives. In order to be legally binding, such directives have to be incorporated and implemented in the individual member countries.

The implementation, control and sanctioning of legislation that is derived from the directives, are mainly matters for national authorities.

The EU Court constitutes an exception. This institution is supposed to supervise and sanction violations of Directives in member countries. However, there is a problem of competence, as the Court does not have any supranational sanctioning authority to lean on. In addition, there are problems relating to the politicization of court decisions.

There are a few examples of the formal decision-making power of interest organizations in the EU, primarily in policy implementation processes. Within agriculture, interest organizations participate in some decisions on prices. The Advisory Committee on the European Social Fund was established to provide advice to the Commission on applications submitted to the European Social Fund. In practice, this body has, in fact, influenced the distribution of grants from the Fund (Lodge 1989: 53). In the labour market area, some institutions of a more corporatist character have been established, but with rather limited powers, one example being the European Foundation for the Improvement of Living and Working Conditions in the EU.

At this point, it is useful to summarize the developments that have been taking place. Since the mid-1980s, there has been a tendency towards a Europeanization of interest articulation within the EU. The system is characterized by unclear principles regulating the formation of mandates for stable interest representation, and it is open to lobbying by many different actors, in relation to many issues. There is a multitude of actors in an open-ended access structure. When assessing the opportunities for influencing the decision-making process, it is important to understand the formal structure, and particularly the decision points where pressure can be exerted. The question that should be asked then, is where do interest groups lobby and why?

In order to understand differences with respect to participation and how actors operate, we also have to look at the policies they try to influence. In our research, we distinguish between five main types of lobbying, related to:

1 principles for constructing the community
2 making technical rules
3 making rules and systems work
4 getting access to funds and locations of projects
5 taking care of externalities.

As we have stressed earlier, the whole system is at a formative stage. An important part of lobbying is directed towards the construction of the EU institutions, regulations, directives and decisions. This is a political task and lobbying is mainly directed towards national governments and the European Parliament. This type of lobbying includes also attempts to strengthen the general awareness of the EU institutions concerning certain issues such as the environment and certain industries or geographical areas of the EU.

A large proportion of the EU rule-making consists, however, of quite specific technical matters. Questions relating to such issues as harmonization of free competition rules and environmental protection involve not only general principles. They also raise very detailed technical issues.

At the same time, it seems to be easier for lobbyists to influence technicalities as advocates of general principles. With regard to technical questions, the representatives of industry or affected societal interests seem to have more legitimacy. In these issues areas, they lobby the Commission.

Recent research has confirmed the old problem that the EU has of getting the different rules they make implemented and respected in the member states (Knill 1998). We have found a substantial amount of lobbying directed towards that aim. The main reason why the Danish ship-owners' association sent a lobbyist to Brussels was to lobby the Commission, the European Court and national courts in the hope of getting EU rules implemented and obeyed by European ship-owners.

A special type of policy decision involves the granting of Commission contracts and projects to individual firms, research institutes or national governmental agencies. This category includes also the locating of European institutions or projects in various localities within the member states.

Finally, we have also witnessed increased lobbying directed towards safeguarding against unintended consequences of a free-market and economic growth-oriented strategy in relation to such areas as the social dimension and worker participation. These externalities are either related to a specific product or they are more general. The Parliament was the main target of lobbying in relation to general externalities, but this is increasingly an important concern for the Commission and the Council as well.

The neat question concerns the variations that exist according to policy area when we look at the actors, the way in which they participate and the types of policy decisions taken. In the following section, we first discuss degree of segmentation in EU policy-making and link this to the question of institutionalization of EU policy-making. We then discuss to what extent the degree of embeddedness of sectorial interests may explain structural variations across sectors; focusing in particular on patterns of interest articulation around agricultural and financial services policies. Finally, we will briefly discuss patterns of political mobilization in cross-cutting functional policy areas, like the environment.

EU-lobbying and segmentation

Lobbying is often viewed as a special type of activity or pattern of political mobilization. An alternative perspective is to see the developing of lobbying in the EU as a process of institutionalization that may lead to various degrees of segmentation. By segmentation we mean the tendency towards stable patterns of participation or networks where participants share basic values, beliefs, norms and expectations (Egeberg et al. 1974). This process is associated with the autonomy of the political sectors in relation to the wider political system and with the fact that the actors are allowed to behave with a certain degree of autonomy in relation to the associations and institutions they represent (Olsen 1978). As a consequence, outsiders find it hard to penetrate and participate in policy-making: i.e. closure of the system (Damgaard and Eliassen 1978). Another element is the degree to which opinions on issues are actually taken seriously and do carry weight. This raises interesting questions concerning the political sector segmentation in the EU.

Studies of political segmentation have mainly focused on how degrees of segmentation influence policy-making. In this report we are concerned with how segmentation can be viewed as a process of institutionalization towards more stable patterns of political participation and reduce uncertainty: i.e. to what extent the actors are able to establish negotiated environments (Olsen 1978, March and Olsen 1984).

What are the basic factors underlying the segmentation process in the nation states? Most fundamentally this is a polity 'constituted by its basic institutions – shared practices and rules embedded in structures of meaning (moral and causal ideas), and resources – which over extended time periods are taken as given by a large majority' (March and Olsen 1995). Secondly, nation states are characterized by clear and accepted boundaries of their institutions and reasonably stable patterns of societal interests and their articulation into politics. Within such political systems it is possible to remove some basic controversies and uncertainties from politics.

As a consequence, within a political sector, there is scope for the institutionalization of shared beliefs, values, language and expertise in an area and thus the relative autonomy of sector actors. The degree to which we find segmentation varies considerably across policy areas. In such a situation it is unlikely that we will find the kinds of sectoral segmentation which we usually see in the member states, with the possible exception of agriculture. At best we will find that institutionalization involves some of the dimensions that define segmentation. Below we will briefly discuss this in relation to existing research on EU-lobbying.

Although specialized expertise in policy making is more important in the EU than in member countries the result is not institutionalization of clear patterns of participation. The role of expertise limits the ways one can express political arguments. However, it can also be seen as an extension of political discourse that allows actors without shared languages, values, etc. to be accepted as legitimate participants. Thus, experts tend to discipline the discourse without establishing boundaries of political participation. In principle anyone holding the relevant expertise or who is able to buy it has access.

To the extent that we find stable policy networks, they tend to be partial and non-exclusive. Some actors will tend to identify with an EU-level policy-network, but they do not seem to enjoy the same degree of autonomy from their associations or institutions as in national systems. In other cases actors involved in policy-making at the EU level, identify with central EU institutions and arenas, rather than their national sector basis. Thus, although the nature of issues, processes and outcomes may be hard to predict with any reasonable accuracy, in some areas we may be able to identify a set of core participants.

The major exception to this is agriculture. The reasons for this are two-fold. This sector has, because of uncertainties in production, more similarities across countries than do other sectors. In addition it is an old, traditional sector with a high degree of institutionalization in all countries. This has produced a corporate type of interest representation in all countries and thus also at the EU level (Buksti 1980). As Van Schendelen (1993: 276) points out, the agricultural sector has acted independently in the EC decision-making system.

This discussion illustrates how the development of EU lobbying is consistent with fundamental insights about institutionalization. One general hypothesis is that the higher the level of institutionalization of a political system (in terms of polity, key institutions, etc.), the easier it is to institutionalize a new area. Established conceptions, rules and practices shape new areas. Another general hypothesis is that the institutionalization of a political issue area will be harder, the more complex and open-ended they appear. In the case of EU-lobbying we find both that there is a lack of a clear and specific institutional framework and that even the simplest sectoral issues may have wider system implications. This is an important reason why EU-lobbying appears complex, fragmented and fluid as described in the articles reviewed.

This complexity, fragmentation and fluidity is discussed by Van Schendelen (1993: 11). Parts of what we find in the area of EU-lobbying can be accounted for in terms of general mechanisms of institutionalization. For instance, the reduction of uncertainty through negotiated environments (March and Olsen 1984, 1989), mimicking of supposedly successful strategies, and the symbolic importance of being present in Brussels, although the real gains may be unclear (Meyer and Rowan 1977, Thomson 1987). The problem is that the rapid expansion of the system makes it hard to identify or limit 'systemic' forces at play. Processes and outcomes seem to be weakly determined. Wide variations seem possible, if not likely, before more stable patterns emerge. The question we ask, therefore, is more modest: Is there anything that may frame or guide institutionalization processes in a way that can tell us something about the broad nature of future outcomes?

Is Embeddedness the Key?

Given this situation, what may be an alternative way to identify underlying structural forces? All political systems will attempt to establish some degree of order and predictability. Also the rather unstructured pattern that we find in EU lobbying should be interpreted in this perspective. It may be that the system is too new and contains too many new elements for it to be possible to extract clues of specific future developments. However, it might be possible that something could be said about the basic directions of such tendencies. What could be a point of departure for this? Andersen and Eliassen (1991, 1998) introduced the idea of embeddedness as a key variable underlying the emerging pattern of EU lobbying.

The notion of embeddedness introduces a framework for understanding different opportunities of political resources mobilization within different sectors. Variations of this kind may be useful in accounting for historical trends or emerging systems. The concept is most easily applied to economic sector policy-making and some associated functional policy-areas like social policy and environmental policy. Some political sectors like culture, foreign affairs and gender may not be accounted for in this way. We will leave such sectors aside here and concentrate on lobbying patterns related to different economic sectors in the EU. Because of the importance of this internal market, economic sector legislation has attracted most attention both in terms of the number of lobbyists attracted and the studies of lobbying undertaken.

In most economic sectors actors seek to further their interests through both collective and individual strategies, but the relative weight of the two strategies varies. The reason why actors in certain sectors pursue collective rather than individual market strategies can be explained by the impact of economic and social constraints.

While economic and social factors often are treated independently, they both refer to an underlying dimension that we have termed embeddedness. We can thus define embeddedness with the aid of a two-dimensional continuum with sunk costs or specification of capital along one dimension and social and legal constraints along the other. The concept of embeddedness thus incorporates both sociological and economic elements within a theory of strategic behaviour. However, strategic responses are here institutionally bonded so far as social embeddedness takes into account, that interests are articulated and legitimated within a given social matrix. To simplify, we can present these dimensions in a two by two table (Table 3.1).

Table 3.1   The two dimensions of embeddedness

The economic dimension	The sociological dimension	
	High social/ legal constraints	Low social/legal constraints
High sunk costs	High level of embeddedness: agriculture, fisheries	Medium level of embeddedness: capital intensive industry
Low sunk costs	Medium level of embeddedness: cornerstone enterprises	Low level of embeddedness: finance

Source: Andersen and Midttun 1989: 135

The general argument is that a high degree of embeddedness provides private actors with incentives for collective action as an alternative to individual business strategies. Vipond (1995) argues that the opening of markets introduces considerable risks as well as opportunities. To cope with this, economic actors need information about economic and political conditions in the EU available though business associations, as well as direct contact with central EU institutions. Successful political protection of sectoral interests, however, assumes that organizational efforts at the industry level are matched by the concern of relevant authorities. What most often characterizes embedded sectors is their susceptibility to regulatory control. One can hardly offer the general argument that embedded sectors are particularly attractive in terms of valuable assets and that state interference reflects the economic self-interest of the state. This may vary considerably: on the one hand, we have subsidized agriculture, while on the other there is the extraction of valuable natural resources like petroleum and hydropower.

We define segmentation along four main dimensions:

1   stable and closed participation in the decision-making process
2   shared values, beliefs, norms and expectations among the participants
3   shared and exclusive sector expertise
4   a dual form of autonomy, i.e.
    –   independent sector control over problems and
    –   autonomy for actors in relation to their associations and the institutions they represent.

In the EU, as an emerging political system, we do not find a full-fledged segmentation of this kind. However, we do find elements of it. Andersen and Eliassen (1991) compared variations across economic sectors at the European level measured as degree to which:

1   arenas are dominated by a few core actors (mainly national authorities or European associations) or open 'for all'
2   sector values are shared rather than being imposed by universalistic regulatory principles
3   expertise is sectoral rather than general, but specialized, across sectors (competition law, social policy regulation)
4   actors operate with a certain autonomy from home governments and national associations.

These indicators measure elements of institutionalization that vary considerably between policy sectors. If we look at associations and lobbying interests permanently represented in Brussels, we expect to find a large number related to the most embedded sectors such as agriculture. In this sector, with its orientation towards regulation and redistribution, there is a strong need for central co-ordination within specialized subsectors, such as dairy products and feedstock. At the same time, the comprehensive administrative system in the agricultural sector can be expected to be open to lobbying by different national interests who are trying to increase their share of resources. This may be done both through the national ministers in the Council and by direct interaction and consultation with the central administration.

In contrast to the agricultural sector, the financial sector is oriented towards general regulations to strengthen market stability and efficiency. There are few policy modifications based on special interests, and rule-making is governed by a strong technical and professional orientation. In such a situation, we expect the general interest to be represented by only a few European level organizations, particularly at the stage of rule-making. However, even when general rules of the kind we find in this sector are to be implemented, the room for lobbying by national interests is much more limited than in the agricultural sector.

The actual representation of actors in the two sectors fits our expectations very well. In the agricultural sector there are 22 European-level organizations, while the majority of the national interest associations have a permanent representation in Brussels. In the banking sector, on the other hand, we find only one Euro-association for commercial banks, one for savings banks and no permanent national level of representation in Brussels.

Concerning the regulation of participation, we expect to find more formal rules relating to the *agricultural* sector than to others. It is subject to a comprehensive body of rules and regulations and a considerable administrative machine. The process of bureaucratization has had time to mature, and this has been reflected in the demands made on interest associations and lobbyists who want to make themselves heard.

In the financial sector, with its strong emphasis on professional arguments, there is less need for formal procedures. To a much larger extent than in the agricultural sector, the advancement of special interests must be presented as part of a general argument. Also, at the present time the number of actors is small and the sector is new. When the implementation stage is reached, it may be open to more specific interests related to the elaboration of specific issues, and the manner in which these are enforced.

The more EU competence increases, the more lobbying occurs.

Lobbying Cross-cutting Policy Areas

The economic policy sectors may be viewed as part of a strategy for growth through market liberalization. Agriculture is in a special position, since it has proved to be a very difficult area for that liberalization. Some important policy areas cut across sectors, such as consumer, environmental and work and safety issues. These areas emerge around a certain kind of unintended consequences produced by a successful economic growth strategy.

Some consequences are specific, in the sense that they may be related to special products. In such cases, producers may be held responsible as part of sector regulation. Sometimes they are taken care of by a sector's actors who see it as their responsibility. One example is the case where the use of chemicals in agricultural production over time leads to high concentrations in food products.

In both the examples above, unintended consequences may be handled as a part of a sectoral policy. Initiatives may be taken by actors involved in the related sector or by external pressure groups. The lobbying associated with this is part of the sectoral pattern directed mostly towards the Commission.

The European associations of consumers (the BEUC), employees (the ETUC), and for the environment (the EEB), may direct their lobbying towards the Commission. However, a prominent characteristic of these issue areas is that they are genuinely political. They involve values and priorities that cannot be decided on the basis of technical expertise. For this reason, these organizations direct a major part of their energy towards the European Parliament.

The BEUC has a reputation for being very effective. Interestingly, it does not limit its activities to traditional consumer affairs. It has also played a very active role in relation to environmental issues. The weakness of the environmental lobby is that it is very heterogeneous and many of the political views that the lobbyists hold lie outside the bounds of traditional party politics. The position of the ETUC is also characterized by many different traditions and ideological orientations.

Environmental policy may have been the fastest growing area of EU policy over the last decades. From 1965 to 1975, the number of items of EU environmental legislation totalled about five per year. In the 1980s the number had grown to more than twenty items per year, increasing even more during the 1990s. Environmental policy is channelled to become one of the key areas of EU policy-making. Marks and McAdam (1996: 113) argue that the environmental movement has benefited from the integration process to a greater extent than other new social movements.

An interesting element in this cross-sector lobbying is that the various groups have common interests with the European Parliament in strengthening the representative political authority in the EU. The Parliament thrives on political issues that cannot be reduced to technical issues. Because of the way the EU system is constructed the cross-sector policy area related to the social dimension may carry more weight than it would otherwise have done. However, it is worth noting that the influence of both the Parliament and the interests of consumers and environmentalists is presently weaker at the EU level than it is in the member states. To summarize, it can be said that our expectations seem to fit the actual pattern of interest representation and lobbying in Brussels quite well. However, we must keep in mind the fact that finance is a new sector still in formation. The picture of policy areas cutting across sectors stresses the relationship between lobbying as such and inter-institutional rivalry.

So far we have discussed the role of various interests and how they can influence different phases of the EU decision-making process. Such possibilities for direct influence have been linked to the general pattern of changes in the EU institutional set-up and decision-making system. In the next part of the book we will take a closer look at how policy-making is made in some important sectors. These policy areas are all characterized by a movement towards a higher degree of European integration. However, they differ with regard to how fast and how far supranational institutions and authority have been established. They also differ with respect to the driving forces underlying such develop-ments. Integration may reflect generalized belief in market solutions (rail and transport), strong pressures from technology and market forces (telecommunications), the weight of the established institutional setting (energy), shared visions and requirements of the internal market (education) and the pressures created by the four freedoms (police and home and justice co-operation). In the third part of the book – The Future of the EU – we will discuss integration processes that transcend sector perspectives.

PART 2

EUROPEAN POLICY STUDIES

CHAPTER 4

RAIL AND TRANSPORT POLICY: NATIONAL PARADIGMS AND SUPRANATIONAL STRUCTURES[1]

Frank Dobbin

Introduction

The story of EU rail and transportation policy is about the inter-relation between economic and political integration. The European Union is often seen as a structure for enforcing discipline on governments in a free market. The idealized market is driven by transcendental economic laws of exchange that determine what is efficient and what is not, and that help to shape social institutions. The modern social institution that has done the most to promote modernization and progress – the state – plays no role in the constitution of market efficiency. On the contrary it can only act to disrupt primordial or natural markets. The great expectation that analysts hold for the EU is that it can negotiate modern states out of the economic picture. The argument in this book, in contrast, is that economic integration under a single European market will not be as simple as eliminating industrial interventions that interfere with natural markets, but will involve national paradigms concerning: (1) how and where markets produce efficiencies, and (2) the role of the state in the constitution of various markets. This will demand not a withering away of European states, but the imposition of a new supranational structure that will affect some particular, as yet unfinished vision of the market.

This chapter explores the European Union's emerging high-speed train policy, which is modelled on the recent British privatization experiment – an effort to move from 'hierarchy' back to 'market', in economist Oliver Williamson's (1985) terms. The idea is to take apart a vertically integrated industry, composed of national railroad monopolies,

---

1 Thanks to Svein S. Andersen, Kjell A. Eliassen and Kathleen Thelen for comments on an earlier draft. The other contributors to this volume also provided helpful suggestions.

and subject its component parts to competition. Rail car production, reservation services, train service, track construction and maintenance, rolling stock repair – the idea is to privatize all of these stages of production and open them to competition. The Union's emerging policy is to effect this strategy across Europe, permitting national railroads and new private firms to compete for business on all European routes, as airlines now do. Although the potential technical, economic and social gains are generally perceived as huge, different national visions of the state–market interrelationship has complicated and prolonged the process.

The principal goal is to describe the forces that have led the EU toward a common policy of privatization and free competition. The policy choice is striking, in part because it is novel for most countries, in part because the most recent trial – in Britain – has been an unmitigated failure, and in part because it flies in the face of what has been the conventional wisdom about railroading for a hundred and fifty years.

The first part of this chapter reviews the Union's emerging high-speed rail policy. The Union heard several proposals for a high-speed rail system, including some based on the highly successful French experience with the TGV. Why did the EU move toward a British-style plan? It is argued that the particular structure of the Union favours a neo-liberal policy – just as the American federal structure favours similar policies. Thus, the French policy solution was kept off the EU table by its incompatibility with the Union's institutional structure. Europe's initial decision to adopt a federal system thus constrained its industrial policy, for the French model depends on a state with a capacity for leadership and with substantial technical expertise.

The second part of the chapter considers the evolution of the high-speed rail policies of Britain and France, which served as the models from which the Union chose. These countries began not with a market and a statist orientation, respectively, but with two very different ideas about how states and markets are related. Their railroad systems represent two different visions of the market, not a market and a non-market. During the 1970s and 1980s, both countries pursued public high-speed train projects. Perhaps the most interesting theoretical implication is that EU members have very different visions of market forces, and thus that when they speak of unleashing 'the market' they have very different things in mind.

Finally, another goal of the chapter is to remind the reader of what any European traveller knows; that the French model has been the more successful of the two. Given its failure in practice, it is all the more striking that the Union has embraced the British model. The Union's decision to follow Britain's failed approach rather than France's stunningly successful approach to high speed rail holds clear implications for the future. One is that the federal structure of the Union will play an important role in 'selecting' policy paradigms (Hall 1993, Dobbin 1993a) for consideration, and in deselecting others. If in any industry there is a case for the French model, it is in railroading.

The European Community's Fast-train Policies

For many years, Europe's national railroads operated on a single broad model. Railroading was presumed to be a natural monopoly, and hence it was thought to be best organized as a state enterprise or as a highly regulated public utility. Public subsidies were thought to be inevitable, as the public subsidized competing forms of transport by building roads and airports. This model was challenged even as Europe was facing integration, on one side by France's great commercial success with public high-speed rail, the TGV, and on the other by Britain's aggressive effort to divide the national railroad up into dozens of privately held companies.

High-speed train service first reached Europe in 1981, when the French opened the newly constructed TGV line between Paris and Lyon. Since then, many new routes have been added. The German Intercity Express (ICE) began operation in 1991, and within a few years service on the Würzburg–Hanover and Mannheim–Stuttgart routes was added. Italy began offering a high-speed 'diretissima' service in the 1980s between Florence and Rome, and it now serves Milan, Genoa, Venice, and Turin. Spain opened a high-speed rail service using the French TGV technology on the 471 km route from Madrid to Seville (*Economist*, 29 October 1994: 23). In 1995, the Eurostar service connected London with Brussels and Paris via the channel tunnel, winning 25% of London–Paris air traffic in its first three years (*Engineering News Record* 1998, *Travel Trade Gazette* 1997). Sweden's tilting trains have been operating at high speeds since the late 1980s. Notably missing from this list is Britain, which modified diesel trains to run at 125 mph but which has yet to upgrade tracks or buy high-speed trains. Even Eurostar runs at low speeds on the British side of the channel.

As early as the mid-1980s, the European Union, the UIC (Union Internationale des Chemins de fer), and the European Conference of Ministers of Transport proposed a master plan for European high-speed rail, and actively debated the advantages of alternatives (ECMT 1986). By the end of the 1980s, members of the Union were firmly behind a new high-speed rail system covering all of Europe, and had proposed an international system of high-speed routes, with an estimated cost of 60 billion pounds (Black 1990, Hoop 1991). The hopes for such a system were two-fold. Some saw great economic promise in such a system, which was expected to generate new traffic, to alleviate airport congestion, and to stimulate commerce generally. Others saw great political promise in such a system, which could join the disparate regions of the Union into a single community. This vision of political and cultural integration is drawn directly from nineteenth-century France, where boosters heralded the capacity of rail lines to integrate regions with diverse cultures into a unified nation. Belgian railway chief Daniel Desnyder recently outlined a new proposal for a 30,000 km high-speed rail network, linking up all of Western Europe, with another 15,000 km of track to complete connections to Russia (*Travel Trade Gazette Europa* 1997). The plan builds on the model of France's LeGrand Star, which connected the far-flung provinces of France to Paris via trunk lines (Doukas 1945). Desnyder's plan depends on gateway cities to each of Europe's peripheral regions, and he promotes it with prose that could come directly from France's nineteenth-century plan. High-speed trains are as important to European integration as the single currency, Desnyder argues: 'High-speed must be the key development of the European network of tomorrow' (*Travel Trade Gazette Europa* 1997: 9).

European transport ministers came to the table with very different visions of how the industry should be organized. Some promoted the elaboration of the existing set of bilateral service agreements among countries, a solution based in the international relations model rather than in any particular economic model. Others used the arguments of economists to promote two more innovative models. Some promoted the public-utility model that had been most successfully developed by France. This model had widespread support among transport economists, who viewed the industry as a natural monopoly, by dint of its high sunk costs, low marginal costs, and demands for managerial co-ordination. Still others promoted the airline model of competing service providers that was then being implemented in Britain. This model had the support of Chicago School economists, who view competition as the best way to manage all transactions.

Directives from the EU Transport Ministry make clear that the British airline model is emerging as the winner. My contention is that the decision to adopt a federal system more or less determined the course of industrial policy, even if participants did not realize it at the time. There were compelling efficiency arguments to be made for each of the three models. A natural experiment, in which each of the models was tried in different contexts, suggests that, of the three, the British model was least likely to succeed. In recent decades, bilateral service agreements had been used on most international European routes, with substantial success. The French public-policy model had been put to a thorough test in France, and had succeeded by virtually all accounts. The British airline model had been put to two tests: one in the 1970s when Britain tried, and failed, to pursue a neo-liberal approach to high-speed trains; and one in the 1990s, with the privatization initiative, which thus far has been an unmitigated failure. We take the two main proposals, discussing the efficiency rhetoric behind each and recent evidence of its viability.

The Two Competing Models

The French favoured an EU rail policy that looked like their own. There were strong technical arguments in favour of a single, integrated, high-speed rail system, having to do with the need for vertical as well as horizontal managerial co-ordination in the industry. There were strong economic arguments as well, having to do with the EU's capacity to use its good credit to raise capital at low cost. And there was good evidence that an aggressive, state-led, high-speed rail network could be a financial success. But the French plan barely received a hearing.

The French model calls for an integrated international high-speed rail network, with one operator, one technology, and one international trainset supplier. The integrated strategy would follow the model of the channel tunnel – in essence a joint venture between British, French, and Belgian units – but would impose a single technology. The tunnel is operated by a unified management team, using a single train technology adapted to operate on three different kinds of infrastructure. Under the French-model proposal, a single technology for track, signalling, and rolling stock would be chosen for all of Europe. Airbus operates on a similar joint-venture model. For fast trains, the problems of technical incompatibility can be complex. Choices of train and track technologies are not independent, because non-tilting trains like the TGV can run at high speeds only on special routes that minimize turns, whereas tilting trains can run on serpentine routes. The choice between tilting and non-tilting trains, then, is linked to the choice between using existing freight/passenger lines and building new, dedicated, high-speed tracks. Signalling system standardization is also demanded by high-speed trains, which are computer-guided. A single, unified, system operated by the European Union would resolve all of these problems.

The model is based on a variety of different economic assumptions. A central assumption is that the industry is essentially a natural monopoly, due to its high sunk costs and low marginal costs. These characteristics lead to predatory pricing under conditions of competition. Predatory pricing drives small competitors out of the market, and leads toward monopolization. Introducing competition is self-defeating under these conditions. A second assumption is that, as Alfred Chandler (1977) has argued, the industry has compelling natural requirements for integrated management. Vertical integration under a single management hierarchy produces the best co-ordination, and hence generates the lowest prices and best service. This was the logic the French expressed for their own system. That this system has been a resounding success is perhaps the best evidence that it is viable.

The French have more or less conceded the fight, but they continue to believe that the neo-liberal model will not only poorly serve Europe, but will undermine the efficiencies to be found in the current French rail system. Most French leaders continue to argue for the efficiency of their own model. Louis Gallois, head of France's national railway (SNCF), argued in 1996 that the EU's 'ill-conceived liberalism' was a threat to French railroads (*Economist* 1996: 73). French officials have opposed the cornerstone of the airline model, of separating track from operations, in the belief that this would destroy the efficiencies that vertical integration brings (*Economist* 1996). France has responded to the apparent success of the neo-liberal model by leading the charge to establish high technical standards for the new EU routes. With high standards, the French national railroad will retain a comparative advantage and will rebuff market entrants with poor technologies (*Transport Europe* 1995).

The second proposal followed the recent British privatization experience, begun in a piecemeal fashion in the early 1980s and realized between 1994 and 1997. Under this scheme, the EU would allow independent operating companies, including national railroads and private concerns, to offer competing service. Rail lines would be financially separated from operating companies, with the lines holding regional monopolies and renting the use of track to users. The airline analogy comes from the independent and competitive character of operators, and from the role of the state in providing infrastructure (directly, or via private concessionaires) in return for user fees. Predictably, in the early 1990s, Britain's Tory Transport Secretary Malcolm Rifkind was a leading advocate: 'I would look forward to the day when any railway operator within a single internal market in Europe . . . was free to provide services' (Freeman 1991). By 1991, the EU had issued a directive that set the stage for such a system in freight. It eliminated international barriers, so that any freight operator could compete for business between Manchester and Milan or Madrid and Berlin (Freeman 1991). The European Community Task force, Group Transport 2000 Plus, backed such an arrangement for fast passenger transport, which would charge national governments, or private sector concessionaires, with maintaining the rails in return for user fees, and would permit any and all comers to operate trains (Hoop 1991).

Since late 1991, the Union has pressed national railroads to separate track maintenance from passenger operations, or at the very least to make accounting transparent (so that user fees might be estimated), as a first step toward this model. Under the system, broad technological standards are established by the EU, but service providers are free to operate in an entrepreneurial way. Train-building, reservation services, maintenance, and other functions would be opened up to market competition.

The current plan builds on the privatization scheme that John Major pushed through in Britain, in March of 1994. British Rail was broken up into nearly one hundred separate companies, with several dozen private carriers competing to offer service on inter-city routes, a separate company (Railtrack) maintaining the track on a fee-for-service basis, and distinct companies handling rolling stock and maintenance. Privatization was largely complete by April of 1997, with a number of private carriers, such as Virgin, offering service and promising to implement high-speed service on high-volume routes. But in the first three years of operation, reliability and punctuality have declined, and formal complaints have risen to unprecedented levels. Speculation has made fortunes for some early bidders in the privatization scheme, and by most estimates the Major government gave away vast amounts of public capital at fire sale prices in order to speed the privatization through. *The Economist*, usually a champion of privatization, describes the experience as an overwhelming failure, largely due to a set of perverse incentives that fail to reward private companies for achieving economies and for improving service. The potential for such a model, it appears, depends entirely on the incentives built into public policy – policy can create market-like incentives, or preclude them.

One might expect that the British opponents of privatization would now be claiming victory, and championing a public model. This is far from the case. The architect of the EU policy is not John Major, but Neil Kinnock, former Labour Party leader and subsequently the EU Transport Minister. Kinnock, who opposed Major's plan to privatize Britain's railroads, now argues that railroads 'should be first and foremost a business'. His EU ministry issued a report in 1996 calling for the separation of passenger rolling stock and track in all countries, and the opening up of competition in all markets to service providers from throughout Europe (*Economist* 1996). In a speech in February of 1998, he argued: 'the EU has a challenging policy agenda, notably in promoting revitalisation of the railways through pragmatic liberalisation and through establishing a coherent framework for infrastructure pricing, which should have a major impact on both the volume of traffic and its cost' (Kinnock 1998). Some analysts have noted that EU policies in many domains emerge not through democratic processes, but by the 'stealth' of EU officials, who sneak new policies through under the broad mandate of the Union (Weale 1997, see also Andersen and Eliassen 1996). Under the broad mandate of opening up markets, Kinnock's transport ministry has made substantial progress toward implementing this new model.

The EU and the National Experiences

The Union, and national governments, have made substantial progress towards implementing this model. In air transport, they moved ahead quickly, setting a precedent for rail. The airline industry was 'liberalized' in April of 1997, when the industry was 'deregulated' so that any airline from any of the fifteen member states, plus Norway and Iceland, could compete for business on any route (Lewis 1997). Putting its faith in the market and the Court of Justice to work out the details (in a manner reminiscent of American regulation), the Union deregulated airlines before addressing a myriad of problems facing policymakers. Among those problems there is regulatory 'harmonization', airport slot allocation, value-added taxes on airlines, user charges, and a unified European aviation authority.

In railroading, national governments have anticipated the competing-provider model by moving to privatize parts of national railroads. They build new routes with joint public–private financing, destined for operation by private firms. With capital support from the Union, governments are moving responsibility for new infrastructure projects out of the offices of national railroads and into the offices of separate, public–private, agencies (*Tunnels and Tunnelling* 1997a).

Sweden was the first to separate train service from track maintenance, in 1988, followed by Norway, Switzerland, Britain, the Netherlands, and Germany (*Economist* 1994). Sweden has reorganized Swedish Rail on a business model, with private-sector managers, bonuses linked to performance, profit centres for each of its units, pricing structures borrowed from airlines, and new and refurbished trains. And Swedish Rail lost its monopoly in July of 1996, which opened the road for competition. In Germany, the national rail company, Deutche Bahn (DB), brought in a manager from Daimler-Benz, and began, in 1996, an eight- to ten-year programme of restructuring before the scheduled privatization of its passenger, commuter, and freight services. The Dutch government has phased out rolling stock subsidies, in a first step toward operating on a business model.

The airline model does not mean, as one might expect, that rail-roading is expected to become fully self-supporting. Instead, it permits the coexistence of a neo-liberal model of railroad operations with a very statist model of infrastructure investment. The EU is not getting out of the railway business, as the US government sought (but failed) to do when it created Amtrak to handle passenger business and Conrail to handle freight. By separating infrastructure from service, the EU is able to underwrite construction without appearing to subsidize the industry – in stark contrast to the situation in the USA, where infrastructure and operations are united and thus where infrastructure subsidies are indistinguishable from operational subsidies.

This approach allows the Union to promote a new high-speed rail network for its political advantages, while maintaining free-market rhetoric. The Union has an ambitious French-style plan for a region-wide system, which will facilitate travel between the centre and peripheral regions, such as Spain, the north of England, and Sweden (where a bridge/tunnel link between Copenhagen and Malmo ties or 'connects' Sweden to the rest of Europe by rail). In 1994, at a summit in Corfu, Europe's leaders ratified a plan for high-speed rail that prioritized nine inter-regional networks. By late in 1995, the list had risen to 14. As the *Economist* summarized the goals of this network: 'The commission wants among other things to help tie peripheral regions of the EU closer to the economic heart: high-speed rail has become a fashionable means to that end' (*Economist* 1994). The first network, the PBKAL (Paris, Brussels, Cologne [Köln], Amsterdam, London) has the main components in place (*Economist* 1994). Other priorities include: Munich–Verona, Paris–Brussels–Cologne–Amsterdam–London, Madrid–Barcelona–Montpelier, Madrid– Dax, Paris–southern-France–eastern-Germany, Lyons–Turin, Netherlands–Germany (*Tunnels and Tunnelling* 1997a). All told, leaders at the Corfu summit estimate that the cost of the 23,000 km network, half of which comprises upgraded track and half of new track, will exceed 200 billion ECU (*Economist* 1994). Many of these lines, including Madrid–Barcelona–Montpelier and Lyons–Turin, will depend on public–private financing, with routes themselves maintained not by national railways but by international concessionaires. Regional lines as well are increasingly depending on joint financing, as in the case of Italy's Rome–Naples and Florence–Bologna lines, for which the state takes a minority stake, with private sources and the EU making up the difference (*Tunnels and Tunnelling* 1997b). Work on many of the new lines has already begun.

The choice of this system was ultimately determined by the federal structure of the EU, and by the coincidental popularity of neo-liberal ideology. Neo-liberalism offered a rationale for the British-inspired model, despite a lack of good evidence that the model can succeed. Federalism made the French model impracticable, because it requires a state with the managerial and technical capacity to operate a huge, vertically and horizontally integrated, enterprise. The fact that the French capitulated so quickly, accepting the British model, suggests that they understood well that the EU did not have the institutional capacity to carry out such a project. As compared with the existing system of bilateral service agreements, the British model has several advantages. One is that it coincides with neo-liberal ideology, by subjecting the various parts of the industry to market competition. The other is that it allows for rhetoric of neo-liberalism to be espoused, at the same time that the EU subsidizes the infrastructure on routes it considers to be of political importance. The book's cover says it is by Milton Friedman, but the text could be Louis XIV.

Two Visions of the Market

In this section, we review the British and French high-speed rail policies and their underlying assumptions. These were the models that the Union's transport ministry was confronted with. It will be shown that the two models do not represent a statist approach in the first case and a market approach in the second. Rather, the two models represent two different conceptions of the market, and of the role of the state in the market. Those different conceptions led to policies that made the French approach successful, and the British approach a failure.

British and French high-speed rail policies of the 1970s and 1980s were designed to constitute disparate sorts of consumer markets, capital markets, producer markets, secondary markets, and international markets. Their policies in these realms illuminate the very different ways in which the two countries understand markets. Policies in both countries appeal to market forces, but whereas, in Britain, public policy is driven by the notion that markets are exogenous to, and prior to, the state, in France, policy is driven by the notion that markets are produced, stimulated, and guided toward national goals by the state.

There is little question of the relative efficacy of the French and British high-speed rail policies of the 1970s and 1980s. By 1990, France was operating state-of-the-art 300 km/h trains on a new network of rail lines dedicated to fast passenger service, and making money doing it. Britain was operating 1960s-technology 200 km/h trains on the nation's undependable, and failing, nineteenth-century freight/passenger network, and losing money. Political observers have put down these differences to France's 'statist' approach and Britain's 'market' approach, but upon close scrutiny this typology breaks down. Policy-makers in each country pursued a set of policies that, they believed, would properly constitute a market for high-speed rail. And policymakers in each country effected these policies through a nationalized railroad. The state–market dichotomy simply does not describe the French and British approaches. These countries worked with entirely different conceptions of state and market.

By the end of the nineteenth century, French and British policies contained very different visions of the role of state and market in the economy (Dyson 1983, Andersen 1992, Hall 1992, Dobbin 1993a, 1993b, 1994) – one in which the state is integral to the market and generates private economic activity, and another in which the state is quite distinct from the market and can only respond to the private economy. Their different 'policy paradigms' suggested very different mechanisms underlying growth. Britain's policies symbolized entrepreneurial drive as the source of economic dynamism, and symbolized positive state action as a threat to entrepreneurialism, markets and growth. They represented the market as a natural outgrowth of society. France's policies gave state technocrats a key role in transforming entrepreneurial drive into progress. They symbolized the state as creator and nurturer of markets. Whereas in British policy, the state was represented as exogenous to the market, in French policy, the state was represented as endogenous.

High-speed rail policies followed the logic of these nineteenth-century policies, despite the fact that rail industries in both countries had been revolutionized by nationalization. Next the very different ideas about markets found in the two countries' early high-speed rail policies are outlined.

The success of Japan's high-speed Shinkansen line, opened in 1964, stimulated both Britain and France to adopt fast train programmes by the end of the 1960s, under their nationalized rail systems. France's Société Nationale des Chemins de Fer (SNCF) established a Research Department in the mid-1960s, and in 1972 the state committed itself to building a high-speed rail link between Paris and Lyons. The line went into service in 1981, with TGV (literally, high-speed train) trains produced by a public–private joint venture under the Compagnie Générale d'Electricité.

Across the channel, British Rail (BR) initiated two new in-house high-speed train projects in the late 1960s. The 'High Speed Train' project produced the InterCity 125 (designed to run at 125 mph) by making minor modifications to existing train technology. The more ambitious Advanced Passenger Transport (APT) project was to build a much faster train. In 1982, after three trial runs that brought minor technological problems to light, BR dubbed the APT project a failure and abandoned research, arguing that the state lacked the capacity to manage the development of such a complex technology (Potter 1989). While BR's technical task was somewhat greater than SNCF's, because BR had determined to build a train that could run on existing sinous track by tilting into the curves, the Italian and Swedish experience showed that such a train was feasible (Flink 1991, 1992). BR spun off its rolling stock division (BREL) to privatize the problem, and later moved to a strategy of competitive tendering for high-speed train technology which made BREL one among private equals (Potter 1993). The end result is that Britain has no high-speed rail service, and France has the most elaborate and successful system in the world.

What caused the French to succeed and the British to fail? Both sought to develop high-speed rail through nationalized railroads, but the French had a vision of the market in which the state was an appropriate and potentially successful actor. The British had a vision of the market in which the state was nothing more than a disequilibrating force. In every market realm, the British vision prevented the state from succeeding.

Consumer and Capital Markets

Where does demand come from? Both French and British policies were predicated on estimates of market demand, but those estimates were based in different ideas about the origins of demand. French policy treated markets as a product of state action, and demand as a *result* of public policy. From the 1960s, the French state gave the SNCF substantial autonomy to act as they saw fit when it came to planning new railroads (Faujas 1991d). They embraced France's 'free market' approach to public monopolies, which suggested that they behave entrepreneurially to stimulate demand. This strategy was outlined in a widely read government report, the Nora report, which was inspired by the experiences of Electricité de France (Beltran 1993: 4). The SNCF thus underwent an 'intellectual makeover' which 'resulted in their no longer reasoning as a monopoly but as one element in a highly competitive sector' (Beltran 1993: 1). They sought to create demand.

In accord with this entrepreneurial approach to nationalized enterprises, the SNCF staffed its new Research Department with highway transport economists who held three very entrepreneurial ideas. First, they assumed that a new technology could bring new riders, and thereby produce economies of scale. Second, they assumed that demand was not a linear function of speed. Dramatic increases in speed could draw large numbers of passengers from other means of transport. Third, they assumed that an aggressive transport policy could not only draw riders from airlines, but could *create* demand. These assumptions suggested that public policy could generate legitimate, new, demand. With rosy projections in hand, SNCF economists could make compelling arguments for the viability of new rail lines (Polino 1993). The Paris–Lyons line's success proved them right, and the Government soon gave the go-ahead for high-speed rail lines connecting Paris with Lille, Calais (and the channel tunnel), and Brussels to the north; with Le Mans, Tours, and Bordeaux to the south-west; with Nancy and Strasbourg to the east; and with Marseilles and Cannes to the south (Neher 1989).

British policymakers, by contrast, began with the premise that demand was a function of characteristics of the private economy that were not within the control of the state, and thus was impervious to government manipulation. They assumed, as well, that government efforts to increase demand would disrupt an efficient equilibrium – they would disrupt free markets. Decisions regarding the future of the railways were politicized so that BR could never develop its own independent plans for promotion of railroads. British Rail used conservative estimates of demand, presuming that public policy could not draw riders from air transport, could not reduce costs through scale economies, and could not generate additional demand for transport. The Ministry of Transport's projections were based on the effects of incremental increases in speed on the West Coast line after its electrification in 1966, which suggested that for each 1 mph increase in speed they could expect ridership to increase by 0.8 per cent. As *The Economist* wrote in 1985, 'The ministry of transport denies that a better service would attract many new passengers' (1985d: 26). As late as 1985, they refused to consider evidence from the Paris–Lyons line as applicable (May 1992), and refused even to accept evidence from the success of their own 125 mph trains. As *The Economist* wrote:

> Trains can benefit from the gloss provided by novelty: the introduction in Britain of the HST125, the world's fastest diesel train, resulted in traffic increases far greater than could be accounted for by traditional forms of measurement. [However] the ministry of transport [still] refuse to allow the word "image" into their financial equations. (*Economist* 1985b: 30)

In consequence, the Ministry of Transport consistently estimated that demand could not support French-style high-speed rail transport, and discouraged the creation of a system. This contributed to the under-funding of technology research, and to the demise of the APT programme in 1982.

Both SNCF and BR relied on private capital to finance railway development, but they approached private capital markets very differently. In France, SNCF behaved entrepreneurially to attract bond investors to its early projects. It went to international capital markets, seeking funds on the promise of the project, and not on the basis of government guarantees of private capital. Prospective investors used the same criteria they used when considering private projects. This approach was a striking success. For the Paris–Lyons line, a third of the capital came from New York banks alone, and for the Paris–Atlantic line, 70% of the 13-billion-franc capitalization came from international markets (*Economist* 1984, Macdonald 1991). The debt for these first two lines was paid off quickly, and this made future issues attractive to investors. To attract capital to its later ventures, SNCF invited two hundred financiers to travel on the latest record-breaking train between Paris and Angers to hear a financial pitch. SNCF finance director Pierre Lubek argues: 'SNCF's main priority is to build up large, liquid lines of stock in the French market that will attract investors from abroad as well as locally' (Macdonald 1991).

France's later financing strategy made the private sector not merely a source of capital, but a co-owner. SNCF financed the TGV-Est, from Paris through Strasbourg, in a consortium with private developers that will lease the line to SNCF for a period of thirty years, whereupon it will become the property of the state (*International Railway Journal* 1990). To pay for rolling stock, SNCF arranged to sell new trainsets to a banking consortium and lease them back (Black 1991a). Underlying these strategies is the belief that the state can generate legitimate demand in private capital markets – that, for a promising transport project, the state can be as good a capitalist as anyone. The banking community has bought this approach. As one British banker put it: 'In the TGV, SNCF has a good product that makes money. If they want to borrow to build more of them, I don't see there being a problem finding investors' (Macdonald 1991).

British policymakers, by contrast, began with the assumptions that the state cannot generate legitimate demand in capital markets and cannot be a competent entrepreneur. Successive governments argued that public projects are inherently uncertain, and that to protect investors from the state's incompetence, it must guarantee private capital. Because guaranteed bonds come under Parliamentary limits on national debt, this meant that British Rail could collect little private capital (Black 1990). One British Rail executive argued that BR should no more guarantee loans than SNCF should: 'Why should they? . . . If banks are prepared to lend to Poland or Brazil, why not to SNCF, or us? Is SNCF likely to collapse? France is likely to collapse first. These loans would be "gilt". And if you give us access to the capital markets, the whole argument for privatization collapses' (Black 1991b).

During the 1980s, administrators at British Rail sought to circumvent public borrowing limits by following the French model, of selling train-sets to a consortium and then leasing them back. Government economists rejected the deal, arguing that such arrangements should be counted against the national debt limit (*Financial Times* 1992). This caution is peculiar to British rail policy, for as the Labour Party's John Prescott pointed out, private investment is common 'in European railway systems, and it is only ideological nonsense and Treasury daftness that prevents us doing it in this country' (Freeman 1991). 'Ideological nonsense' or not, the British inclination to think that any rail expansion will be the financial responsibility of the state is not limited to Conservatives. The last Labour government cancelled a link from London to the channel tunnel because cost–benefit analyses, based on the conservative techniques discussed above, showed that the line would not pay off bondholders (*Economist* 1988). In late 2000, some six years after Eurostar connected London with the continent, Britain has yet to build a high-speed link between London and the tunnel, which would reduce the London–Paris journey by more than half an hour, to less than two and a half hours. The rosiest projections are that the link will be completed in 2007 (*Economist* 1994). The British state, convinced of its own incompetence as a capitalist, repeatedly tied its own hands in order to protect prospective investors.

Production Markets

Who will provide railway service? In France, the state holds an unchallenged monopoly and few policymakers see advantages in a private production market. Transport minister Paul Quiles summed up the French position: 'Our analysis shows there is no advantage to the community – privatisation is not on the agenda. Our aim is to have a railway in a sound financial state, meeting the demands of the community. Good management is in no way at odds with the concept of a public company' (Black 1991b). State technocrats argued, along the lines of Alfred Chandler (1977), that the industry has unique problems of co-ordination. They concluded that a vertically integrated structure best suits the industry. And they saw the state as the most able manager of such a system. Even when an economic downturn prompted Mitterand to delay the construction of the Paris–Atlantic line, which was projected to turn a healthy profit, fast-train advocates never suggested privatization to solve the problem (*Economist* 1984). In France, private production of rail service is not generally seen as efficient.

By contrast, Britain began to try to privatize rail services several decades ago, and succeeded in the 1990s with a push from John Major. The argument behind this policy is that public managers are simply incapable of running enterprises efficiently because they are not driven by the profit motive. Privatization makes anything more efficient, even if it is not accompanied by competition.

Even before the dramatic privatization scheme enacted by John Major's government, Britain took a number of small steps. First, after privatizing its rolling stock division, in 1991 British Rail put out tenders for bids for the new HST250 (to run at 250 km/h) train, in an effort to stimulate private production (Flink 1991, 1992, Potter 1993). Second, in the 1980s, BR was reorganized according to private management principles, into a set of 'profit centres' based on the M-form approach of cost accounting in which separate divisions keep independent books. The aim was to produce distinct, competitive, divisions as a first step toward privatization (Black 1991b). The success of the new regional operating divisions was heralded by *The Economist* in 1985: 'it is noticeable that the lines in Cornwall and Scotland have shown a good deal more enterprise since they were granted a degree of independence' (*Economist* 1985a: 60). Third, from 1982, BR tried to spin off divisions that were profitable enough to attract buyers, selling the National Freight Company, British Rail Hotels and, as mentioned, the rolling stock company BREL. Transport Secretary Rifkind described privatization as a panacea for inefficiencies in the system: 'Many of the criticisms against BR are justified. I would like to see as much of BR as possible privatised in the next Parliament' (Black 1991b). Fourth, several proposals were mooted for full privatization even before the Major government took action, including a proposal that would have created private regional operating monopolies. As Tory MP Robert Adley argued in a debate over how to privatize: 'All that we have to do in order to do what the Japanese are doing is the following: we build 2,000 kilometres of mainline railway for high-speed trains at public expense. Then we transfer British Rail, free of charge, to six non-competing regional monopolies, financed by the public sector. Having done that, we write off all BR's debts and financial commitments' (Black 1990). The Japanese embassy insisted that this is not Japan's policy at all, but Adley articulated the sentiments of many. Under this scheme of privatization without competition simply putting the railroads in private hands was expected to make them more efficient. In May 1992 the Government announced an alternative strategy to create private, regional monopolies. The new plan would allow private firms to run trains on British Rail track, in direct competition with BR service. The 'airline' model of rail organization would make BR only one among competing producers of rail service. The state would maintain the network in return for user fees, and the government's InterCity trains would be ineligible for further government funding (*Financial Times* 1992, Potter 1993). From 1994, BR was broken into nearly a hundred different companies.

The plan that finally succeeded included both privatization and competition. Proposals now under consideration include privatization of British Rail as a single enterprise, privatization of separate regional operating companies as monopolies, and the break-up of BR into a public rail network and private operating companies (Roche 1991). In previous efforts to effect privatization, and in the current scheme, British policy-makers characterize private ownership as efficient in and of itself because it induces efforts to maximize profits. Indeed the privatize-the-whole-thing plans as well as the spin-off-regional-monopolies plans would simply transform a public monopoly into one or more private monopolies – but with profit motives. For British policy-makers, BR is incapable of acting entrepreneurially. While the French have shown no inclination to believe that private parties would do a better job than the SNCF, the British have consistently tried to move the railroads into private hands.

Secondary and Export Markets

Approaches to the secondary economic effects of railroads differ markedly. In France, it is the role of the state to create and foster markets for goods and services. As a result, secondary effects are part of the calculus of infrastructure development. As in Britain, French rail projects are expected to produce a net return of 8%, but in France, projects with important secondary effects are subsidized when the need arises. A case in point is the TGV Est, connecting Paris with Strasbourg, which was projected to return 4.5%. Rather than scrap the project, SNCF organized public capital infusions that would be forgiven, on the principles that regional growth would more than compensate for public outlays and that the line will have public-relations value because it will connect Paris with Strasbourg, where the parliament of the European Community is located (*International Railway Journal* 1990). France has continued to subsidize TGV rolling stock research as well with a logic of secondary effects – that improved trains will expand ridership Despite the remarkable financial success of the first TGV lines, the state has continued to finance research and development on TGV trains, to the tune of 66 million European Currency Units for the period 1990–94, in the belief that the new technology will have beneficial secondary effects. It will generate increased internal demand through improved comfort and speed, and will attract international buyers(Neher 1989). French policy has been oriented to the notion that transport policy can, and should, generate secondary growth in non-rail markets.

In the French model, secondary economic effects of public investments are part of the calculus of infrastructural development, while in the British model the primary economic effects of public investments are all-important – new projects must be profitable in themselves. In France policy-makers believe that it is the role of the state to fund projects that will have positive secondary economic effects on the economy. Under this logic, it is the duty of the state to do what it can to promote the growth of secondary markets by undertaking infrastructural transport projects that might not show primary economic returns. In Britain a very different view of the role of the state in secondary markets emerges. Public projects must be profitable on their own. In the British calculus, the market should decide which projects the state undertakes because only the market can discipline the state.

The British have a very different approach to secondary economic effects. As *The Economist* assesses British policy:

> Whereas the British Treasury insists on treating railways as an industry that has to earn a commercial return on its capital, countries such as France and Germany take the view that railways produce benefits to the community at large . . . that should be recognised when making investment decisions. The British view, that such benefits have to be captured in the fare paid by the passenger, has had the effect of ruling out any building of completely new lines for high-speed trains in Britain. (*Economist* 1994: 23)

Long before the Conservative Party's privatization flurry in the 1980s, British policy-makers contended that railways should be self-supporting, and that the state should not second-guess markets by subsidizing rail. Thus, far from treating railroading as a locomotive of growth, the state sought to streamline British Rail so that only profitable portions would survive. By the beginning of the 1980s, British Rail benefited from public subsidies that amounted to only 0.29 per cent of GNP; whereas her continental peers (Germany, France, Holland, Spain) averaged 0.7 per cent of GNP. By 1990 British Rail subsidies amounted to only 0.12 per cent of GNP (Black 1991b). 'The British philosophy is that people who use the railways should pay the lion's share of the costs "up front" in fares' (Black 1991b). This logic was linked to the test of 'commercial viability' that was applied to new rail projects during the 1980s (Black 1990). Margaret Thatcher responded to the idea of using public capital for the channel tunnel link by arguing that private parties would finance the line if it were worth building: 'We don't believe we should subsidise international rail services' (Black 1990). As one analyst concludes, high-speed rail in Britain was stalled by the 'insistence of the British Government that any investment in improved InterCity rail infrastructure must be wholly commercially viable' (Nash 1993: 7).

This approach is predicated on the idea that public capitalization of projects that would lose money constitutes a misallocation of the nation's resources, regardless of what the secondary effects might be, and threatens to create externalities that are ultimately inefficient.

Railroads are not generally thought of as an export commodity. But the visionaries behind France's TGV project saw it, from the very beginning, as a potential source of international revenue. Despite the rapid proliferation of national projects to design high-speed trains – Germany, Sweden, and Italy brought projects to fruition – the SNCF was determined to make its technology the industry standard. The national railroad built the Paris–Lyons line as a full-scale advertisement for the TGV, and even before the Lyons line opened in 1981, SNCF and the train-maker actively promoted the technology in international markets. Since 1981 they have engaged in unabashed boosterism; inviting foreign dignitaries to ride on the TGV, nurturing fast-train proposals from infancy in a wide range of countries, and developing comprehensive TGV proposals for markets around the world. In 1989 they convinced Spain to buy the technology. They succeeded in promoting modified TGV trains connecting London, Paris and Brussels via the channel tunnel. In the USA they have promoted TGV technology for systems in Florida, the Midwest, California/Nevada and Texas. In a consortium with the Quebec trainmaker, Bombardier, they won the Florida contract, only to have the funding pulled out by the state. They have wooed Australia, Canada, Korea and Taiwan (Agence France Presse 1991; Menanteau 1991, May 1992, Schmeltzer 1992). The costs associated with competing internationally have been large, because as Hubert Autruffe, undersecretary of the Ministry of Transport, argues:

> a TGV cannot be exported in the same way an Airbus can, which requires only an airport: TGVs require a particularly costly, heavy infrastructure that

demands two to three years of preliminary studies that only the most advanced countries are capable of conducting. The required experience – to design in Texas one of the most important infrastructural projects ever realized in the United States – our clients simply do not possess. (Menanteau 1991)

In their determination to remain internationally competitive, the state and GEC-Alsthom, now jointly owned by British GEC and French Alcatel, have continued to fund research to ensure that the TGV remains at the cutting edge of technology (Neher 1989). Recognizing the benefits of tilt-train technology, GEC-Alsthom joined with the Quebec train-maker, Bombardier, to provide the first tilt trains for the American market, due to begin operation on the Northeast Corridor in 2000.

While British Rail's early tilt-train technology potentially enjoyed a much larger market than the TGV, because tilting trains can operate at high speeds on existing tracks throughout the world (whereas the TGV requires special, new, tracks), British policymakers rarely discussed the Advanced Passenger Transport project as a possible source of international income. Sweden and Italy embarked on tilt-train projects when Britain did, and both are now marketing trains to other countries. Sweden lost a close competition with Quebec's Bombardier for the trainsets that will serve the Washington–New-York–Boston route in the USA, and both Sweden and Italy have sought British contracts from the new, private, service providers (Flink 1991, 1992). The decision to kill the promising APT project was predicated on the belief that the state would not be able to market the technology abroad to recoup initial research and development costs. There is no small irony in the situation, because BR developed the initial bogie innovations that made France's TGV possible, yet BR did little to exploit the technology save for installing it on conventional trains to create the HST125 (Potter 1989: 103). British Rail has presumed from the start that the state would not be able to market its rail technology internationally – meanwhile, governments in France, Italy and Sweden have assumed otherwise, as has Quebec's private Bombardier.

Conclusions: The State and the Market in Fast-train Policy

The two model policies that the Union chose from, then, were based in very different visions of the role of the state in the market. First, French policy is motivated by the belief that the state can and should generate demand for transport; whereas British policy is motivated by the belief that the state neither can nor should generate demand. Second, French policy is motivated by a belief that the state is a competent economic actor; whereas British policy is motivated by a belief that the state is an incompetent economic actor. Between French and British policies we do not simply see a continuum of intervention, but very different conceptions of how markets work and the role of the state in the market. This section underscores the success of the French public-utility model, and the failure of Britain's 'airline' model. It would be wrong to conclude that the airline model cannot succeed, because it has not been given a fair chance. But it is striking that the EU never fully considered the French model, which was such a clear success, and chose a model that had not been put to the test. Perhaps the most interesting conclusion to be drawn is that nations and groups have very different ideas about what a market is and where it comes from, and that these may not readily converge in the Union.

In the first half of this chapter, we took into consideration the path that the European Union's high-speed rail policy has taken. Three different proposals were heard for how high speed rail should be organized: one for an expansion of the previous system of bilateral service agreements; one for a single, publicly run, system modeled on the French experience; and one for competitive service, modeled on the new British policy. The model that has taken hold, did so without a sustained discussion of the options. The competitive service model has been pushed by the EU since 1991, and it is now widely accepted as inevitable. National governments everywhere, even in France, have reoriented national rail policies to this model, separating track construction and maintenance from service provision in anticipation of opening up service competition to all comers. A similar 'neo-liberal' model was put into effect in EU air transport in 1997.

What is striking about this model is that there is poor empirical evidence to suggest that it was the best of the three options, and that some important actors initially opposed it. France, which has the most successful high-speed rail system in the world, opposed it on grounds of efficiency – the industry's demands for coordination make competitive service impractical. Some industries, the French argued, are best organized from the top down. The best empirical evidence against this model comes from Britain. On the one hand, Britain's neo-liberal approach to high-speed rail doomed its own project in the 1980s. On the other hand, the recent British privatization experiment in railroading has been disastrous, with high levels of speculation, low levels of competition and abysmal service. This experience suggests that the received wisdom about railroading from the nineteenth century, which is that the industry cannot sustain real price competition because of its high fixed costs and low marginal costs, may still hold. As Charles Francis Adams, Massachusetts' first railroad commissioner and later President of the Union Pacific Railroad, wrote in 1893: 'There are functions of modern life . . . which necessarily partake in their essence of the character of monopolies . . . Wherever this characteristic exists, the effect of competition is . . . to bring about combination and closer monopoly. The law is invariable. It knows no exceptions' (Adams 1893: 121). This line of thinking led nations throughout the world to nationalize private railroads into integrated systems. The EU seeks to reverse the trend, and to surmount the problems associated with high fixed costs by separating the track from the running of trains. But barriers to entry will remain high, as they are in the airline industry. In short, the French model had produced the best and most profitable high-speed rail system in the world. The British model was based on an economic theory that had been proven wrong in real-world tests dating back to the nineteenth century.

Why, then, does the British model appear to be succeeding in the EU? Institutional analysis offers insights. The EU's federal system, like the American system, is not structured to facilitate government leadership in industry. The EU lacks a professional cadre of technocrats. It lacks a centralized political structure, which can bring a visionary policy to fruition. And it lacks the kind of revenue-collecting authority at the heart of France's high-speed rail policy. Instead, the EU's federal structure, and dependence on the Court of Justice for enforcement, give it the core administrative features of the US government. In the United States, early state leadership in the economy was undermined by the same administrative weaknesses that plague the EU. Congressional efforts to stimulate the rail industry via land grants, in the 1860s and 1870s, produced graft and a backlash against public leadership, in large measure because the federal government lacked the administrative structure, and professional expertise, to plan and manage the land grant projects.

In the United States, the federal structure spawned a series of industrial policies, under the umbrella of antitrust, that made the state a referee in the market. Policies regulating competition were well suited to the American state, because they required little more of the state than that it set out abstract rules and because they relied on private actors to use the courts to compel their competitors to comply with those rules. The neo-liberal model succeeded in EU high-speed rail because the Union has virtually identical institutional capacities. Why did the French not insist on imposing their own approach to fast trains on Europe? It was clear that the Union did not have the capacity to undertake such a programme. What alternatives were left? The only alternative that received serious consideration was the neo-liberal 'airline' model.

The Union's administrative capacities in effect kept the French model off the table. For the proponents of the 'airline' model, it was fortuitous that American-style neo-liberal rhetoric swept the world in the decade after 1989. That rhetoric emerged from the American experience, as economists sought to derive economic laws that naturalized the American industrial policy regime. As Fligstein and Mara-Drita (1996) argued in the case of the Union's adoption of the Single Market Programme, the EU high-speed rail policy depended not only on what was rational – for all three proposals were oriented to rationality – but also on cultural and social factors. The proposal that appears to have won was structurally compatible with the EU's federalism, and culturally compatible with the new wave in public policy, neo-liberalism.

In the second half of the chapter, a review of the history of British and French high-speed rail policies of the 1970s and 1980s traced the origins of two models considered by the Union. French and British policies were built on different sorts of market logics. The French have a vision of the market in which the state is endogenous, charged with creating markets and industries. In virtually every realm, in consequence, the SNCF behaved as custodian of the nation's future, but also as an entrepreneur. The French presumed not only that their state could be an effective capitalist, but that their state could do the job better than the private sector, given the industry's large needs for capital, unusual demands for co-ordination across time and space, and particular importance for the rest of the economy. By contrast, British policy was consistently oriented to the idea that the state exists outside of the market, and that assertive public policy will produce inefficiency and will disrupt the natural economic equilibrium. These ideas doomed Britain's early high-speed rail experiment.

The French and British experiences support the efficacy of the French system and throw into question the efficacy of the British 'airline' model. France's high-speed rail network is not only the most advanced in the world, but the most profitable. Britain pulled the plug on its own high-speed rail programme after minor setbacks, in 1982, and is alone among the large European countries in still lacking a high-speed rail system. We do not argue that this evidence suggests that the EU plan will necessarily fail, but that, in the French approach, the EU had a proven product that it chose to ignore.

Corporate governance varies dramatically in form across societies, showing little tendency to converge despite the fact that most economic theories predict convergence (Fligstein and Freeland 1995). Until recently, the case of railroading was an exception. Throughout the world, railroads that began on very different tracks, converged on the track of public monopolies. The economics of the industry were thought to demand this. The great power of neo-liberal rhetoric and the privatization movement has changed all of this, although what we are seeing is not exactly convergence, for even privatization takes very different forms across settings (Starr 1989). It is likely that the European rail industry will not move toward a new equilibrium, of privatization, but toward a mixed system, with public ownership dominating in some countries, private ownership in still others, and mixed ownership elsewhere. The regulatory system that the Union has created does not preclude any of these alternatives, but it does seem to preclude the sort of state-first approach to industrial policy that has served France well. This illustrates the close relationship between political and economic integration in Europe.

CHAPTER 5

TELECOMMUNICATIONS POLICY: INTEREST CONVERGENCE AND GLOBALIZATION

Kjell A. Eliassen and Marit S. Marino

Introduction

In contrast to the sector of rail and transport the telecommunication sector is characterized by a high degree of success. A powerful Pan-European supranational regime has been established despite strong and diverse traditional models. This chapter discusses why this has been possible within a relatively short time and with little conflict. We will also discuss what effects the new regime has on industry structure. The telecommunications sector is on the one side a highly technical sector, with significant importance for general economic development and for research and development in advanced technologies. On the other side, it has traditionally been a highly politicized sector, where the nation-states claimed total sovereignty until the end of the last decade (Eliassen and Sjøvaag 1999). As such, it is a good case study for the development of politics (both national and European) in a context increasingly dominated by economic globalization and technological improvements.

The theoretical framework of this book suggests that European policy-making can best be characterized as a complex, multi-level process where the success of the implementation of policies hinges not only on their correct interpretation into national legislative systems, but also on the participation and acquiescence of the various actors in the up-stream formation of policy. Also in this respect, telecommunications is a good illustration. The current policy-making arena in the field of telecommunications will be characterized as complex by any observer. It is indeed multi-level, since the main actors include such different organizations as the nation-states' representatives (especially through the Council of Ministers, which has played an important role in the process), the European Commission (and several of the DGs within), the industry, and also to some extent the consumers.

The success of the implementation cannot be attributed to the Commission alone. As we will demonstrate, when the EU made its first moves to constitute a European policy in the 1980s this corresponded in time with similar moves in several member states, an aspect which undoubtedly assured the relative ease with which the directives were implemented.

In order to highlight the process that has taken place, we will first give a brief overview of the history of liberalization in the telecommunications sector in Europe. To demonstrate the multi-level characteristics of the process, a discussion of some of the member states' domestic reforms succeeds the description of the process within the European Union. The technological complexity of the sector requires us to set out certain issues in greater detail, such as interconnection and universal service, to allow us to comment on the recent and future challenges in the regulation of the sector. Furthermore, it is the case that this process takes place in an arena larger than the European Union, which is why we also include some comments on the global development.

The History

The 1st of January 1998 saw the final barriers to competition in the European telecommunications industry lifted. Aside from some brief derogations for countries with less-developed telecommunications infrastructure, there now exists a Single Market for telecommunications of all types within the European Union. The last fifteen years have therefore seen a radical change in the way the telecommunications sector operates, and the regulatory regime within which it works (Melody 1997, Pelkmans and Young 1998).

There are two types of logic that have been important in the liberalization process in the EU. First, the project of creating a Single Market for the EU member states required trans-European communications systems. It is easy to find similarities between the liberalization of telecommunications and the general logic of the Single Market. The two processes have corresponded in time as well as on the level of ideas.

Second, technological development has undoubtedly provided an important set of constraints on policy-makers, as well as undermining the possibility of keeping the old monopolistic order. Digitalization implied that it was no longer possible to clearly distinguish between voice telephony and transmission of other signals, and satellite communications challenged the system of purely national regulation and provision.

These two factors together provide the main driving-forces for the liberalization process (Pelkmans and Young 1998: 2). That is not to say that national political actors have had no impact on the process, far from it, but the coupling of new technology and the embracing of the free-market ideology at the European level has found its logical conclusion in telecommunications liberalization.

Recent history of telecommunications regulation in Europe is really a history of the European Union's gradual progression towards liberalizing a sector which was based almost entirely on national monopolies of networks, infrastructure and equipment as late as the beginning of the 1980s. The contrast could not be starker with the current regulatory regime, which is designed to remove monopolies and ensure that telecommunications in Europe are administered in the spirit of the competition rules as laid down in the Treaty of Rome.

The sector has also taken on a European character, as the EC has deliberately fostered a Europe-wide culture of both co-operation in development and infrastructure, and competition for contracts and customers. However, the EC, as in so many areas, has had to feel its way slowly towards this goal, as technology has developed at a dizzying pace and the regulatory regime has had to run to keep up. This is evidenced by the flood of Commission framework documents and proposals, as well as the myriad of technical groups and advisory panels involved in the process. It is therefore a story of incrementalism, but incrementalism towards a clearly defined goal of competition, which has now, to a large extent, been achieved. In a simplistic sense, the process has been to apply EC competition laws to the telecommunications sector, but as the chapter will show, the Commission has, in many ways, taken a far more radical, proactive course of action which has attempted to institute a dynamic and vibrant cross-European industry. The Full Competition Directive opened up the European market, and many companies are now offering competing services which are both cheaper and more advanced than before.

The Situation Prior to Liberalization

In order to give some indication of the profound change that took place during the 1980s and 1990s, it is necessary to sketch the situation as it existed in member states prior to any liberalization.

The telecommunications networks in virtually every European state – with the exception of Sweden – were operated as Post, Telegraph and Telephone administrations (PTTs), which formed part of the governmental administration. They were usually integrated with postal services, many of them administered directly by ministries and staffed by civil servants. The PTTs held a de facto monopoly over the national telecommunications infrastructures, and had a double role as both regulators and suppliers. Telecommunications policies were heavily politicized, because they touch both the security, economic, educational, and social policies of a country (Morgan and Webber 1986).

These monolithic creatures completely dominated the telecommunications industry, even extending to 'cosy' patent-sharing agreements with the manufacturers of customer premises equipment (CPE), the physical terminals necessary for the operation of the networks. Contracts were awarded in a political manner – i.e. there existed a deliberate policy of backing 'national champions' in each member state (Grupp and Schnöring 1992). There were companies such as GEC/Plessey in Britain and Siemens in Germany. Each PTT had its own arrangement with the relevant company, and since the contracts were awarded by governments with the express intention of building up one company to the exclusion of others, it was hardly a case of 'open and fair competition'.

The economic importance of the telecommunications equipment manufacturing sector, as well as its role in the research and development of a country's technological industry (including military industry), had, through the tacit definition of the telecommunications sector as belonging to the 'hard core' of national autonomy, ensured its exclusion from the competition rules in the Treaty of Rome from the beginning. Traditionally, the need for national security and complete national coverage at 'equal and affordable prices' (what was later to be called universal service) in communications was used as an additional political argument to keep both telecommunications and the postal monopolies well within the competencies of the nation-state (Morgan and Webber 1986).

Regulation of telecommunications in the context of the European Communities received little attention until the Green Paper of 1987. The speed with which this was done after 1987 provides an interesting study of the way the EU has extended its influence to a national sector where it previously would have been unable to act.

The system of 'national champions' was increasingly seen as restricting the European equipment manufacturers' ability to compete in design and innovation with the American and Japanese, and that some kind of co-ordination in research and development was necessary to avoid a European slump in the sector. The earlier system of national-level regulation was gradually replaced by a system in which the European Commission played a central role.

The First Steps – Harmonization rather than Legislation

The EC's initial strategy was *not* to use legislation to regulate the sector. In the early 1980s it lacked both the legitimacy and the resources to do so. Instead, it chose to encourage harmonization of networks and equipment. This was achieved by means of pan-European standardization bodies, set up as a part of the EC strategy to harmonize technical standards throughout the region, in order to prepare for one single market in which goods could flow freely. This strategy was continued and integrated in the Trans-European Networks programmes.

In the Commission, a Special Task Force was set up within DG III to advise Commissioner Davignon about the prospects for reform. At this stage, the Commission laid the seeds of a genuinely European system, and its efforts were successful with many of the actors involved in the process. Commissioner Davignon played an important role during the early years of the process, to the extent that he could be called a 'visionary' of a Europe with a truly harmonized telecommunications sector. He was instrumental in gaining the crucial support of industry for the principle of EC-defined standards, and it was this, coupled with the zeal shown in persuading national governments of the benefits of collective action, that enabled many of the advances to take place.

The effect of telecommunications on numerous other branches of activity was recognized from the late 1970s. Several bodies were set up during these early years, predominantly composed of both officials from the Commission and also representatives of the member states, emphasizing the Commission's need to work in close partnership with the national governments (Dyson 1986). The industry, too, co-operated in establishing these standards, since there was a widespread recognition of the benefits from a 'research and development' point of view.

The Commission had in its Community Action Programme on Telecommunications in 1984 identified three directions for Community effort in the field of telecommunications: first, network development for advanced services; second, a Community-wide market for equipment; and third, emphasis on forefront research and development. The only genuinely cross-national body in existence prior to this was CEPT (The European Conference of Postal and Telecommunications Administrations) which was effectively a lobby group for the European public telephone operators, and concerned with neither liberalization nor European co-operation.

The Commission also sought to promote trans-European co-operation through the establishment and co-funding of ambitious R&D programmes. The most important and long-running example of this would be the ESPRIT (European Strategic Programme for Research and Development in Information Technology) and RACE (Research and Development in Advanced Communications) programmes. These can be seen as Commission attempts to gain a central position in the development of technology (Dyson 1986: 16–17) but also as a recognition by many member states that their national markets individually were too small to sustain the investment needed to keep their 'national champions' at the forefront of technology. However, there is little doubt that the Commission played a significant role in mobilizing co-operation in the field.

First Legislative Strategies in Face of International Challenges

In the early 1980s the European telecommunications equipment industry was starting to lose out to its American and Japanese competitors. The American telecommunications arena, which for voice telephony provision until then had consisted of the monopolist AT&T in addition to the state regulator, underwent drastic changes as the New Right administration under President Reagan had decided on a 'big bang' deregulation programme. AT&T was forced to divest into several regional organizations (so-called 'Baby-Bells'), and its monopoly was removed, paving way for a more meaningful competition in a way which was impossible in Europe at that time (Hills 1986).

The US deregulation programme affected the European situation in two main ways. First, it was an example of the way a liberalization process could succeed and bring with it real benefits. Second, the US government insisted upon reciprocal liberalization of the European market. If European firms should be allowed to compete freely in the American market, then American firms should have the possibility to enter the European market – which was impossible under the regulated monopolies of the public phone operators (Dang-Nguyen 1988). It was not so much the providers of 'plain old telephony service' who wanted to access the European market. The real pressure came from the manufacturing and especially the computer industry, mainly in the form of the American computer manufacturer IBM.

Meanwhile, the first privatization programme took place in Britain, as the Thatcher government began to sell off the telecommunications wing of the GPO (General Post Office) under the name of British Telecom (Thatcher 1994). British Telecom thus became the first European operator to be privatized. The British experience clearly showed the need for sector-specific regulation in a liberalized market (for a full account of the situation in Britain, see Thatcher 1999), a lesson that was not missed by the European Commission.

There were other impetuses for the European Commission to intervene in the European telecommunications market, especially in the area of CPE. Despite Europe's relatively strong performance in innovation, American and Japanese companies were becoming increasingly, and ominously, competitive in the field of advanced technology. Two British writers were eulogizing the free market when they described the American/Japanese threat as 'a spectre haunting Europe' (Dyson 1986).

The Commission realized that the only way the European companies could keep up would be by the twin means of co-operation across Europe, and a Single Market for CPE within it. The creation of a Single Market would ensure a large enough 'domestic' market for European producers to sustain the investment needs. Hence this external pressure contributed to the Commission's attempts to liberalize this sector, arguing that the industry had to rationalize in order to survive. The single-market approach resulted in an increased trade in CPE Europe-wide, but attempts to build genuine cross-national alliances between companies in this area, despite the European research programmes, were less successful. The Commission was worried about the prospect for European technological companies, and its efforts were directed at preventing complete American/Japanese dominance of the sector.

The first real Commission initiative came with the 'lines of action', which it proposed to the Council at the beginning of 1983. These lines of action formed the basis for a telecommunications action plan, approved by the Council in 1984. It is important to note that this was a Council approval, which endorsed the action plan by the representatives of the member states. For future implementation efforts, this was a significant measure and signalled the Member States' willingness to reform.

The lines of action were a continuation of the previous strategy, and laid great stress on the research and design aspects of the sector. At this point in time no proposal was forwarded to change the status of the public telecommunications operators, illustrating that the Member States were determined to keep the status quo intact. There was not yet sufficient momentum for the entrenched national systems to be reformed.

What the package did do was to lay down the basis for the liberalization of the market for terminal equipment. EC standards were to become the norm for this equipment, a prerequisite for introducing Europe-wide offerings of contracts for telecommunications equipment. This 'functional' strategy is an example of the Commission's use of technological advance to secure a more 'political' end – a technique which it would use more often in the following years.

The Commission also practised breaking the sector down into segments and thus regulating slices of the industry separately and at different times, rather than attempting to legislate for the industry as a whole. They broadly distinguished between three components: the *network*, i.e. the physical cables and switches which enable the data or sounds to be transmitted, including satellites; the *services*, including voice telephony, value-added network services (VANS – of which banking services is a much-cited example) and data-transmission; and third, the manufacturing of *customer premises equipment* (CPE), i.e. equipment such as modems, fax machines and switching equipment (Thatcher 1994).

The Member States' Perspective

During the 1980s, all European countries were forced to re-evaluate their policies towards telecommunications. While it was the Commission that attempted to meld the differing debates in each country into a set of concrete proposals and directions in the 1987 Green Paper, it would be instructive to look at a number of the strategies considered by individual member states at this time.

The Witte Commission in Germany is a useful illustration of a member state seeking to reform its telecommunications system on its own terms (Witte 1988). Its rationale for action was the increasing fragmentation of demand for telecommunications services, the need for a rapid implementation of an innovative infrastructure, and the pressing necessity of delineating the role of state-owned entities in relation to the emerging competitive environment (Witte 1988: 22–3). In addition, it was clear that Deutsche Bundespost would have difficulties meeting the new demands without substantial change. 'As the present legal status of the Deutsche Bundespost would make it difficult to adopt [the necessary flexible] approach, the need for action aimed at removing the obstacles to an active market policy on the part of Deutsche Bundespost becomes evident' (Witte 1988: 27). The Witte Commission suggested that the telecommunications branch should be administratively separated from the postal service and set up as DBP Telekom, with greater autonomy from governmental control. However, it would be allowed to retain its monopoly on the basic network and on voice telephony (which amounted to around 90 per cent of all business).

This approach was indicative of many of the European states' initial antipathy towards 'true' liberalization, as they preferred to retain some degree of privilege for the national carrier. Germany, however, met specific difficulties with the re-unification in 1990. The cost of improving the East-German telecommunications infrastructure was huge, and a modernization programme (Telekom2000) was instigated to invest DM55bn over the period 1990–97 (Schmidt 1991). This hampered the domestic reform process, and the stressed economic situation of Deutsche Telekom also contributed to an increase in politicians' willingness to introduce private capital into the company.

In France, the government opened up for limited competition in CPE in the mid-1980s (Dang-Nguyen 1988), but the socialist government in power from 1981 to 1986 was reluctant to introduce competition in the sector. The operation of telecommunications was under the administration of a 'functional office within the state administration', in 1988 given the name of France Télécom. As late as 1990, the French government was reaffirming the right of France Télécom to retain a monopoly over the basic telecommunications services.

The French counterpart to the German Witte commission was the Prévot Commission, which recognized the need for increased flexibility in the sector, but in line with traditional French political order was eager to reconfirm the role of the State (Prévot 1989). It was also the French state that opposed the Commission's right to issue the directive on liberalization of the terminal equipment market, as discussed below. What has been interesting since the new regime was introduced in France in 1997, however, is the pragmatism with which they have pursued liberalization (Eliassen and Sjøvaag 1999).

The Benelux countries also undertook cautious programmes of reform, whilst leaving the significant services immune from competition (Verhoest 1995). Only in Britain did the government institute any degree of a meaningful liberalization of the core services during these years, but BT's status as a private company meant that there was far less political risk attached to this strategy (Marsh 1991). Besides, weak regulation and a long period of transition from monopoly to competition meant that BT was able to maintain its dominant status comfortably during these years. One should remember that the British case was not so much about liberalization as about privatization in the early years (Thatcher 1999). What has sometimes been hailed as an example of liberalization was in reality a change from a publicly to a privately owned monopoly, and the regulator, Oftel, became instrumental in introducing a competitive regulatory regime only after the initial public offering.

The 1987 Green Paper on Telecommunications

The 1987 Commission Green Paper on Telecommunications was the bedrock on which all subsequent reforms were built, and marked the point of departure for the liberalization of certain segments and for systematic EU legislation. It was an ambitious document, emerging from a Commission that had finally begun to believe that it could legislate to achieve its desired ends. The Commission was now acting with a great deal more authority and autonomy, and the scope of the paper reflects this. It marked an important step in the Commission's drive to make Member States aware of the benefits of, and need for, liberalization, and demonstrated its willingness to legislate actively to ensure that the process of liberalization took place.

At this time, the general feeling towards liberalization in Europe changed from hostility to curiosity and even 'hospitality', and many of the Commission's free-market proposals might have emanated directly from the national administrations. Expressed at EU level it reduced the possibility of controversy at the national level. The Paper was therefore both a crystallization of many of the national positions in the debate at this time, and also reinforced and extended many of the Commission's previously stated aims and objectives.

The principles of the Paper are worth examining in some detail since they provide a full and clear explication of the Commission's objectives, and all future developments must be understood in this context. The main rationale for this document was the long-standing view that the competition provisions in the Treaty of Rome needed to be applied to the telecommunications sector. The industry as it stood was in breach of, or at least going against the spirit of, the competition clauses in the Treaty of Rome. The PTTs represented an unacceptable monopoly in their sector, whilst the 'cartel' system relating to the national champions was particularly restrictive. The 1987 Green Paper set out to remedy this.

One should also note the consultative nature of this exercise – consensus was reached with the member states on most, if not all of the Commission's proposals. However, the document should be seen as much as a strategy for advancing and improving the telecommunications sector as a doctrinaire application of the EC's competition policy.

It is important to bear in mind that the Green Paper did not require a fundamental change in the status of the PTTs – they could remain as public bodies and retain their monopoly on basic telephone networks and infrastructure. This was in accordance with the findings of almost all the policy review bodies in the member states, such as the Witte Commission in Germany, and demonstrated that the member states were not yet ready to surrender the monopolistic position on basic services, nor be bounced into the kind of privatization measures introduced in Britain and the USA.

There was also concern that preserving a universal service would require cross-subsidization between services, since the policy hitherto in most countries had been to substantially overprice long-distance calls to the benefit of access charges, as well as to use the telecommunications operators as 'cash cows' for the Treasury. However, the Commission recognized the need at this point for investment in the telephone infrastructures, and saw that this could best be achieved with the PTTs in public ownership and receiving sufficient revenue to make this possible.

The most far-reaching and influential of the provisions in the Green Paper are related to Open Network Provision (ONP), laying down rules for access to the transmission network. Access to the means of trans-mission is crucial to the development of competition. This provision remains the bedrock for the liberalization and diversification of the telecommunications industry. ONP was designed to ensure that the public network operators were inhibited from frustrating competition by limiting access to the networks, thereby retaining their dominant market position not by efficiency and innovation, but by non-competitive practices.

Under the new ONP regime, any service provider could connect to the network as long as its equipment met the ETSI-defined standards. This harmonization of access conditions to the network had the twin benefit of allowing new, smaller companies the crucial foothold neces-sary to begin meaningful competition, and also allow the PTTs in each country to take advantage of the European market as a whole, thereby increasing their competitiveness. The ONP-provisions were to be crucial as the European market liberalized fully in the 1990s, when all services were opened to competition.

The other crucial requirement for this new regime was that the roles of market regulation and service provision were split, to ensure transparency in the sector. The idea of separation of regulation and operation had been forwarded in several countries, and resulted in administrative changes in many Member States around the turn of the decade, whereby operators were either defined as separate units, or (later) corporatized. Later, the ONP directive demanded the establishment of a National Regulatory Authority (NRA) independent from the industry, which in most cases (with the exception of Italy) has resulted in an independent agency.

Liberalization of CPE, Satellite and Mobile

The Terminal Equipment Directive – the first use of Article 90[1] in the telecommunications sector

In 1988, the Commission turned its attention to the legislative liberalization of CPE. The main objective of the 1988 Terminal Equipment Directive (EEC/88/301) was a gradual opening of the market for terminal equipment.

This directive was issued as a directive under the Treaty of Rome Article 90(3), which empowers the Commission to issue directives that will be directly applicable in the member states, without the approval of the Council of Ministers. This means, clearly, that the non-elected, bureaucratic organization that is the European Commission can decide upon development of national regulation on its own initiative. The rationale for introducing such measures into the Treaty was that the Commission is to be the guardian of the Treaty. The directive was immediately contested by some member states, and was brought before the European Court of Justice (Scherer 1998). The main claim was that the Commission by applying Article 90 in this context had acted outside of its competencies.

The legal process took almost 30 months to complete, but in March 1991 the Court of Justice stated that the Terminal Equipment Directive was to be upheld, at least in its most central parts. In particular, the Court

---

1 This article received a new number with the implementation of the Amsterdam Treaty. It is currently numbered Art. 85. Since it was still Art. 90 at the time we are describing here, we have chosen to use the old name.

held that the Commission had within its competencies to specify the relevant obligations of the member states under the Treaty including the specification and limitation of exclusive rights, and that the abolition of exclusive rights in this field also was justified with reference to the principle of free movement of goods. One should also note that the Court of Justice in the same ruling limited the use of Article 90 to issues concerning *state measures*, and as such cannot be used to regulate anticompetitive behaviour of the relevant undertakings themselves.

The directive obliges the member states to abolish all 'exclusive rights' of their telecommunications operators regarding use and marketing for terminal equipment; to ensure that private suppliers can participate in the terminal equipment market; and to ensure that users have access to new public network termination points. In order to ensure a European market in terminal equipment, directives have been issued that establish the principle of full mutual recognition of type-approval. Hence, equipment that is approved in one member state can freely be sold throughout the European Community.

The Commission's use of Article 90 in its efforts to initiate the liberalization process has been used by scholars to argue the paramount importance – indeed, the ultimate requisite – of the institution's role in the process (Webber 1998). One should not forget, however, that the ONP directive and a host of other liberalization directives have been issued by the Council of Ministers, and that although the Commission has been important, it has by no means been the only institution responsible for the development.

Satellite and Mobile Communications

In 1990 the Commission published its Green Paper on satellite communications ('Towards Europe-wide system and services'), designed to establish a more flexible regulatory system and foster the growth of satellite services. The case of satellite communications offers a good example of the difficulties in separating between regulation and operation of services, notably because of the many levels of interested parties. Regarding distribution of televized programmes, the regulatory authority lies within the nation-states, whereas access to the means of satellite communications was organized through international organizations such as Eutelsat, Intelsat and Inmarsat.

This 'institutional confusion' resembles what one later found with the convergence between IT services and telecommunications, where different providers, regulators and politicians which have formerly been concentrating on their special segment (such as public broadcasting, newspapers, or private, one-to-one telecommunications), met in an attempt to form common policies. The sheer number of institutions involved has made this difficult, in addition to the fact that these institutions normally have their own way of thinking and shaping policies (Levy 1997, Blackman 1998, Clements 1998).

The Commission proposed in its Green Paper on satellite communications to extend the principles of abolition of special rights, of free and unrestricted access, and of harmonization, to the satellite segment. These measures were seen to be paramount if a European market in satellite services was to be achieved. The ensuing directive legislated according to these principles.

The mobile communications market was an area where the EC started regulating very early in its development, through the setting of a European technical standard, the GSM (Global Systems for Mobile Communications.) Prior to 1987, five different systems for mobile phones had been developed in the EU member states. As a consequence, mobile phones had low penetration throughout Europe. The exception to this was the Scandinavian countries, where the NMT (Nordic Mobile Telephones) standard had been in use since the early 1980s. In 1987, the Council of Ministers adopted a recommendation for the introduction of the GSM standard.

The Mobile Directive (EC/96/2) entered fully into force in November 1996, and abolished the remaining exclusive rights within this market segment. The directive requires that mobile licences be put out to competitive tender. In 1997, eighteen DCS1800 licences were granted amidst fierce competition. This sector is widely predicted, along with Internet technology, to be one of the fastest-growing areas of telecommunications in the next decade, both in terms of technology and volume of subscribers (Englund 1999).

Some Technological Terms

It is difficult to discuss the future of European telecommunications regulation without including the terms of 'interconnection' and 'universal service'. The former is determining whether fair competition is feasible, the second demonstrates where telecommunications meets social policy.

Interconnection is necessary if subscribers to different networks are to communicate with each other. Under the old regime, pricing of interconnection took place on a bilateral basis, between the national telecommunications operators. They determined prices for calls from abroad, prices that were in no way based on costs (Andresen and Sjøvaag 1997). Rather, the old policies aimed at subsidizing local call tariffs and network access through overpricing of long-distance calls. This, coupled with the monopoly situation of the national operators, turned these international interconnection agreements into secure sources of revenues for the operators.

With the new ONP regime emerged a need for just and transparent interconnection prices (Garfinkel 1994), which was far from easy to implement. Not only was there no tradition for calculating the costs of interconnection, there were also huge uncertainties in how to account for the sunk cost in the networks of the old monopolies. This was an area where the British situation, because of its early occurrence, provided the European countries with useful experience. However, although interconnection tariffs ideally should be accorded upon by all interested parties, this became an area where the newly established national regulatory authorities became crucial. Both in France and Germany the NRAs set interconnection tariffs that were significantly lower than those proposed by the incumbent operators (see below).

'Universal service' was originally an American term, its most basic meaning being 'full geographical coverage' (Dordick 1990, Mueller 1993). In the European context, however, the term has taken on a more extended meaning and includes a condition that the basic services shall not only be the same throughout the national territory, but also be provided at 'affordable prices' (Hart 1998). The intention is to avoid so-called 'cream-skimming' of densely populated areas to the disadvantage of users in rural areas. Universal service can be seen as the regulatory safeguard from states that were used to providing telecommunications services as part of their public service, when the operators are being privatized (Skogerbø and Storsul 1998).

It is interesting to note that in the case of France, where the universal service provisions have been heavily emphasized all along the regulatory reform process because of their traditions of *service public*, the regulators tend to regard the question with less fear of failure as liberalization proceeds (ART 1999). The problem with a liberated market does not seem to be that the 'isolated customer living on a hilltop far away' doesn't get his or her services provided. Rather, in the information society, equal access to information is a broader challenge, and the disadvantaged are more likely to be illiterates in information technology and the poor living in city centres than citizens living far from the metropolis.

The Advent of Full Liberalization

The most significant measure to have influenced the hitherto last round of Commission directives was the EU Telecom Review's consensus in 1993 that full liberalization could not be restricted to the areas of VANS and other more marginal services. It would have to extend throughout the entire sector – local, long-distance and international calls, and all services and infrastructure. This was, of course, the logical extension of the Commission's position since the 1987 Green Paper. Ever since the Paper had recommended partial liberalization in certain areas, the then 'reserved services', namely voice telephony, were the obvious next port of call as circumstances allowed. This required a revision of the ONP provisions, since they were originally designed to ensure an open market for VANS rather than voice telephony. It remains, however, the natural framework for the interconnection and access to infrastructure under the new fully liberalized regime.

The new regime was laid down in the ONP Interconnection Directive, passed in 1997. This replaced the concept of the monopoly network operator with the idea of many public network operators acting in competition. The Commission reintroduced the idea of rights and duties for these operators, with the rights referring to unfettered market and network access, and the duties to the obligation to guarantee universal service. Those companies with 'significant market power', defined as over 25 per cent of the market share, have a 'general duty to supply'. Universal service means that every citizen has a right to access to a certain set of basic telecommunications services at 'affordable prices'. The exact content of the concept of 'basic services' is left to the member states to decide upon. For the time being, only the incumbent operators have sufficient market share to fall under the obligations of universal service.

There is, however, considerable political leverage in this question, as the question of 'affordable prices' is seen to entail a need for subsidization of certain users. The problem of settling the debates about who should pay is handled differently in different countries. In France, a universal service 'fund' was established simultaneously with the opening of the market, a fund to which all dominant operators will contribute. In Germany, however, there are legal provisions in place for the establishment of such a fund, but this will come into power only when no operator volunteers to supply the services. Taking into account that the operators then will have to contribute a certain percentage of their turnover to this fund, it seems reasonable to predict that no such fund will exist in Germany for a long time yet.

It must be noted that despite its long gestation period, the Full Competition Directive was still ambitious in setting an absolute deadline for every member state to liberalize their telecommunications completely. Many states sought derogations from the Commission, claiming that their industries were simply not ready to liberalize. Some of these were granted, as in the case of Ireland. The national carrier, Telecom Eirann, had carried out a massive development of its network, and the investment necessary had led it into debt. Thus the immediate effect of a fully competitive market would have been disastrous to the company, as it needed the revenues from its continuing monopoly to justify its investment in the network. Similar 'structural' issues were claimed by other states, notably Greece, which was granted an extra year to carry out the necessary reforms. So the European states varied in their ability to implement the directive.

For those member states who did not comply with regulation within the time frame, the Commission took action, first in the form of informal talks, and in more severe cases by taking member states to court. This illustrates the 'guiding principle' of the DG IV in this question, that it is better to start the process on time even if the result is not perfect, rather than to await completely harmonized implemented legislation in all member states. The final deadline for full liberalization was 1 January 2000, even with the derogations.

Post-1998 – Implications for Industry

Let us now examine the 'brave new world' of a liberalized telecommunications sector. With the Full Competition Directive implemented and all barriers to trade lifted, the industrial actors face a competitive environment. Special and exclusive rights over networks and services have been removed, with obvious implications for industry.

The most visible effect of the liberalization has been the proliferation of new actors in the market. Small firms have been given the chance to compete with the previously dominant operators, and many such companies are taking the opportunity to undercut the larger operators and offer new and innovative services such as combined entertainment–Internet–telephony applications. The mobile market in particular has seen an explosion in the number of companies bidding for licences and providing services. Moreover, operators previously restricted to operating within their national boundaries are now expanding their markets and forming joint ventures and alliances with other companies.

The former public telephone operators themselves have undergone tremendous changes since the start of the regulatory reform in the 1980s (Curwen 1997: 183–7). Less than fifteen years ago the majority among them were public administrations, contributing to state revenues, and with little if any direct link between their costs and the pricing of the services they provided. Now most of them have been sold (at least partly) to private interests, giving them a new set of stakeholders. They operate under private law, and are regulated not by their Ministers, but by an independent agency. They meet competition in their home markets, where they before had exclusive rights, and they also access foreign markets to compete abroad. They form alliances and joint-ventures, and have (or are about to) transformed their organizational structures in line with modern management principles. And they have to satisfy clients who are increasingly sophisticated and demanding both with regard to quality and price of old as well as new services.

In addition to these established actors we find a plethora of new entrants wishing to deliver telecommunications services or networks. Some of these are enterprises that have been created solely to enter the telecommunications industry, others are companies with long experience from other sectors, typically public utilities such as electricity and railways. The years 1998 and 1999 have seen a frantic activity of companies creating alliances, dissolving them, and buying each other in order to gain foothold in the various markets. It is no longer that easy to determine whether a company is German or Italian, whether it is principally a network or service provider. The convergence between traditional telecommunications and information technology also gives rise to alliances and mergers between software companies and mobile operators.

While the new entrants are finding their feet and establishing niches in the market, it appears that life beyond the 1998 market will be equally challenging for the former incumbent operators and dominant players. Many are having to face the uncomfortable realities of declining market share as the corporate sector in particular begins to take advantage of the services and savings offered by liberalization. British Telecom's market share is expected to drop to 'only' 62 per cent in the early years of this decade, and other incumbent operators are suffering similar or worse falls as the competition bites into their domestic markets. Cable companies have proven keen to expand their communications activities into telecommunications areas, and are routinely offering prices 10–20 per cent lower than on the conventional networks. The German regulator set its interconnection rates a good deal lower than Deutsche Telekom had anticipated (Werle 1999) – a clear sign that the older companies, at least in some countries, cannot expect preferential treatment from the newly empowered regulators.

In any sector being liberalized the actors – both old and new – will accumulate knowledge of the new regulatory regime through trying and failing. The speed of search for partners, which has been high in the telecommunications industry over the last two years, will undoubtedly slow down in the future. We believe that the 'new' landscape will consist of relatively few large infrastructure providers, hosting a large number of service providers. The resulting companies will have a view of their environment different from 'traditional' enterprises, and the concepts of 'competitor' and 'customer' are becoming less stringent, because in a networking environment such as telecommunications, different actors can take on different roles at different times (Fjeldstad 1999). And these companies will be acting not in a national or even a European arena, but globally.

The Global Context – and the WTO Agreement

World trade is increasing. This is especially true in services industries such as telecommunications where, in terms of market capitalization, the industry now ranks third in the world behind health care and banking. Indeed, telecommunication and office equipment was the fastest growing sector of merchandise exports during 1995, and the global value of trading in telecommunications services has been evaluated as US$600bn, of which cross-border trade is estimated to amount to US$100bn (http://www.itu.org). The global nature of the telecommunications sector strengthens the need for a world-wide regulatory framework, and increasingly one which is not only bilateral in nature, but can reduce uncertainty for multinational and multidomestic companies. The two main organizations for global co-ordination are the International Telecommunications Union (ITU) and the World Trade Organization (WTO).

The ITU grew out of the need for an overarching framework for securing interconnection between different national telegraph and telephone networks. Its main functions are to co-ordinate and regulate the use of the frequency spectrum, and to ensure the interoperability of telecommunications networks across national borders through standardization of equipment and systems. Furthermore, the ITU is working to promote telecommunications in the less-developed countries. However, the organization does not possess direct sanctioning powers, except for the rules laid down in international law, of which the ITU regulation forms a part, and have little power to enforce policies. It therefore works mainly as a forum for international discussion and documentation, in conformity with its intentions, relying on the mutual benefit for its members to follow its recommendations.

Of more immediate importance for trade agreements and the mutual opening of markets is the WTO. In 1997, the WTO telecommunication agreement opened the way for a multilateral framework for freer trade, market opening and competition. At the end of the negotiations on basic telecommunications there were 69 signatory governments to the Fourth Protocol, which sets out a global framework for mutual market opening in the sector. These countries together constitute more than 90 per cent of the global market for telecommunications services.

The WTO parties have agreed on a set of principles relating to competition safeguards, interconnection guarantees, transparent licensing procedures, and the independence of regulators. They have also established a 'dispute settlement procedure', an innovation in multilateral dispute settlement. Offers and commitments are binding on governments, and are practically irreversible. Thus a return to a system of national monopolies is excluded and the situation increases international interdependence.

However, the effectiveness and efficiency of the WTO as a forum for international dispute settlement will obviously depend on the members realizing the mutual benefit of co-operation. Since carriers operating in non-liberalized markets profit from the existing system, at least in the short term, they have few incentives to abandon it. The most important issue to promote a global industry is market access, which was at the top of the agenda of the Negotiating Group on Basic Telecommunications.

Although the WTO agreement on telecommunications is a clear step towards greater market opening, one should not believe that the process will be straightforward. Implementation at national level is crucial (OECD working paper 79/1995), and both national governments as well as operators will hold on to their competitive advantage in the domestic market as long as possible (Fredebeul-Krein and Freytag 1997). There is, however, little doubt that the WTO holds strong potential for establishing a new regime in the global telecommunications sector (Broadman and Balassa 1993). With a regulatory framework governed by a supranational organization, and member states that stick to its rulings, one can easily envisage a sector where the role of the nation-state is being reduced to the benefit of multinational and also multidomestic firms, and – one hopes – to the benefit of the consumers. After all, we still live in a world where a substantial part of the population never has made a phone call.

Conclusion

What will be the future of European telecommunications regulation? We see three points determining the development. First, technological development will rapidly change the conceptual basis on which regulation is done today. An example of this is the current definition of mobile communications as a basis for regulation, which will become redundant as users demand total flexibility between fixed, mobile and satellite technologies.

Second, continued globalization of the industry will challenge the effectiveness of national regulation and increase the need for regional and global regulatory regimes. Industry prefers a unified system in order to reduce uncertainty and diversity in their market place and wants as few regulatory institutions as possible. This issue will be further complicated by the relationship between sector-specific and general competition regulation. Increased competition will increase the need for decisions based on general competition rules, which the recent cases of mergers and acquisitions both in Scandinavia and in Italy show. Our assumption is, however, that because of the large number of operators at all levels of policy-making, and the multitude of interests involved, the present complicated picture of multi-level and multi-institutional regulation will persist for the foreseeable future.

Third, the speed of the technological convergence between tele-communications, media and information technology will provide important impetus to change the political regime. The same holds true for the changing issues involved in the regulation debate concerning not only frequencies and concessions but also content and ownership.

These points are all issues the policy-makers have to keep in mind in future revisions of the regulatory regime. Studying the process of liberalization from the mid-1980s until now shows the increasing speed of reform, and the principal content of the next regulatory reform might at times seem inevitable. We believe, however, that there is still ample space for politics in the regulation of this sector, even if policy-makers will be required to change their perceptions of basic concepts. The challenge of universal service provision might no longer be territorial coverage, but equal access to information will continue to be paramount for the development of European society.

The complexity of European policy-making is demonstrated in this chapter. Further case studies into different countries' liberalization process will increase the detail of this picture (see Eliassen and Sjøvaag 1999), but such investigations in no way render the presentation less complex. Even if new technology is global, it has to be implemented technically into different systems of infrastructure, and politically into countries with varying traditions for state action and intervention in the economy. In addition, the global arena adds another level for policy-making and co-ordination.

CHAPTER 6

ENERGY POLICY: INTEREST INTERACTION AND SUPRANATIONAL AUTHORITY

Svein S. Andersen

EU Energy Policy: What are the Driving Forces?

The struggle over a common EU energy policy is a special case of Europeanization of policy-making (Usherwood 1998), and up to the 1980s it was regarded as a spectacular failure (George 1985: 100). Energy policy is characterized by strong conflicts between a common policy, on the one hand, and divergent national policies, on the other. The focus here is the emergence of a common EU energy policy during the 1990s. Despite its inclusion in the very first treaties on the European Community, energy was until very recently more or less unaffected by common market legislation, and few energy policy decisions were taken at the central EU level (Schmitter 1996). The most important changes in the last few years are related to the internal market directives on the electricity and gas markets (Hancher 1998).

This chapter does not intend to identify all EU regulations that affect energy. Neither does it deal with the impact of national energy policies, which has played a key role in the sector. Rather, it focuses on the inter-relationship between attempts to create a common EU energy policy, on the one hand, and the institutional development of the EU (and its predecessors), on the other hand. We can distinguish four stages in the development of EU energy policy, as follows.

In the first, from 1946–57, energy supply was a major problem facing the (then) six members (of the ECSC). Energy was mostly indigenous coal supplies. Energy co-operation fuelled wider economic and political co-operation. In the second period, from 1957–72, energy was not regarded as an issue of great concern. Cheap imported oil replaced coal, and although this was a period of marked advances in European co-operation, this was not reflected in the energy sector. In the third period, 1972–85, energy re-entered the EU agenda and this time as a problem of oil prices and supplies. Common policies largely failed. The last stage, from the late 1980s to the late 1990s, represents a revitalization of attempts to introduce a common EU policy.

The EU is still far from a common energy policy, but since the late 1980s a number of important EU initiatives have been taken to strengthen the supranational influence on the energy policy (Matlary 1991, Lyons 1992, 1994, Padgett 1992). Energy issues have increasingly been linked to three general perspectives. First, the EU's internal-market programme where competition policy plays a major role. Second, the EU's attempts to establish a common environmental policy with fiscal measures as key instrument. Third, the European Energy Charter and the Charter Treaty which were attempts by the EU to create international market regimes that could support reform in the former Eastern Bloc and thereby secure the EU's energy supplies.

Such initiatives all reflect the desire to establish European policies in areas that before were dominated by national authorities. They were linked to the revitalization of the EU, based on institutional reforms and the general support for increased EU co-operation where liberalization was a key element. Changing perceptions of energy in relation to environmental concerns and with respect to the international supply situation were additional factors. During the early 1990s the proponents of common EU policy dominated the agenda-setting. As will be discussed in detail later, attempts to achieve Europeanization of energy policy experienced serious problems, but there were also some important successes (Matlary 1997a). The new initiatives have opened the way for changes that may make it impossible to preserve important parts of national energy markets in the long run.

One major perspective explains the development of supranational authority and common policy by pointing to the gradual emergence of common and overlapping intergovernmental interests. The process is driven by rational actors building coalitions (Morgenthau et al. 1973, Waltz 1979). This would be consistent with the co-operation over coal (and steel) policy during the post World War II years. The Six (who had lost the war) saw co-operation on coal as a requisite for successful reconstruction, but also in the new spirit of a unified Europe.

The lack of overlapping interests between member countries (and national energy sectors) is consistent with the lack of a common EU policy in the energy sector up to the late 1980s. From the late 1950s to the early 1970s such co-operation did not seem necessary. During the 1970s national interests were too diverse. However, it is not possible to explain the elements of common energy policy since the late 1980s in terms of overlapping interests. On the contrary, such a tendency would seem highly unlikely from this bottom-up perspective since the lack of, or small degree of, overlap is a consistent characteristic of the energy sector.

Important new EU energy policy initiatives have been driven by the Commission, which has exploited institutional rules to take the initiative, to redefine the energy sector in relation to the internal market, environmental policy and foreign policy. The areas to which energy is linked are all areas where supranational institutions have been assigned tasks that the neo-functionalists call inherently expansive (Cameron 1991: 25). This is perhaps most obvious in the case of the internal market and in environmental policy, but also in relation to the EU's ambitions to exercise international leadership during the dramatic transformations going on in the former Soviet Union and Eastern Europe after the end of the Cold War. The new EU initiatives in energy policy did not happen automatically, but seem to have been part of a deliberate plan. Key actors in the Commission and in some member countries wanted to exploit the momentum of success in other areas. Such initiatives managed to reinstate energy policy as an important concern at the EU level.

A key to understanding this development is how the EU – as an institutional framework and a set of central institutional actors – interacts with underlying interests in the energy sector in the different stages of EU development. This interaction demonstrates the close link between EU decision-making, the problem of defining collective interests and the impact of the EU's political cycles. The development of energy – and especially petroleum – policy during the 1990s in the EU is the topic for the rest of the chapter. Central questions are: What drives the development in this policy area? How is a common EU energy policy linked to the development of EU institutions and the movement towards the European Union? Under what conditions can we expect a development of supranational authority and common EU policy?

Common Energy Policy Initiatives

New proposals for common EU energy policy in the late 1980s and early 1990s were closely related to the revitalization of the EU. The Single European Act (1987) and the Maastricht Treaty (1993) strengthened supranational authority in a number of policy areas, although not specifically in relation to energy policy (Wallace and Wallace 1996, Hix 1999). The reforms did, however, create a new dynamic where actors in other policy areas became more active in redefining traditional energy policy issues. Such initiatives represent a form of political spill-over, where resourceful actors exploited new opportunities within a new institutional framework. The new initiatives did not get much support from traditional energy sector interests. New EU level perspectives challenged national policy paradigms and vested interests, and shifted issues over to new arenas with new decision-making procedures. Diverse national energy interests – including new member countries – were forced to relate to new types of games at the EU level.

One important source of change was the EU's internal market programme. This reflected not only the internal development of the EU, but also general policy and international orientations reflected in OECD. The latter had for some time pushed towards more liberal arrangements in the energy sector. The internal market opened up for a number of initiatives in the energy sector, as part of a general deregulation policy (COM 88 174, Matlary 1991). This was an area covered by new rules of majority decision-making, and where the commission had a strong role. In this perspective the question was not whether national energy sectors performed well in relation to various national objectives, but whether the organization of industries was consistent with principles of competition policy and detailed law.

Another major source of policy initiatives affecting energy was environmental policy (Bergesen 1991, Iversen 1992). Initiatives from this sector differed from deregulation in that policies were directed towards the realization of specific objectives with growing popular support. There was, however, no agreement on what would be the best ways to achieve them, except that environmental interests should play a key role in formulating solutions. Also in this area, after Maastricht (1994), it was possible to make decisions according to majority rules, although there were exceptions for issues involving fiscal matters. And with respect to environmental policy relating to international climate negotiations the Commission was empowered by strong political signals from the European Council (Simon and Duhot 1994).

The third policy area was foreign policy, which became linked to the wider EU co-operation through the Maastricht Treaty. There was some uncertainty as common foreign policy objectives were not clear, and decisions should still be firmly controlled by member states according to traditional rules of international co-operation. The changing status of this policy area was, however, reflected in ambitions about a more active leadership role for the EU in international matters. As it turned out foreign policy interests wanted to use energy policy as an instrument in relation to reforms in the former Eastern Bloc countries. Again, however, there was no clear idea about the way that energy policy could best do this. The details were left to those usually involved in EU energy policy formulation, reflecting the tug of war between sector interests and general market perspectives (Dore and De Bauw 1995).

Below we will describe new attempts to create common EU energy policy, distinguishing between policies of deregulation, on the one hand, and initiatives reflecting policy objectives relating to environmental and foreign policy.

Common Energy Policy as Deregulation: The Single Market

The Single European Act of 1987 laid the foundation for the revitalization of the EU and for the conclusion of the internal market before the end of 1992. However, it contained nothing on a common energy policy. This was no coincidence, as energy was regarded as a very problematic area. This did not mean that energy, or any other area of economic activity, was to be exempted from the internal market programme. The energy objectives adopted by the Council of Ministers (Energy) in September 1986 explicitly mentioned the need for greater integration of the internal energy market (SPRU-report 1989, Stern 1990).

Up to this time, energy was partly regarded as a national problem. As for oil and gas, both security of supply and price risk related to factors outside the control of the EU. These were traditional concerns for the EU as well as the member states. At the EU level they had been dealt with through stockpiling of oil and efforts to increase energy efficiency. In member countries oil dependency had been reduced through taxation and comprehensive regulation – often through oligopolistic or mono-polistic arrangements – which had been instruments to reduce demand and promote diversity of energy. Natural gas, which was mostly imported, made it necessary to balance supplies from a small number of sellers. Sometimes energy policy had also been motivated by the desire to preserve regional employment. Such regulation had a price, and this became clear as oil prices fell in the early 1980s.

The internal market in energy was to be realized through three different types of policy instruments (Lyons 1994: 5). First, through specific energy directives removing barriers to competition and trade, by translating general Treaty principles into new sector regulation. Second, general internal-market directives that would also affect energy, like the directive on public procurement. Third, more active application of existing competition law to the energy area. However, the latter also faced political limitations, and rulings could only address specific instances of violations. The following discussion focuses on attempts to introduce specific directives in the energy sector. It is important to keep in mind, however, the interaction among these three sources of change.

Energy policy was discussed in a special *White Paper on Energy Policy* in 1988 (COM 88 174). The Commission took a close look at energy sectors in Europe within the framework of the internal market programme. The study concluded that the (downstream) oil industry was already, with some exceptions, operating within a free market. In addition, coal and nuclear sectors had since the 1950s been covered by detailed Treaty provisions. It was primarily in the gas and electricity sector that there was a need for new directives.

In the coal industry the major problem was to apply Community legislation to reduce subsidies, while there was a need for cost transparency for equipment and components in the nuclear sector. The priorities for the (downstream) oil industry were coupled to general measures of taxation and standards. The Commission's conclusion was that existing law and general internal market directives would solve most of the problems in the energy sector. The exceptions were the gas and electricity industries, and here the Commission focused on downstream activities. In addition came upstream oil, and oil and gas (Lyons 1994: 6/7).

Major parts of the European energy industry were in violation of the internal market principles. The suggestions made were not motivated by positive objectives related to energy, they were part of a general deregulation policy. The point of departure for the Commission's initiative were Articles 86 and 90 in the Treaty of Rome about state-owned and other monopolies and abuses of market power. Such articles seemed especially relevant in the gas and electricity sectors, where the degree of monopolization on the national level was extremely high. These sectors, to a large degree, would have to submit to market forces that would lead to greater efficiency and lower prices. They now became the target for the Commission through a number of directive proposals.

The internal market programme consisted of 279 proposals to create directives that could remove non-tariff trade barriers and create a single market across the EC. In the Commission the push to link energy to the internal market came from Directorate General IV, which was responsible for competition, and Directorate General XVII with responsibility for energy policy. Other Directorates General were also involved, especially DG XXI (General customs union and indirect taxation), DG III (Single market and industry) and, not least, DG XI (Environment). This participation by several DGs in the formation of energy policy reflects two important circumstances. Energy was being coupled to a number of EU policy areas, and the commissioners did not have the same degree of control within a policy area which ministers usually have in a national ministry. The Commission passes all motions by majority votes, and all the (then) 17 commissioners were involved in all policy fields.

The First Conflicts over Electricity and Gas Directives

The Commission had a three-stage approach to the introduction of internal market directives in the energy sector. The initial focus was on the downstream side of the electricity and gas sectors, but the plan was to move upstream as reforms progressed.

During the first stage the Commission wanted to introduce elements of competition into the distribution of electricity and gas. This should be accomplished through the introduction of transparency of prices and investment plans and transit rights for other grid operators. Proposals for such directives were adopted by the Commission and sent to the Council of Ministers (Energy) in July 1989.

The price transparency directive – covering both gas and electricity producers – was uncontroversial. It was adopted by the Council in June

1990 and became operative in mid-1991. The new directive required suppliers to provide the Statistical Office of the European Communities – SOEC – with three types of information on a regular basis: prices, pricing systems and breakdown of consumers and consumption volumes. Based on this the SOEC would publish statistics which would improve the information available to market actors (Lyons 1994: 7). Such a system had been established in Great Britain already in 1988, as the new controlling authority OFGAS pressured the privatized British Gas by threatening to take them to court (Andersen 1993).

Two other directive proposals concerned transit rights for other grid operators in the electricity and gas sectors, respectively (Capouet 1992). The aim was to ensure that a grid operator in one member state should not impede the trade of electricity or gas between other member states. Both proposals were short and simple, basically focusing on procedures for handling of transit requests. The electricity directive was passed in October 1990, and came into force in July 1991. In contrast to other cases the Commission found that the electricity industry, represented by Eurelectric, was co-operative to the proposed transit rights. However, the industry also made it clear that the Commission's ideal of a common carrier system was completely unacceptable.

The proposal for transit rights in the gas sector proved more controversial. It took almost two years before it was adopted by the Council of Ministers (Energy) and entered into force in January 1992. Germany and the Netherlands – with their national monopoly suppliers Ruhrgas and Gasunie – were most actively against. However, there was widespread scepticism against the proposal. These reactions from affected interests may be regarded as a positioning to fight future and more far-reaching Commission proposals.

The fourth of the first stage proposals also signalled that there were clear limitations to what member states would accept in the energy sector. The aim of the investment transparency directive was to ensure exchange of information to achieve a better coherence of large-scale investment projects in the Community. However, at the Council of Ministers (Energy) meeting in May 1990 member states voiced their opposition to this plan. The Commission was forced to step back from the directive approach and, instead, to make better use of existing regulations.

The second stage in the deregulation of the EU's electricity and gas markets introduced more ambitious objectives and more comprehensive regulatory measures. This led to strong political reactions from member countries and their industries (Austvik 1991, Capouet 1992). The new proposals attacked 'the heart of the gas and electricity industries with practising monopolies' (Lyons 1994: 5). The Commission wanted to introduce competition that would fundamentally alter the relationship between suppliers, transmission operators, distributors and consumers (Stern 1992, Austvik 1995).

By that time, it was already clear that many member states and affected industries were opposed. For this reason the Commission established working groups to be part of the Commission's preparatory work. For each industry there was one committee of experts and one consisting of member state representatives. These groups met throughout 1990. Based on their reports the EU Commission prepared directive proposals during the last half of 1991. The proposals were presented to the Council of Ministers (Energy) in January 1992.

The complex proposals basically required that member states did three things (Lyons 1994: 10):

1 Abolish exclusive rights regarding electricity generation and the building of gas and electricity transmission lines
2 Oblige vertically integrated companies to unbundle their accounting and management systems
3 Introduce third party access (TPA) rights to a limited number of high volume gas and electricity consumers so that they could chose suppliers from throughout the Community.

Despite all the consultations that had taken place, more than half of the member countries were against the proposals. On the other hand, the Commission had strong support from big industrial customers. During the autumn of 1992 a stalemate developed between the Commission and its closest ally, Britain, which held the EU presidency, on the one hand, and almost all other member countries and their industries, on the other hand. In an unprecedented move, the Council of Ministers sent the proposal back to the Commission without a comprehensive committee discussion, with detailed political instructions for the future work. It was a deadlock, and it was clear that an agreement on the proposals on electricity and gas markets could not be reached in the short run.

An Early Success: Oil and Gas Licensing

By early 1992 the Commission was well aware of the political problems involved in pursuing an internal market for energy. The second stage faced serious difficulties. This meant that the third stage was delayed. However, in relation to upstream oil and gas the Commission faced fewer adversaries than in the areas of electricity and gas liberalization. This opened the way for a directive proposal for hydrocarbon licensing. This directive was to regulate the granting and use of authorization for prospecting, exploration and production.

The proposed directive would introduce market principles also in upstream petroleum activities. It should no longer be possible to grant special privileges to national or state-owned companies. This would also fill a gap between the proposed directives for gas and electricity movement, on the one hand, and existing public procurement legislation regulating contracts in the oil, gas (and coal) exploration and production industries. The procurement directive from September 1990 opened the way for a simplified procedure in the petroleum sector, if regulation fulfilled the internal market conditions. The full procedure could complicate certain contracts. It turned out, however, that getting exception from it was more problematic than had been foreseen (Lyons 1994: 15/16, Andersen 1995: Ch. 4).

For the Commission – and Britain, which was its close ally in this area – the licence directive was important to keep up the political momentum in the energy sector. The UK, which held the EU presidency during the first half of 1992, made the completion of the licence directive a priority. This would be consistent with reform already carried out in Britain during the early 1980s. The EU parliament was quick to give its first opinion. For this reason it would have been possible to reach a common position in the Council of Ministers (Energy) by the end of 1992.

However, at the Council of Ministers' meeting on 30 November 1992 Denmark managed temporarily to postpone a common position. Eventually, the special interests of Denmark and Norway, as the two major oil and gas producers in western Europe except Britain, managed to delay and alter the proposal substantially. A key issue for Denmark was the preservation of state participation in infrastructure (gas transportation) and the relationship to historical obligation entered into during the early 1960s. Norway was the major petroleum exporter in western Europe and had a strong statist tradition. It was not an EU member, but through the European Economic Area agreement and later membership negotiations it became directly involved with internal EU deliberations.

The licence directive demonstrated, again, that strongly affected minorities might create considerable political problems for the Commission's plans. The fact that a non-member country could achieve access to the EU internal decision-making was another confirmation of the political weight that energy issues were given by member states in the EU, although one could argue that there were special interests at stake for Norway. The licence directive was passed in May 1994 and entered into force in mid-1995. It was the last energy-specific directive-proposal from the Commission. The 'grand plan' from the early 1990s was abandoned, at least for the time being. This reflected not only the opposition in the energy sector, but also more general political problems in the EU.

Counter Mobilization and Limited Success

The licence directive was one of the few directives influencing the structure of the industry, which was actually passed during the first half of the 1990s. The price transparency and transit directives had limited effects in this respect. There were, however, other directives that affected the energy sector. Such directives were mostly related to general efforts of the internal market. The procurement directive has already been mentioned. Another was the harmonization of (minimum) excise taxes for mineral oils in 1992. Parallel to the introduction of directives, the energy sector had been under pressures to change due to the application of existing competition law. For political reasons the Commission had to exercise caution, but a number of cases eliminated deviations from the internal market.

Competition law was, for instance, used to push for liberalization of downstream oil markets in Greece, Portugal and Spain. However, practices in a number of other countries, involving different sectors, were targeted by the Commission. Sometimes the threat to raise a case was enough to bring about changes. In other cases changes were enforced through Court rulings (Lyons 1994: Ch. 3). Such decisions differ from the directive approach in that they limit themselves to the issues at hand, and do not attempt to formulate new general regulations. However, in the long run they create precedence that may open the way for and influence new directives. This interplay between the directive approach and the use of competition law is important in the long run (Stern 1992, Noreng 1994).

The focus of efforts to change the EU's energy markets – through political initiatives or through court decisions – had mainly been transportation systems and concession regimes. National consumer prices vary considerably, and this is likely to be the case for a long time to come.

The process from radical Commission proposals to complicated negotiations, watering down original intents, reflects the duality of the Commission's role in the EU decision-making process. On the one hand, it is supposed to be a radical supporter of the EU's visions. On the other hand, it shall try to reach complicated political compromises. There were strong forces at the EU level dissatisfied with national industries and with national authorities defending arrangements on a collision course with EU visions. On the other hand member states and national industries had strong vested interests. This meant that the Commission's suggestions often would be changed considerably during the lengthy process towards a final passing of a directive.

The formal changes in the EU institutions and decision-making procedures since the late 1980s had been limited, but important. Among other things, the door was opened for majority decisions in the Council

...inisters. The lobbyists swarmed to Brussels and laid siege to EU institutions. This indicates that EU institutions and general EU policy were in the process of being strengthened compared with national interests. The Council of Ministers was still important, but energy policy was no longer the exclusive domain of member countries and national industry. The Commission was on the offensive, not only because of DG XVII and its responsibility for energy matters. DG IV, responsible for competition policy, was often pushing the Commission.

The Failure of Common CO$_2$ Tax

Another tendency in the development of EU energy policy started parallel to ongoing deregulation efforts of the internal market. Again it was not the traditional, national energy actors who were on the offensive. Just as in the area of deregulation the initiatives came from political forces outside the energy sector also at the EU level. Energy was increasingly coupled to environmental protection and foreign policy. Environmental impact from energy had top priority with DG XI (Environment) as well as in a number of member countries (Lyons 1990, Matlary 1991, Andersen 1995).

Around 1990 environmental policy was one of the most important forces behind a new energy policy in the EU (Bergesen 1991, Iversen 1992). The EU had been occupied with environmental policy since the early 1970s. The focus of the first environmental programmes had been special problems of pollution. By 1990 two important changes had taken place. First, environmental policy, in contrast to energy policy, had become part of the Treaty of Rome through the Single European Act reform in 1987. Second, environmental protection had been defined as a horizontal policy area – a general concern to be taken into account in other policy areas. These changes gave the environmental policy greater weight.

The Single European Act established a foundation for environmental policy in the EU constitution, namely articles 130R, 130S and 130T.

The goal of Article 130R is to preserve, protect and improve the environment, and to contribute to better health and a rational use of natural resources.

Article 130S concerns decision procedures, and states that in the Council of Ministers motions are to be passed by unanimity. This was changed to qualified majority after the treaty conference in Maastricht, effective from 1 January 1993.

Article 130T states that the introduction of EU regulations in this field shall not deprive member countries of the right to introduce stronger measures.

In addition, Article 100A concerns the creation of uniform and effective regulations in the EC. It states that regulations shall be based on a high level of protection of health, environment and consumer interests. EU environmental policy comprises air pollution, changes in the climate, water quality, waste disposal, control of chemicals and noise. Pollution and the climate are the fields that until now have had the greatest impact on energy policy.

Demands for reduced pollution were not solely linked to use of energy, but burning of fossil fuels was a serious source of pollution. Energy efficiency and alternative energy had been on the EU agenda for some time. Some directives have been passed to reduce emission from cars and industry. However, the climate policy, which surged to the top of the political agenda around 1990, created a new context for EU energy policy (COM 92 226, Lyons 1994: 53). This led to new demands for cleaner energy forms and regulations. There were strong coalitions outside the energy sector that drove the process onwards, even though the atomic industry had nothing against stronger rules for CO_2 emissions.

International research co-operation led to a strong and united report in 1990 in which climate change was viewed as a major international political challenge. Without a rapid stabilization of climate gas emissions the results would be serious negative and irreversible effects. The report gave momentum to the proponents of environmental policy in the EU, in the Commission as well as in a majority of member states. As a result the EU introduced a stabilization target in 1990 and a radical proposal for a common EU CO_2 (later CO_2 /energy) tax in 1992 (COM 92 226). The EU also hoped to win support for such a tax from all OECD (and other) countries in the Rio Conference in 1992.

A CO_2/energy tax would have introduced substantial energy price increases and also two new price formulas for different energy sources. However, once more the complex decision-making process surrounding the directive proposal ran into difficulties. This was partly because international trading partners were reluctant to support the EU's proposal about a tax, but also due to complex interests within the EU. Political visions that dominated the first years were eventually undermined by the opposition representing energy and general industry interests. In December 1994 it became clear that a common EU CO_2/ energy tax could not be achieved.

The setback for a common CO_2/energy tax does not, however, mean that environmental policy in EU is dead. A number of less radical measures have been introduced. In relation to the CO_2 issue the new monitoring mechanism strengthens those who want to keep up the pressure for action. Also, a number of member countries are actively supporting new initiatives, although it seems that fiscal measures will be introduced on the national level. The new emphasis on unemployment and other economic problems has, to some extent, weakened the commitment to environmental policy. The attempt to link the solution of unemployment and improve environmental protection through a new tax structure was not successful in the short run. However, environmental concern, with strong popular support, may well be an important challenge to energy policy in the years to come.

On the other hand, it is important to keep in mind that taxation of energy is also linked to fiscal interests of the member states. As Austvik (1996b, 1997) has pointed out, since the mid-1980s there has been an increase in consumer taxes on energy, in particular oil products. This has two important implications. The first is that it reduces the import bill, since all member countries, except Britain and Denmark, are dependent on import. The second is that the profits are transferred from exporting to consuming countries. The import of both oil and gas into the EU is expected to increase significantly over the next 20 years. This means that the CO_2 tax initiative is partly realized through other instruments, although not consistently in relation to CO_2 emissions. In some cases the worst polluter in this respect, namely coal, is even subsidized. Tensions of this nature are also reflected in the proposal for a directive on *Restructuring the Community Framework for the Taxation of Energy Products* (COM 97: 30 Final 97/0111).

The Energy Charter Treaty

Another consideration that has increasingly influenced EU energy policy over the last years is foreign policy. This was a result of the Gulf War and, especially, the events in the former Soviet Union and Eastern Europe after the end of the Cold War. In both cases the security of supplies was a central concern. However, the foreign policy concerns also go further than the energy implication. This was most obvious in the case of the European Energy Charter and Treaty (Dore and De Bauw 1995, Andersen 1997b).

The Gulf War created an increased understanding of the fact that war in the Middle East was not a dramatic one-time event, but a symptom of underlying problems which may flare up again at any time. In short: the problem is not a lack of stability in the oil market, but that the Middle East 'does not work'. Such preoccupation strengthened the view that energy is a strategic commodity. This perspective has always been central for the Commission's Directorate General XVII with responsibility for energy questions.

In the short run, the answer to the uncertainty in the Middle East was to create a crises depot corresponding to 90 days' consumption, as in the USA. In a further perspective, creating economic ties between some Arab countries and the EU could have a stabilizing effect. The general idea behind the latter is that increased interdependency will strengthen a communality of interests and increase stability. Such efforts came in addition to the work done on a more effective use of energy in the member countries.

Earlier, the EU's energy risk related to the Soviet Union's dependency on gas import (Moe 1988). This could, in principle, be used to exert political pressure. Now the situation was quite different. The gas industry in Russia had huge infrastructure problems. There had been several great leakages in the pipelines to western Europe. (Some have argued that as much as 30 per cent was lost before the gas reached the market.) Through the Energy Charter and the Treaty, the EU wished to strengthen the framework for market-based solutions and to offer security to foreign investors. In addition, Russia has large oil resources that could reduce dependency on the Middle East (Ebel 1994).

The point of departure was a somewhat unclear political initiative sent to the European Council, the so-called Lubbers Plan in 1990. During the Commission's work on this plan, focus was placed on a mixture of foreign policy, aid programmes and energy policy, which, in the long run, could contribute to lasting and cheap access to energy for the EU. Energy was also one of five sector programmes aimed at assisting the changes in Russia. The last programme aimed at using 105 million Ecu. About 50 per cent would be spent on strengthening security in the atomic industry, 20 per cent would be spent on reducing energy consumption, and the electricity and gas sectors would each get around 15 per cent.

Through these programmes, the EU wished to secure its own future supply. By helping Russia in the energy sector, an important contribution would also be made in relation to the dramatic changes taking place in that country. If the EU programme could contribute to a successful transformation in the oil and gas sector, it could also function as a model for new institutional solutions in the rest of the economy. The oil and gas sector was also one of the few sectors where Russia had export potential, making it a source of much-needed foreign currency incomes.

One element of the Energy Charter was that, to a certain extent, there were overlapping interests between national industries and the EU Commission, in contrast to the adversary orientation which was evident in other fields of energy policy. The Charter and Treaty was meant to strengthen the market framework prevalent in the West, but there was room for solutions with elements of western European traditions, i.e. power concentration around large companies. Also, it was unrealistic to imagine pure market solutions in the energy sectors in the former Eastern Bloc countries. This provided room for a communality of interests between parties that in other areas are strong adversaries.

The preparations for the Energy Charter Conference took about a year. The Charter was concluded within 6 months after the conference opened and signed in December 1991. The negotiations over the Treaty were a time-consuming process, and there were major changes in perspectives and ambitions along the way. The Treaty was signed in December 1994. Some important issues were too complicated to deal with in the short run, and had to be taken out of the Treaty to reach an agreement. These outstanding issues were the subjects for a new round of negotiations that started immediately after the signing of the first treaty. The implementation and effects of the Charter Treaty are still uncertain.

The increased weight of foreign policy was related to institutional changes in a context of radical changes. Foreign policy became formally linked to the wider EU co-operation through the Maastricht Treaty, but without room for Commission activism or majority decisions. However, political ambitions about a more active role for the EU in international politics played an important role. For this reason the European Council – the regular meetings by the EU's heads of state – has been active. Such initiatives have played a major role in connection with eastern Europe.

The Late 1990s: Breakthrough for Electricity and Gas Market Liberalization

The first round of the decision-making procedure on the liberalization of the European electricity and gas markets had demonstrated that these were very controversial issues. In May and November 1993 the Council discussed the proposal which the Commission has introduced already in 1990. Although almost all countries were against the present proposal, the Council stated that electricity and gas markets had to become more open. However, it was not clear how this could be achieved. In this situation the European Parliament – through its energy committee – took an active role in finding a compromise acceptable to both the Council and the Commission. This active role of the Parliament reflected not only that the two major EU institutions were unable to find a workable compromise. It was also linked to a more general struggle for increased influence in the EU. The Parliament's proposal (CERT 1993) was the basis for a new Commission proposal presented to the Council of Ministers in December 1993.

The Commission had invested considerable prestige in the proposal, and went a long way to find compromises that could solve the political stalemate. Compared with the first proposal, changes were substantial. Most importantly the idea of public service obligation was strengthened, and third party access was made voluntary. The latter meant that the Commission had to settle for a solution which was not very different from the existing practice of the industry, although the burden of proof now shifted to the industry when access was denied due to lack of 'free capacity'. The first results were, therefore, a long way from the ambitious objective of common carrier, or free access to the transport systems for everyone (Austvik 1995).

In early 1994, the Commission re-sent a revised version of its proposal. It took into account some of the inputs from the Council and the

Parliament. The changes are reflected in the final directive, and they are related to two areas. The first allowed gas producers to negotiate access to transmission lines. The other established a framework for liberalization providing the member countries with various options. In addition, criteria for third party access to transmission lines were suggested. The following process was complicated, reflecting that member countries had quite different interests at stake reflecting resource base, energy mix, sector arrangements and attitudes to state roles and regulation (Matlary 1997a, Eldevik 1999). The Commission therefore chose to focus on the electricity first, since this was politically easier.

By the end of 1995 there was a Commission agreement to include the French proposal for a so-called single-buyer model (where the company responsible for power procurement and/or transmission system operation was to carry out both tasks). The French were also instrumental in the introduction of public service obligation that, in some countries, may be necessary to ensure security of supplies and consumer and environmental protection (Hancher 1998: 5/7). The Council and Parliament finally adopted the directive concerning a single market for electricity in December 1996, which entered into force on 1 February 1997. It implies a deregulation of both production and transport of electricity. From February 1999, all countries must open at least 25.3 per cent of their market to free competition, increasing to 28 per cent in 2000 and 32 per cent in 2003, and so on (Nylander 1998).

The electricity directives paved the way for key elements in the gas directive. However, the Council (Energy) had to meet four times before all countries could agree. In addition the working group for energy and COREPER had intense meetings to clarify issues of a legal and technical character. In the spring of 1997 the Dutch presidency discovered that important political issues still remained where countries were still far apart. Under the presidency of Luxembourg the member council finally managed to agree, in December 1997. The directive came into force on 22 June 1998, and was to be implemented from 1999. Within two years the member countries must make the necessary changes in national law to open the way for changes. Just as in the electricity directive the liberalization is to be implemented gradually over a number of years. In addition, even more than in the case of electricity, the gas directive is really a framework for national adaptation. To a large extent it is up to the member countries to decide on how fast and effective reforms are to be carried out (Stern 1998).

The contents of the electricity and gas market directives in some ways differ dramatically from the Commission proposals introduced in 1992. It has been a long and tortuous process, but it has lead to a transformation of the European electricity and gas markets. The changes in member state and industry perspectives are in some ways dramatic, and may have radical consequences in the long term. An important precondition for the continued efforts towards liberalization, despite frustrations and conflicts, has been the renewed dynamics of the EU in the late 1990s.

Energy and European integration

This chapter has described the development of a common EU energy policy. When common energy policy finally emerged, it was partly because the traditional energy actors were loosing their exclusive control over the energy arena. In this sense the emergence of a common energy policy has demonstrated the momentum of European integration. Initiatives relating to the internal market and environmental protection have been based on supranational authority, which the Commission and its allies have tried to extend into the energy sector. The premises for the energy policy were also introduced in two new ways: firstly, 'in from the side', on the initiative of other parts of the Commission than DG XVII, such as the DG XI (Environment); secondly, 'from above', through general political summit meeting decisions in the case of CO_2 tax and the Energy Charter initiative.

One may characterize the development in the energy sector as political spill-over, but not in the neo-functional sense. In the latter theory spill-over is based on a concept of interest group politics, where rational actors pursue their interests and there is little concern with contextual factors. The recent development of EU energy policy, on the other hand, demonstrates how interests in a sector have been overwhelmed by actors invoking different policy context within a general framework of EU development, based on broader and more robust supranational authority. It is the dynamic interaction between several policy contexts and the impetus of the more general development that explains the direction of EU energy policy.

Energy is not covered by the Treaty of Rome. The tension between national interests and the EU is the main reason why energy did not formally become a field of common policy during the treaty revisions in Maastricht and Amsterdam. When it was proposed during the negotiations over the Maastricht Treaty, Britain was against it as part of a strategy to limit the scope of supranational authority. This happened despite the fact that Britain had already gone further in the direction of liberalization than the Commission has proposed. This also illustrates the lack of a common vision for a positive energy policy at the EU level.

In this situation the Commission has a certain freedom as to how directives affecting energy should be defined. For example, 'energy' directives may be handled through the decision-making procedure laid down in the Treaty, which requires unanimity; however, they may also be defined in relation to the internal market and the majority rule of decision-making (article 100a) introduced with the Single European Act reform, and further developed in the Maastricht and Amsterdam Treaties. Given the high degree of monopolistic tendencies in the energy sector and the barriers to trade between countries, the Commission here has a strong case for the internal market.

It has been argued that the completion of the internal market seriously undermines the role of DG XVII (Energy), and that energy policy in the future will be dominated by environmental interests (Evans 1998). The position of environmental policy has been strengthened in the Maastricht and Amsterdam Treaties. These treaties also strengthened the basis for joint EU foreign policy. Indirectly this may have increased the capacity of the Community to deal with supply issues. The EU is highly dependent upon import of oil and gas, and this is likely to increase even more in the next decade (Lord 1997).

It is, however, important to keep in mind that EU *policy* is not the only source of change. Policy initiatives will interact with other factors which have more piecemeal effects, but which may be less vulnerable to the political cycles in the EU. The first stems from the interaction between policy-making, the role of the EU court and market strategies. Such interaction is most likely to have an effect on deregulation efforts. However, the Court can also play a role in environmental matters. The other reason is the increased emphasis on subsidiarity, which opens the way for more active national strategies within the framework of general EU principles. The other source of change is that some private companies may pursue strategies that can alter existing market structures. Together such forces of change can open the way for and support new policy initiatives, as has already happened in relation to the electricity and gas market directives. This also means that issues will not necessarily come back onto the political agenda in the same way.

CHAPTER 7

EDUCATIONAL POLICY: INSTITUTIONALIZATION AND MULTI-LEVEL GOVERNANCE

Erik Beukel

Introduction: Europeanization and Education

Education is not among the policy areas that form the basis of the European Union. Ever since the European integration process was initiated in the 1950s and the European Community was created in 1957, economic issue areas have been the nucleus of integration. Being a non-economic issue area, education has not – until the Maastricht Treaty entered into force in late 1993 – been referred to as an independent subject for common policies in the treaties. This reflects that national regulatory and problem-solving capacities are high in the educational field while European capacities are low (Scharpf 1999: 116–20). In contrast to some of the other policy areas treated in this book, like telecom, what characterizes education is that the EU policies mostly come in addition to national policies.

In the most important early treaty, the Treaty of Rome of 1957, only a few educational issues, directly related to the functioning of the common market, were mentioned: provisions for vocational training (art. 41, 118 and 128), and the provision for mutual recognition of certificates (art. 57). However, through the 1980s the Court of Justice replaced its earlier narrow interpretations of these stipulations with broader definitions, meaning that they had consequences for practically all types of higher education (Lonbay 1989: 373f., De Witte 1992, Lenaerts 1994: 4f.). Moreover, aspects of the broad educational issue area that are not directly related to the common market stipulations have also, since the early 1970s, been included in the member states' endeavours to set up a common policy-making process. And most important, in the mid-to-late 1980s the gradual, informal, and tentative steps toward educational co-operation in the EC were boosted into independent educational programmes and initiatives followed by new programmes in the mid-1990s. The result is that today aspects of education policy are an established part of the Europeanization of national policy-making that, compared with other issue areas, is less controversial but, considered in a long-range perspective, reflects and implies significant developments in Europe.

In the Amsterdam Treaty (Conference of the Representatives of the Member States 1997) – entered into force on 1 May 1999 – two articles directly deal with the broad educational issue area: arts. 149–50 on 'Education, Vocational Training and Youth' set out the goals of the institutionalization of education as a Community issue. Art. 149 states that the Community shall:

> ... contribute to the development of quality education by encouraging cooperation between member states and, if necessary, by supporting and supplementing their action, while fully respecting the responsibility of the member states for the content of teaching and the organization of education systems and their cultural and linguistic diversity.
>
> Community action shall be aimed at:

- developing the European dimension in education, particularly through the teaching and dissemination of the languages of the member states;
- encouraging mobility of students and teachers, inter alia by encouraging the academic recognition of diplomas and periods of study;
- promoting co-operation between educational establishments;
- developing exchanges of information and experience on issues common to the education systems of the member states;
- encouraging the development of youth exchanges and of exchanges of socio-educational instructors;
- encouraging the development of distance education.

Art. 150 states that the Community shall:

> ... implement a vocational training policy which shall support and supplement the action of member states, while fully respecting the responsibility of the member states for the content and organization of vocational training.
>
> Community action shall aim to:

- facilitate adaptation to industrial changes, in particular through vocational training and retraining;
- improve initial and continuing vocational training in order to facilitate vocational integration and reintegration into the labour market;
- facilitate access to vocational training and encourage mobility of instructors and trainees and particularly young people;
- stimulate co-operation on training between educational or training establishments and firms;
- develop exchanges of information and experience on issues common to the training systems of the member states.

To contribute to the achievement of the objectives, the Council shall adopt incentive measures (art. 149), or measures (art. 150), in accordance with the procedure referred to in art. 251 (co-decision procedure), excluding any harmonization of the laws and regulations of the member states.

The evolving institutionalization of education represents a case of the increasing complexity of policy-making and multi-level governance in the EU (see Andersen and Eliassen in Chapter 1). The purpose of this chapter is to outline and elaborate main features of the institutional-ization, or Europeanization, of education policy at Community level. The very notion of 'Europeanization of education' causes concern in most countries in Europe, one reason being that it is equated with homo-genization of the educational systems that could imply a loss of national identity. Considered in a global perspective, the similarities between the education systems in Europe are obvious, but viewed in single-state perspectives the dissimilarities are conspicuous (Lenzen 1996). Never-theless, as transnational relations increase the interdependence between the countries in Europe, it is interesting to elaborate the consequences for the education systems and the role of the institutionalization of education in the EU (Tulasiewicz and Brock 1994).

Analysing the institutionalization of educational policy as a Community issue means applying a neo-institutional perspective on the Europeanization of education, that is, examining the crystallization of different complexes of norms, rules and programmes which regulate the way education is dealt with in the EU. The focus is on formal and informal routines that prescribe behavioural roles, constrain activity, and shape expectations in the field of education (Keohane 1988, March and Olsen 1989: 21f. and 1998: 948f., Howlett and Ramesh 1995: 26–8).

To understand the characteristics of the Europeanization process in the educational field it is expedient to simplify the policy process by analysing it into discrete stages (Lasswell 1956: 2, Lindberg 1971: 53, Howlett and Ramesh 1995: 9–15). Four conceptually distinct but empiri-cally intertwined and related policy stages can be propounded: (1) an early pre-decisional stage of problem-recognition and information-gathering; (2) a later pre-decisional stage of formulating action alterna-tives; (3) the decision stage of making a choice between policy alternatives; (4) administration of the policy.

We focus upon two questions: (1) Which stages and aspects of the educational policy process are dealt with in the Europeanization of education? (2) What characterizes the organizational arrangement set up? Does the pattern of activity relate to a pre-decisional stage of the policy process as problem-recognition and information-gathering, or more to the later pre-decisional stage like the formulation of policy alternatives? Or does the Europeanization extend to prescribing, enact-ing and implementing general rules, meaning a direct choice between action alternatives? And how do pre-decisional activities influence the actual policy choice? Who are the policy entrepreneurs and what is the role of member states, compared with the Commission, in the organizational set-up?

Elaborating such questions as to different periods since general education appeared on the public agenda in the EC will provide a basis for explaining certain characteristics of the Europeanization of education policy. Moreover, we hope to elucidate if and when new programmes and initiatives indicate new directions for the Europeanization process in the educational field.

First we review the main features of the early institutionalization, and thereafter the focus is upon the educational programmes and initiatives after the mid-1980s and the changes in the 1990s. After having identified and summarized the distinctive features of the institutionalization of education through 30 years, the dynamics of the process are discussed: How can trends and innovations in Europeanization of education policy be explained? What determines new directions?

The Early Institutionalization

General education first appeared directly as an area of interest to the Community during 1971 when the Commission set up two Working Parties on educational issues. They became responsible to Commissioner Altiero Spinelli (Italy) and initiated work designed to collect data on educational issues and elaborate the need for greater Community effort in the educational field (Suppl. 10/73. 9). At the same time the Council, when adopting a series of general guidelines concerning vocational training – directly referred to in the Treaty of Rome – stated that the 'objective of the programme should be to provide the population as a whole with the opportunities for *general* and vocational education' (see Suppl. 3/74: 5).

The ministers for education from the then six member states held their first meeting in late 1971, with Altiero Spinelli from the Commission participating. The resolution from the ministers' reunion stated that the provisions on educational measures in the Treaty of Rome should be completed by increasing co-operation in the field of education as such. It also mentioned that the 'ultimate aim' was 'in fact to define a European model of culture correlating with European integration' (*European Educational Policy Statements* 1988: 11). A Working Party of Senior Officials from the member countries was set up to consider, together with the Commission, ways for achieving co-operation in the educational field, and what the legal bases could be for this (Neave 1984: 6–7). After the ministers' meeting the Commission stated 'mit Befriedigung' (see Fünfter Gesamtbericht 1971: 7) that, from then on, educational issues were to be considered common policy issues and the Commission hoped for a convergence of the member states' educational policies in order to assure a harmonious development in the Community.

From early 1973 education figured for the first time as part of the responsibility of one of the members of the Commission, Ralph

Dahrendorf (Federal Republic of Germany). He presented various ideas in the Commission on how initiatives on, for instance, language teaching, teachers' and students' movements among member countries, and how the development of the study of Europe as part of the school curriculum could increase understanding in Europe and promote European integration (*General Report* 1973: 369–70). The first Communication on education from the Commission to the Council, 'Education in the European Community' (Suppl. 3/74), was presented in 1974, and it elaborated the reasoning for developing educational co-operation in the Community.

A main argument is that the promotion of educational co-operation is an integral part of the overall development of the Community. This does not mean, the Communication added, that there must be a common European policy in the education field as in the sense applicable to other sectors. The objective of harmonization would be as undesirable as it would be unrealistic. But a Community perspective in education is increasingly important, and what is required is a common commitment to the development of educational co-operation and a systematic exchange of information and experience. Among specific proposals mentioned were increasing mobility in education and the development of a European dimension in education.

The ministers of education held their second meeting also in 1974, and the resolution from the meeting stated that education must on no account be regarded merely as a component of economic life. Allowance must be made for the traditions of each country and the diversity of their respective educational policies and systems. A number of priority spheres of action that did not directly originate in the Treaty were outlined, and the ministers set up an Education Committee, composed of representatives of the member states and of the Commission. The chairman of the Committee came from the country exercising the office of President of the Council (*European Educational Policy Statements* 1988: 15–16). The Education Committee prepared the Community Education Action Programme that was adopted in February 1976 (*European Educational Policy Statements* 1988: 23–7).

The Action Programme established the Education Committee as a permanent body and the organizational centre of educational co-operation. Thus, measures to be implemented at Community level should be undertaken by the Commission 'in close liaison' with the Education Committee. The exposition of the programme contained six headings that pointed to central aspects of the Community's educational activities more than twenty years later: better facilities for the education and training of nationals and the children of nationals of other member states and non-member countries; promotion of closer relations between educational systems in Europe; compilation of up-to-date documentation and statistics on education; co-operation in the field of higher education;

teaching of foreign languages; and achievement of equal opportunity for free access to all forms of education. At the same time the Action Programme was marked by an extensive use of non-committal wordings and suggestions like exchange of information and experiences, study visits, strengthening of contacts, pilot projects, preparation of reports, examination of this or that problem, and so on.

During the following years, the implementation of the Action Programme was characterized by the arrangement of a vast number of pilot projects, meetings, seminars and the like (De Witte 1989, Beukel 1992: 27–37). Primacy was given to a number of functional measures like the transition from school to work, the development of co-operation between educational administrators and labour market institutions, the development of co-operation between institutions of higher education, and the introduction of new information technologies. Another significant feature of the implementation was the extensive involvement of administrators of educational systems together with labour market institutions throughout the Community, including the first joint session of Ministers of Labour and Social affairs and Ministers of Education in 1983 (Neave 1984: 43–55, *European Educational Policy Statements* 1988: *passim*, Suppl. 3/74: 7).

In the late 1970s, disagreement over the implementation of a European dimension in education did result in cancelled meetings between the ministers of education for a couple of years. However, that split had no impact on what can be termed the day-to-day and low-key dealing with various aspects of the pre-decisional stages of the educational Europeanization process.

The Boost from the mid-1980s

From the mid-1980s the institutionalization assumed new characteristics. The primary change was that the Council adopted independent educational programmes to be implemented by the Commission in co-operation with a number of intergovernmental institutions, established for specific educational purposes. Another notable change was that for some years in the late 1980s and early 1990s a new wording was applied in resolutions adopted by the ministers for education, giving the term 'Europeanization' an ideational substance as well. The three most important programmes (Rosenthal 1991: 273–83), adopted through 1986–89, were: (1) COMETT (Community Programme for Education and Training in Technology), (2) ERASMUS (European Community Action Scheme for the Mobility of University Students) and (3) LINGUA, the Language and Training Programme.

COMETT I, covering the period 1986–89, was adopted by the Council in 1986. The resolution referred to art. 128 on vocational training and art. 235 on supplementary actions (*European Educational Policy Statements* 1988: 157–63). COMETT II, covering the period 1990–94, was adopted by the Council in 1988, and that resolution referred only to art. 128 (*European Educational Policy Statements* 1990: 57–63). Whereas COMETT I was endowed with a budget of 45 million Ecu, COMETT II had a budget of 200 million Ecu, i.e. more than a quadrupling of the annual budget. The objective of COMETT was four-fold: to give a European dimension to co-operation between institutions of higher education and industry in the area of new technologies; to foster joint development of training programmes, exchange of experience and optimum use of training resources at Community level; to improve the supply of training at local, regional and national levels; and to develop the level of training in response to technological and social changes. This was to be achieved especially by creating a network of university–industry training partnerships, to be used for transnational exchanges of students, the development of transnational projects for continuing training and multimedia training systems.

ERASMUS I, covering the period 1987–89, was adopted by the Council in 1987 (*European Educational Policy Statements* 1988: 187–93), following long and, at times, bitter negotiations during the 17 months after the Commission had submitted its first proposal in 1986. The resolution referred to art. 128 and art. 235. ERASMUS II, covering the period 1990–94, was adopted by the Council in 1989, this time only referring to art. 128 (*European Educational Policy Statements* 1990: 109–13). Whereas ERASMUS I was endowed with a budget of 85 million Ecu, the budget for the first three years of the new period is more than doubled to 192 million Ecu. The objective of ERASMUS was to increase substantially the number of students spending an integrated part of their study period at an institution of higher education in another member country, and generally to promote broadly based, intensive co-operation at all levels between the institutions of higher education. The wider aim was to improve the quality of education and training, ensuring the development of a pool of trained personnel with direct experience of intra-Community co-operation and thereby contribute to the strengthening of a 'People's Europe'. To realize the aims various actions were outlined, like programmes for exchanging students and teachers and increased student mobility between member countries.

LINGUA was an action programme to promote foreign language training and skills. It was adopted by the Council in 1989, referring to art. 128 and 235, with an estimated budget of 200 million Ecu for the period 1990–94 (*European Educational Policy Statements* 1990: 89–97). Before the adoption the programme had been the subject of controversy in the Council in that some countries (Britain, Denmark and Germany) expressed the view that the Commission's original proposal marked an excessive extension of the competence of the EC. Hence, the member states' primary responsibility for education and the supplementary character of the Community's measures were emphasized.

Each programme was to be implemented by a committee composed of two representatives from each member state, with a representative from the Commission as chairman. The Commission was to perform the secretarial functions and was assigned an important role in the implementation of the programmes. Concerning the geographical scope of the programmes, agreements on the EFTA countries' participation in COMETT and ERASMUS were concluded in the early 1990s.

Concurrent with the adoption of specific educational programmes in the second half of the 1980s, the Council passed resolutions on the educational co-operation that placed it in a general European and ideational context. Some of these ideas were hinted at in the early 1980s, in the 'Solemn Declaration on European Union' signed by the heads of state or governments in 1983 (*European Educational Policy Statements* 1988: 99). However, the tendency to argue for educational co-operation in terms of *European* ideas and interests became most evident towards the end of the decade. Thus, in 1988, the Council adopted a resolution on the European dimension in education that was characterized by a marked attachment to European culture and European ideas: young people should be strengthened in their consciousness of being Europeans and realize the value of European ideas, such as democratic principles, social justice and human rights. To give substance to the European dimension in education, the member states should, within the frame-work of their educational structures, implement actions as to teaching plans in schools, teaching material, teacher education, and the stimulation of contacts between pupils in different countries. The Commission was asked to carry out various measures concerning exchange of information, teaching material and teacher training (*European Educational Policy Statements* 1990: 19–21).

The predilection for stressing the role of educational co-operation within a broad conception of the political structure and role of Europe became most evident in a resolution adopted by the ministers in the autumn of 1989, during the time of the seminal events in eastern Europe (*European Educational Policy Statements* 1990: 101–2). After the democratic revolutions in the formerly totalitarian half of Europe, the need for extending educational co-operation to the new democracies in central and eastern Europe came into focus, and in spring 1990 the TEMPUS (Trans-European Mobility Programme for University Studies) programme for exchanges in higher education was adopted (Official Journal No. L 131/21–6, 23/5/1990, Pertek 1992b).

Hedges and Expansions in the 1990s

In the mid-1990s the educational programmes were rearranged and expanded. In 1994 a new programme for vocational training was adopted and the following year an umbrella programme for actions at all educational levels. The programmes represent a continuation in that they reiterate and elaborate the stipulations of the Maastricht Treaty arts. 126 and 127 (which correspond to arts. 149 and 150 of the Amsterdam Treaty, p. 125) and the three programmes adopted 1986–89 (COMETT, ERASMUS, and LINGUA). However, at the same time the new programmes represent both hedges and expansions: the references to respecting the responsibility of the member states and excluding any harmonization of laws and regulations are emphasized, while the budgets are increased compared with the earlier educational programmes.

An action programme for vocational training, named LEONARDO DA VINCI, referring to art. 127 in the Maastricht Treaty and covering the period 1995–99, was adopted by the Council in December 1994 (Official Journal No. L 340 29/12/1994). The programme shall ensure the implementation of a Community vocational training policy that consists of three parts: measures to sustain the quality of member states' systems, arrangements, and policies; measures to support innovative capacity in actions on the training market; and networks and accompanying measures for promoting the European dimension (Curwen 1998). Originally it had a budget of 620 million Ecu that later was increased to 800 million Ecu. The Commission shall implement the programme in consultation with the member states and assisted by a committee composed of two representatives from each state, chaired by the representative of the Commission.

The action programme for co-operation in the field of education, SOCRATES, was adopted, on the basis of the co-decision procedure, by the European Parliament and the Council of Ministers in March 1995, referring to arts. 126 and 127 and covering the years 1995–99 (Official Journal No. L 87 20/04/1995). It comprises three chapters: higher education (ERASMUS); school education (COMENIUS); and horizontal activities in the areas of language skills in the Community (LINGUA), open and distance education, and promotion of the exchange of information and experience (including EURYDICE and ARION). Originally SOCRATES had a budget of 850 million Ecu that later was increased to 920 million and 1000 million Ecu. Also this programme has to be implemented by the Commission in consultation with the member states and assisted by a committee composed of two representatives from each state, chaired by the representative of the Commission.

The last mentioned stipulation is the result of a very contentious inter-institutional process of negotiating and bargaining, however, which was marked by disagreements about the relative influence of the Commission and member states on the programme's implementation. The European Parliament demanded that it and the Commission should be put on equal footing with the Council, while the Council attempted to extend the role of the member states. Actually, as SOCRATES was amongst the first cases where the then newly introduced co-decision procedure was applied, it became an opportunity to test the inter-institutional balance of power in the new European Union, and considered in that light the dispute between the institutions was a drawn game. As to the scope of the education activities covered, SOCRATES represents an extension to new areas in the Europeanization of education policy like introducing the European dimension in schools and to adult education (De Groof and Friess 1997, Hermans 1997).

Following the stipulations in the Maastricht Treaty, arts. 126.3 and 127.3 (repeated in the Amsterdam Treaty) that the Community and the member states shall foster co-operation with third countries and the competent international organizations, both programmes apply to Iceland, Liechtenstein, and Norway in the framework of the European Economic Area Agreement. From 1998 onwards, they apply for the associated countries of central and eastern Europe as well as Cyprus and Malta. Also, collaboration treaties on higher education and vocational training have been concluded with Canada and the United States, and so the pan- and extra-European aspects of the Community's education policy have been strengthened.

Features of Europeanization over 30 Years

It is a general feature of the Europeanization of educational policy at Community level that while the early institutionalization was marked by an exclusive dominance of the pre-decisional stages, the institutionalization since the mid-to-late 1980s has also included some actual choices on education policies. Representing that change in more elaborate terms, the main characteristics of Europeanization of education policy can be highlighted by emphasizing seven features:

1 While the first institutionalization in the early 1970s operated with a problem-recognition that entertained norms and ideas about education policies converging toward some vaguely defined European education policy, such norms were abandoned after a couple of years and replaced by an interest in gathering information and formulating action alternatives.
2 The increased institutionalization of education after the late 1980s, moving from solely bearing on pre-decisional operations to also including educational policy choices in the form of Community action

programmes, primarily concerns newly established measures which cannot be decided and implemented at single state level.

3   The increased institutionalization is rhetorical and ideational as well but at the same time very different from the first institutionalization in the early 1970s, particularly as to the norm emphasizing member states' responsibility for the content of education and dissociations from harmonization.

4   An important aspect of the actual policy choices is that the new programmes directly bear on a much broader group of people engaged in European educational systems than the pre-decisional, information-gathering institutionalization that dominated for about 12 years and primarily concerned administrators in the educational and related sectors.

5   Therefore, since the late 1980s a greater part of the educational demands and expectations will be directed at the Community. Otherwise expressed, what has been top-down intergovernmental and supranational initiatives will lead to bottom-up transnational demands.

6   The increased budgets for the educational programmes adopted for the late 1990s indicate a more prominent role of Community programmes in the overall structure of education in Europe. However, this does not affect the general characteristic that the predominant institutionalization and problem-solving capacities in the educational field occur on a single-state level.

7   Compared with the early institutionalization when the Education Committee was the organizational centre, the establishment of different organizations for directing and implementing the new Community programmes means that the organizational structure has become more complex.

Dynamics of Europeanization

Given the divergent findings as to the growth and character of institutionalization through the period since the early 1970s, it is expedient first to focus briefly on the initial dynamics of Europeanization in the first years of the 1970s. Thereafter I consider factors that may explain the growth in institutionalization since the mid-1980s, including the specific features of Europeanization of education and its continuation in the 1990s. I then discuss the role of policy entrepreneurs compared with broader economic, cultural, and political trends.

As to factors that stimulated *the initial institutionalization* in the first half of the 1970s, it is difficult to pinpoint the exact sequence of events. Available data seem to indicate that the Commission played the decisive role inasmuch as specific members of the Commission took the critical initiatives. Thus, in the summer of 1971, Altiero Spinelli led the establishment of the two bodies (see above) that were given the role of considering general educational issues. Later in 1971, he also played an active role when the ministers for education held their first meeting and agreed on the need for a 'European model of culture correlating with European integration' (see above). During the following years, Ralph Dahrendorf was clearly the active promoter. Noting this, it also has to be registered that it is evident from the Commission's manifestations later in the 1970s that it would have preferred the institutionalization to proceed beyond the measures implemented in the mid-1970s.

The significance of these observations is that the Community's most distinct supranational institution may account for the early institutionalization of some pre-decisional stages of the member states' general educational policy. However, the mere initiation of the Community's occupation with education did not mean that the Community's activities from then took on the role of prescribing and enacting rules in the general educational field. Thus the European-minded policy entrepreneurs in the Commission were able to initiate the Europeanization process as to education policy, but there were evident limits to their influence, even if the ministers for education initially shared the inclination. The effecting of pre-decisional policy activities did not, by itself, lead to the decision stage.

Considered in the light of the Treaty's provisions and the then dominating views in the member countries about the role of the EC during the 1970s, the lack of further institutionalization of education is not surprising. The process of institutionalization and integration was not automatic once it had been initiated (Beukel 1994). The more or less openly expressed desires of the Community's most distinctive supranational institution were not sufficient to carry on a strong process of Europeanization.

Concerning the growth in institutionalization after the mid-1980s, a more detailed examination (Beukel 1992: 14–19) indicates that factors directly related to the Community system did not play a significant role. That is, the pre-decisional activities did not automatically lead to decisions. The dynamics of the new Europeanization (independent programmes and pro-European resolutions) have to be looked for by examining changes in the Community's environment. We refer to changes that posed to the member states and the Council economic and political challenges to which they reacted by strengthening educational institutionalization.

During the late 1970s and early 1980s *changing international economic structures* altered the EC countries' options in the way that long-term changes in the economic strength of different countries and regional groupings accumulated to a critical point. Most important, as the relative economic position of the United States had declined through more than a decade, it was no longer a viable option for Europeans just to follow in the wake of the United States and adapt to that country as the economic engine. In the early 1980s, the Reagan administration's economic policy was strongly criticized by European politicians, including people who otherwise supported the American–West-European partnership. Besides, there were several other economic bones of contention on both sides of the Atlantic Ocean that prompted European decision-makers to question a continuing European reliance on American economic leadership (Ginsberg 1989: 270f.).

As to the European position in the international economic structure, different indicators pointed to different conclusions (Patel and Pavitt 1989). It was an oversimplification simply to refer to the development as Europe's decline, but there was widespread talk of eurosclerosis in the early 1980s. The European countries that were members of the EC began reconsidering their economic possibilities and strategies. Various elites in governments, business and the Commission during the first half of the 1980s began contemplating new economic, technological and political strategies that could reinvigorate European integration and meet the different challenges (Sandholz and Zysman 1989).

Evaluated in this context, the Community's new institutionalization of the educational field can be seen as one part of a more extensive endeavour to reinvigorate Europe in response to changes in international economic trends which became apparent in the early-to-mid-1980s.

Another dynamic factor concerns consequences of *the changes in communication and information technologies* that may be encapsulated by the phrase 'from industrial society to the information society'. The essential point is that, while the technology of industrial societies is based on mechanical systems aiming at mass production, technology today moves toward being based on knowledge. The post-industrial society is a knowledge society where knowledge as the social centre of gravity is shifting to the knowledge worker who is collecting and using information in order to comply with heterogeneous demands in society (Toffler 1990: 368–71). Critical economic processes depend on information-based organization, i.e. the use of systematic information, imagination and other abilities that are culturally conditioned. Flexibility, knowledge and education are rewarded in a way very different from the traditional industrial society, and it all takes place concurrent with increasing interdependence between governments, business enterprises and citizens across national boundaries.

For educational systems this has far-reaching consequences. They must be open systems as transnational and interdisciplinary activities become much more significant, and the basis for strictly national educational systems is undermined. The economic, educational and cultural interplay between educational institutions and economic life in different countries is strengthened. The socio-political content and meaning of these processes is ambiguous but it does follow the new institutionalization of education that is closely related to the growth of the information society.

The last factor relates to *Europe's role between the United States and the Soviet Union*. European wishes for a more independent European role in relation to the American ally and vis-à-vis the Soviet opponent have been among the motives for European integration ever since its initiation in the early 1950s. During the Carter administration (1977–81) and the first Reagan administration (1981–85), many Europeans shared a more or less undefinable feeling of uneasiness about the American Soviet policy as too confrontational. However, ten years earlier many Europeans were apprehensive spectators to the Soviet–American détente. Where the Soviet–American relationship was concerned, and regardless of whether the incumbent administration in Washington stressed confrontation or détente, Europeans thought their interests were disregarded. As noted in an Indian proverb – quoted by Pierre Hassner in a study of Europe and the contradictions in American policy (Rosecrance 1976: 72) – two fighting elephants will trample the grass, but it is equally true that two loving elephants will do the same.

It all meant that, from the early 1980s, more and more Europeans across the political spectrum expressed the view that western Europe and the Community ought to be moving away from their traditionally passive political role of just complaining – 'Americans decide, Europeans complain' – towards a more active and independent role. This occurred concurrent with a growing interest among European elites – authors, journalists, politicians – for identifying a common European identity, an all-European 'Europeanness', described by noting its historical roots and its cultural and political characteristics, often in rather woolly terms (Buzan et al. 1990: 50–7). Central Europe was rediscovered, and the Soviet military and political hegemony in eastern Europe was increasingly questioned. Doubts were expressed by political movements who a few years earlier had perceived Europe's problems solely in terms of détente, disarmament and opposition to nuclear weapons, and the consequent political actions as simply a matter of opposing the United States.

The growing quest and support for a European cultural and political identity through the 1980s, and the related greater interest for Europe's role in relation to the United States and the Soviet Union, implied positive attitudes to the concept of Europeanization. Support for European norms and ideas became a natural part of the political manifestations from a wide political spectrum and a notion of 'unity in diversity' (Ryba 1995) was a critical element in the European self-image, implying a significant change compared with the early 1970s.

Concluding Remarks

The notion 'Europeanization of education' causes concern among many Europeans because it is equated with homogenization of educational systems and the loss of national identity. The Amsterdam Treaty's stipulations on educational co-operation clearly reflect endeavours to reduce that concern, such as the reiteration that the EU shall fully respect the responsibility of the member states for the content of teaching and the organization of education systems. In the same way, it is emphasized that harmonization of laws and regulations is excluded. And the broader concern for the loss of national identity is met with the stress on the Union's respect for member states' cultural and linguistic diversity. Thus it is obvious that both the Treaty makers, namely the fifteen governments, and the Commission have caught the message from concerned Europeans: Don't proceed too fast and don't touch the critical national core areas; hedges concerning the range of educational co-operation are prominent in the late 1990s.

However, when the evolution in educational co-operation in the Community is considered in the long term, namely since general education first appeared as a Community issue almost a generation ago, it is striking that the 'big jump forward' – the new educational programmes during the last years of the 1980s – was not caused by the Community institutions' sudden pro-European inclinations. It has to be related to fundamental changes in the Community's environment, namely the European urge to manifest its position vis-à-vis the United States and, most important, the need to meet the crumbling Soviet empire in the other part of Europe that made it 'politically correct' to emphasize *European* ideas and norms and prepare *European* (educational) programmes. That is, the most important new direction since the educational field was included in the common policy-making process can be explained by changes in the Community's environment rather than by the institutions' initiatives. Of course, the institutions' *reactions* to changes in the environment are significant, but it is *re*actions – rather than independent *actions* – which are important.

At the same time it is worth noting that the range as well as the character of the EU's involvement in the educational field hold several seeds of strife, between member countries and between transnational political groups. One matter in dispute might be the more exact definition of a 'European dimension in education', which is a natural candidate in the educational field for the stronger scepticism vis-à-vis institutionalization at the EU level (Ryba 1995). Also, the combination of economic internationalization and cultural decentralization, as well as the evolution of the information and communication society, include factors which may make an apparently obvious dividing line between primary education as a national issue and transnational EU issues more blurred.

The new slogans in EU politics – nearness and subsidiarity, i.e. that decisions have to be taken as closely as possible to the citizens – will definitely be applied as an argument in that strife. The same holds for the Union's obligation to contribute to the development of quality education and to respect the member states' responsibility for the content of teaching and the organization of education systems (De Groof and Friess 1997: 12ff.). All these arguments can refer to stipulations in the Treaty on the European Union. And they may lead to divergent conclusions concerning the expediency of new EU measures in the educational field.

It follows that there is a natural tendency to exaggerate the independent meaning of not only specific Treaty stipulations and the Commission's inclinations but also the fifteen member governments' policies when it concerns the direction of the educational field as an aspect of Europeanization. More critical dynamics are outside the Union's range, however. In a period with rising concern for national identities this could be a new source of concern. However, education is an area where the creation of a new institutional setting has made it possible to develop a common policy despite different national interests.

CHAPTER 8

POLICY ON JUSTICE AND HOME AFFAIRS: FROM HIGH TO LOW POLITICS

Ellen Ahnfelt and Johan From

From Co-operation to Integration

Police co-operation and Justice and Home Affairs have traditionally been regarded as 'high' politics, and presumably outside the scope of EU common policy. This changed with the Amsterdam Treaty in 1997. There, it was decided to integrate parts of home and justice affairs and police co-operation (and also parts of the Schengen agreement) into the First Pillar of EU co-operation. This also implies the full involvement of EU institutions in these areas as in other areas of 'low' politics.

This chapter, however, deals mainly with the growth of police co-operation between the members of the EU, and the integration of police co-operation into a wider policy context, that of Justice and Home Affairs. Over the last decades there has been a considerable expansion and development in European police co-operation both within and outside the EU. The most ambitious elements are the forms of co-operation which have developed between the EU member states in parallel with the structural changes that have taken place within the EU.

The point of departure for this chapter is that there are two main driving forces that have influenced this development. On the one hand, changes have taken place with regard to the threat that international criminality poses, or the perception of that threat. On the other hand, there is the area of EU development and integration during this period.

Development of a common, and exclusive, police co-operation among the EU countries began in the 1970s. With the signing of the Maastricht Treaty in the early 1990s, this development was both formalized and institutionalized. The treaty created both the foundation for a police office at a European level – Europol – and an integrated, wide-scope and formalized collaboration that embraced Justice and Home Affairs in what has been designated as the Union's 'Third Pillar'. The signing of the Amsterdam Treaty further strengthened this collaboration. Under that treaty the co-operation is described in greater detail and the Union's institutions are given greater influence. But decisions on police co-operation matters still require unanimity.

A protocol added to the Amsterdam Treaty also dictated that co-operation set forth in the Schengen agreement – previously a separate structure for co-operation concerning internal borders, external border surveillance and, among other things, policing – would be integrated into the EU. In the autumn of 1999 the fight against organized crime was for the first time a major topic at the EU's top-level meeting in Tampere, and the EU's justice and home affairs ministers agreed beforehand to support Germany's proposal to create a unified EU police academy. 'Our police officers must be better trained in order to meet these new challenges' stated Germany's Minister of Home Affairs, Otto Schilly.

Before pre-negotiations took place for the Maastricht Treaty, however, significant development also was underway. Until 1985, police co-operation was clearly separated from the EU's institutions and was strictly intergovernmental. When the Single European Act was passed in 1986, new challenges and new possibilities were given scope. Open borders for persons were to be gradually followed by reductions in passport checks at borders and the resultant 'security deficit', for which there was in any case political agreement, would be replaced by 'compensatory measures'. These would be in the form of common border checks, measures to fight illegal immigration, and police collaboration. Greater co-operation in closer association with the Community was also facilitated by the fact that the EU's level of competence and its decision-making effectiveness were vastly improved on all matters regarding the inner market. With regard to police collaboration, was earlier defined as a compensatory measure in relation to reductions in border checks. As concerns the EU's collaboration on police co-operation and in the area of Justice and Home Affairs, there is considerable indication that this definition has lost focus. In the first decade of the new millennium, the Union's common interests can be looked upon in an entirely new way and many previous barriers to closer police co-operation can be seen to have been breached.

The EU's development in this area also has substantial potential impact on countries outside the EU. For countries applying for EU membership, the area of justice also requires certain criteria to be met, including the raising of standards in general, and specifically those involving a level of crime-fighting that will not result in problems the EU presently regards as a threat. The shape of EU policy, for example as it applies to external border checks, is also regarded as a model for applicant countries. In countries where police authorities are responsible for border checks this will have a direct impact on policing and the use of police resources.

The development also has a 'Nordic dimension'. Since the last edition of this book the Nordic Passport Union and the Schengen area of free movement of people have been linked together through a co-operation agreement between the Schengen countries and Norway and Iceland, the Nordic non-EU members. Through the agreement Norway and Iceland actually very nearly became full members of the Schengen co-operation. The Amsterdam Treaty integrates the Schengen co-operation into the EU, which necessitated a new institutional co-operation agreement between the EU countries and Norway and Iceland. Since the Amsterdam Treaty went into force on 1 July 1999, Norway and Iceland have participated on Schengen relevant matters within the EU co-operation on Justice and Home affairs, through a so-called Mixed Committee structure. This adds to the complexity of the co-operation that faces the EU countries in this area after the Amsterdam Treaty, and at the same time represents a new challenge to the Nordic countries.

Perspectives on Policing and Home and Justice Affairs

It is important to emphasize that significant barriers, or opposition, exist with regard to the development of police co-operation. Police activity may at the outset be characterized as *high politics*, a policy area which has traditionally been seen as the prerogative of the state (Hoffmann 1965). A Europeanization of police co-operation therefore represents the elevation to EU level of a policy area in which the influence of the individual state has traditionally been very important.

According to classical political theory, a monopoly of the legitimate use of force is a fundamental characteristic of the nation state, and in democratic countries the police force represents the state's central implementing agency in the internal exercise of legitimate power. The strong connection between the nation state and control of the police force, and between police functions and the area of state jurisdiction, at once constitutes a barrier both to cross-border operational police co-operation, international co-operation on a political level, and in particular to supranational co-operation involving the relinquishing of power and control at the national level.

It is also possible in this context, however, to speak of high and low *policing* as a parallel to high and low *politics* (Brodeur 1983). This signifies that certain police functions which do not directly affect the integrity of the state are more readily transferable from the national level to e.g. an institution within the Community, while responsibility for areas such as the maintenance of law and order as well as security, is strictly retained at the national level. It should therefore be possible to visualize a comprehensive international police co-operation which goes beyond an informal level in 'low policing' areas, without necessarily implying Europeanization of core national politics.

The growth in international police co-operation from the 1970s onwards was earlier often understood in an exclusively rational context; fresh initiatives and forms of co-operation were seen as functional and necessary responses mainly to the increase and development of international crime.

In order to understand development within the EU, this perspective is inadequate. Closer collaboration between EU institutions cannot be understood on the basis of growth in international crime alone. Nor can the significance of this development in criminality be understood solely on the basis of a purely rational perspective.

It is not sufficient to argue that the increase in international crime, or the perception of an increasing threat from crime, has been of significance in legitimizing intensified police co-operation. Political and public awareness is a prerequisite if international crime is to trigger initiatives in police co-operation (Gregory and Collier 1992). These may, however, be induced if the threat of crime is linked with other factors and interests. With regard to police co-operation within the EU, two factors are presumptively of particular importance. First, there is the reduction of border controls in the expectation that such reduction will encourage a cross-border flow of criminal activities within the EU, which legitimized compensatory control measures. Second is the wish to secure the Union's external borders against internationally and globally organized crime, but in particular to control immigration from the poorer regions to the south and east of the EU in order to prevent illegal immigration and an increase in the number of applications for asylum on false premises (Bigo 1992).

It has here been argued that integration within the EU also makes itself felt as an *independent* driving force in the development of police co-operation. Influence over the development of police co-operation can be of importance to the EU system for several reasons. The attainment of power and influence over functions related to control and implementation, as progressively new policy areas are incorporated into the EU, is integral to EU rationale. EU crime, for instance in the form of fraud directed against the Union, is an increasing problem. Furthermore, problems related to the Union's external borders and the growing identification of the Union as a single unit which is being threatened from outside by increasing criminal activity and illegal immigration, also promote an acceleration of the centralization of police co-operation. Furthermore, institutional development at the Union level will strengthen the EU as a unit in relation to its constituent members.

Enhancement of police co-operation at the EU level may in turn also act as a means of promoting integration. Police co-operation can reinforce the process of integration in several ways: by providing the basis for reducing border controls as described above, but also because integration is augmented when new policy areas come under the Union's authority;

in particular does this apply to policy areas which have traditionally been central to state control.

When a level of understanding binds elements which include the development of international criminality – particularly the EU's special needs in this context – and integration within the EU and interest groups connected to it, it is time to make demands on a complex perspective in order to understand the origins of the process of development and to comprehend its results:

> Governments and police authorities see a functional requirement for closer European cooperation with the completion of the internal market and the abolition of many controls at the frontier but they are engaged in a process of probing and bargaining from which both the scope of cooperation as well as the institutional form of cooperation will emerge. (Anderson 1992)

The process of probing and bargaining within the EU primarily concerns the relationship between solely intergovernmental solutions and those of a supranational character. In this development there will be a number of players at the national level and within the EU who have different positions with regard to integration in the EU, different interests related to development and different approaches regarding understanding of the problem. Police co-operation has traditionally been the domain of professionals and experts. Nonetheless, due to increasing political influence and stronger ties to other areas of political activity, the door is now open for different opinions regarding what type of co-operation is needed, what institutional solutions would be most effective, what would be feasible, what would be desirable, and what problems should be prioritized.

The main question in this chapter is how far integration in the EU has come with regard to police co-operation. To answer it, two points of departure are used: the institutional organization of the co-operation, and what type of co-operation is to be established.

As concerns institutional organization, we will look more closely at how police co-operation during the different phases is integrated into the EU's institutions and how tight the integration is. To what extent has the development of police co-operation, from the establishment of TREVI in 1975 until the enforcement of the Amsterdam Treaty, led to an integration of policy formulation in this field, i.e. through a closer linkage to EC institutions and the wielding of stronger influence on the part of the Community? And what will the 'Nordic dimension' mean in this development? Will the co-operation with Norway and Iceland increase the influence of the Nordic countries within the EU in this field? Or will the co-operation actually mean increased Europeanization of policy formulation in these non-EU member countries?

The content of the police co-operation established by the EU and how it is legitimated are also important because this is a politically sensitive area for the national state, and some forms of co-operation are more sensitive than others. Growing bilateral police co-operation within the framework of the EU can be explained as being a result of the individual country's needs, and can be simplified by reducing traditional barriers and hindrances to effective cross-border co-operation. This can be effective in relation to the fight against crime without representing a broad-range threat to the state's monopoly on legitimate use of force. State sovereignty first and foremost becomes an issue in connection with a country's police being allowed to cross the borders of another country and on what conditions. The right to carry out police activity is very closely associated with state sovereignty. Supranational co-operation on policing – i.e. the employment of police authority on the basis of decisions made at Union level and under the power of the EU – would represent a complete breach with the concept that police authority is deeply rooted in the national state. One major question is whether such a reality within the EU has become closer to realization since the Amsterdam Treaty came into effect. Should activities within the EU to a greater degree focus on police co-operation as a response to common demands, and the types of police co-operation reflect this, it would at the same time reflect the level of integration within the EU.

Early Forms of Co-operation

TREVI was the first EC forum for police co-operation. At the initiative of the British and the Germans, TREVI was established by the Council of Europe in Rome in 1975 as an intergovernmental forum for the EC Ministries of Justice and Home Affairs, and designed to co-ordinate counter-measures against terrorism. TREVI's ambit of functional responsibility was gradually extended from combating terrorism and exchanging information, to embracing general police matters, international crime, and post-1992 compensatory measures. These areas were the responsibility of, respectively, the working groups TREVI I, II, III and TREVI 1992. TREVI III, which was responsible for measures against international crime (illegal trafficking in drugs, illegal trafficking in weapons, computer crime, armed robbery, money-laundering), was established in 1985. The direct cause of this extension of TREVI's responsibilities is not entirely clear, but it has been linked to growing acknowledgement of the complexity of international crime, a stronger tendency to regard international crime as a threat to the internal security of Europe, and a step on the road to greater European integration (Fijnaut 1991). The most important alteration of TREVI nevertheless started with the Single European Act in 1986.

The Single European Act and the EU countries' declaration on closer co-operation concerning entry and residence for persons from third countries, combating terrorism, drugs, illegal trading in art and antiques and other organized crime, as follow-up on the intention to introduce free movement of people, had considerable impact as a fresh stimulus to police co-operation and for closer co-ordination of police, immigration and judicial co-operation. This significance has been expressed in various ways. For example, the Single European Act can be seen as a catalyst in relation to the Schengen Agreement. In 1988, the European Council established the so-called Co-ordinators Group. It was designed 'to co-ordinate, stimulate and promote all the work being performed at inter-governmental and Community level in relation to the free movement of people'. The Co-ordinators' Group singled out TREVI, the Ad Hoc Group on Immigration and the Judicial Co-operation Group, the latter organized as a part of the European Political Co-operation, as the most important responsible fora, thus opening the way for later linkages between these. In a subsequent report submitted to the European Council meeting in Maastricht, the Co-ordinators' Group recommended that co-operation in the judicial area be given a structural framework which could promote greater efficiency, a recommendation which was followed up by the Maastricht Treaty.

Simultaneously with the creation of the Co-ordinators' Group in 1988, TREVI was instructed to assess what impact the removal of border controls would have on international crime, and this resulted in the establishment of the working group TREVI 1992. Its mandate was later expanded to include the planning and preparation of necessary compensatory measures in this connection. The resultant Programme of Action was adopted by the TREVI Ministers in 1990, and subsequently provided the groundwork for the organization's activities.

The Programme of Action was based on 'the Minister's conviction that new co-ordinated measures are called for as a follow up of the Single European Act, as is the intensifying of security measures at the external borders of the EC'. The programme included proposals on which *areas* of co-operation between the police and security services within the Community ought to be strengthened, *methods of co-operation*, and the precise modus of *implementation*. The most important areas of co-operation were to be combating terrorism, drug trafficking, organized crime and illegal immigration; co-operation in the technical and methodological spheres; and the conduct of joint training programmes.

The responsibility for laying the basis for the removal of border controls led to the Commission's being given observer status in TREVI 1992, and at TREVI's meetings at Senior Officials level whenever these dealt with issues related to the establishment of the Internal Market. The Commission thus achieved what it had frequently requested but repeatedly been denied ever since the establishment of TREVI in 1975.

The grounds for refusing to allow the Commission to participate had all along been the strong emphasis on TREVI's intergovernmental status and the crucial significance of the police and the judiciary for the sovereign state. There was moreover considerable scepticism among the member countries at the time when the Commission was admitted to TREVI 1992, and at the first meetings the representatives of the Commission and the Secretariat of the Ministerial Council were consigned to inconspicuous back benches.

The relationship between the Commission and TREVI had differed markedly from the relationship between the Commission and the EC's intergovernmental co-operation on immigration, which was initiated in 1986. Here the Commission has all along participated as observer, and had for example been involved in formulating proposals to the EC convention on asylum (the Dublin Convention). The explanation probably lay partly in the fact that immigration co-operation was established at a different stage in the development of the EC, and partly that co-operation on immigration came to be so strongly emphasized as a common problem for all member countries after the decision to create the frontier-free Internal Market.

Part of the follow up of the Programme of Action was a plan for a step by step establishment of a European Drugs Intelligence Unit (EDIU). Germany proposed that at some stage in the process, EDIU should also be accorded executive police authority. However, this proposal aroused so much opposition among the representatives of the other eleven member countries that it was omitted from the plan which was put before and adopted by the TREVI ministers (the ministers of justice or internal affairs of the EU countries) at their Luxembourg meeting in May 1991.

The implementation of the Maastricht Treaty called for transformation of TREVI to the extent that it hardly would be correct to say that it survived. Police co-operation formed part of the collaboration on Justice and Home Affairs, and came under the jurisdiction of the Council of Ministers. Hence, the new Council of Justice and Home Affairs replaced the ministerial level in TREVI. The Commission got observer status in all former TREVI working groups, of which the structure continued to exist, and the Council Secretariat took over the secretariat functions. TREVI's tasks and activities were thus adapted so as to fit into a new structure with closer links to the Community, as well as with other areas of policy, first and foremost immigration. All provisions in the forum exclusively for police co-operation were gone.

The Schengen Agreement

The Schengen Agreement had as its goal the creation of a Europe free of internal borders, as set out in the Single European Act, and had thus a completely different point of departure than TREVI. Schengen represented intergovernmental co-operation for the gradual removal of border controls, preceding the establishment of the Community's Internal Market. Co-operation was based on two conventions, the first being the Schengen Agreement signed in 1985, and the second the subsequent Implementation Agreement entered into in June 1990. Schengen thus had a different and more formalized legal foundation than TREVI, with police collaboration representing only one element of joint action.

When Schengen in 1999 was integrated into the EU, only the United Kingdom and Ireland among the EU member states were not included. There are several reasons for the reluctance of these member states to sign the Agreement, the chief of these being that measures governing border controls and compensatory measures were mutually inter-connected in the Schengen Agreement, and these countries do not wish to dismantle border controls.

The rationale behind the Schengen Agreement was the notion of *compensatory measures*: when the borders are opened for the free flow of people and goods, internal security can only be maintained if the border controls are compensated for by the introduction of alternative measures. Conversely, compensatory measures in the form of intensified external controls and increased police co-operation should not be implemented independently of abolition of border controls at the internal border. This coupling made the Schengen Agreement into a bargaining card against those countries which were reluctant to eliminate border controls.

Schengen is usually deemed to have served as an important stimulus with regard to integration within the EU. The participating countries have described the negotiations as experiments in the devising of models for external border control, police co-operation and the other compensatory measures. The co-operation has been likened to a laboratory, a first proof, a recipe book, etc. for the reduction of border controls and for integration. This function had an important bearing on the member countries during the preparatory stage of Schengen, and to a large extent served to legitimize the negotiations. The Schengen co-operation may consequently be seen as a precursor to closer co-operation in the areas of Justice and Home Affairs within the entire Union.

The Agreement embraces a number of key measures relating to areas that have traditionally been reserved to the state.

The most important point here is apparently that it set the foundation for common control routines in connection with border controls. The Schengen Agreement requires that external border control be carried out on the basis of common regulations for border control, and at the same level. This intrudes on the individual state's monopoly situation in a key control area, as well as putting constraints on the shaping of national policy and use of resources. It also concerns areas of activity that in a number of countries are carried out by the police or related authorities.

The Agreement also represented the most ambitious attempt before the Maastricht Treaty towards the evolution of a model for European police co-operation, as well as towards its formalization. The Agreement encompassed co-operation on several levels: it covered legal and constitutional issues inclusive of allowing policemen to cross the border to another country on certain conditions, an advanced information system, the Schengen Information System (SIS), partly for border control and partly for police investigative functions. Agreement between the member states on the aim of collaboration, namely the abolishing of border controls, evidently made it possible to agree on measures which at the time would have been unacceptable in other contexts.

The negotiations concerning the Schengen Agreement ran into difficulties on several issues. While France was strongly opposed to granting foreign policemen any authority whatever on French soil, Germany argued for the right to pursue criminals across borders. Extradition, visa collaboration and a common policy on asylum were other areas of contention. Also the Agreement as to where the Schengen Information System should be located was contentious. Negotiations on the Agreement were originally finalized in December 1989, but the signing was delayed as a result of the developments in eastern Europe. For instance, Germany felt that it first needed a clarification of its role in relation to control of its borders with East Germany, and in particular the issue of controlling the influx of immigrants from other eastern European states (den Boer 1991).

In 1994 Germany had ratified the Schengen Agreement and the signatory parts decided that the co-operation should enter into force on 26 March 1995. This put Denmark in a difficult position. At this time Denmark was one of three EU members not participating in the Schengen co-operation, and at the same time was a member of the Nordic Passport Union.

Nordic implementation of the Schengen acquis and the resulting activation of the Schengen co-operation is planned for the first half of the year 2001. Norway's expenses are stipulated to come to 260 million Norwegian crowns in investments and 160 million crowns in annual operating costs. The expenses will go to strengthening border controls along the coast – which will be the EU's external border – developing Schengen Information Systems, strengthening controls along the Russian border and implementing other necessary measures for the Schengen acquis. Complete implementation – such that the Schengen member countries' border controls with the Nordic countries are dismantled – also requires that the measures put into effect are approved by the other Schengen/EU countries.

Police co-operation within Schengen after the Agreement took effect has been centred to a great extent on strengthening and simplifying bilateral co-operation between countries. Bilateral co-operation has also been stimulated by the dismantling of border controls. Greater co-operation has been established, among other areas, at the French–German border. One example is that French and German police have a shared police station in Strasbourg. The Schengen Implementation Agreement's decisions regarding police permission to cross borders on hot pursuit are, in accordance with the Agreement, supplemented with bilateral agreements between the countries. With regard to how far into the individual country Agreement articles apply and what powers of attorney the police will have is left up to the nations themselves to negotiate. Guidelines have been developed in the form of a handbook for police co-operation and an overview of the individual country's legal systems, as well as police competence and regulations with regard to controlled delivery of narcotics. No initiative was taken with regard to the development of common institutions such as Europol. Larger co-ordinated actions have been carried out to some extent, such as with co-ordinated control operations in the different countries, for, among other things, narcotics.

The Maastricht Treaty: Co-operation on Justice and Home Affairs

The Maastricht Treaty or Agreement on the European Union reached final negotiations in December of 1991 and was signed on 7 February 1992. The result was an extensive expansion of co-operation within the EU and a completely new structure for the co-operation. Negotiations took place on two courses, two different treaty conferences in which the one addressed the framework for political union and the other addressed economic and monetary co-operation. Negotiations on the Justice and Home Affairs Pillar were part of the conference on political union, but originally not as a major issue. Chancellor Kohl and President Mitterand formulated a letter to the Italian EU Executive Committee in 1991 in which they stated that negotiations should include the scope of the Union's and the Community's competence, with emphasis on the following.

> Certain issues that are currently handled in an intergovernmental context could enter the scope of the union: immigration, visa policy, right of asylum, anti-drug actions and measures to fight organized crime. Consideration could be given to setting up a Council of Interior and Justice Ministers. (Agence Europe 10–11 Dec. 1990)

The point of departure for police co-operation being drawn into the Union was to a certain extent an expressed desire for further integration. Moreover, there was to be increased focus on, among other things, organized crime and illegal immigration as an external threat to the EU countries. Internal security would be a part of the foundation of the Union according to the introduction to the Maastricht Treaty in which the Heads of State confirm: 'Reaffirming their objective to facilitate the free movement of persons, while ensuring the safety and security of their peoples, by including provisions on justice and home affairs in this Treaty'.

The Maastricht Treaty encompassed a more extensive and more formalized co-operation in the area of Justice and Home Affairs than had so far existed. Police co-operation became an area of co-operation within the Union.

During the Maastricht negotiations, Germany strongly advocated that the arrangements for such co-operation should be incorporated in the supranational EC, but this did not get the necessary support of the other member states, and the provisions were placed in the so-called Third Pillar, with the consequence that this aspect of co-operation would be co-ordinated at intergovernmental level.

Co-operation on visas, however, was an exception, as the regulations governing visa policies were subsumed under the EC's supranationality as one of the Community's new policy areas (Section III, Art. 100 C). The regulations on visa policies are more far-reaching than in the other new policy areas, thus underlining its importance for the EC. The adoption of uniform visa regulations was seen as a precondition for the common external border control and a reduction of controls at the Community's internal borders, again underscoring the crucial significance of immigration policy for the EC.

Within the European Union, the Council of Ministers decides which third world citizens require visas for entering the Community (Art. 100 C). Initially resolutions on this should be unanimous, but from 1 January 1996 it has been in the Council's power to make decisions on visas, with a qualified majority. As in other policy areas, such proposals have to come from the Commission after a round of hearings in the European Parliament. Article 100 C emphasized that the Commission is obliged to lay recommendations from a member country affecting this area before the Council, if requested to do so by a member state.

The common visa policy may be regarded as a precursor paving the way for other judicial and internal affairs being brought under the supranational Community, as the text of the Treaty specified that the Council of Ministers could decide that the rules on procedure contained in Article 100 C should also be applicable to other measures in a number of Third Pillar policy areas. This applied to policies affecting asylum, immigration, the combating of drug-related crime, international fraud and judicial co-operation in civil matters. Such decisions had to be unanimous.

The EC's new intergovernmental co-operation in the fields of Justice and Home Affairs was justified on the grounds of a need for closer co-operation if the goals of the Union were to be realized, in particular those related to *the free movement of people* (Section IV, Art. K).

The following policy areas were encompassed:

1 Asylum policy;
2 Rules governing the crossing by persons of the external borders of the member states and the exercise of controls thereon;
3 Immigration policy, and policy regarding nationals of third countries:

   (a) Conditions of entry and movement by nationals of third countries on the territory of member states
   (b) Conditions governing residence of third country nationals within member countries, including regulations governing family reunion and the right to gain full employment
   (c) Combating unauthorized immigration from third countries, residence, and employment while within the borders of member states;

4 Combating drugs (when not covered by 9);
5 Combating international fraud;
6 Judicial co-operation in civil matters;
.7 Judicial co-operation in criminal matters;
8 Customs co-operation;
9 Police co-operation for the purposes of preventing and combating terrorism, unlawful drug trafficking and other serious forms of international crime, including if necessary certain aspects of customs co-operation, in connection with the organization of a Union-wide system for exchanging information within a European Police Office (Europol).

These important and sensitive areas were linked and accorded a higher degree of formalization in relation to the EC's institutions than earlier, even though such co-operation was to continue having the status of being intergovernmental. Status in relation to the EC as well as the degree of organization had earlier varied from area to area. While police co-operation had been the responsibility of TREVI without any participation on the part of EC institutions (apart from the Commission's observer status in TREVI 1992), immigration issues had been taken care of by the so-called Ad Hoc Immigration Group, in which the Commission had observer status since its inception in 1986. In the field of immigration co-operation, the Dublin Convention, among others, had been success-fully negotiated to a conclusion. EC co-operation in civil and criminal law matters had been formally organized as part of the European Political Co-operation, which also took place at intergovernmental level. Combating drug abuse had been the responsibility of CELAD (European Community Drugs Coordination), which was an EC ministerial co-ordinating group, while the Community's customs co-operation had been organized through MAG, later MAG 92 (Mutual Assistance Group) since the end of the 1960s.

In addition to the stipulations relating to the Third Pillar, two concluding declarations were incorporated in the Agreement concerning respectively police co-operation and asylum policy. The declarations could be seen as a political addendum to the text of the Treaty, and revealed something about the relative importance attached to the different areas within the pillar. Matters related to asylum were to be given high priority, and aspects of asylum policy were to be harmonized before the beginning of 1993 (Declaration on Asylum). This was in turn linked to the goal of removing internal border controls and, as a precondition, reinforcing the external ones. As far as *The Declaration on Police Co-operation* was concerned, Germany received political support, the partners expressed agreement on *the objectives* which formed the basis for the proposals forwarded at the meeting of the Council of Europe in Luxembourg in 1991. It was at this meeting that Chancellor Kohl first put forward his proposal for the establishment of Europol, a proposal which was appreciably broader in scope than the one which was ultimately adopted.

Co-operation in the fields of Justice and Home Affairs was hence to continue to take place at the intergovernmental level, after the introduction of the Maastricht Treaty. The different policy areas however became more closely integrated, and the relationship to the EC's institutions altered. The Maastricht Treaty formalized the framework for the co-operation, which had evolved in the various sectors since 1975, and facilitated uniform and closer ties to the EC system in these areas.

A 'new' Council of Ministers with responsibility for the entire area was established. The highest political level responsible for police co-operation became the Council of Ministers instead of the EC's Ministers of Justice or Home Affairs serving in their capacity as TREVI ministers. However, by virtue of being a fully intergovernmental Council, its decisions had to be unanimous.

The Commission's position was enhanced in many respects. It was determined that the Commission should be 'fully involved', even though the co-operation was to be intergovernmental. More precisely, the Commission, in line with the constituent member countries, got the right to initiate policies in the areas of asylum, border control, immigration policy, narcotics, countering international fraud, and judicial co-operation on civil matters. With regard to co-operation in the spheres of criminal matters, customs co-operation and police collaboration, only the member states were entitled to initiate proposals to the Council of Ministers. However, the Commission would not be without influence here either, as it was accorded observer status in appropriate fora. In the sphere of police co-operation this implied that the Commission would no longer be confined to having observer status in relation to the former TREVI 1992, but also in working groups on police matters. As to the wielding of influence, its lack of expertise in this domain was evidently a greater problem for the Commission than its lack of powers of initiation.

The Maastricht Treaty also to some extent explicated the role of the *European Parliament*. The Presidency of the Commission should progressively keep the European Parliament informed on current progress in the area (Art. K.6). The Parliament was furthermore to be consulted on the principal aspects of activities, and the Presidency should ensure that Parliament's views were duly taken into consideration. This implied that matters relating to Justice and Home Affairs constituted a domain in which the Parliament would have a *minimum level of influence*. The Parliament got the right to raise queries and make recommendations to the Council, and was to make an annual review of progress in the area of Justice and Home Affairs.

The Maastricht Treaty established, as we saw above, the formal foundation for the establishment of Europol (Art. K.1, point 9).

As has previously been emphasized, the establishment of Europol represented the most significant step so far in elevating regular police co-operation to EU level, as Europol was intended to become a *police institution* while simultaneously forming an integral part of the EU. Europol had a lengthy prehistory. Since the 1970s, Germany had attempted to initiate a reorganization of European police co-operation and the creation of a Europol Unit (Fijnaut 1992). Views on whether the unit should be part of intergovernmental co-operation or be subordinate to the EC's institutions had, however, differed, and the relationship between Europol and Interpol, as well as the role to be played by Interpol had been the subject of debate.

Chancellor Kohl's proposal at the Luxembourg meeting in June 1991 for the establishment of Europol should be seen against the background of Germany's earlier interest in the matter, and the already existing plans for the prospective EDIU under TREVI. The decision to establish Europol marked the first step on the road to a more operational police co-operation between the EU member states, but it was by no means a foregone conclusion that the unit would ever have operational police competence devolved upon it. In the Maastricht Treaty, Europol was only loosely defined, and its responsibilities were limited to the exchange of information. In the final declaration, Europol was not explicitly mentioned. A number of areas relevant to an expanded co-operation were, however, listed, and the member states committed themselves to consider a broadening of the framework for such co-operation during the course of 1994.

Tasks which were accorded particular mention in this connection were: assistance to the national authorities responsible for investigative and security tasks in order to facilitate co-ordination, the establishment of databases, crime analysis and undercover work, as well as developing investigative methods, the collection and systematization of national preventive programmes with a view to sharing information in order to organize these at a European level, extra training, research, forensic techniques, and anthropometry.

A majority of the EU's member countries held the opinion that Europol – as plans were for phase two – would have to be established on the foundation of an internationally binding treaty because, among other things, Europol would then be able to exchange sensitive investigative information. In June of 1993, the EU's Ministers of Justice a nd Home Affairs approved an agreement that would serve as the foundation for the establishment of a Europol Drugs Unit (EDU). This was the predecessor of Europol. EDU began its activities in The Hague in January of 1994. This is a clear sign that there was increased focus on organized crime as a common problem for the EU countries. The Europol Convention was nonetheless not completely negotiated until 1995. Ratification was completed first in 1998, and the Convention took effect on 1 October 1998. Europol was not operative until the summer of 1999. Consequently, EDU – or Europol phase 1 – had a life span of nearly six years, and with dynamic German management the institution played a very significant role in the development of police co-operation within the EU. Increased focus on the issue of criminality as a common problem was also signalled by continual expansion of EDU's mandate. From illegal drugs it was expanded to trafficking nuclear and radioactive substances, crimes involving clandestine immigration networks, illicit vehicle trafficking, trafficking in human beings and illegal money-laundering activities in connection with these forms of crime.

Co-operation within the Third Pillar has experienced continuous development since the Maastricht Treaty took effect, and measures directed against crime have been in focus.

The European Council in Dublin on 13 and 14 December 1996 underlined its absolute determination to fight organized crime and stressed the need for a coherent and co-ordinated approach by the Union. It decided to create a High Level Group of national experts to draw up a comprehensive action plan containing specific recommendations, including realistic timetables for carrying out the organization. The group was requested to examine the fight against organized crime in all its aspects, on the clear understanding that it would refer any issues involving Treaty changes to the coming Intergovernmental Conference. The group should complete its work by March/April 1997.

The plan contained a proposal including 30 recommendations and 15 political guidelines, i.e. proposals for recommendations that the group considered to be so important that the Council ought to adopt them as its own. The proposals embrace a wide area of police co-operation, legal co-operation, criminal law harmonization and other measures.

It was also suggested that the Council should reiterate the view that Europol should be given operative powers together with national authorities. Without prejudice to the outcome of the Intergovernmental Conference, Europol should be enabled to facilitate and support the preparation, co-ordination and carrying out of specific investigative actions by the competent authorities of the member states, including the operational actions of joint teams comprising representatives of Europol. It should also be enabled to ask the competent authorities of the member states to conduct specific cases and develop expertise that may be put at the disposal of member states to assist them in investigating cases of organized crime. Europol should be instrumental in the collation and exchange of information by the law enforcement agencies of reports on suspicious financial transactions.

A majority of the recommendations in the plan were approved by the Council, such that the foundation actually was laid for further development of the co-operation in these areas before the Amsterdam Treaty came into effect.

The Amsterdam Treaty

The Amsterdam Treaty was signed on 19 June 1997 and came into effect on 1 July 1999. The Treaty contains a number of changes with regard to co-operation in the fields of Justice and Home Affairs. Co-operation in the fields of Justice and Home Affairs covers, as we have seen, a number of different areas that were clearly delineated in the Maastricht Treaty and gathered together in the Third Pillar. These different areas are not so easily identifiable in the Amsterdam Treaty. The treaty can be said to divide the areas of co-operation into three domains. The first domain includes Free Movement of persons in the specific context of the dismantling of person controls at the internal borders. The area includes a common regime for the carrying out of person controls at the external borders, the development of a common visa policy, conditions for free movement of third-country citizens living in the Union, common strategies for illegal immigration and a common policy on asylum and the treatment of applications for asylum. These are, as we have seen, to a certain extent areas that can have distinct significance for the forming of policy in the member countries, especially concerning regulations for external border controls.

The other domain includes provisions on police and judicial co-operation in criminal matters, which, to a much greater extent than previously, has been gathered under the heading 'compensatory measures'. Special emphasis is put on organized crime, and the area covers co-operation between law enforcement authorities, the judiciary and approximation of legislation in that context.

The third is the domain of international private law, which includes judicial co-operation, rules on jurisdiction and conflicts of laws, and the approximation of substantive and procedural legislation.

The Maastricht Treaty contained the basis for co-operation now stipulated by Treaty in the three domains. In the Amsterdam Treaty the co-operation seems considerably wider in scope; the individual articles are more detailed and descriptive. The degree of detail also gives the impression that the Union is given much more competence than under the Maastricht Treaty, especially in the second domain. This is not necessarily the case, because the Amsterdam Treaty to a great extent reflected the Council's working programme as it was already developed within the framework of competence the Maastricht Treaty gave the Union. The degree of detail concerning description of further measures on the issue of asylum and visa routines, police co-operation and legal co-operation would nonetheless indicate that further guidelines in these areas are now regulated by Treaty.

One major change is that both the domain concerning freedom of movement and decisions concerning civil rights co-operation are transferred to the First Pillar, the supranational co-operation. This means that the Community's decision-making mechanisms will apply for these areas. But the drafters of the Amsterdam Treaty have at the same time accepted some departures from the pure Community method in these fields. For a transitional period the member states will have a joint right to initiative with the Commission, the Court of Justice will have only limited competence, and unanimity for adoption of legislative acts will be the rule rather than the exception.

As concerns the domain which in principle remains at intergovernmental level in the Third Pillar – the Provisions on Police and Judicial Cooperation in Criminal Matters – the Community's institutions are given greater competence. The Commission is given full rights of initiative on a par with the member states and both the Court of Justice and the Parliament are given more influence than previously. In accordance with the Treaty, the Court will initially have full jurisdiction 'to give preliminary rulings on the validity and interpretation of framework decisions, and decisions on the interpretation of conventions established under this Title and interpretation of the measures implementing them' (The Amsterdam Treaty, Art. K.7 1.). One of the limitations is that 'The Court of Justice shall have no jurisdiction to review the validity or proportionality of operations carried out by the police or other law enforcement services of a Member State or the exercise of the responsibilities incumbent upon the Member States with regard to the maintenance of law and order and the safeguarding of internal security' (The Amsterdam Treaty, Art. K.7 5.). The influence of Parliament is expanded by replacing the hearing procedures in the Maastricht Treaty with a consultation procedure.

It cannot necessarily be said that co-operation on Justice and Home Affairs is given new foundation in relation to what had been established on the basis of the Maastricht Treaty. The significance of co-operation in the field of Justice and Home Affairs is nonetheless further emphasized; in the terms of Article 2 of the TEU:

> The objective of The Union is to maintain and develop The Union as an area of freedom, security and justice, in which the free movement of persons is assured in conjunction with appropriate measures with respect to external border controls, asylum, immigration and the prevention and combating of crime.

This is a new unifying political concept in the context of the EU which encompasses the entire area of Justice and Home Affairs co-operation. Perhaps this to some extent can be seen as compensation for the provisions in the area now between both the EC and the EU Treaty.

The contents of the provisions on police and judicial co-operation in criminal matters are more greatly elaborated in the Amsterdam Treaty than was the case previously. Focus is on internal security, something that must be seen in connection with the fact that the regulations concerning control at the external borders have been transferred to the First Pillar. The goal of this co-operation is now to provide citizens with a high level of safety within an area of freedom, security and justice, by developing common action among the member states in the fields of police and judicial co-operation in criminal matters and by preventing and combating racism and xenophobia.

Both the articles concerning police co-operation and legal co-operation are extensive. The Treaty reflects the fact that considerable emphasis is given to the strengthening of co-operation on criminal law with regard to police co-operation, something which has been attempted previously in the history of the EU, but which has always proven difficult. This in itself is a sign of Union development.

Common action in the field of police co-operation shall include operational co-operation to the prevention, detection and investigation of criminal offences.

Considerable emphasis is given to financial crime, which is an area of substantial common interest for the EU since collection, storage, processing, analysis and exchange of relevant information, including information held by law enforcement agencies on reports concerning suspicious financial transactions (in particular through Europol), are referred to in a specified decision (Art. K.2 (b)). Europol is also given a role that was previously more exclusively taken by the Unit for the Co-ordination of Fraud Prevention, UCLAF, which is organized within the Community.

The co-operation will moreover include co-operation and joint initiatives in training, the exchange of liaison officers, secondments, the use of equipment and forensic research and common evaluation of particular investigative techniques in relation to the detection of serious forms of organized crime. These are traditional measures in bilateral and interstate police co-operation that among other things seek to reduce barriers towards co-operating, such as different languages, differences in the organizational structures of the police and the legal systems. In light of the decision to establish a common police academy within the EU, noted at the beginning of this chapter, extensive collaboration of this sort can be confirmed as a target for the EU.

The extended competence for Europol, which were proposed in the plan from the High Level Group on Organized Crime, are embraced in the Treaty. Over a period of five years, Europol will be given the competence described previously and will consequently be given scope to encourage member countries to investigate special cases and to set up and participate in teams that investigate cases that concern several member countries. In addition, the Council will promote liaison arrangements between prosecuting and investigating officials specializing in the fight against organized crime in close co-operation with Europol.

The Amsterdam Treaty also integrates the Schengen co-operation into the EU, through the protocol, annexed to the EC and EU Treaties, on the integration of the Schengen acquis (the Schengen protocol), which states that the Schengen acquis immediately applies as a matter of the law of the European Union, between the thirteen signatory states to the Schengen Agreement.

In this fashion the Schengen acquis will become a part of the EU's regulations. It will also be divided between the First and Third Pillars, thus keeping the same structure as that introduced by the Amsterdam Treaty. Schengen's regulations concerning external border controls, which previously in this chapter have been noted as having significant consequences for national policy and use of resources in a sensitive area, have consequently become a part of the supranational co-operation. Nonetheless, this does not mean that the Schengen regulations will apply to all of the EU countries. The UK and Ireland – which have previously not wished to participate in the Schengen co-operation, because of the absolute link between the dismantling of person controls at internal borders and the establishment of common external border controls – were granted the possibility to 'opt out' of the relevant decisions.

A very insistent disagreement between the UK and the other EU countries has thus been eliminated by 'coming to agreement about being in disagreement'. The UK has accepted that free movement of people will also apply to third-person citizens living in the EU, which has been an aspect of its grounds for not wanting to remove person controls.

By integrating the Schengen acquis the EU has achieved a set of regulations for external border controls, something that has previously proved impossible to attain. The EU's negotiations on a convention on external border control deadlocked early in the 1990s due to the UK's position on the matter and to conflict between the UK and Spain concerning who should be responsible for the border controls on Gibraltar. The former Schengen regulations will not apply to the UK and Ireland, but they will apply to the two non-EU countries, Norway and Iceland!

The integration of the Schengen acquis, the opt-out for the UK and Ireland, Norwegian and Icelandic participation (and the Danish opt-out that will not be discussed here) provide an extremely intricate pattern of decision-making and participatory involvement.

The Schengen protocol required an association of Iceland and Norway with the activities of the Union in the field of the Schengen acquis on the basis of the Agreement signed in Luxembourg on 19 December 1996.

This was nonetheless not without problems, not as seen by the EU nor by Norway and Iceland. Seen from the point of view of the EU, the co-operation model established in the Luxembourg Agreement would have to match the special requirements of the institutional framework of the European Union, and in particular the fact that the signatory states to the Schengen Agreement are members of the EU, whereas Norway and Iceland are not, as well as the fact that the Schengen co-operation defines its own sphere of activities, but the scope of the Union/ Community, even in the field limited to matters of Justice and Home Affairs, is wider and covers matters not related to Schengen.

Norway and Iceland wanted an agreement that gave them equal access to participate in the decision-making process as they had under the Luxembourg Agreement, i.e. that participation should be on an equal basis at all levels, including the Council, when Schengen issues were treated. For the EU, this was completely unacceptable.

The result of the negotiations is an institutional agreement that gives Norway and Iceland access to participate in the decision-making process through a 'Mixed Committee structure'.

In connection with the issue of integration, substantial work has been put into defining what the Schengen acquis embraces, and what is no longer technically applicable. Subsequently, an important question is where the decisions should apply in relation to the EU's legal foundation, which in effect would divide them between Pillars I and III. In addition, efforts were made, during German chairmanship in the spring of 1999, to unite organizational structures in the former Schengen co-operation with structures within the domains that now make up EU co-operation on Justice and Home Affairs. The result is that individual Schengen groups are implemented in their entirety, while others are to be combined with existing groups in the EU.

Within the co-operation there will be working groups within which Norway and Iceland will never participate, groups which, when they treat Schengen issues, will also meet as Mixed Committee and groups that only treat Schengen questions and as such always meet as Mixed Committee. In the autumn of 2000 there still remain many open questions and considerable 'probing and bargaining' as concerns how this structure will function. One important point is obviously the understanding of which issues represent further development of the Schengen acquis and which do not. Police co-operation in this context is an example of an area in which it is not so easy to decide what is a Schengen relevant matter and what is not. Some aspects are nonetheless clear. Europol in this context is not relevant to Schengen, while continuing co-operation with regard to the Schengen Information Systems is. There are nonetheless many grey areas. This necessary statement looks for the moment to result in further development concerning the division between elements in the EU's police co-operation that can be seen as compensatory measures and those that concern the internal security of the Union.

Conclusion

The different political areas within Justice and Home Affairs area are, as we have seen from the Amsterdam Treaty, now divided between the EU's First Pillar, supranational co-operation, and its Third Pillar. At the same time, a highly complex decision-making structure was established, containing certain digressions from the strictly Community-related decision-making model in the supranational EU, and a greater degree of influence for the Community's institutions in the Third. The right for the UK, Ireland (and Denmark) to opt out of certain areas has also been accepted, while two non-EU countries, Norway and Iceland, will participate in the former Schengen area through a Mixed Committee Structure. Co-operation on Justice and Home Affairs thus emerged as less coherent than after the Maastricht Treaty. Nonetheless, the degree of integration is higher, and the model can be seen as a step in the direction of supranationality in several of the areas within the Justice and Home Affairs area.

One interesting aspect of the co-operation is that the conditions for and the regulations for border controls have become a part of the EU's supranational area. This is a political area that has significant importance for the shaping of member countries' border control regimes and consequently represents a Europeanization of policy development at the national level. In this context it is important that the integration of the Schengen co-operation entails common regulations for operative border controls for the Union. Within the EU the co-operation on border control regulations is understood as being clearly separated from police co-operation. At the same time it can be seen that these regulations have consequences for national border control tasks that in certain countries are carried out by the police. This is the case for the two non-member countries participating in the co-operation and previously bound to the former Schengen acquis. On the basis of the decision-making model that has been established, there appears to be little likelihood that these Nordic countries will have significant potential to influence further development of the co-operation.

This also applies to the actual police co-operation within the EU. Integration of the Schengen acquis and the co-operation's various working groups has, as has been noted previously, resulted in a process in which definition is necessary concerning what further development is relevant to Schengen and what is not. As regards police co-operation, it looks as if the most important line of division will concern which co-operative strategies can be tied into the dismantling of border controls and which will be tied into strengthening the Union's internal security. Norway and Iceland will only be able to participate in relationship to the former. Inasmuch as the EU is putting more and more emphasis on the Union's internal security as a grounds for police co-operation, it can be expected that what was previously regarded as 'compensatory measures' will be less and less important.

Europol, which is now operative, has, since the Maastricht Treaty was signed, represented the most important force with regard to common police activities at a supranational level. The EU has still not established any common police authority under supranational instruction, something that would, as noted in the introduction, represent a total breach with national sovereignty in this area. Europol remains intergovernmental and has not been granted police authority, but a step has been taken in this direction. Europol shall assist member countries in the investigation of organized crime, as well as encourage investigation in the member countries. Europol's mandate also embraces the fight against terrorism, which is a high policing area, and several aspects of financial crime that, with regard to the issue of fraud, remain an internal EU affair.

The EU is also expanding its co-operation in low policing areas to a greater degree. This applies to bilateral co-operation, such as, for example, the secondment of liaison officers. In this connection it is interesting to note that this type of co-operation is also used in the area of legal co-operation, wherein the secondment of representatives for the prosecuting authority is planned. Police co-operation and legal co-operation in the EU now go hand in hand to a greater extent than previously.

The exchange of experience and training is also within the framework of traditional bilateral police co-operation and can be characterized as a low policing area. In light of the proposal to establish a common police academy within the EU in order to raise the EU countries' competence in relation to organized criminality, there is, at least, confirmation that within the EU this type of wide-scope co-operation is being targeted. When police officers are trained to be experts on organized, cross-border criminality, what is created in practice are police officers who can work with high policing tasks. What is also a possibility is that in this way a 'Europolice' can be developed by stimulating cultural similarities, common expertise and loyalty to the EU.

How far has integration come in the EU with regard to police activity, an area of 'high politics' and a sensitive domain with regard to co-operation at the national level? Development – from the establishment of TREVI in the mid-1970s to the implementation of the Amsterdam Treaty in the autumn of 1999 – has come a long way. The Union's institutions have gradually achieved a greater degree of influence. Co-operation has been expanded significantly, both in breadth and depth. We have seen that the Single European Act represented an important threshold because it created the foundation for united police co-operation and other related areas of politics in one structure, while tying those areas to the establishment of the inner market. This created the opportunity for the Union's institutions to obtain access to police co-operation, the first occasion being the Commission's being granted access to participate as observers in the co-operation. When, after the Amsterdam Treaty, the Commission achieved the right to initiative on equal footing with member states in the domain that includes the Provisions on Police and Judicial Co-operation in Criminal Matters, this was a major step. The Maastricht Treaty also represented significant progress, inasmuch as police co-operation was instituted as a part of the Union, and the Third Pillar was a first step in the direction of a common legal area within the Union.

PART 3

THE FUTURE OF THE EU AND EUROPEAN INTEGRATION

EUROPEAN MONETARY UNION: ECONOMIC VERSUS POLITICAL INTEGRATION AND THE LIMITS OF SUPRANATIONALISM[1]

Miriam L. Campanella

Requirements and Possibilities

This chapter focuses on EMU fiscal discipline and centres on the question: Why have EU member governments chosen to submit their own domestic public budget to 'collective monitoring, surveillance and enforcement'. Students of public budget, such as Wildawsky or Buchanan, would probably suggest that the best way to balance a budget is through domestically based constitutional regulation. Students of EMU are likely to suggest that EMU fiscal discipline belongs, as with other arrangements such as the creation of the European Central Bank, to the area of international political economic relations (Molle 1994, Crawford 1996). National convergence policies constitute the major issue facing the European Union, and are likely to provide a test of the willingness of EU countries to adopt ever-closer political-economic integration. EMU fiscal discipline does not interfere with the capabilities of national fiscal authorities in their own way to raise taxation and govern expenditure. However, it was deemed necessary to place limits on public spending and to adopt an international monitoring, surveillance and enforcement policy in order to avoid a free-riding problem (Gros and Thygesen 1998).

With a certain nonchalance towards the convergence criteria, 11 EU countries proceeded to fix irrevocably their exchange rates. From 1 January 1999 the Euro became a parallel legal tender for 270 million Europeans. It will become their single currency in 2002. Nonetheless, EMU fiscal criteria remain a highly controversial issue in that fiscal consolidation continues to be a difficult objective to achieve. In 1999, a year after the introduction of the new currency, public deficit was running at 1.6 per cent of GDP on a yearly base, while public debt was estimated to have declined only to 72.9 per cent (against the EMU requirement of 60 per cent). Meanwhile, member countries such as

Belgium and Italy are still bearing a 120 per cent debt ratio to GDP (*ECB Monthly Bulletin*, January 2000). These figures are especially striking when compared with those for the United States and Japan.

The share of government expenditure in GDP is significantly larger in the Euro area than in either Japan or the United States, at 49 per cent against 39 per cent and 34 per cent, respectively (*ECB Monthly Bulletin*, January 2000). Persistent high government expenditure in the Euro area shows that the problem of fiscal discipline is not obsolete, as many economists would allow (Corsetti and Roubini 1993). The choice made by EU countries to adopt an international monitoring, surveillance and enforcement policy to solve the problem of fiscal discipline within the EMU area is a distinctive character of the EMU project, and a sign of the peculiarity of the EMU arrangements.

The EMU provisions have set limits to fiscal deficit such that it has to be less than 3 per cent of GDP on a yearly base. In addition, a 'co-ordinating' body – the European Commission and the Council of Ministers – is given the power to monitor and to enforce the rules. When comparing the EMU approach to domestically based constitutional regulation, the EMU enforcement mechanism appears to be weaker and prone to colluding practice. As the Council of Ministers is given the role of taking the final decision in a case of an acknowledged violation of the agreed rule, a question arises: Who enforces whom? A political body is unlikely to inflict penalties on one of its member governments.

The above question raises a second one: Why have EU countries adopted such a weaker enforcement mechanism? A response provided in this chapter is that the EMU model serves better the objective of the participating countries to circumvent market assessment, so as to leave more room for manoeuvre for deficit-spending-prone governments seeking political survival. The 'international market pressure' argument is, indeed, central in understanding the EMU arrangements and member countries' approach to making policy in the Euro area (Andersen and Eliassen 1999: 10). The approach is very similar to other EMU practices, like the monetary policy that EMU countries have delegated to the supranational European Central Bank (ECB). Though the technicalities are different, the delegation of monetary policy to the ECB and the delegation of fiscal discipline to a supranational set of bodies, represent a solution to the time inconsistency problem (Campanella 1998).

The chapter's major tenets are as follows:

1   The provisions of the international Pact of Stability and Growth[2] address the time inconsistency problems which affect the Euro-zone countries in their attempt to ensure international market credibility (long-term benefits) without upsetting the short-term calculations essential to their own political survival. Thus, a solution to the credibility problem is provided.

2 Under fiscal discipline, the market constituency believes that peer countries are willing to monitor sovereign debtors, and eventually to bail them out in case of liquidity crises.

3 Under the supranational monitoring and punishment provisions, the Euro nations have found a solution to a 'free-riding' problem. In fact, admission to the EMU third stage has not solved the problem of deficit-prone countries, as the latter, given their past negative fiscal record, could continue suffering from higher interest rates. Although a fixed exchange rate will place some constraints on inter-European competition, deficit-prone governments can take a breath as they are likely to enjoy reduced debt servicing costs and at the same time gain greater space for manoeuvre at a domestic level.

EMU in Practice

The general principles and procedures of the Treaty have been spelled out in detail in secondary legislation, which forms the so-called 'Stability and Growth Pact'.

Article 104c of the Treaty on European Union at the outset states that, in the third and final stage of EMU, 'Member States shall avoid excessive government deficits'. The compliance of a member state with the budgetary discipline requirement will be assessed *inter alia* on the basis of the level of the government deficit as a share of GDP in relation to a reference value set by the 'protocol on the Excessive Deficit Procedure' (Protocol 5 of the Treaty) at 3 per cent of GDP.

When there is an excessive deficit, a procedure aimed at reducing the deficit is initiated. This includes several steps involving increasing 'pressure' on the member state through recommendations and notice to take effective measures to correct the excessive deficit position. If such a correction does not take place, the Treaty foresees that sanctions may be applied to the member states participating in the EMU.

The 3 per cent threshold can be exceeded without causing an excessive deficit, but only under a restrictive set of conditions. In particular, three conditions must be met:

1 *exceptionality*: the origin of the excess has to be outside the normal range of situations;
2 *temporariness*: the deficit is allowed to remain above 3 per cent of GDP only for a limited period of time;
3 *closeness*: the deficit must remain close to the reference value.

In practice, the Treaty prescribes that the original cause of the rise of the deficit above the 3 per cent ceiling must be exceptional, that the deficit must not, in any case, exceed this threshold by too much, and must promptly return below it, once the initial cause no longer applies. These three conditions have to apply simultaneously. The extent of the subset of events that does not give rise to an excessive deficit depends on the degree of restriction with which these conditions are interpreted. The Treaty, however, does not specify the exact content of the three constraints. The Stability and Growth Pact gives a more precise interpretation of the first two conditions listed above.

The core elements of the Stability and Growth Pact include:

- setting time limits to the various steps of the Excessive Deficit Procedure so as to speed it up, and where appropriate, impose sanctions within the calendar year in which the decision on the existence of the excessive deficit is taken;
- defining the meaning of the exceptionality and temporariness conditions;
- specifying the conditions in which sanctions will be applied and their scale.

The starting point of the Pact is that the EMU members should set medium-term budgetary targets which are 'close-to-balance or in surplus', thus enabling them to respect the 3 per cent ceiling even during economic downturns. The exceptionality clause (condition 1) can be called upon when the excess of the deficit over the reference value is due to an unusual event outside the control of the member state in question and which has a major impact on the financial position of the general government. It can also apply if the deficit overrun takes place in the presence of a severe economic downturn. The latter case is considered 'exceptional' if there is an annual fall in real GDP of at least 2 per cent.

An annual fall in GDP of less than 2 per cent could nevertheless be considered exceptional in the light of other evidence, such as the abruptness of the downturn or the accumulated loss of output relative to past trends. In any event, in evaluating whether the economic downturn is severe, the member state will, as a rule, take an annual fall in real GDP of at least 0.75 per cent as a reference point. This condition recognizes that, in the event of a harsh and persistent recession, the room for budgetary manoeuvre between close-to-balance and a deficit of 3 per cent of GDP may not be sufficient to cushion the negative effects of the shock in economic activity.

As to the temporary nature of the excess of the deficit over 3 per cent of GDP (condition 2), the Pact allows it only insofar as the 'exceptional' conditions mentioned above persist. If the Commission's budgetary forecast indicates that the deficit will not fall below the reference value in the year following the recession, the country will also be considered to be in a situation of excessive deficit in the year of the recession because it has violated the 'temporariness' clause.

The Pact does not deal with the closeness condition (condition 3, above).

Problems are graded in order of 'seriousness':

1 the no-problem case, in which, in spite of the recession, the deficit remains below the 0.75 per cent threshold;
2 the limited-problem case, in which, the deficit exceeds 3 per cent of GDP during the recession, but remains close to it and returns below it immediately after the recession; the three conditions mentioned above apply, hence no excessive deficit occurs;
3 the violation of the closeness condition, in which the deficit is pushed up well above the reference value, but promptly moves below it as soon as the recession is over; the country is in excessive deficit during the year of the recession, but no sanctions are imposed on it;
4 the violation of the temporariness clause, in which the deficit remains fairly close to the 3 per cent ceiling during the recession year, but as it does not move below it in the year after the recession, the country is in excessive deficit during the year of the recession and, unless effective measures to correct the deficit are implemented, there is a presumption that sanctions will be applied;
5 the double-violation case, in which both the temporariness and closeness conditions are not respected; there is an excessive deficit which, as in the previous case, could eventually lead to sanctions.

The decision as to whether or not an excessive deficit existed during the year of the recession is taken on the basis of figures for the recession year which are reported one year later. In order to avoid the imposition of sanctions, the member state considered to have an excessive deficit has to take immediate action in the year in which the decision on the existence of an excessive deficit is taken. The correction of the deficit should be completed in the year following the identification of the excessive deficit; i.e. in order to avoid sanctions, the member state concerned should bring its deficit below the reference value within two years' and one year after its identification, unless special circumstances are granted.

The surveillance and enforcement service defines the 3 per cent deficit target as an absolute target which must be met in every fiscal year, exemptions being approved in very rare circumstances. It includes an enforcement policy that requires non-interest-bearing deposits for members found (during a six-monthly deficit review) to have a deficit in excess of 3 per cent of GDP. A fine can be imposed if the deficit violation persists for more than two years. The enforcement mechanism is structured as follows.

Early warning system: monitoring and surveillance

The Commission and the Council will 'study these programmes and monitor Member States' budgetary performances with reference to their medium-term objectives and adjustment paths with a view to giving early warning of any significant deterioration which might lead to an excessive deficit'. Once the Excessive Deficit Procedure has been initiated the Council will, in accordance with paragraph 11 of Article 104c of the Maastricht Treaty, 'impose sanctions on a prescribed scale'.

Triggering the procedure

The Commission, invited to commit itself to prepare a report whenever the actual or planned government deficit exceeds the 3 per cent reference value, will, as a rule, consider an excess over the reference value resulting from an economic downturn to be exceptional only if there is an annual fall in real GDP of at least 2 per cent.

The Economic and Financial Committee will formulate an opinion on the Commission's report within two weeks. Where it decides that an excessive deficit exists, the Council will make recommendations to the member state concerned 'with a view to bringing that situation to an end within a given period' (Article 104c (7)). If a member state fails to act in compliance with the successive decisions of the Council under paragraphs 7 to 9 of Article 104c, the Council will impose sanctions including a non-interest-bearing deposit. These sanctions would be imposed within ten months of the reporting of the figures notifying the existence of a deficit. The Stability Pact foresees an 'expedited procedure . . . in the case of a deliberately planned deficit which the Council decides is excessive'.

Structure and scale of sanctions

The Commission can take the following action on establishing that a government has not complied with the agreement.

1 Levy a non-interest-bearing deposit.
2 Convert the deposit into a fine after two years if the deficit of the government concerned continues to be excessive.
3 When the excessive deficit results from non-compliance with the government deficit reference value, the amount of the deposit or fine will be made up of a fixed component equal to 0.2 per cent of GDP, and a variable component equal to one tenth of the excess of the deficit over the reference value of 3 per cent of GDP. There will be an upper limit of 0.5 per cent of GDP for the annual amount of deposits. The amount of the sanction will be based on outcomes for the first year in which the excessive deficit occurred.

Implementation

The implementation of *excessive deficit procedure* is subject to a 'European Council Resolution' being issued. Such a resolution would give strong political guidance to the Commission, the Council and the member states on the implementation of the procedures. Furthermore, the Pact introduces two regulatory provisions: one on strengthening the surveillance of budgetary positions as well as the surveillance and co-ordination of economic policies, and another one on speeding up and clarifying the implementation of the excessive deficit procedure.

Why Converge?

Current literature on EMU fiscal discipline mirrors the intrinsic difficulties of the problem. Three main questions are of interest to this chapter: (a) whether or not a fiscal discipline is desirable, and for what purpose; (b) whether the Pact can increase mutual trust or produce negative effects on relations among EMU members; (c) whether or not the objectives of public budget discipline have been seriously sustained by appropriate institutional provisions.

All three questions rank high in EMU political economic literature but perhaps only the last two are of direct interest to EU policy-makers. The first obviously relates to the economic performance that the introduction of a balanced budget discipline can bring to economies that have only recently started their transition to an open-market policy. The second one relates appropriately to the political relations among member states, and between them and their domestic electorate, which has not been allowed to express its own preferences for a single currency through the ballot box. The third question relates to the effectiveness of the fiscal institutions when they are embodied in a macroeconomic policy; favouring a macro discipline can raise doubts about the real willingness of these institutions to follow through with their announced objectives.

A declared objective of the Stability Pact is to insulate the future ECB from possible inflationary pressures. For this reason, hard-currency countries recognize that the relationship between monetary and fiscal policy plays a crucial role. As anticipated by Sargent and Wallace (1981), the way in which monetary and fiscal policy is co-ordinated affects the Central Bank's ability to control inflation. Fiscal deficits can be financed either by seignorage (inflation) or by bond sales. If monetary policy dominates fiscal policy, then the monetary authorities can set monetary policy independently, and the fiscal authorities would have to finance the deficit by a fixed amount of seignorage (determined by the monetary authorities) and by bond sales. As monetary authorities (independent central banks) are free to choose the path for the monetary base, they can permanently control inflation. If, however, fiscal policy dominates monetary policy, the fiscal authorities could set the budget deficit independently, and the monetary authorities would be constrained to finance the difference between bond sales and the budget deficit. In this case, the monetary authorities would have less power to control inflation (Brociner and Levine 1991: 8).

Sargent and Wallace suggest that 'monetary policy be designed to dominate fiscal policy, for the control of inflation'. EMU treaties have created the ECB, as the monetary authority, which should decide on monetary policy independently, so that the fiscal authorities (or authority) would then be limited in the financing of their deficits. 'Knowing that they would have no recourse to monetary financing would also impose a discipline on the fiscal authorities to set a deficit compatible with their available source of financing. And the ECB could more reputably, and therefore successfully, achieve its goal of price stability' (Brociner and Levine 1991: 20).

Arguments in favour of the introduction of a Community-wide fiscal discipline originate from the various governments' long-lasting divergent behaviour in public spending, net government lending, and gross public debt in the 1980s and 1990s. At the beginning of the 1960s, as Von Hagen finds, 'there was a remarkable similarity among the six EC Member States and Ireland, Denmark and the UK. Expenditure varied between 25 and 35 per cent of GDP' at the end of the decade. After the oil shocks in the 1970s, there was an acceleration of expenditure relative to GDP. In the early 1980s expenditure ratios peaked, except for 'Greece, Spain and Italy [which] maintained positively trending expenditure ratios throughout the decade' (Von Hagen 1993: 43).

The need to protect participant countries in the single currency area from the consequences of an excessive borrowing country is assessed in different ways in economic literature. Some authors detect negative externalities of excessive borrowing in three main sectors:

1 If a country's level of public debt becomes unsustainable, other members may be politically obliged to bail out the member in crisis – despite the 'no-bail-out clause' provision of Article 104 of the Maastricht Treaty – thereby creating generalized 'moral hazard' incentives for all nations to over-borrow.
2 Because of financial interdependencies, a failure to affect a bail-out may lead to a Community-wide banking and financial crisis.[3]
3 Bail-out issues aside, excessive borrowing by one member nation may raise government interest rates elsewhere in the Community, a pecuniary externality with real (but secondary) effects when inefficient taxes have to be levied to repay debt.

The scope and range of the EMU discipline has raised doubts on whether a numerical target of 3 per cent is tenable in economic terms.

Though estimation of average public expenditure in the EC is acknowledged to range around 3 per cent of GDP, some economists question the economic rationality of the deficit criterion as it 'implicitly amounts to a current balanced budget rule, i.e. the current revenues should equal current expenditure' (Corsetti and Roubini 1993: 119). Regardless of the fact that institutions imposing fiscal discipline are warmly recommended at a national level (Von Hagen 1993), they are rejected at a Community-wide level on the premise that they cannot perform appropriately (Eichengreen and Von Hagen 1996).

Firstly, restrictions on public deficits seem to be unnecessary if member states in a 'federal union' still control taxes (Bayoumi et al. 1997). According to Eichengreen and Von Hagen (1996), the act of declaiming a fixed benchmark is the same as intensifying pressure at Union level to offset country-specific shocks that an unrestrained national budget would have managed autonomously. In the present EU, Eichengreen and Von Hagen (1996) consider fiscal restrictions to be redundant and dangerous. By controlling the overall level of taxes in the EU, there will be the option of no default and therefore no pressure for bailing out. In the event of financial difficulties, governments can resort to a 'third' option: to raise their own taxes. 'The fact that this third option exists will buttress the credibility of the ECB's no bail out rule.'

Secondly, the excessive deficit procedure, as Von Hagen argues, 'is worse than redundant: it will aggravate the very problem it is designed to avert. If tax-smoothing and automatic-stabilization capacities of national governments are hamstrung, national officials will lobby for these services to be provided by the EU, leading to the transfer to member states' (Von Hagen 1993: 137). Political pressures on the EU institutions, the EU Commission and Council are likely to increase.

In a different way, students who focus attention on political biases in fiscal policy appreciate the introduction of a fiscal benchmark. The tendency of political governments to run 'excessive' fiscal deficits, which is likely to take place in the run-up to an election, can discourage fiscal competition (Alesina and Perotti 1996). Others, such as Alexander and Anker (1997), and Crawford (1996), who focus attention on time inconsistency problems make a similar assessment. In their case, the lower interest rates, which are expected in the new currency area, will probably encourage a looser budget policy.

A further rationale often called on to maintain Community-wide discipline derives from the political problem of how to reassure the domestic electorate that no harm will come to the whole area from the different national attitudes towards political beliefs and the size of national debt before entry. The underlying rationale of the fiscal criteria is that convergence regarding those reference values will make the European economy more efficient and subject to fewer variations in prices and production. However, important benefits from EMU will depend on how national budget policy adapts to the more demanding situation: solving domestic problems (budgetary autonomy) and responding to overall EC macroeconomic policy (co-ordination).

Compliance with the fiscal criteria, however, can be limited in scope and consequences.[4] This is because it can be a straightforward instrumental policy aimed at winning credibility in financial markets so as to enjoy the benefits of lower interest rates. As is shown in the Italian case, the 2.7 per cent deficit of GDP which has gained Italy admission to the first (and indeed large) group of EMU, has been obtained principally because of the increased credibility that financial markets have won for the country. The payoff has even been doubled as the political coalition in power has not been forced to avoid cutting social transfers, a fact that has rescued its political unity from erosion (Alesina 1998).

The real payoff seems to come on the front of lower interest rates, while it does not seem to have led the EMU participating countries to introducing any irreversible structural changes in the dominant pattern of their distributive policies. The major difference can be synthesized very accurately in that, before Maastricht, distributive policies were funded by high public deficits and, after Maastricht, they are funded by raising the tax burden.

How can appropriate 'virtuous' budgetary behaviour be encouraged at a national level? Are governments able to resist political pressures to run a virtuous budget policy if unemployment rates continue to increase? The first problem consists in assessing whether or not the two criteria (3 per cent deficit and 60 per cent debt to GDP) are linked together. The specialized literature on public spending has not yet reached a clear assessment. At least three main reasons are generally discussed – positively or negatively – when linking fiscal criteria (dimension of public debt and public deficit) to monetary criteria, the interest rate, inflation rate and exchange rate. First, a country's 'excessive' (unsustainable) indebtedness may provoke a financial and fiscal crisis, such that other member states are obliged to relieve the member's debt crisis and this despite the 'no bail out provision' of Article 104b of the Maastricht Treaty – a provision that is rooted in the principle that each member state is fully responsible for its own public deficit. However, EU member states or the ECB may be obliged under political pressures to bail out the guilty. Second, as a special case of the first, excessive indebtedness can affect price stability. In the case that an insolvency crisis does hit the whole European financial system, the ECB may be forced to inject liquidity into the system in order to guarantee that the payment system works. The ECB should act in such a case as a 'lender of last resort', and the rescue may affect price stability in the Union. Thirdly, excessive indebtedness may cause harmful externalities. This is the case where the excessive borrowing of one member state is likely to attract increasing shares of EU savings and as a consequence cause interest rates to increase in the other EU countries as well.

To summarize, at least two rationales make reference to fiscal discipline, as shown in Boxes 9.1 and 9.2.

Box 9.1 Fiscal discipline: two rationales

1 The deficit limit is aimed at controlling potentially adverse *fiscal externalities* to the EU member states due to excessive borrowing by a single member state (a) causing the ECB to pump up interest rates for all the area in order to offset inflationary pressures; or (b) drawing speculative and investment capitals from other member countries. Expected outcome would be generating fiscal virtue plus economic co-ordination, and last but not least, trustworthiness.
2 The deficit discipline strikes at the heart of the position of *state intervention* in the EU member economies. By self-restraining public budget policy, the budget discipline calls for public expenditure and tax cuts, as well as for governments to be excluded from the economy at large.

Box 9.2 Fiscal discipline: three approaches

1 Market discipline: capital liberalization and risk premium on governments' obligations.
2 Constitutional rules: binding governments by means of constitutional budget-balancing regulations.
3 Supranational institution: peer group multilateral surveillance.

As the EMU has adopted a mixed stance in which some aspects of each of the above points are considered (Bayoumi et al. 1995: 1047), it is right to ask whether the results conform to the announced objectives.

The Market Discipline Hypothesis

The market discipline hypothesis offers a reply to those who argue that it is necessary to introduce a formally defined fiscal discipline to protect the ECB from inflationary pressures. This literature proposes that the Pact's objective of safeguarding monetary stability can be achieved better by private markets, which can exert a considerable amount of discipline on individual countries. In the EMU, as countries cannot finance a deficit by printing money, they have to sell bonds. A country's credit-worthiness will be reflected in the real rate of interest (including a risk premium) set to attract investors. As the rate rises with the risk, the interest rate acts as a discipline imposed by the market mechanism on individual countries, thus making it difficult to co-ordinate fiscal policy.

The market discipline hypothesis, however, is more relevant under the Exchange Rate Mechanism (ERM) than under the EMU. In a mechanism that manages exchange rate parities, part of the risk premium in the real rate of interest reflects the anticipated depreciation of the currency. Under a regime of fixed exchange rates, as the possibility of devaluation is removed, so is the associated risk premium. Moreover, as capital markets become integrated and capital becomes more mobile, only a small rise in the real rate of interest will be needed to attract capital. In an EMU regime, the integration of capital, an important aspect of capital globalization, implies that a country that wants to finance its deficit by borrowing can draw on the savings of all member countries. But if all countries were to borrow, the fiscal deficits would lead to higher interest rates for all member countries (Bisignano 1996). This free-rider problem represents an inefficient externality[5] which could be removed by fiscal co-ordination. Such a conclusion favours an institutional solution as 'much of the market's discipline on member governments will be lost with monetary union' (Brociner and Levine 1991: 11).

In the opinion of Giovannini and Spaventa (1990), the credibility gain from an EMU regime would facilitate a reduction in inflation without the cost of fiscal discipline. They also express doubts whether the market will exert much fiscal discipline. Applied to US states, the 'market discipline hypothesis' has proved to be successful in placing constraints on the States' 'debt wish' (Sbragia 1996). As Bayoumi et al. (1995: 1052) argue, the market discipline hypothesis poses problems even in the vintage American Federal context on two key-levels: '(1) By how much and how quickly do sovereign borrowers respond to [market-imposed default premiums] incentives? (2) Are the incentives provided . . . sufficient?'. These are two weak points that sovereign borrowers can exploit, making things worse, or that can lead to an uncontrollable situation.

In conclusion, the limits of the market discipline approach are evidence that this approach is untenable at least in the initial period of EMU. Though it should be (and eventually will be) the favoured approach to national fiscal policy in the EU, national governments will continue to have fiscal responsibility for the foreseeable future. At the moment, however, it would seem that a 'pure' and laissez-faire market discipline is not a sufficient spur to fiscal discipline.

Another important section of the market discipline hypothesis relates to interest rate movement under the conditions of a single currency.

Economic literature on the Stability Pact has focused attention on the consequences that a single interest rate is likely to have on the borrowing policy of EMU countries.

According to economic theory, in a system of fixed exchange rates with no possibility for realignments, all national interest rates for loans of identical quality (time to maturity and risk liquidity) must be the same. Alexander and Anker (1997) focus on the convergence of interest rates in the 15 member countries before and after 1999 and question whether a single interest rate is likely to materialize in the Euro area.

Analysis of the interest convergence before 1999 shows a continuing spread between the 15 EMU countries. The authors observe a correlation between the volatility of exchange rates and the convergence of interest rates. They analyse the developments of short-term (3-month) interest rates in Italy and Germany in two distinct periods of time. In the period 1987–92 when no realignments took place, and 1992–95 when successive speculative attacks on the lira put a lot of strain on the Italian currency. They find that the spread of interest rates is low in the period of stable exchange rates and is high in the period of frequent exchange rate realignments. Evidence from the period 1996 (November) to 1998 (February) after the lira's re-admission to the ERM shows that the Italian interest rate spread steadily narrowed. In conclusion, the authors assume that before 1999 the interest spread correlates 'to a large extent [with] expectations about exchange-rate changes', while after 1999, with fixed exchange rates and the exclusion of realignments, and no country-specific risk premium, interest rates should tend to be the same. Under this new condition, however, lower interest rates can give rise to a situation in which weak governments extend their deficits by issuing bonds at the lower European interest rate.

Following the 'market discipline hypothesis', the response of the markets should be to raise nominal interest rates against the excessive national borrowers. The higher interest rate is believed to place enough constraints on national governments so as to stop them from continuing debt-prone behaviour for a long time. Without considering for the moment the vagueness of this statement, which is analysed in the 'time inconsistency dilemma', the rise of interest rates in the excessive borrowing countries is likely to cause spillover negative externalities as well. Raising nominal interest rates on a country's bond increases the expectations of a risk of default for these bonds. The first consequence is its effect on the balance of payments and the implications of future fiscal deficits. Spillover effects are observed in the global capital markets. Under conditions of growing liberalization of capital markets, governments are largely inclined to finance budget deficits through foreign borrowing. A case often mentioned is that of the USA in the 1980s, which resorted largely to foreign borrowing to finance deficit budgets. At that time in the mid-1980s, rising USA interest rates and high deficit obliged

European central banks to raise interest rates, and eventually led for calls for a single currency (Henning 1995).

Under the specific EMU conditions, the incentive to foreign borrowing could be further enhanced by a uniform interest rate set by the ECB and the absence of credit risk in the borrowing country.

This situation, described in the Mundell–Fleming hypothesis, states that 'where there is free movement of capital and an immutably fixed exchange rate, fiscal expansion becomes more efficient because (1) the interest-elasticity of demand for the government's debt is greatly increased, due to the lack of the need for a devaluation-risk premium, and (2) the expansion is not choked off by a rise in exchange rate, as would occur with variable exchange rates if the central bank does not monetize the deficit' (Alexander and Anker 1997). Such concerns could be of little importance and rather trivial in the case of a temporary fiscal expansion which the markets expect will be reversed. As Crawford argues,

> Its importance lies in an expansion (or contraction) which markets expect to be sustained for a long time. . . . Fiscal measures that are expected to be temporary do not carry the risk that the extra debt may have to be monetized, and therefore, where devaluation is possible, there need be no devaluation premium. Hence there is no difference (up to this point) between the EMU and the variable-rate scenarios in the case of a temporary expansion. But if a temporary expansion raises the level of prices and wages (relative to those in other countries) it will, in the EMU case, reduce real rates of interest in the country that takes the financial initiatives, since interest rates in all EMU countries are the same. This is not for long in a variable-rate scenario because nominal interest rates would rise as the demand for monetary and credit rose (due to both fiscal expansion and lower real rates of interest). (Crawford 1996: 298)

In conclusion, the market discipline hypothesis will be reversed, as markets are likely to accommodate the sovereign borrower's demand.

Domestic Constitutional Regulation or International Co-ordination?

This section discusses EMU fiscal discipline against the background of a domestically based model, i.e. the Balanced Budget Rule model. Following studies of fiscal discipline (Buchanan, Wildawsky and others), the model is based on the principle that fiscal discipline should be enforced by constitutional regulation at domestic level. Students of optimal contract add evidence to the above thesis and suggest that policy co-ordination would be enforced by 'domestic institutional arrangements, not by an international agreement, and would not raise problems of sustainability, neither any country would have an incentive to deviate from the optimal contract' (Persson and Tabellini 1995 in Muscatelli 1997: 123). Similar conclusions can be drawn from comparative studies of the Balanced Budget Rule. Von Hagen (1993), following Buchanan and Wildawsky, finds that fiscal discipline is pursued better through domestic institutions and at a constitutional level.

When the Stability Pact is analysed against the background of these results, students observe that the EMU peer surveillance policy and the procedure of punishment are substantially managed by those to whom the Pact assigns the responsibility of imposing the final (if any) punishment. Inman (1996) spells out the weaknesses of the trigger mechanism embodied in the Pact and argues for a mid-range solution that can improve its enforcement performance. In his conclusion, the Pact's enforcement mechanism is politically biased, which means that it is unlikely to provide an effective fiscal discipline (Inman 1996).

Comparative studies on fiscal institutions find that budget procedures and budget institutions do influence budget outcomes. Budget institutions include both procedural rules and balanced budget laws. Analysts of Balanced Budget Rules claim that for a balanced budget rule to be effective some important provisions are essential. These should be: (1) ex post deficit accounting; (2) constitutionally grounded rules; (3) enforcement by an open and politically independent review panel or court which can impose significant sanctions when there are violations; (4) a costly amendment procedure (Bohn and Inman 1996, Inman 1996). EMU budget fiscal discipline can be correctly compared to a balanced budget rule case as it establishes that a public deficit lower than 3 per cent is the benchmark of public borrowing and there is a set of enforcement policies. When these procedures, however, are compared to the standard strong balanced budget rule, EMU discipline appears to be a mix of weak and strong features.

EMU fiscal discipline as a balanced budget rule is considered to be strong as the timing review is required ex post: it should also be considered as strong because override cannot be approved through majority rules. The amendment process is strong too, in that it is difficult and costly.

EMU fiscal discipline as a balanced budget rule is weak in that it sets a feeble enforcement procedure: access is closed, the enforcer is partisan and the penalties, though large, are difficult to assess. Those weaknesses are particularly important as they come from the institutional and political framework within which the Stability Pact is set. Zooming in on the 'institutional environment' within which the decision procedure is to be initiated, politically self-interested parties are introduced:

1 Access to the violation procedure is closed, as it is limited to the Commission's initiative. The Commission Report to the Council of

Ministers is peremptorily designed to initiate the excessive deficit procedure against a nation that violates the deficit benchmark (Article 104. C.2).

2 Though the Commission is generally defined as a supranational institution, it plays 'as a partisan enforcer, whose interest is to seek the largest possible EMU' (Gros 1995). Evidence of this inclusive attitude comes from the Commission Report on third stage convergence (March 1998) which is more benevolent than the European Monetary Initiative Report. Though the two institutions seem close, in that they share 'supranational features', the Commission has a stronger interest to pursue an all-inclusive and no-conflict policy which will allow it to gain momentum as the depository of the European political design.

As Inman predicts, the Commission is 'unlikely to interpret the guidelines strictly to allow open access to others to bring a balanced budget rule violation. Even if charges of violation are made, the inability of the Council of Finance Ministers (ECOFIN) to impose even modest spending guidelines on current violators (e.g. Greece) suggests the political will is lacking to act as an independent enforcer of a balanced budget rule' (Inman 1996: 28).

3 Penalties are also weak. Violating nations are required to disclose additional fiscal information before issuing new debt. The European Investment Bank may withhold funds, but only a few EU countries receive significant funding from the Bank. Finally, the Council Ministers may impose fines or call for non-interest-bearing deposits, but these are unlikely to be significant with a partisan enforcer.

As Gros concludes: 'With closed access, a partisan enforcer, and small penalties, the EMU current 3 per cent rule is, at best, a weak balanced budget rule' (Inman 1996: 30–1). Though the Amsterdam Conference made an attempt to attenuate the concern and the increasing signs of disaffection of the German public against EMU and Euro, the Stability Pact shares several features with its predecessor; it differs as to budgetary position in that it is now subject to a more severe monitoring, which includes a compulsory mini budget when a divergence is detected with the approved Stability Programme. The procedure of enforcement has been speeded up and more severe sanctions are imposed on violating member states. The new fiscal discipline has been strengthened in three ways:

1 *Timing*. The *initiating actor*, the *Commission*, which is the institutional agenda setter for all decisions to be made by the Council, expresses an opinion and makes a recommendation to the Council. The *policing actor*, the *Council of Ministers*, establishes a deadline for the correction of the fiscal budget, which 'should be completed in the year following

its identification unless there are special circumstances'. The Council's recommendation is made public immediately after the deadline set in accordance with Article 3 expires.

2 *Warning policy.* Early warning and *public* recommendation.
3 *Pecuniary sanctions.* Section 4 Arts. 11, 12, 13, 14, 15, 16. Deposits or fines will be made up of a fixed component equal to 0.2 per cent of GDP, and a variable component equal to one tenth of the excess of the deficit above the reference value of 3 per cent of GDP. There will be an upper limit of 0.5 per cent of GDP for the annual amount of deposits. The amount of the sanction will be based on the outcome for the year in which the excessive deficit occurred.

When the new provisions are assessed one question immediately comes to mind: Is it possible to strengthen the enforcement procedure?

At first glance, it seems that the only very new factor that adds real pressure on a violating nation seems to be the decision to make the recommendations of the Commission and the Council public. Publicity can indeed open the eyes of public opinion a little more, especially of private markets so as to re-admit them as 'a market enforcer'. Though to a small degree, publicity can add some strength to the Commission's and Council's early warning. The remaining two provisions, which are indeed huge if they are really applied, have to get political approval, which means a deadlock which can only result in a politically induced delay.

To summarize, against the background of standard strong balanced budget rule, the new EMU fiscal discipline does not really reverse the assessment made above about the Excessive Deficit Procedure 1. The enforcement procedure is not strengthened by tougher pecuniary sanctions, it is still enfeebled by a triggering mechanism left in the hands of the European Council, a political institution *par excellence* which is unlikely to seriously self-inflict the announced sanctions.

Though this final Section does not claim to cover all possible alternative interpretations, it argues that cartel gains and collusion will eventually prevail in the future workings of EMU policies.

Implementation and Enforcement

Balancing the nation's public budget is a rather recent economic imperative in advanced industrial countries. For over five decades, since the end of the Second World War, the fiscal policy of most of the industrialized countries was inspired by Keynesian deficit spending and a certain propensity to run higher state deficits. As opponents to Keynesian theory would admit (Buchanan et al. 1978), unanticipated political bias, due to pressures and incentives in government, parliament, and in the administrations, towards over-expansion in public expenditure and deficit finance, have produced a misinterpretion of the scope and the aims of the original objective of Keynesian theory.

As several students have shown, bureaucratic and ministerial pressures towards increased expenditure have even been reinforced by constituency level pressures, which in continental Europe have been translated into expensive 'acquis sociaux' following a general convergence of left and right coalitions towards a model of a 'social market economy'.

Buchanan, Burton and Wildawsky focus on the political process of drawing up public budget policy, the conflicting interests emerging in the process of writing financial laws, and the way the latter substantially affect the level of taxation and expenditure. In this context, students of 'public choice' have collected historical series of public deficit figures, which show that higher public deficits are associated with events in the political cycle (elections). As Buchanan comments, 'fiscal policy is deeply involved with budgetary manipulation', and as a consequence there is a necessary 'linkage between any macro policy objectives and the whole process of public sector allocation'. The linkage indicates how difficult it is to introduce an independent watchdog institution (delegation) designed to protect fiscal and budget policy from the consequences of the political cycle. As Buchanan asserts: 'Given this necessary linkage, and given the institutional-political history, it seems today unreal to suggest that any shift of authority over fiscal policy would be delegated to either a discretionary or even to a rule-bound authority. It seems highly unlikely that fiscal policy, in any sense, would be removed from the ordinary procedures of democratic decision-making, with divided legislative and executive responsibilities and roles in its overall formulation' (Buchanan et al. 1978: 51).

When assessed against a Buchanan-like model, EMU fiscal discipline clearly lacks 'democratic determination'. In this regard, the EU appears to be an 'undefined' political object. *Firstly*, the EU is not yet (or never shall be) an accomplished polity.

- It lacks a central and political (elected) government. Such a fully fledged institution does not yet exist, and the Commission of European Communities, given its bureaucratic (non-elected) nature, is unlikely to match it.
- The European Parliament, the central and political (elected) body, is not provided with appropriate control over member states' public budgets.

Secondly, differences with the USA relate to the effectiveness of the way in which to accomplish the objective of fiscal discipline. Though the EMU has also provided the European Central Bank with legal independence

(Campanella 1996), the 'principle of delegation' has not been granted to the European Commission, the monitoring and warning body of the Stability Pact. If effectiveness were to be the real objective, the political bodies (the Council of Ministers) should be left very little room to man-oeuvre on decision-making (Inman 1996). Such a provision is perfectly compatible with multilateral surveillance, as 'commitment technologies' (Von Hagen 1993) can be given the task of monitoring for the objectives of 'macroeconomic co-ordination'. This, however, is not found in the Stability Pact that, instead, has left the power to initiate and to pursue the major steps of the enforcement procedure in the hands of the European Commission and of the Council of Ministers (Eichengreen and Wyplosz, 1998).

In a few words, the enforcement policy, which is the key point of any 'international agreement', lacks an appropriate independent enforcer, yet one is necessary if the policy is going to be successful. The political 'intergovernmental' body, i.e. the Council of Ministers, which is designed to monitor and eventually take action against violating member coun-tries, is unlikely to be given the necessary autonomy and independence that an independent enforcer requires.

Concluding Remarks

A major rationale for fiscal discipline is to prevent externalities arising from independent fiscal policies that can be too expansionary or sub-optimal (Brociner and Levine 1993). In the case studied in this chapter, fiscal discipline among EMU countries has taken the shape of fiscal co-ordination, especially when the enforcement mechanism is left in the hands of the interested parties (member governments in the Council of Ministers). Muscatelli (1997: 116) warns about fiscal co-ordination: 'If we want to explain what motivates fiscal policy, we ultimately have to look to political preferences and electoral objectives as key driving forces. Thus, governments may pursue distorted policies as they have partisan objectives (policy objectives which match the preferences of a part of society), or because they are office-motivated and are pursuing short-term benefits for electoral purposes. When co-operating over fiscal policies such governments may collude against the interests of the private sector'. This means that the latter and the declared objectives of the international agreements cannot openly proclaim to counter private market economy in their capability to impinge on fiscal policy-making, which is crucial to politicians in power. Colluding against the private sector can easily be a joint Pareto payoff that nobody is willing to give up.

Though the Stability Pact sees some other European supranational institutions become involved in the assessment of fiscal performance, it has been left to the European Commission to take initiative on the enforcement mechanisms. As a consequence, two distinct problems arise regarding the efficacy of the EMU fiscal discipline: (1) politicization of the triggering mechanism, which enfeebles the implementation of the sanctions; (2) The 'left-out players problem' which raises doubts about the democratic legitimacy of international macroeconomic policy. International agreements as far as they do not take into account the consequences that their policies are likely to cause to parties not involved in the negotiating process can originate colluding practice (Vaubel 1985: 25). Though neo-realist theories seem to account for so many aspects of EMU grand projects, they can be unequipped to face the colluding practice that is implied in 'joint Pareto gains'.

This chapter has analysed the case of the Excessive Deficit Procedure 2, which is intended to strengthen the fiscal discipline within the Euro area. It has raised doubts on the capability of a supranational institution-alist approach to explain why the EMU governments have committed to fiscal discipline by means of an international institute and why they have purposely weakened it by retaining power on final decision. What supranational institutionalism could describe in terms of 'Pareto (improving) joint gains' might easily turn out to be a move to obtain 'cartel gains' or simply to arrange for 'collusion'.

Notes

1 First drafts of this Chapter have been presented in a Seminar at the West European Studies Program and at the ECSA Conference in Seattle (1997). The author thanks Franco Reviglio, M. Guglielmina Tenaglia-Ambrosini, Alberta Sbragia, and Roland Vaubel for useful comments.

2 The Pact of Stability and Growth was subscribed to by the Council of European Ministers in July 1997 in Amsterdam. The fiscal discipline embodied therein is referred to here as Excessive Deficit Procedure 2. The fiscal discipline embodied in the Treaty of Economic and Monetary Union, Maastricht 1991, approved January 1992, is referred to here as Excessive Deficit Procedure 1.

3 McKinnon (1996) suggests that a bail-out risk will be most intense at the start; Eichengreen and Von Hagen (1996) argue that it will be least at the outset.

4 A major critique of the importance of the balanced budget rule is raised by M. Friedman (1995) who remarked that he would prefer living in a world in which the government spends $1 trillion a year and finances its spending partly through borrowing, to one in which the government spends $2 trillion a year but keeps its budget in balance. In Friedman's reasoning, it is clear that the harmful effects on the economy are caused by current spending and current taxes and not by the public budget deficit *per se*. See also Razzolini and Shughart II (1997: 216).

5 In a letter to the author, Prof. Roland Vaubel suggests that the impression is false that international interdependence through the world capital market has to be viewed as an 'inefficient externality' and a source of 'free-rider problems'. I agree with this suggestion and with the statement 'Spillovers through the market are efficient unless you assume that governments have, and ought to have, more targets than instruments' (Vaubel 1998 personal communication).

CHAPTER 10

THE COMMON FOREIGN AND SECURITY POLICY: LIMITS OF INTERGOVERNMENTALISM AND THE SEARCH FOR A GLOBAL ROLE

Helene Sjursen[1]

Re-defining Foreign and Security Policy

The Common Foreign and Security Policy (CFSP) of the European Union is often overlooked and sometimes even ridiculed in studies of European integration. Until recently it was not unusual to argue that the EU did not have a foreign policy, that is, to describe the CFSP as a 'myth'. Integrating in this area of so-called 'high politics' has often been described as synonymous with 'surrendering sovereignty' altogether. When put to the test, national perspectives seemed to prevail over efforts to conduct a common European foreign policy. Nonetheless, at the end of the 1990s, efforts to establish a common foreign and security policy were speeded up. So-called 'pillar two' issues emerged on top of the policy agenda of the EU. Compared with other areas of increased European integration, the developments in the CFSP seem primarily to be problem-driven rather than a spill-over from the institutional setting.

A crucial question then becomes to what extent this development can be seen as lasting or whether or not it is only a passing phenomenon, dependent on a particular and temporary state of affairs. This chapter will suggest that the tendency to ignore the CFSP in studies of European integration is closely connected to a specific perspective on international relations, to one specific understanding of the international system. This perspective would also lead to the conclusion that the changes in the late 1990s are temporary. There is a danger, however, that important dimensions of the EU's foreign policy are ignored or not understood when this approach is used. In order to capture these 'lost' dimensions,

1   The author would like to thank Svein S. Andersen and Erik Oddvar Eriksen for comments and advice.

the chapter suggests that it is necessary to employ a different perspective on international relations. In turn, this will also lead to different conclusions on the question of the durability of change in the EU's foreign and security policy.

The chapter starts out by tracing the gradual building of the CFSP. It looks both at the policy-content of the CFSP, its institutional structure and its relations with other Western institutional networks. It emphasizes in particular the seeming inconsistency over time in external observers' assessment of the future prospects for establishing a common foreign and security policy in the EU. Then the chapter turns to discuss what might be the driving forces in foreign policy co-operation in the EU. In order to do so, it highlights two different analytical models. The first one would see the CFSP as a product of competing interests, the second one would argue that it is also influenced by shared ideas and values.

Building a Common Foreign and Security Policy in the European Union

Historically, co-operation on foreign and security policy has been a sensitive issue for the EU. The development of a foreign and security dimension to the EU has been dependent on two factors in particular: The first is the EU's relations to the United States and NATO, the second is the internal EU disagreement and insecurity about the general purpose of European integration. Traditionally, closer co-operation or integration on foreign and security policy has been connected to the idea of a Political Union. Hence, the issue has been difficult for those member states who were primarily interested in the economic dimensions of European integration, as well as for those who have been concerned with protecting national sovereignty from the intrusion of supranational institutions in Brussels. At the same time, the debate about the development of an EU foreign and security policy reflects conflicting views inside the EU on what kind of influence the United States should have on European affairs. This has meant that the dividing lines on the EU's security and foreign policy co-operation have often been different from those in other policy areas.

France has often played the role of the driving force in foreign and security policy, but has received far less enthusiastic support from Germany here than on other issues. This is primarily because of Germany's close ties to the United States in security and defence (Rummel 1996). The UK and The Netherlands have been particularly sceptical about the development of an independent security and defence role for the EU. In the case of Britain, this scepticism must be seen as a consequence partly of the country's close ties to the United States and partly as a consequence of British reservations about developing a

European organization with a strong political dimension. To the extent that Britain has supported the development of a foreign and security policy in the EU it has been on the condition that this policy will be formulated on the basis of consensus amongst member states and without interference from the Commission and the Parliament. As for The Netherlands, it has traditionally supported the idea of Political Union and wished to see the EU develop into something more than a free-trade organization, yet the Dutch have been sceptical about security and defence co-operation because of a concern that this might weaken the ties to the United States and reduce future American involvement in European security and defence (Pijpers 1996).

After a failed attempt at establishing a European Defence Community (EDC) and a European Political Community in the early 1950s, further efforts to make foreign policy co-operation into the core of European integration were abandoned.[1] Security and defence co-operation was defined into an Atlantic context: Nato became the central organization for security and defence in western Europe, and the United States became guarantor of European security. As for foreign policy, it remained within the realm of the nation state. The Europeans focused on using economic instruments as a tool to integrate at the European level (Gerbet 1983). This did not mean that the idea of European co-operation on foreign and security policy disappeared. At the EU summit in The Hague in 1969, the idea of political co-operation was relaunched, and led to the establishment of European Political Co-operation (EPC) in 1972. After this, the system of foreign policy co-operation was gradually expanded, both in terms of its institutional framework and its policy content. EPC became important in the Helsinki process which was launched in the early 1970s, both in terms of co-ordinating the positions of western European states and in setting the overall agenda. EPC also developed a distinct position on the Middle East, most clearly defined in the Venice declaration of 1980 (Ifestos 1987). EPCs capacity to react to situations of crisis was strengthened in the early 1980s (Hill 1992). Still, all these developments took place outside the treaties. It was only with the Single European Act that EPC was formally included in the treaty framework, and that the commitment of the member states to consult and co-operate in foreign policy became a legal obligation.[2] Also, EPC developed in the shadow of NATO and the Cold War problematique. Security and defence were excluded from its discussions.[3] To many, this meant that the EC could not be a serious actor in the international system (Bull 1982). The image of EPC as the insignificant 'brother' of transatlantic co-operation and European integration was reinforced by the maintenance of the intergovernmental mode of decision-making in EPC. What then, did the end of bipolarity mean for foreign policy co-operation in the EC?

The End of the Cold War: Strengthening Institutions and Adding Security to Foreign Policy

The end of the Cold War changed the security framework in Europe radically. From being potential enemies, the previous Warsaw Pact states became potential partners both to the EU and to NATO. Assessments of the most important security challenges for Europe were gradually redefined: the likelihood of European, in particular western European, states needing to turn to military power to defend their territories appeared as minimal or non-existent. Focus shifted to more 'diffuse' security challenges, such as international crime, ethnic conflicts, terrorism, spread of nuclear weapons as well as humanitarian and environmental crises. In parallel, a debate developed in Europe about the legitimacy of using military power in other contexts or for other purposes than to defend national territory. In this context, the EU emerged as a natural security actor in particular in situations where collective solutions were sought as well as in situations where there was a need for political and economic instruments and not military force. In a sense the EU can be seen as the embodiment of the co-operative approach to security encouraged by the 'new' European security agenda. In key respects it has successfully 'domesticated' security amongst its own member states. NATO, on the other hand, which was built on a traditional perspective on security and defence, was expected to have outlived its role. The statement of the Luxembourg foreign minister Jacques Poos during the Luxembourg presidency of the EU in the first half of 1991: 'This is the hour of Europe, not the hour of the Americans' (*Financial Times*, July 1991) is symbolic for this period.

The Treaty of Maastricht, which was ratified in late 1993, was a turning point for the EU's foreign and security policy. The more modest EPC was left behind and replaced with the so-called Common Foreign and Security Policy (CFSP). The aim of developing a policy that covered 'all areas of foreign and security policy' and that should be supported 'actively and unreservedly by its Member States in a spirit of loyalty and mutual solidarity' was written into the Treaty. Security and defence were also explicitly included in the CFSP. The Treaty promised to develop a 'common security and defence policy' and perhaps also 'a common defence'. The recently revitalized West European Union (WEU) was singled out as the defence arm of the EU.[4] Thus, as distinct from the Single European Act, the Maastricht Treaty went further than to just write existing practice into the Treaty, and actually laid out new patterns for development in foreign and security policy (Edwards and Nuttall 1994).

As a follow-up to the Maastricht Treaty, the WEU started to strengthen its own institutions and develop military capabilities. In 1992, the co-called Petersberg declaration, which defined the WEU's security tasks to include peace-keeping, crisis-management and 'soft security', was issued.[5] Institutional adaptation to external change did nonetheless not take place with the expected, or desired, efficiency. The definition of security seemed to change more rapidly. The 1990s were dominated by intense discussion about 'alternative security architectures' in Europe. Different institutions often appeared to be competing over the same tasks (Forster and Wallace 1996). It also became evident that even though the security challenges to Europe had changed, the actors' preferences for solutions were still influenced by some of the same factors as during the Cold War. These were the views on the United States' role in Europe and on the purpose and future development of the EU as an organization. Behind the formulations in the Maastricht Treaty, there were still divergent views, not only about how to develop a European security policy, but whether or not the EU should have such a policy at all. The text of the Maastricht Treaty was vague enough to satisfy both the maximalists, such as France, who wanted to see stronger integration in security and defence, and the minimalists, most importantly Britain, who wished to continue with the status quo. The question of whether or not the EU could give direct instructions to the WEU was particularly unclear. The Maastricht Treaty also stressed that the development of a common European security policy should not in any way prejudice or challenge Atlantic security co-operation.

Expectations about the disintegration of NATO after the 'loss' of its enemy did not come true. In fact NATO, under General Secretary Manfred Wörner, turned out to be far more efficient in redefining its role and its organizational structure after the Cold War than the EU. From being a traditional military alliance whose purpose it was to protect the territory of its member states against an external threat, NATO developed a more flexible strategy, which amongst other things would allow it to conduct peacekeeping operations outside NATO territory. The continued relevance of NATO to European security was strengthened at the NATO summit in Berlin in June 1996, where it was decided that a European Security and Defence Identity (ESDI) should be developed inside the framework of NATO.[6] A central element in this strategy was the creation of mobile forces, the so-called Combined Joint Task Forces (CJTF). It was agreed that these forces would be available to the WEU for European operations, in situations where the United States itself would not wish to participate. This decision was interpreted as a victory for the Atlanticists in the struggle over the development of security structures in Europe (Duke 1996, Cornish 1996). Any European use of NATO forces was dependent on recognition from the Atlantic Council. In other words on agreement from the United States, irrespective of whether or not the United States would take part in the operation (Sjursen 1998). Hence, it looked as if the WEU would foremostly be connected to NATO rather than become the defence arm of the EU. The Berlin agreement was to a large extent made possible by France's decision to move closer to the military co-operation within NATO.[7] This was interpreted as a signal that France had abandoned its ambitions about developing a European security policy with the EU at the core, and chosen instead to expand the European security identity inside NATO.

This struggle about the development of EU foreign and security policy was also influenced by external political events, in particular the war in Bosnia and the question of enlargement of Western institutions, both the EU and NATO, to central and eastern Europe. The EU's treatment of these issues was heavily criticized and often, to its disadvantage, compared with NATO's approach. The EU appeared hesitant in the face of requests for enlargement of the EU to eastern Europe whereas the United States quickly decided to enlarge NATO. After the EU's failure to negotiate peace in Bosnia, it was NATO that was seen to have found a solution to the conflict (Kintis 1997). As a result, expectations about EU capabilities in foreign policy in the early 1990s were more and more frequently described as unrealistic (Hill 1998). The 'new NATO' was presented as an organization which was far better suited to tackle the challenges that Europe was facing at the end of the Cold War than the EU.

Inside the EU attempts to follow up the ambitions of the Maastricht Treaty moved slowly. The 1996–7 Intergovernmental Conference, which resulted in the Amsterdam Treaty, was expected to clarify some of the uncertainty about the relationship between the WEU and the EU. Nonetheless, the result was seen as a victory for the Atlanticists. The independence of the WEU was maintained and the organization seemed more and more as a protection against a too independent security role for the EU rather than as a defence arm directly subordinated to the EU. To what extent did these difficulties in security and defence have a knock-on effect on efforts to strengthen the institutional set-up of the CFSP?

Limited Institutional Change

The Amsterdam Treaty did not change the fundamentals of decision-making in foreign and security policy. A careful attempt was made at expanding qualified majority voting in the second pillar of political co-operation by writing into the Treaty that, after unanimous agreement on common strategies, the Council may proceed with majority voting for 'joint actions' and 'common positions'. This provision was restricted by a provision allowing member states 'for important and stated reasons of national policy' to oppose the adoption of a decision by qualified majority voting. Incidentally, this means that the French interpretation of the Luxembourg 'compromise' of 1966 was for the first time formally included in the Treaty, even though in a particular policy area. The principle of flexibility, which allows member states to refrain from participation in certain policies, has sometimes been presented as a solution to the difficulties and complications resulting from increasingly divergent views on the further integration within the EU. This principle was not extended to the CFSP. Nonetheless, the possibility of 'constructive abstention' that was introduced in the Amsterdam Treaty does in practice allow a limited number of states to take initiatives in foreign policy without the full participation of all member states. How, and whether or not, this will be practised remains an open question.

Another way of strengthening integration and efficiency in foreign policy decision-making would be to strengthen the role of the Commission. At the same time, this would also help resolve the problem of inconsistency between pillars in external policy. From being almost completely excluded from the former EPC, the Treaty of Maastricht had increased the Commission's influence in the CFSP. Although the changes fell short of the Commission's own ambitions in foreign policy, it did for the first time become 'fully associated' to all aspects of the EU's foreign policy and was given the right to propose policies (Nuttall 1996). In response to this increased recognition, the Commission's services were reorganized. A group composed of the six Commissioners with involvement in external affairs (popularly referred to as the 'Relex Group') was established and began to meet regularly under the chairmanship of the new Commission President Jacques Santer (Cameron 1998). A new DG was also established to deal specifically with the CFSP and to prepare the Commission for participation in foreign policy co-operation. However, this trend towards a stronger role for the Commission was not taken any further with the Amsterdam Treaty. It has even been suggested that Amsterdam represented a setback for the Commission in foreign policy, after a period of gradual encroachment on the territory of the Council and the Political Directors (Allen 1998). It is possible that the Commission's active role in the early 1990s produced a backlash, with the member states again being more reluctant to increase its influence in foreign policy (Smith 1995: 398, Allen 1998). The ability of the Commission to play an effective role in foreign policy was also hampered by problems of legitimacy. With no real democratic accountability for the Commission and little sense of clear EU foreign policy interests which the Commission could claim to represent, it has often been considered difficult to justify the Commission's taking centre stage (Nuttall 1996). The new Commission, under the leadership of Prodi, seems to be making progress in terms of strengthening its legitimacy. In the longer term this might facilitate a stronger role for the Commission in foreign and security policy.

In terms of enhancing the cohesion and efficiency of the CFSP pillar, leadership is important. So far, the Presidency has played a crucial role in this respect. Nonetheless, it has been difficult to ensure consistency in the EU's external representation with leadership rotating every six months. There is some concern that this will become even more of a problem after the enlargement to eastern Europe. The EU will then have an even larger number of smaller member states. Furthermore, there are some signs that the larger member states have increasing reservations about subordinating their foreign policy to the successive leadership of the smaller member states. It was not possible for the EU member states to agree on Presidency reform at the 1996–97 Intergovernmental Conference. However, an effort was made to strengthen the cohesion in the EU's external representation, and to give the EU a single visible voice in the international system. It was decided to nominate a 'High Representative' of the EU (a Mr or Ms CFSP) in the person of the Secretary General. This reform is considered, by the Commission as well as by France and Britain, to be potentially the most important change to the CFSP that came through in the Amsterdam Treaty. Still, the authority and influence of the High Representative depends much on the personality nominated. Hence, some member states such as Britain argued for a long time that the post should be filled by a civil servant, whereas others, such as France, would like a senior politician to take the lead. Benefits were expected from the nomination of a 'Mr CFSP' in the person of Javier Solana, former Secretary General of NATO. He is assisted by the new Planning Unit, composed of representatives from the Commission, the WEU and the member states, which is intended to help provide the EU with a long-term perspective in foreign policy.

Overall, the first assessments of the Amsterdam Treaty were fairly negative. Most observers stressed that the member states had only made minimal adjustments compared with the Maastricht Treaty and that the principal weaknesses in the CFSP framework were still there. At the same time, it was argued that one should not exclude the possibility that the Treaty would allow the EU to develop a more cohesive foreign policy. Much was seen to depend on the way in which the institutional changes proposed were implemented, as well as on the political commitment of member states to use the new provisions. Regelsberger and Wessels (1996: 42–3) for example considered many of the problems of the CFSP to stem not from the rules or institutions alone, but from the member states' reluctance to 'play by the rules of the game which they themselves established'.

A British U-turn

An important turning point came in the autumn of 1998, when Britain under the leadership of Tony Blair declared its support for a more independent security role for the EU and thus abandoned its position as defender of the political independence of the WEU. With the Franco-British 'St Malo declaration', work on strengthening the EU's security and defence capacity was given new life.[8] In turn, this also increased the speed in implementing the institutional provisions of Maastricht and Amsterdam. The changes in the British position were partly a result of Blair's desire to lead an active European policy, partly a result of increasing British frustrations with the USA. Foreign and security policy is one of the areas Britain most easily can promote in order to strengthen its own influence inside the EU. In this area the Franco-German axis is weaker, and France does in many ways have more in common with Britain than with Germany on foreign and security policy. As permanent members of the UN Security Council, with strong overseas interests and with a military capacity that includes nuclear weapons, France and Britain distinguish themselves from most of the other EU member states in this policy area. At the same time, co-operation in this particular policy sector is far less sensitive domestically in Britain than some aspects of economic integration, such as monetary union. In security and foreign policy it is still possible to talk about 'co-operation' instead of 'integration' – hence, it is possible to claim that British sovereignty is not under threat. Britain's frustrations with the United States were triggered by discussions on Western policies in the former Yugoslavia. The British government was particularly disappointed with what it considered to be American sabotage of the Vance–Owen plan for Bosnia.

As a result of the change in the British position, one of the most important blockages to the strengthening of the CFSP was overcome. The St Malo declaration was followed by systematic discussion amongst the member states of the EU on the practical shaping of co-operation in security and defence. At the European Council meeting in Cologne in June 1999 a new course was identified. The Cologne summit conclusions stressed that the EU must develop the necessary capabilities to fulfil the objective of a common security and defence policy, and that the EU must have the capacity to act autonomously and be supported by credible military forces.[9] Furthermore, the EU's own capacity for analysis and intelligence should be strengthened. In this connection the German presidency suggested 'regular (or ad hoc) meetings of the General Affairs Council, as appropriate including Defence Ministers.' In addition plans were made for a permanent body in Brussels (Political and Security Committee) consisting of representatives with political/military expertise, an EU Military Committee consisting of Military Representatives making recommendations to the Political and Security committee, an EU Military Staff including a Situation Centre, and other resources such as a Satellite Centre.[10] With regard to the role of the West European Union, the expected outcome was that it would disappear as an independent institution. Security policy in Europe will then be developed through discussions between the EU and the United States inside NATO or through independent EU initiatives. The content of the EU's security policy is still defined with reference to the 1992 Petersberg declaration. In other words, it is concerned with crisis management, peacekeeping and peacemaking operations.

Despite these changes and clarifications, the relationship between NATO and the EU remains ambiguous. This is obvious if one compares the texts issued at NATO's Washington summit in April 1999 with the declarations from the EU summit in Cologne. In the NATO declaration, European use of NATO capabilities is described as dependent on acceptance by the Atlantic Council, and the EU's security policy is presented in a way that suggests that it is only a supplement to NATO.[11] The Cologne summit on the other hand signalled ambitions about developing separate European resources and capabilities so that the EU can act independently of NATO. Another difficult point has been the position of European NATO states which are not members of the EU.

The CFSP has changed both in terms of its institutions and in terms of the content of policy. The changes in the content of policy are fairly unambiguous. From concentrating exclusively on foreign policy, the CFSP now also discusses security and to a certain extent defence policy. This change is connected to broader developments in the international system. The main purpose of security policy is no longer seen to be to defend the territory of nation states from an external threat. It is expected that European security tasks in future will focus increasingly on non-territorial threats and operations in third countries. This change is evident when one looks at the EU's efforts to define its security role. The role of the EU is linked exclusively to these 'new' security tasks. The EU's purpose is not to become a military alliance in the traditional sense. However, this change is also evident inside NATO. Thus, the institutional changes have been less important than what was expected in the immediate aftermath of the Cold War. Likewise, the institutional mechanisms of the CFSP have only been marginally adjusted. NATO continues to be an important security institution in Europe. At the same time, it is no longer the only security institution in Europe. The role of the EU, both independently and as a forum for co-ordinating a European position inside NATO is strengthened.

What is perhaps most striking about the developments in EPC/CFSP in the 1990s are the extreme swings in the assessment of its future prospects. The optimism with regard to the strengthening of the CFSP in the immediate aftermath of the Cold War, which was replaced by pessimism after the Amsterdam Treaty, has, after the St Malo declaration, returned. Thus, the 'story' of the CFSP outlined above requires some disentangling. To what extent then can developments in foreign and security policy in the late 1990s be considered durable? Both internal and external factors will influence the future development of the EU's security and defence policy. Assessments of which factors should be considered most important do, however, depend on what kind of process we consider the EU to be. They depend on what kind of driving forces we see as most influential in the development of the CFSP. It is possible to distinguish between two fundamentally different perspectives on political processes in the international system: a realist perspective and a cosmopolitan perspective. These should be seen as analytical models, not empirical descriptions of reality. Thus, they are 'ideal types' that provide different concepts allowing us to analyse different dimensions of foreign policy co-operation in the EU. If one restricts oneself to one of these basic perspectives, some dimensions of the EU's foreign policy are likely to be ignored, because we lack the concepts necessary to capture them. The first approach tends to see co-operation as interest driven whereas the second approach focuses on discourse and sees the increased co-operation as the product of the spread of supranational norms and identities. These two analytical models are thus likely to have diverging perceptions of the question of the resilience of the CFSP.

Foreign Policy as Interest-driven

From the perspective of the first analytical model, policy is seen as driven by material self-interest. From a classical realist perspective, interests are defined in terms of power (Morgenthau 1946). Here, the international system is seen to be composed of sovereign states that act on the basis of material self-interest, without reference to common norms, identities or values. The international system is defined as anarchical, in other words; there is no overarching authority to identify common rules. Order is considered to be maintained as a result of a balance of power rather than as a result of a common authority as is the case in domestic politics. What counts in the end is power, measured in material terms as economic or military capabilities, not an assessment of whether or not actions are normatively right or 'good'. International institutions are not attributed any independent role in this perspective. Co-operation will only be possible if states face a common external threat, as they did during the Cold War, or if their national interests coincide. When their interests cease to coincide, co-operation will also disintegrate. When other groups of states emerge as more attractive in terms of serving the national interest, loyalty to the EU will disappear. Many studies of the CFSP, although not always explicitly theoretical, implicitly rely on the basic assumptions of this perspective (Ifestos 1987, Pijpers 1991, Hill 1996). In these studies, a clear distinction is drawn between the classic 'community method' of pillar one and foreign policy co-operation in pillar two. The intergovernmental structure of the CFSP decision-making process is seen as a manifestation of the limits to foreign policy co-operation in the EU.

The CFSP is often criticized for having a slow decision-making system and for being incapable of acting decisively, in particular in situations of international crises, such as Kosovo, Bosnia or the Gulf War (Kintis 1997). The CFSP is often also seen to be incapable of letting words be followed by action. An often-quoted example is the Venice declaration of 1980 where the EU officially recognized the Palestinians' right to self-determination. This happened at a time when the United States was far from accepting such a principle. Yet, it was not followed up with concrete policy initiatives. The United States was still seen as the actor that determined the policy-agenda in the Middle East, and any symbolic value of the EU declaration was not considered. The CFSP has also been criticized for failing to take the lead in European politics at the end of the Cold War (Allen 1998). This role was filled by the United States, it is argued, not by the EU and its new Common Foreign and Security Policy. These difficulties and weaknesses with the CFSP can easily be understood with the help of interest-based theories. The institutional network of the CFSP can from this perspective only be seen to reflect the interests of its member states. It can not be expected to put any limits on the foreign policy initiatives of the member states, to shape their interest or bring them to stick to the common framework if it collides with their own interest. However, it seems likely that EU membership will modify the unlimited effects of states' self-interest also within the foreign policy and security area.

Most importantly, interest-based perspectives have difficulties explaining why the CFSP occasionally succeeds, or why it exists at all. They do not explain why the CFSP has proven to be so durable. It becomes difficult from this perspective to understand the criticisms that emerged towards Germany after its decision to unilaterally recognize Croatia as a sovereign state. If one expects that the CFSP will not create any ties on member states and that states at all times will act according to their own interest, this kind of action should neither be perceived as surprising nor unacceptable, but rather as a legitimate and logical action.

The classical power politics perspective has been further elaborated upon and modified into the neo-realist and neo-liberal perspectives on international relations. A central difference with the power-based theories is that from the neo-realist and neo-liberal perspectives, the different strategies of negotiation, the calculations of actors, also contribute to explaining the outcome in international politics. In the older, or 'classical realist', perspectives the focus is mostly on the power resources of actors. Negotiation strategies are usually not taken into consideration. Amongst themselves, neo-realists and neo-liberals disagree on the likelihood of co-operation. Both perspectives accept that the anarchical nature of the international system put particular constraints on co-operation. Yet, neo-realists consider international anarchy to represent a greater hindrance to inter-state co-ordination than the neo-liberals do. The two perspectives also disagree on whether or not states have a common interest in co-operating: the neo-realists consider states to be mostly interested in relative gains, whereas the neo-liberals stress states' interest in maximizing their absolute gains. Nonetheless, when it comes to their basic assumptions about what are the central driving forces in international politics, the differences between these perspectives are small (Risse-Kappen 1995, Mansbach 1996). According to Risse-Kappen (1995: 26) neo-liberal institutionalism should not be regarded as part of the liberal paradigm. This 'co-operation under anarchy' perspective shares all realist core assumptions, but disagrees with structural realists on the likelihood of international co-operation among self-interested actors'. Furthermore, their starting point, that material interests are the central driving forces in foreign policy, is one that they share with the classical realist perspective. Actors are seen to calculate rationally on the basis of their interests. Indeed, it has been suggested that the difference between the classical realists and the neo-realists is principally one of methodology (Linklater 1995).

Neo-realist and neo-liberal perspectives have rarely been applied directly to the CFSP or the EU. Nonetheless, one of the dominant theories of European integration, neo-liberal institutionalism, draws on elements from both these approaches (Moravcsik 1998b). Neo-liberal institutionalists pay little attention to the CFSP, arguing that foreign policy co-operation in the second pillar is different in character from the first pillar. In other words, the idea of a fundamental distinction between high and low politics and a separation between the two pillars, based on differences in their decision-making system is maintained in some of the most influential present-day theories of the EU. Hence, in terms of providing an alternative perspective from the classical realist position on the CFSP, these recent theories are of limited use. In order to highlight such issues, we need a different perspective on international politics altogether. This perspective takes as its starting point that the international system is more complex than interest-based theories assume.

Towards a Europeanization of Foreign and Security Policy?

Europeanization of foreign and security policy has two dimensions. The first relates to interaction internally, amongst the EU member states. The second relates to the status and role of the EU in the international system. The underlying assumptions of the 'Europeanization' perspective stand in contrast to the view of states as 'billiard-ball' actors whose interests are defined exogenously and where the decision-making process is characterized by intergovernmental bargaining and unlimited state interests. In order to identify a process of Europeanization the effects of ideas, values and identities that are often set aside in the rationalist analytical tradition, have to be taken into consideration. It is necessary to discuss to what extent such factors influence policy and institutions in a particular area. Applied to the CFSP, such approaches would suggest that foreign policy-making within the EU is a dynamic process where interests and objectives are not exogenous but emerge as a result of interaction at the national, European and international level. The clear distinction between the 'national' and the 'European' might gradually be blurred, even in the area of 'high politics'. A process of 'Europeanization' of foreign policy in which shared norms and rules are gradually accumulated might be closer to describing accurately the CFSP than the image of rational bargaining leading to agreement on a policy of the lowest common denominator (Hill 1996).

Some evidence of a 'Europeanization' of foreign policy can be found. Tonra (1997: 197) has found that, in the cases of Ireland, Denmark and Holland, 'political co-operation improved the effectiveness, broadened the range and increased the capabilities of foreign policy making'. Hill and Wallace (1996) refer to an engrenage effect in foreign policy co-operation: They point out that the preparation of foreign policy now takes place in the context of European consultation and that, as a result, 'Officials and Ministers who sit together on planes and round tables in Brussels or in each others' capitals begin to judge "rationality" from within a different framework' (Hill and Wallace 1996: 12). A classic example would be the so-called 'co-ordination reflex' between Political Directors so often mentioned even in the early literature on EPC.

There are also further indications of change in European foreign policy that cannot be captured by concentrating exclusively on the intergovernmental characteristics of the CFSP. One dimension to the changes taking place in European foreign policy is what Allen (1998) has referred to as the process of 'Brusselization' of European foreign policy. Although foreign and security policy remain formally in the control of the nation state and have not been transferred in any substantial way to the European Commission, it has in practice become more difficult for the foreign ministries of the member states to control the foreign policy process. Foreign policy is increasingly made in Brussels, by national representatives. This gradual transfer of decision-making from national capitals to Brussels has developed in parallel with efforts in the Treaties of Maastricht and Amsterdam to increase cohesion between the first and the second pillar. One consequence has been that rivalries have developed between the Political Directors (who traditionally deal with the CFSP) and the Permanent Representatives. The important point however is that this tendency towards Brusselization suggests that centrifugal forces within the EU are quite strong and that the foreign policies of member states undergo important changes as a result of membership in the EU and participation in the CFSP.

It could be argued that without the corresponding development of a shared identity, the 'Brusseliztation' of foreign policy is unlikely to lead to a cohesive foreign policy. In this area, the signals are mixed. It is difficult to argue that there is a European foreign policy identity. Nevertheless, the identities of Europe's 'nation states' seem increasingly ambiguous. Laffan (1996) has suggested that issues of identity have re-emerged at three levels in Europe: within states, in the European Union and at the wider European level. It is often argued that the nation state is too small to handle the consequences of economic globalization on its own. According to Laffan's thesis there is a parallel development according to which the nation state is too large for issues of identity, which now emerge at regional level. Consequently, we must at least reflect on the possibility that the very fundament of national foreign policy is changing. It is not clear that this will lead to a transfer of loyalty to 'Europe' or to an effective 'European' identity, comparable to national identities, that may underpin the CFSP. Instead, what this change in European identities might open the way for is alternative ways of legitimizing foreign policy.

Traditionally, the EU's external identity has been built around the notion of a civilian power (Duchêne 1972). According to Waever (1996), the efforts to build a European identity are now given a slightly different meaning. He argues that efforts to build a European identity are increasingly being linked to the issue of security. This, according to Waever gives a sense of urgency to integration: its alternative – fragmentation – is presented as destructive to the whole European project (Waever 1996: 123). Looking at the EU's enlargement policy towards central and eastern Europe, there are signs of efforts to build an international identity based on ideas represented in a model of deliberative democracy.

There are indications of a tendency to link the EU's international role to certain general ideas and values in international politics. Hence, at the height of the war in Yugoslavia, public opinion called for Europe to 'do something' to stop the war, thus suggesting a view, in the public at large, of the EU as a community of values with a right and duty to take initiatives in foreign policy. This is consistent with a cosmopolitan perspective that would, from the outset, define the international system as complex, both with regard to which actors are involved in influencing the political agenda and which policy areas dominate the policy agenda (Eriksen et al. 1995). Most importantly, political, legal and normative dimensions are considered to have a direct influence on states' behaviour at the international level. Thus, rather than focus exclusively on rational calculations aimed at satisfying material self-interests, a cosmopolitan model would underline the role of laws, principles and processes of deliberation within an institutionalized system. The nation state, although legally sovereign, is seen as woven into a complex network of mutual dependency with other national states as well as transnational actors and international organizations. From this perspective the absence of a hierarchy both between actors and issues in the international system would be important.

Military power is, in other words, not attributed a privileged position on top of the hierarchy as it is in the realist perspective. Military power is not seen as the ultimate arbiter in international relations, which gives actors a particular weight in the international system. On the contrary military power is set alongside economic and political power. Consequently the nation state looses its privileged position in the international system. This privileged position is seen to grow out of their sovereign right to use military power. When this right no longer is particularly important, the possibility arises of considering other actors as equally important and influential in international politics. In such a system of mutual dependency, it follows logically that order is seen as established through a network of agreements rather than as a result of a balance of power. In other words, one would see a network of norms and rules at the international level creating limits for the behaviour of states and giving indications of what is acceptable behaviour in the international system.

Although the international system post-1989 has obviously not transformed itself into a cosmopolitan democracy there are elements of change in the international system that point to an evolution in this direction. It is often argued that neither the nation state nor the international system is what they used to be, or what the realist perspective claimed that they were. The privileged position of the state is challenged both domestically and internationally. The state can no longer control political, economic and in some cases even military movements across national borders. The nation state is not, either, able to draw on the same type of loyalty from domestic actors as it has previously been able to. Actors' loyalties will follow other logics and be defined according to other premises than loyalty to the nation state. At the same time, the state has to relate to an increasing number of international agreements that put constraints on its behaviour.

In the case of the EU, a cosmopolitan perspective could help us understand what an increasing body of literature already points to: the considerable influence exerted by the EU, if not in the international system, then at least in Europe. Despite the EU's obvious difficulties in handling international crises, it is often seen as a key force in the longer-term reshaping of international politics in Europe after the end of bipolarity. The vast number of applicants wishing to join the EU is a further sign that external actors perceive the EU as an influential actor in the region. In other words, the empirical 'reality' does not seem to fit entirely with interest-based theories of international relations and European integration. Political co-operation has actually proved extremely durable.

Several authors have taken these observations as their starting point in analysing the EU's international role. Allen and Smith have emphasized the difficulty in studying western Europe's international role as long as 'the notion of a "foreign policy" carries with it a conceptual framework which is inseparable from the state-centric view of world politics' (Allen and Smith 1990: 95). They claim that we tend to get stuck in this state-centric view when analysing European foreign policy, and therefore find it difficult to account for the growing significance of the EU's international role. They suggest that by using the concept of international 'presence', it is possible to study the impact of the EU in different policy areas of the international system, and to show that the EU 'has considerable structure, salience and legitimacy in the process of international politics' (Allen and Smith 1990: 116).

Building on the notion of the EU's 'presence' in the international system, as well as Sjøstedt's (1977) analysis of the EC's international actor-status, Hill has suggested that the EU is best seen as a system of external relations in which 'the Europeans represent a sub-system of the international system as a whole . . . a system which generates international relations – collectively, individually, economically, politically – rather than a clear-cut "European foreign policy" as such' (Hill 1993: 120). This European sub-system has three dimensions to which we should pay attention: (1) the national foreign policies of the member states, (2) the CFSP and (3) the 'external relations' of the first pillar. Such interpretations of the EU's international role are often referred to as 'non-rationalistic' (Matlary 1997b). Nonetheless, what they seem to have in common, rather than a belief in 'irrationality' is (1) a view of interest as endogenous to the policy process; (2) a view of politics as based on other factors than pure material interest. It is in other words the particular definition of rationality that interest-based theories build upon that is questioned in the 'non-rationalistic' literature. Actors can be rational even if they do not seek to enhance their own material gains.

The CFSP is not a common foreign policy in the sense prescribed by the Treaty of Maastricht. According to the Treaty, the CFSP shall be 'supported actively and unreservedly by its Member States in a spirit of loyalty and mutual solidarity'. Further, the CFSP is supposed to cover 'all areas of foreign and security policy'. It would be naive to pretend other than that national foreign policies remain strong and that reaching a consensus, in particular in situations of crisis which require rapid responses, remains difficult. Identifying shared interests and reconciling different national foreign policy traditions is a challenge. Thus, this literature does not confirm traditional neo-functionalist assumptions about integration.

Central to neo-functionalist analysis is the view of a spillover, which is expected to take place as an unintended consequence of economic actors' pursuit of their own interest. One would thus have to show that integration in foreign policy has taken place as a functional spillover from the wider integration process at work in the Community. This might be the case mostly in external economic relations. There does not seem to exist an automatic link between economic integration and the development of a common foreign policy. This literature does not suggest, in neo-functionalist fashion, that it is only a matter of time before control of foreign policy is moved from the national to the supranational level. It suggests that it is possible to detect a gradual process of change even in foreign policy-making. Furthermore, it suggests that we need to pay closer attention to the dynamic interaction between the national and the European levels in order to understand political co-operation. We do not know the end station of this process and we must reflect on the possibility that it may never lead to one single European foreign policy in the traditional sense of the word.

Most of the so-called reflectivist literature is not explicit in identifying the driving forces in the political process. In order to specify these, the cosmopolitan model might help by providing an alternative model of human action. Rather than focus exclusively on rational calculation aimed at satisfying material self interests, it would underline the role of laws, principles and processes of deliberation within an institutionalized system. The intergovernmental character of the CFSP may not then be the most important element, but rather the quality of the processes that take place inside them, and whether or not these can be seen as processes aimed at coming to a shared understanding through arguing, or simply a process of bargaining between self-sustained interests. A situation of arguing can be seen to take place in institutions that respect the participating parties as actors with equal rights. Thus relations within the CFSP could be seen as based on reciprocally recognized norms, rather than on a balance of power.

Conclusion: the Future of European Foreign and Security Policy

This chapter has outlined the EU's efforts to build a common foreign and security policy and discussed the extent to which changes in this particular policy sector can be seen as durable. The question of the significance and future prospects for the EU's foreign and security policy is particularly pertinent because of the expected enlargement of the EU to central and eastern Europe. It is common to assume that the CFSP will be even more atomized as a result of the increase in the number of member states in the EU. Cohesion will obviously be more difficult with 25 than with 15 member states. An assessment of the consequences of

EU enlargement for the future evolution of the CFSP will nonetheless have to be explicit about what one considers to be the central forces that drive further integration in foreign and security policy. What is the type of glue that keeps the member states of the EU together? The chapter has used two different analytical models to discuss the significance of developments in this particular policy-sector. The first one sees politics as exclusively oriented towards satisfaction of self-interests. The second model views politics as a system with rights and duties, placing additional requirements on actors than simply the one of satisfying self-interests. This is related both to the member states' position in the wider EU integration process and the EU's emerging role in an international liberal political context. If only unlimited self-interests are the driving forces – then atomization is a logical consequence. This chapter has suggested an alternative perspective providing a different answer to this question, where recent developments in the CFSP may be a step on the way towards further European integration.

Notes

1 The EDC was rejected by the French Parliament in 1954, despite the fact that the project was the result of a French initiative.

2 For a thorough overview of the historical developments of EPC see Simon Nuttall (1992).

3 The Single European Act admitted that EPC could discuss the 'economic implications of security'.

4 Treaty on European Union, Art. J4.

5 Petersberg Declaration, West European Union Council of Ministers, Bonn 19 June 1992.

6 Ministerial Meeting of the North Atlantic Council (1996), Final Communiqué, Berlin.

7 France pulled out of the military dimension of NATO in 1966 but remained part of the political dimension of the Alliance.

8 'Franco-British summit – Joint declaration on European defence', 4 December 1998.

9 Declaration of the European Council on strengthening the common European policy on security and defence. Press release: Brussels (03-06-1999) Nr. 122/99.

10 Presidency Report on strengthening of the common European policy on security and defence. Press release: Brussels (03-06-1999) Nr. 122/99.

11 Washington summit communiqué. Press communiqué NAC-S (99) 56, Washington, 24 April 1999.

EU ENLARGEMENT: INTERESTS, ISSUES AND THE NEED FOR INSTITUTIONAL REFORM

Finn Laursen

In recent years we have seen a debate in Europe on 'Deepening versus Widening' (Wallace 1989, De la Serre 1991, Wessels 1996). In the past, widening, i.e. enlargement, was often linked with deepening. The first enlargement agreed at the summit in The Hague in 1969 was for instance linked with the creation of European Political Co-operation (EPC), the foreign policy co-operation among the member states, which started in 1970. Spanish and Portuguese membership came in parallel with the Single European Act (SEA). The last enlargement as of 1 January 1995 was made on the basis of the Maastricht Treaty, which deepened integration in various ways, *inter alia* by outlining the phases towards Economic and Monetary Union (EMU), by giving the European Parliament a right of co-decision in a number of areas, and by adding a number of new policy chapters.

The enlargement to the east differs from earlier expansions of the EU in three ways. First, the present enlargement is motivated by the wish to use the process actively to stabilize and stimulate democracy and economic development in future member countries. Second, the present process has a radical scope; it aims at doubling the number of member countries and redefining the concept of Europe. Third, in the ongoing enlargement the present member states are reluctant to extend all commitments to new members in the short run.

The Maastricht Treaty foresaw an intergovernmental conference (IGC) to review the Treaty in 1996. This conference, which produced the Amsterdam Treaty, was seen as the conference which would make the next enlargement possible, namely with some central and eastern European countries (CEECs) and possibly Cyprus and Malta (Ludlow et al. 1995). The latter two countries applied in 1990 for membership. There are now 10 CEECs which have applied for membership. They did

---

This chapter relies on earlier writings by the author, especially Laursen (1996, 1997 and 1998).

so in the following order: Hungary, 31 March 1994; Poland, 5 April 1994; Romania, 22 June 1995; Slovakia, 27 June 1995; Latvia, 13 October 1995; Estonia, 24 November 1995; Lithuania, 8 December 1995; Bulgaria, 14 December 1995; The Czech Republic, 17 January 1996; Slovenia, 10 June 1996 (*Europe Documents* 1996).

Furthermore, there has been an application from Turkey already in from 1987, but the Commission said that Turkey, although in principle eligible, was not ready for membership (EC 1989). This changed in late 1999, when Turkey was accepted, in principle, as a candidate country.

The Development of EC/EU Enlargement Policy

The Maastricht Treaty dealt with enlargement in Article O, which stipulated:

> Any European State may apply to become a Member of the Union. It shall address its application to the Council, which shall act unanimously after consulting the Commission and after receiving the assent of the European Parliament, which shall act by an absolute majority of its component members.
>
> The conditions of admission and the adjustments to the Treaties on which the Union is founded which such admission entails shall be the subject of an agreement between the Member States and the applicant State. This agreement shall be submitted for ratification by all the contracting States in accordance with their respective constitutional requirements.

The Amsterdam Treaty has added that 'The Union is founded on the principles of liberty, democracy, respect for human rights and fundamental freedoms and the rule of law' (Art. 6).

The old Article O was procedure oriented. The basic procedure has not changed. The European Parliament must give its assent, which is a power it has had since the SEA. Given the fact that unanimity is required in the Council, each member state, as well as the European Parliament, has a veto. A member state must be European. Morocco, which applied in 1987, was told that it cannot join because it is not European. Although the Commission opinion on Turkish membership in 1989 was negative, the question of eligibility was answered in the affirmative. So Turkey can hope eventually to join, once certain political and economic obstacles have been removed.

The European Council meeting in Maastricht in December 1991 also issued a short statement on enlargement, saying 'that any European State whose system of Government is founded on the principle of democracy may apply to become a member of the Union'. In reality democracy has been an implied principle from the beginning. This condition is now confirmed by the Amsterdam Treaty.

In December 1991 the European Council invited the Commission to prepare a report on enlargement for the Lisbon summit in June 1992 (*Agence Europe*, 12 December 1991).

The Commission presented this report on 'Europe and the challenge of enlargement' to the meeting of the European Council in Lisbon in June 1992. It referred to a new context, partly because of the completion of the internal market and signing of the Maastricht Treaty, partly because of the end of the Cold War. The integration of the CEECs was now seen as 'a historic opportunity'. It could contribute to the 'unification of the whole of Europe' (EC 1992).

The Lisbon Report set the following conditions of membership:

- democracy and the respect of fundamental human rights
- acceptance of the Community system and capacity to implement it, including a functioning and competitive market economy, and an adequate legal and administrative framework
- acceptance and capacity to implement the Common Foreign and Security Policy 'as it evolves over the coming years'.

The report, however, still mainly dealt with the EFTA applicants. At the time of the Lisbon summit none of the CEECs had applied for membership. Association agreements, known as Europe Agreements had been negotiated with Poland, Hungary and Czechoslovakia, and negotiations on similar agreements were taking place with Bulgaria and Romania. Trade and Co-operation Agreements had been signed with the three Baltic states and Albania.

The Europe Agreements acknowledged that membership was the goal of the CEECs, but the EC side did not offer such membership at the time. The subtle language used, for instance, in the Hungarian agreement, was: 'HAVING IN MIND that the final objective of Hungary is to become a member of the Community and that this association, in the view of the Parties, will help to achieve this objective . . .' (OJ L 347, 31 December 1993).

Concerning membership for the CEECs a break-through came at the Copenhagen meeting of the European Council, 21–22 June 1993, where the heads of state and government agreed that 'the associated countries in Central and Eastern Europe that so desire shall become members of the European Union'. The economic and political conditions were listed in the following way:

> Membership requires that the candidate country has achieved stability of institutions guaranteeing democracy, the rule of law, human rights and respect for and protection of minorities, the existence of a functioning market economy as well as the capacity to cope with competitive pressure and market forces within the Union. Membership presupposes the candidate's ability to

take on the obligations of membership including adherence to the aims of political, economic and monetary union. (EC 1993)

The Presidency conclusions then went on:

The Union's capacity to absorb new members, while maintaining the momentum of European integration, is also an important consideration in the general interest of both the Union and the candidate countries.

Put differently, both the EU and the candidate countries had to be ready. Widening was linked with the EU's capacity to continue the process of integration, although different member states had different perspectives on what this meant.

The Essen European Council in December 1994 adopted a pre-accession strategy, the most important part of which was the idea of a White Paper on the integration of the CEECs into the Internal Market. This paper was endorsed by the European Council in Cannes in June 1995.

The Madrid summit, 15–16 December 1995, again dealt with the issue of CEEC membership of the EU. The European Council now said that 'Enlargement is both a political necessity and a historic opportunity for Europe'. It reiterated that accession negotiations with Malta and Cyprus would start six months after the conclusion of the 1996 Intergovern-mental Conference (IGC), as promised by the Corfu meeting of the European Council in June 1994. Concerning the CEECs the European Council confirmed in Madrid 'the need to make sound preparation for enlargement on the basis of the criteria established in Copenhagen and in the context of the pre-accession strategy defined in Essen' in December 1994. The pre-accession strategy would have to be intensified. The Madrid conclusions continued:

[The European Council] asks the Commission to expedite preparation of its opinions on the applications made so that they can be forwarded to the Council as soon as possible after the conclusion of the Intergovernmental Conference, and to embark upon preparation of a composite paper on enlargement. This procedure will ensure that the applicant countries are treated on an equal basis. (. . .)

Following the Conclusion of the Intergovernmental Conference and in light of its outcome and of all the opinions and reports from the Commission referred to above, the Council will, at the earliest opportunity, take the necessary decisions for launching the accession negotiations.

The European Council hopes that the preliminary stage of negotiations will coincide with the start of negotiations with Cyprus and Malta. (EU 1995b)

The debate concerning the question whether some CEECs would join sooner than others was left unanswered. For the moment the official policy was that the applicants would be treated on an equal basis and the European Council hoped that accession negotiations could start six months after the IGC.

The Florence summit of the EU in June 1996 stressed 'the importance of the strategy for preparing for accession, which now incorporates Slovenia', and went on:

> Recalling its Madrid conclusions, it reiterates the need for the Commission's opinions and reports on enlargement as called for at Madrid to be available as soon as possible after the completion of the Intergovernmental Conference so that the initial phase of negotiations with countries of Central and Eastern Europe can coincide with the beginning of negotiations with Cyprus and Malta six months after the end of the IGC, taking its results into account. (*Agence Europe*, 23 June 1996)

At Madrid the heads of state and government 'hoped' (as they now used the terminology) that negotiations 'can' start six months after the IGC. Under pressure from the CEECs the language was slowly and subtly changing.

The IGC that had to be completed before enlargement had started during the Italian presidency in the first part of 1996. It continued during the Irish presidency in the second part of 1996, and a draft treaty was proposed by the Irish at the end of the year. The difficult issue of institutional changes was not dealt with, however. Negotiations were continued during the first part of 1997 under the Dutch presidency. The British elections in May and the emergence of a new Labour government led to a speeding-up of negotiations, and they were concluded in Amsterdam in June. The Amsterdam Treaty, however, did not solve the institutional issues.

In July 1997 the Commission published its opinions on the ten applicant CEECs, and at the Luxembourg meeting of the European Council in December 1997 the heads of state and government worked out a strategy for the accession process. A screening process of all ten CEEC applicants started in the spring of 1998, and in the autumn of 1998 'real' negotiations started with the five front runners: Estonia, Poland, the Czech Republic, Hungary and Slovenia.

Profile of the CEEC Applicants

Most CEECs are relatively small, the main exceptions being Poland with about 39 million inhabitants and Romania with about 23 million. The GDP per capita is relatively low. In 1991 the Commission gave figures varying between 4,500 and 7,000 Ecu per capita. The share of employment in agriculture remained high, up to about 26–7 per cent in Poland for instance. Among the Mediterranean applicants Turkey is a big country (about 55 million inhabitants), poor (a GDP per capita of about 1,309 Ecu in 1989), and about 50 per cent of the population employed in agriculture (EC 1991).

Figures for GDP vary quite a lot. *The Economist* gave the following 1994 GDP, at purchasing-power parity exchange rates: The Czech Republic $7,910; Slovenia $7,020; Slovakia $6,660; Hungary $6,310; Poland $5,380; Latvia $5,170; Estonia $4,519; Bulgaria $4,230; Lithuania $3,240; and Romania $2,920. This should be compared with an average of $18,170 for the fifteen EU members. The figures given for the Mediterranean applicants were: Cyprus $10,260; Malta $7,460; and Turkey $4,610. Very roughly we can say that the average GDP of the CEECs is about a third of the average GDP of current EU members.

Table 11.1 gives figures for 1996 as they were given in the Commission reports on progress towards accession published in November 1998. In terms of GDP per capita at purchasing-power parity exchange rates, the Czech Republic and Slovenia remain in front followed by Slovakia. Agriculture as share of the labour force is lowest in the Czech Republic, Hungary and Slovakia, highest in Romania, Bulgaria, Lithuania and Poland.

Whatever the exactness of the figures, they give rough indications of the costs of enlargement of the EC/EU. It is clear that membership of the CEECs will have budget costs because of financial transfers from the EU's structural funds and through the Common Agricultural Policy (CAP). The latter includes expensive price support for producers. In its

Table 11.1 CEEC population, income and agricultural shares, 1996

	Population (millions)	GDP per capita (Ecu)[1]	Agriculture share of labour force (%)
Czech Republic	10.3	11,600	6.3
Hungary	10.2	7,800	8.3
Slovakia	5.4	8,200	8.9
Poland	38.6	6,900	22.1
Slovenia	2.0	12,200	10.1
Estonia	1.5	6,100	10
Latvia	2.5	4,700	18.3
Lithuania	3.7	5,300	24.2
Bulgaria	8.3	4,600	34.4
Romania	22.6	6,100	38
EU-15	372,654	17,264[2]	5.3

1 At purchasing-power parity exchange rates.
2 1995 figure.

Sources: Commission Reports, Progress Towards Accession, November 4, 1998; *Agence Europe*, 7 January 1998; 'Selected Statistics' supplement to *Agence Europe*, 12 January 1998.

1991 report the Commission estimated that Poland, Hungary and Czechoslovakia would be entitled to receive 6.5 billion Ecu and Turkey 5.4 billion Ecu through structural fund transfers. The 1991 EC budget for the EC poorer regions was 7.4 billion Ecu. The Commission report in 1991 did not try to put figures on the costs in the agricultural sector, but expected great problems.

An independent study by Baldwin estimated that the costs of admitting the four Visegrad countries, Poland, the Czech Republic, Slovakia and Hungary, would increase annual EU spending by 63.6 billion Ecu on the basis of then existing policies (Baldwin 1994). The implication of this is pressure for reform of the most costly EU policies prior to an eastern enlargement. In particular the CAP, which was already reformed in 1992, largely because of GATT's Uruguay Round, would need further reform, it was recognized.

If we look at the political side of the profile of the CEECs, they have embarked on a process of political reforms after the end of the Cold War. But democracy is not easy to establish from one day to the next. It depends on a certain political culture that takes time to develop. In the 1991 report the Commission officials suggested that the democratic tradition was weak in Poland, Czechoslovakia and Hungary and practically 'none' in Romania and Bulgaria. How quickly could one then expect democracy, including the rule of law and respect of human rights and rights of ethnic minorities, to take root in these countries?

A further dimension of this was of course that the administrations in these countries at the time of accession will have to be able to implement Community law. Since this was already creating problems for some of the current members of the EU it was clear that preparation, including training of officials, was necessary.

Table 11.2   CEEC growth, unemployment and inflation, 1996

	Growth (% GDP)	Unemployment	Inflation
Bulgaria	− 10.1	13.7	123.0
Poland	6.1	12.3	19.9
Romania	3.9	6.7	38.8
Slovakia	6.6	11.1	5.8
Slovenia	3.1	7.3	9.7
Czech Republic	3.9	3.5	8.8
Hungary	1.3	9.2	23.6
Latvia	3.3	18.3	17.6
Lithuania	4.7	16.6	24.6
Estonia	4.0	10	23.1
EU-15		10.7	2.5

Sources: Commission, Reports on Progress Towards Accession, November 4, 1998; *Agence Europe*, 7 January 1998.

Table 11.2 gives some macro-economic figures for the CEECs. Poland and Slovakia both reached a growth rate of over 6 per cent in 1996. But Bulgaria still had negative growth. Unemployment was above 10 per cent in many of the CEECs. The Czech Republic had the lowest unemployment at 3.5 per cent. Slovakia had the lowest inflation rate at 5.8 per cent. The Czech Republic and Slovenia also had one-digit inflation. Bulgaria and Romania still had very high inflation.

Table 11.3 gives an overview of economic reforms in the CEECs by the mid-1990s. It is based on estimates from the European Bank of Reconstruction and Development (EBRD), the IMF and OECD. It suggests that Poland, Hungary, the Czech Republic and Estonia had gone furthest in the process of economic transition, followed by Slovakia and Slovenia.

The Europe Agreements

Current relations between the EU and the CEECs are mainly based on the so-called Europe Agreements. They were initially proposed by the Commission in August 1990. Negotiations with Poland, Czechoslovakia and Hungary took place during 1991 and later with the other CEECs. They include political dialogue, economic, cultural and financial co-operation and aim for free trade for industrial products as well as free movement of services and capital over a ten-year transition period. They do not include free movement of people, only some rights for legally established workers. The transition to free trade is asymmetrical, with the EU moving faster than the CEECs. Most EU customs duties should be abolished after five years. Liberalization periods were longer for sensitive products, especially steel and textiles, where 6–7 years was foreseen. Because of the CAP there is no liberalization of trade with agricultural products, only some improvements in market access (Maresceau 1993).

The Europe Agreements also established institutions of association, an Association Council, an Association Committee and a Parliamentary Committee. Through these institutions, bilateral meetings between the EU and the respective CEEC have taken place.

Thanks partly to the Europe Agreements the EU has become the most important trading partner of the CEECs, increasing its share from about 30 per cent in 1988 to about 55 per cent in 1993. Trade with the former Soviet Union decreased drastically in the same period. There was also an important fall in intra-CEEC trade (Denmark, Ministry of Economics 1996).

EU imports from the CEECs increased from 16.2 billion Ecu in 1991 to 41.7 billion Ecu in 1995, an annual growth varying between 17 and 27 per cent. EU exports to the CEECs increased from 17.7 billion Ecu in 1991

Table 11.3 The most important structural reforms in the CEECs, 1989 to mid-1995

	Privatization and Restructuring			Liberalization			Reforms	
	Privatization of small enterprises	Privatization of large enterprises	Restructuring of companies	Prices & wages	Trade, competition	Financial system	Tax system	Pension/social
Poland	+++	++	++	+½	+++	+	+½	½
Hungary	+++	+++	++	+	+++	+	+	
Czech Rep.	+++	+++	++	+	+++	+	++	++
Slovakia	+++	++	++	+	+++	+	+	½
Bulgaria	++	+	+	+	++	+		
Romania	+++	+	+	+	+½	½	+	
Estonia	+++	+++	++	+	++½	+	++	+
Latvia	+++	+	+	+	++	½	+	
Lithuania	+++	++	+	+	++	½	+	
Slovenia	+++	++	++	+	++½	+	+	+

0 = none or few steps; + = ongoing/early stage; ++ = fast progress/approaching completion; +++ = nearly successful completion; ½ indicates that the classification is probably underestimated in relation to other countries in the same group.

Source: Denmark, Ministry of Economics, 1996.

to 49.3 billion Ecu in 1995, an annual increase between 21 and 32 per cent. During the whole period the EU's trade surplus kept increasing, reaching 7.6 billion Ecu in 1995. Roughly half of this trade, however, is between Germany on the EU side and Poland and the Czech Republic on the CEEC side (EUROSTAT 1996).

The Pre-accession Strategy

The meeting of the European Council at Essen in December 1994, outlined a pre-accession strategy for the CEECs. It was to consist of the Europe Agreements as well as new multilateral 'structured relations'.

The Council of Ministers had prepared a report for the Essen meeting. It emphasized that an essential element of the pre-accession strategy would be 'the phased adoption of the Union's internal market acquis'. This involves a 'complex process of approximation of legislation, norms and standards' (EC 1994). Eventually a White Paper published in May 1995 would outline this process in detail.

The EU's PHARE-programme would assist the CEECs in preparing for accession. Among short-term measures we found a promise from the EU to inform any associated country before initiating anti-dumping proceedings, a promise to improve access to the EU's textiles market, and improvements in respect to rules of origin. On the CEEC side a 'satisfactory implementation of competition policy and state aids control' was emphasized as being especially important. The CEECs were expected to draw up an inventory of their state aids. The Commission would provide guidance and set up a competition policy training programme (EC 1994).

In respect to agriculture the EU promised to examine 'the effects on agriculture in these countries of all subsidized exports'. The Commission was asked to present a study during the second part of 1995 on the relations between the EU and the CEECs in the agricultural field.

The Council report also included rather general sections on promoting investments, and second and third pillar co-operation, including co-operation to prevent conflicts related to issues such as borders and frontiers and co-operation in combating all forms of organized crime. The convergence of environmental policies and approximation of environmental legislation were mentioned as priority items. The CEECs would be integrated into the Trans-European Networks, including rail and road projects.

Co-operation in culture, education and training, as well as financial co-operation through PHARE and the European Investment Bank (EIB) were also mentioned.

The strategy finally encouraged intra-regional co-operation, 'bon voisinage', and free trade among the CEECs.

These various more or less concrete measures which had already to a certain extent been covered by the Europe Agreements were linked with a so-called structured relationship, which meant a 'multi-lateral framework for strengthened dialogue and consultation', i.e. regular meetings at all levels between the EU and all the CEECs. There were to be annual meetings of heads of state and government, semi-annual meetings of foreign ministers, annual meetings of agricultural ministers, transport, telecommunications, research, and environment ministers, semi-annual meetings of justice and/or home affairs ministers, and annual meetings of cultural affairs and education ministers (EU 1994).

In May 1995 the Commission then published the White Paper on 'Preparation of the Associated Countries of Central and Eastern Europe for Integration into the Internal Market of the Union'. The first part outlined the general philosophy of the White Paper. The Annex listed the EU legislation that the CEECs would have to adopt to prepare for participation in the Internal Market. It covered the following 23 areas: Free Movement of Capital, Free Movement and Safety of Industrial Products, Competition, Social Policy and Action, Agriculture, Transport, Audiovisual, Environment, Telecommunication, Direct Taxation, Free Movement of Goods in Harmonized or Part-Harmonized Sectors, Public Procurement, Financial Services, Personal Data, Company Law, Accountancy, Civil Law, Mutual Recognition of Professional Qualifications, Intellectual Property, Energy, Customs and Excise, Indirect Taxation and Consumer Protection (EU 1995a).

Each section listed the regulations, directives and decisions that the CEECs were advised to adopt and implement to prepare for participation in the internal market and gave recommendations concerning the sequence of introduction of this legislation.

The White Paper stressed the need to set up relevant administrative structures in the CEECs and that technical assistance would be necessary. To meet the latter need the Commission has established a Technical Assistance Information Exchange Office (TAIEX) since the beginning of 1996. From May 1996 four services were operational: documentation and legal advice, a workshop programme, a study visits service, and a pool of national experts (Interview with Commission officials).

A fifth service to be set up was a database which would store information on available technical assistance and progress on legal approximation in the CEECs.

Some of the problems detected in the CEECs by the Commission included poor policy co-ordination, poor economic impact analyses, partly because of poor consultation of industry, and inadequate administrative structures. The CEECs have created central EU departments that are well-staffed and equipped, but the dissemination of information to line ministries remains poor. TAIEX therefore has tried to go to the line ministries, too, only to discover that few officials here speak English, French or German. So language is a practical problem.

Language is also a problem when it comes to getting the existing Community legislation translated well into the languages of the CEECs. Often freelance translators use different terminology. There is thus a need for quality control, uniform glossaries, databases of terms, and training programmes for translators.

Another problem of the administrations of the CEECs has been a tremendous drain of officials to the private sector, which offers better opportunities and salaries.

In May 1996 TAIEX sent a questionnaire with 170 questions to the CEECs. They had a July deadline, which they all met. The answers, which were confidential, were used to prepare the opinions on membership which the Commission had to prepare. These opinions were published in July 1997 after agreement on the Amsterdam Treaty in June 1997.

Agenda 2000

Agenda 2000 is the name given to the opinions and composite documents on enlargement published as a series of communications from the Commission on 15 July 1997. Volume I, entitled 'For a Stronger and Wider Union' gives an overview. Volume II is entitled 'Reinforcing the Pre-accession Strategy'. Also included were the individual Commission opinions on the 10 CEEC applicants. All the documents were put on the Internet the same day. They were published later as supplements to the *EU Bulletin*.

Since the Amsterdam Treaty was supposed to prepare the Eastern enlargement(s) of the EU, it is natural that the Commission commented on the outcome of the European Council meeting in Amsterdam, 16–17 June. Overall the treaty was seen as 'a new step on the road to the unification of Europe' and the Commission was of the opinion that it allowed 'to start the enlargement process'. However, 'the institutional reforms were only partial and need to be completed before the forthcoming enlargements'. More specifically, a date should be set 'for the reform regarding the weighting of votes in the Council which must accompany the reduction in the number of Commissioners to one per Member State prior to the first enlargement' (EU 1997a: 4).

Apart from the introductory institutional considerations Volume I had three main parts: the policies of the Union, the challenge of enlargement, and the new financial framework for 2000–2006. The need for reforms of the EU's Common Agricultural Policy and structural policies was acknowledged.

Concerning the applicants the Commission concluded that Poland, the Czech Republic, Hungary, Estonia and Slovenia were closest to meeting the membership criteria set up at the European Council meeting in Copenhagen in June 1993. It was therefore recommended to start accession negotiations with these five CEECs. The remaining five should receive further assistance through a reinforced pre-accession strategy.

In respect to the political criteria set up at Copenhagen, i.e. democracy, the rule of law, human rights and respect for and protection of minorities, Slovakia was the one country that had problems:

> A democracy cannot be considered stable if the respective rights and obligations of institutions such as the presidency, the constitutional court or the central referendum commission can be put into question by the government itself and if the legitimate role of the opposition in parliamentary committees is not accepted. (EU 1997a: 30)

The Commission also noted that 'the Hungarian minority faces a number of problems in exercising its rights' (ibid.: 31).

In respect to economic criteria, i.e. functioning market economy and capacity to cope with competitive pressure and market forces, the situation was more differentiated. Five countries, the Czech Republic, Estonia, Hungary, Poland and Slovenia, could be considered to have market economies. Slavakia came close 'in terms of legislation and systemic features, but lacks transparency in implementation' (ibid.: 32). In respect to capacity to withstand competitive pressures, Hungary and Poland should satisfy the criterion in the medium term, 'provided they stay on the current course'. The Czech Republic, Slovakia and Slovenia 'should be in the same position on condition that they strengthen their efforts and avoid policy reversals.' Further, 'Because Estonia has modernized and radically liberalized its economy, it comes close to this last group, but its large external imbalance is a cause for concern'. On the remaining countries the verdict was this:

> Latvia, Lithuania and Romania have made great strides recently, but will require further consolidation of their efforts. Bulgaria is shedding the difficult legacy of the past; it has made considerable progress very recently and is on course to join the others during the next decade. (ibid.: 33)

In conclusion then, politics put one country into the second group and economics four, leaving five that should start negotiations first.

The proposed financial framework was based on the assumption that the first eastern enlargement with five CEECs would take place in 2002. This means that the budgetary costs of the CAP and structural policies will only partly be felt during the seven years of the framework. On the further assumptions of average annual economic growth of 2.5 per cent among the current member states and 4 per cent among the applicants the Commission concluded that the financial framework for 2000–2006 could be kept under the current ceiling of 1.27 per cent of the GDP of the member states (ibid.: 51).

For the new member states the Commission included the following figures. For CAP market measures, expenses would increase from 1.1 billion Ecu in 2002 to 1.4 in 2006. Specific rural development accompanying measures would increase from 0.6 to 2.5 billion Ecu over the same period. For those CEECs not joining in the first group, pre-accession support was set at 0.5 billion in 2000 increasing slightly to 0.6 billion in 2006 (current prices). Expenses for structural operations for new member states would increase from 3.6 billion Ecu in 2002 to 11.6 billion in 2006. Pre-accession aid for structural operations was set at 1.0 billion Ecu per year from 2000 to 2006 (1997 prices) (ibid., tables 1–4, pp. 60–3).

Agenda 2000 also suggested a new instrument of Accession Partnership to 'mobilize all forms of assistance to the applicant countries within a single framework for the implementation of national programmes to prepare them for membership of the European Union'. Accession partnerships would involve 'precise commitments on the part of the applicant country, relating in particular to democracy, macro-economic stabilization, nuclear safety and a national programme for adopting the Community *acquis* within a precise timetable, focusing on the priority areas identified in each opinion' (ibid.: 5).

The Luxembourg Summit

The differentiation proposed by the Commission between the five front runners plus Cyprus (5 + 1) and the remaining five in a second group led to a fair amount of discussion during the second part of 1997. In order to prevent certain countries from feeling excluded, Denmark and Sweden jointly submitted a proposal to the Luxembourg presidency that the EU should begin talks with all applicants in 1998 while negotiations would begin in January 1999 with the best-prepared countries. At that point negotiations could be 'extended to other applicant countries which have made adequate progress during the first phase of negotiation' (*Agence Europe*, 1 December 1997). The proposal basically tried to avoid a premature differentiation. Presumably the Scandinavians hoped that Latvia and Lithuania would have time to join Estonia in the first group.

The Luxembourg Presidency adopted the idea of a 'single starting line'. There would be, explained European Council President Jean-Claude Juncker, 'detailed negotiations with the six best prepared candidates and negotiations focusing more on efforts to be pursued with the others', and 'those making rapid progress could then enter into the more advanced type of negotiations' (*Agence Europe*, 4 December 1997).

Another issue faced by the EU was what to do with the Turkish application. On this point the French had suggested a European Conference which could include all applicants, including Turkey.

Prior to the meeting of the European Council the Foreign Ministers reached consensus on a plan which included the idea of a European Conference and joint start of negotiation with the other 11 candidates. Among the Eleven formal negotiations would start with the Six and preparatory negotiations with the Five (*Agence Europe*, 10 December 1997).

The European Council then 'decided to launch an accession process comprising the ten Central and East European applicant States and Cyprus'. The accession process would be launched on 30 March 1998 by a meeting of the foreign ministers of the Fifteen and Eleven. There would be an enhanced pre-accession strategy including accession partnerships and increased pre-accession aid. This aid would have two priority aims: the reinforcement of administrative and judicial capacity (about 30 per cent of the overall amount) and investments related to adoption and application of the acquis (about 70 per cent). Bilateral intergovernmental conferences would be convened in the spring of 1998 to begin negotiations with Cyprus, Hungary, Poland, Estonia, the Czech Republic and Slovenia. At the same time 'the preparation of negotiations with Romania, Slovakia, Latvia, Lithuania and Bulgaria will be speeded up in particular through an analytical examination of the Union acquis'. There would be a review procedure. 'From the end of 1998, the Commission will make regular reports to the Council, together with any necessary recommendations for opening bilateral intergovernmental conferences, reviewing the progress of each Central and East European applicant State towards accession in the light of the Copenhagen criteria, in particular the rate at which it is adopting the Union acquis' (*Agence Europe*, 15 December 1997).

The Luxembourg European Council characterized enlargement as a 'comprehensive, inclusive and ongoing process, which will take place in stages'.

The European Council also decided to set up 'a European Conference which will bring together the Member States of the European Union and the European States aspiring to accede to it and sharing its values and internal and external objectives':

> The members of the Conference must share a common commitment to peace, security and good neighbourliness, respect for other countries' sovereignty, the principles upon which the European Union is founded, the integrity and inviolability of external borders and the principles of international law and a commitment to the settlement of territorial disputes by peaceful means, in particular through the jurisdiction of the International Court of Justice in the Hague. (ibid.)

Initially the EU would invite the 10 CEECs, Cyprus and Turkey to take part in this European Conference. The European Council confirmed 'Turkey's eligibility for accession to the European Union', and suggested a European strategy for Turkey, including the development of the possibilities afforded by Turkey's association agreement, intensification of the Customs Union, implementation of financial co-operation, approximation of laws and adoption of the Union acquis, and participation in some EU programmes and agencies. In a section on conditions for strengthening Turkey's links with the EU, the European Council also mentioned 'the alignment of human rights standards and practices on those in force in the European Union, respect for and protection of minorities, and the establishment of satisfactory and stable relations between Greece and Turkey' (ibid.).

In the end Turkey decided not to take part in the inaugural session of the European Conference on 12 March 1998.

The Official Start of the Accession Process

The accession process formally started on 30 March 1998 with a meeting between the EU and Eleven applicants. Council President Robin Cook reminded the applicants that membership implied the full acceptance of the acquis communautaire as well as its effective application. It also implied the full acceptance of the common positions, common actions and other acts in the context of CFSP as well as common actions, common positions, conventions and other acts agreed within the framework of the Justice and Home Affairs Pillar (*Agence Europe*, 30 March 1999).

On 25 March 1998 the Commission had approved Accession Partnerships for the 10 applicant CEECs. The priorities set out in these are divided into short-term and medium-term priorities. The Commission will report regularly to the Council and the European Council on progress made in the different CEECs. Prior to the official opening of the accession process the EU had also created two new pre-accession instruments for agriculture and structural policies totalling nearly 11 billion Ecu for the period 2000–2006 (*Agence Europe*, 27 March 1998).

After the formal opening of the accession process, accession negotiations officially started with the 5+1 within the framework of six separate IGCs on 31 March (*Agence Europe*, 1 April 1999). But for the first months of the process all Eleven went through a 'screening process' which started on 3 April. The Commission had established an Enlargement Task Force, headed by Klaus van der Pas, which was in charge of screening of the six in the first group. Officials of DG IA, headed by François Lamoureux, were responsible for the other five applicants. Said Commissioner Hans van den Broek at the opening of the 'screening':

'Even if the timeframe and the arrangements of the screening process vary for the six countries already in negotiation and for the five others, you will all be participating on an equal basis' (*Agence Europe*, 8 April 1999).

Screening was what had also been called 'analytical examination' of the acquis. The purpose was to identify problems and identify legislative areas where additional efforts should be made. The technical phase of this screening started on 27 April 1999. Between 27 April and the end of September the first group finished screening of the following 13 chapters: research, telecommunications, education, culture and audiovisual policy, industrial policy, small and medium-sized enterprises, CFSP, company law, consumer protection, fisheries, statistics, the free movement of goods and external relations (*Agence Europe*, 1 October 1999).

On 10 November 1998 real negotiations started with the members of the first group on the first seven chapters that had been covered during the screening process. The main problems to be negotiated included transition periods requested for the telecommunications and culture and audiovisual chapters (*Agence Europe*, 30 October, 1999).

First Progress Reports and the Vienna Summit

On 4 November 1998 the Commission adopted progress reports on the 10 CEECs as well as Cyprus and Turkey. Although the Commission did not recommend starting negotiations with any of the Five in the second group the progress in Latvia, Lithuania and Slovakia was especially noted. At the same time the Commission issued a warning to the applicant countries in the first group which had already started negotiations. The Commission especially expressed concern about the slowdown of the adoption of the acquis in the Czech Republic and Slovenia.

A composite paper summarized the situation. In respect of the political criteria there were no new problems or setbacks. Overall, however, 'the problems of minorities continue to raise concerns'. The situation of the Roma remained problematic in many CEECs. Estonia had not yet adopted the Citizenship law that would allow stateless children to become citizens. In respect to the rule of law 'a common problem for all the candidate countries remains the inherent weakness of the judiciary' (EU 1998b: 3–4).

Looking at the economic criteria there was also progress. Concerning the existence of a functioning market economy the Commission found that the Czech Republic, Estonia, Hungary, Poland and Slovenia could be regarded as functioning market economies. Latvia and Lithuania had made 'substantial progress' and Lithuania had made 'important progress'. Bulgaria also had made 'substantial progress' but could not yet be regarded as a functioning market economy. Only Romania had not improved with respect to this criterion (ibid.: 6–7).

Concerning the second economic criterion, capacity to withstand competitive pressure and market forces within the Union, the Commission found that Hungary and Poland had continued to improve their ability and should be able to satisfy this criterion in the medium-term. Slovenia should also be able to cope with competitive pressure and market forces in the medium-term. So should the Czech Republic, 'even though it lost some ground compared with last year'. The prospects of Slovakia were good, and Estonia was in a very similar situation. Latvia had made 'great strides', and Lithuania had made 'similar strides'. Bulgaria had also made progress recently although the privatization process appeared to be slowing down. Romania's situation had deteriorated due to the government's lack of commitment to structural reforms (ibid.: 8–9).

Looking at the adoption of the acquis the Commission concluded that Hungary, Latvia and Estonia had maintained a good pace of legislative approximation. Bulgaria and Romania had stepped up their efforts, albeit from a lower base. Poland and Lithuania had a mixed record. But, the general pace of transposition had slowed significantly in Slovakia, the Czech Republic and Slovenia. In all the candidate countries progress in the competition, standards and certification and environment sectors had been limited. The area of state aids remained of particular concern (ibid.: 16).

Concerning administrative and judicial capacity to apply the acquis, Hungary had 'developed a consistent and strong track record'. Latvia, Estonia and Lithuania had made progress. But Poland, the Czech Republic and Slovenia, although starting from a relatively solid base, had 'not made significant progress since the Opinions' of 1997. The process of administrative and judicial strengthening had stalled in Slovakia, and the capacities remained weak in Bulgaria and Romania (ibid.: 18–19).

On the basis of the reports the Commission did not feel it necessary to make new recommendations 'on the conduct or extension of the negotiations'. But the Commission did highlight the particular progress of Latvia: 'If the momentum of change is maintained, it should be possible to confirm next year that Latvia meets the Copenhagen economic criteria and, before the end of 1999, to propose the opening of negotiations'. Lithuania´s 'considerable progress' was also mentioned, but additional measures were necessary before Lithuania could be said to meet the Copenhagen economic criteria. 'The new situation created in Slovakia following the elections also allows for the prospect of opening negotiations on condition that the regular stable and democratic functioning of its institutions are confirmed'. On the other hand, Romania had not made further progress since 1997, and its economic situation gave 'cause for concern'. And the slow-down in certain states which had started negotiations, in particular Slovenia and the Czech Republic, was characterized as 'worrying' (ibid.: 29).

A meeting of the General Affairs Council on 7 December 1998 examined the Commission's progress reports, welcoming these. However, the Council did not make any recommendations to the European Council to extend the accession negotiations. The Vienna European Council, 11 and 12 December 1998, endorsed this attitude (EU 1998c).

The EU's Capacity

Obviously the progress in the applicant countries is an important variable in the enlargement process. But the Copenhagen criteria also mentioned 'the Union's capacity to absorb new members' as a factor. How prepared then is the EU side?

On the policy side the questions of agricultural policy and structural policy and their budget implications were singled out as especially important. In respect to these a CAP reform was agreed in March 1999 and a new financial perspective was agreed in March 1999 during the German Presidency.

The CAP reform included reduction in base price for beef meat (20 per cent in three stages), price cuts for milk combined with specific quota increases and lower intervention prices for grains (20 per cent in two stages). Overall it did imply extra costs of about 6.9 billion Euro compared with the financial framework of 307.1 billion confirmed by the Heads of State and Government at a prior meeting at Petersberg (*Agence Europe*, 12 March 1999 and 18 March 1999).

Final agreement on all the chapters of Agenda 2000 was reached at the Berlin summit in March 1999. The CAP reform was slightly diluted by a postponement of the reform of the milk sector and a change in the reduction of the intervention price for cereals to 15 per cent. Structural policy was also an issue at the Berlin meeting. In the end the Cohesion Fund appropriation was increased from 15 billion to 18 billion Euro over the 2000–2006 budget framework period (*Agence Europe*, 27 March 1999).

It took 20 hours of difficult and sometimes acrimonious negotiations in Berlin to reach the agreement. The total expenditure for agriculture would increase from 40,920 million Euro in 2000 to 41,600 million in 2006 (1999 prices). Structural operations would be slightly reduced from 32,045 million Euro in 2000 to 29,170 million in 2006. Pre-accession aid would remain at 3,120 million Euro through the period. The budgeted amount for new members starts with 4,140 million Euro in 2002 and increases to 14,220 million in 2006. This should reduce appropriations for payments as percentage of GNP from 1.13 per cent in 2000 to 0.97 per cent in 2006 (*Financial Times*, March 27/28 1999).

The agreement was welcomed as paving the way for enlargement.

There is, however, another aspect of the EU's capacity to absorb the applicant countries which remains unsolved, viz. the institutions. If the current candidates all join we will move from a Union of 15 to a Union of 27 or more states. Can such a Union function on the basis of the current institutions, originally designed for a Community of Six? Collective action considerations suggest that decision-making becomes more difficult as the number of members increases if decision-making procedures are not improved in parallel (Laursen 1994).

The EFTA enlargement (Austria, Finland and Sweden) took place on the basis of the Maastricht Treaty, which also led to some deepening of integration. But a dispute erupted in the spring of 1994 in connection with this enlargement about the necessary redefinition of a qualified majority vote (QMV) in the enlarged EU. Among the Twelve, 23 votes (of a total of 76) could form a blocking minority in the Council of Ministers. The UK and Spain wanted to keep the blocking minority at 23 even if the total number of votes by including Austria (4 votes), Sweden (4 votes), Finland (3 votes) and Norway (3 votes) would become 90. Eventually it was agreed at a meeting of the Ministers for Foreign Affairs in Ionnina, Greece, on 26 and 27 March 1994, to increase the blocking minority to 27, on the condition that the Council would try to reach a satisfactory solution if between 23 and 26 votes opposed a proposal. Since, in the end, Norway did not join, the blocking minority among the Fifteen was set at 26 out of 87 votes (the QMV being set at 62). Before the 1995 enlargement two big countries plus one small country could form a blocking minority. This was no longer the case after the 1995 enlargement.

If existing weights were to be used for the CEECs it has been estimated that a Union of 27 members will have a total of 131 votes. Projecting the current weights, the new QMV would be 93 votes and a blocking minority vote would be 39. The 10 CEECs would have 40 votes and thus be able to constitute a blocking minority (see Table 11.4).

The question of voting in the Council was on the agenda of the 1996–97 IGC. Some of the bigger countries tried to get their number of votes increased relative to the smaller countries. There were also suggestions for a double majority, where a majority of votes would also require a majority of populations for a measure to be adopted.

In the end the Amsterdam negotiations did not solve these and other institutional issues. The Dutch presidency suggested a re-weighting of the votes in the Council, but no agreement could be reached. The Treaty has a protocol on the institutions which states that 'at the date of entry into force of the first enlargement of the Union . . . the Commission shall comprise one national of each of the Member States, provided that, by

Table 11.4   **Extrapolation of the current voting system to a union of 27 members**

	Population (millions)	Votes	
Union of 15 members	371	87	
Poland	38.5	8	
Romania	22.8	6	
Czech Republic	10.3	5	
Hungary	10.3	5	
Bulgaria	8.5	4	
Slovakia	5.3	3	
Lithuania	3.7	3	
Latvia	2.6	2	
Slovenia	2	2	
Estonia	1.5	2	
Cyprus	0.7	2	
Malta	0.4	2	
Union of 27 members	477.6	131	
Qualified majority		93	(70.99%)
Blocking minority		39	(29.77%)

Source: Commission Doc SN 612/96 (C 4).

that date, the weighting of the votes in the Council has been modified'. A second article in the protocol stipulated that 'at least one year before the membership of the European Union exceeds twenty' an IGC should be convened 'in order to carry out a comprehensive review of the provisions of the Treaties on the composition and functioning of the institutions'.

A new IGC is now foreseen in the year 2000 to try to solve the institutional issues.

Flexibility or Classic Enlargement?

There is strong pressure for enlargement towards eastern Europe. So we will get a much wider EU in the near future. The CEECs that have concluded Europe Agreements are now officially in line for membership. Slovenia and Turkey are the latest to join this group. Other former Yugoslav republics, especially Croatia, may soon join this group. Albania may also join some time in the future. On the other hand, the former Soviet republics, apart from the three Baltic countries, are not being offered association agreements, but so-called Partnership and Co-operation agreements, which do not include free trade, at least for the moment, and which are not supposed to prepare these countries for EU membership.

If 10 CEECs and Cyprus and Malta join over the next decade or so, we will move towards an EU of 27 members. Obviously such an EU will have greater diversity of interests and a greater multiplicity and complexity of problems to be solved. This is the reason why a solution of the institutional issue is necessary. Without institutional reforms we could get a wide, but weak Union. We could also get a Union with more multi-speed integration and variable geometry. We have that phenomenon already. In the current EU the UK and Denmark have the right to decide later whether they will join the third phase of EMU or not. The UK got an opt-out on social policy in the Maastricht Treaty. Ireland and Denmark are not members of the Western European Union (WEU) which is supposed to be the defence arm of the EU. Nor have Austria, Sweden and Finland joined the WEU as full members after they joined the EU. Most CEECs will probably have problems with EMU convergence criteria for many years to come.

The problems with the Maastricht Treaty and the prospective enlargement (or enlargements) has led to a discussion of various forms of flexibility in recent years: multi-speed integration, variable geometry, hard-core Europe, *à la carte* integration, etc. (CEPR 1995, Pisani-Ferry 1995, Curtin 1995, Jacquemin and Sapir 1996, Maillet 1996).

There are degrees of flexibility. The idea of two-speed integration has been accepted in connection with past enlargements in the form of transition periods, varying from a few up to 10 years. But so far new members have had to accept the *acquis communautaire*, i.e. existing rules and regulations. This has been the classical method of enlargement since the first enlargement was agreed in 1972.

The basic philosophy of the Maastricht Treaty on EMU is multi-speed. It is a question of economic capacity which will decide which states will take part in the third phase of EMU. However, the arrangements allowing the UK and Denmark to decide later whether to join or not opens the possibility of some EU members permanently staying out of EMU for political reasons. This opens the possibility of variable geometry.

The UK opt-out on social policy was the best recent example of variable geometry. It has now been closed since the UK decided to join the common social policy under the Amsterdam Treaty.

If we were to reach the point where all members freely can pick and choose what they want to take part in we will have *à la carte* integration. The Commission and most member states are strongly against *à la carte* integration but recognize that some degree of variable geometry may be necessary.

The idea of hard-core Europe, where a group of countries move ahead of the other countries, was suggested by German CDU/CSU politicians in 1994. In the text entitled 'Reflections on European Policy', signed by Karl Lamers and Wolfgang Schäuble, it was stated:

> ... the countries of the hard core must not only participate as a matter of
> course in all policy fields, but should also be recognizably more Community-
> spirited in their joint action than others, and launch common initiatives aimed
> at promoting the development of the Union. Belgium, Luxembourg and the
> Netherlands must therefore be more closely involved in Franco-German
> cooperation. . . . (Lamers 1994: 17)

A hard core can exercise leadership and the laggards can join later
when they are ready.

The same document recommended enlargement in stages. 'Poland,
the Czech and Slovak Republics, Hungary (and Slovenia) should become
Members of the European Union around the year 2000' (ibid.: 23). It is
now clear that the year 2000 was unrealistic for the first eastern
enlargement, but the idea of enlargement in stages is clearly realistic.

To avoid the dangers of *à la carte* integration it is important to reach
agreement on central policy areas where all members must participate.
There is broad agreement that these should include the internal market.
For the internal market and some flanking policies the members must
fully take part and accept the Community method, including supranational elements in decision-making. It has also been argued that
structural policies and the CAP should be included in the common policy
base, while it is not necessary to include EMU in such a base as long as
there is some macro-economic co-ordination (CEPR 1995). Within CFSP
a coalition of the willing may be sufficient, it has been suggested.

The Amsterdam Treaty has now included rules on flexibility. Indeed,
the rules are so restrictive that they will only be usable in marginal cases.
Enlargement, it seems, will still follow the classical method of requiring
full adaptation of the *acquis communautaire*. This process will create
radical changes in the EU, but it will probably take time. We should also
not rule out that this will create serious problems for the EU both in
relation to internal decision-making and failures of specific countries to
carry out the necessary changes.

CHAPTER 12

CONCLUSION:
MAKING POLICY IN THE NEW EUROPE

Svein S. Andersen and Kjell A. Eliassen

The Path of European Integration

This book is about the way policies are made in Europe. The EU represents a new type of complex, multi-level and loosely coupled decision-making and implementation system where processes often have strong elements of informal influence. It might be regarded as an experiment with new types of political structure (Laffan et al. 1999). During the 1990s, EU policy-making has increased in scope, depth and volume. This is reflected in a growing number of contributions to the study of the EU that in various ways have been pursuing such ideas (Richardson 1996, Hix 1999, Peterson and Bomberg 1999, Wallace and Wallace 2000). The introduction of the Euro, the revitalization of the CFSP, the new dynamics of the enlargement, and the increasing importance of EU citizen rights and values have created new challenges for the study of EU policy-making.

The first edition of this book was published at a time when the Maastricht Treaty was about to be implemented. At this time the internal market was almost completed. It was an unprecedented success bringing the EU and the EU agenda back onto the main stage in Europe. The completion of the Maastricht Treaty reflected the optimism created by this success, but mainly among political and business elites. However, the concept of a strengthened political integration was at first well received by the majority of voters. After the Treaty was signed by the Heads of States and Governments in December 1991, political leaders experienced, to their surprise, considerable scepticism from the public. The total lack of national parliamentary debate prior to the negotiations on the plans for a European political union caused a great deal of uncertainty in the member countries. Such problems were reflected in the narrow majority in the French referendum and the rejection of the treaty revision at the first referendum in Denmark. As it turned out, there was a lack of basic legitimacy for the elements of deeper political integration in many member countries.

The ratification and final implementation of the Maastricht Treaty took place in a political climate characterized by euro-pessimism. One issue in the political debate was the question of the role of the Commission as an activist for integration, and as a response to this the principle of subsidiarity was reactivated on the EU political agenda. Another issue concerned the lack of citizen involvement not only in the treaty negotiations, but generally within EU decision-making. A third point of discussion was whether political integration was at all feasible and desirable. Some saw the Maastricht Treaty as the delayed response to the Cold War threat, and thus not sustainable in the long run. The context for these discussions was that effects of the intensified competition in the new internal market were felt at the same time as Europe went into an economic recession. Consequently, when looking at the future of European integration in the early 1990s the prospects were uncertain and somewhat gloomy.

Many observers feared that the EU, after a period of dynamic and successful change, would slide back into a period of stagnation. In the short run a key question was whether the EU would be able to incorporate the EFTA countries. The next challenge was the new version of the old problem of deepening and widening at the same time: how to enlarge to the east without loosing the momentum created by the Maastricht Treaty. Institutional reform and the successful launching of the Euro were considered a precondition for this. The Amsterdam Treaty failed to solve the institutional issue, but the three-pillar structure was partly revised.

Most of the content of the third pillar was moved into the first pillar (asylum policy, immigration policy, combating fraud on an international scale, customs co-operation, juridical co-operation in civil matters) and in addition the Schengen agreement was incorporated within the EU's first-pillar structure. Within the second pillar the institutional structure of the CFSP was strengthened. The most important sign of the new EU dynamism was that the Euro was introduced by 1 January 1999. Subsequently, the second pillar was revitalized partly as a result of the Balkan experience and in particular the Kosovo war. All these changes had substantial implications for the everyday policy-making in the European Union and the structure of central EU institutions, the establishment of the European Central Bank, the internal reorganization of the Commission and the new institutional set-up of the home and justice affairs and the Schengen co-operation.

In the longer perspective these issues have been explored by the Forward Studies Unit of the Commission that has drawn up five scenarios for the union of 2010:

- The first scenario, *Triumphant markets*, discusses a situation where European integration primarily is driven by liberal market integration. The Union is enlarging rapidly and widely but is sliding towards a European economic area with reduction in EU budgets.

- The second scenario, *The hundred flowers*, emphasizes how new technologies allow for European societies to develop in different ways reflecting their past. As a result Europe moves towards a highly fragmented assembly of states and regions.
- The third, *Shared responsibilities*, sees the business elite as the defender of European values, initiating social reforms within new forms of partnership with authorities. The result is a Europe with shared values and social responsibilities including most of the eastern European countries.
- The fourth scenario is called *Creative societies*: Here, the political elite unable to carry out necessary reforms experiences widespread social mobilization and unrest. The result is a Europe with less wealth, but with as strong social awareness. Enlargement to the east is delayed.
- In the fifth scenario, *Turbulent neighbourhoods*, the EU experiences serious instability in its immediate surrounds, including armed conflict. Globalization slows down and there exists a growing public discontent. As a result the nation state is strengthened as a source of political legitimacy and the EU becomes more intergovernmental.

These five scenarios are not only quite different from each other; they also suggest trajectories that differ considerably from the development of the last decade. Such scenarios are not meant to predict outcomes, but rather to create more sensitivity about the factors that may shape the future of the EU. In the context of this book, it is interesting that the scenarios represent a relatively high degree of openness about future development.

Making Policy in Europe

Here we deal primarily with a selection of policy areas that exemplify a movement towards Europeanization. These sectors have different points of departure. Transport, for example, is an old EC core business, being one of the three sectors mentioned in the Treaty of Rome. Other policy areas, like energy and education, move on different tracks and at different speeds. In the telecommunications industry, national governments strongly support EU-wide liberalization and standardization. In the area of police co-operation, on the other hand, nation states have only reluctantly and painfully started a process towards increased EU co-operation, and this area was not moved to the first supranational pillar after Amsterdam.

Three of the studies in this book look at strategic sectors which are prerequisites for the effective functioning of the internal market, namely deregulation in the transport and energy sectors and liberalization in the telecommunications industry. Two studies deal with what we may call supporting sectors, although they also have an agenda of their own.

Europeanization in these sectors is necessary in order to deal with the effects of a Europe without frontiers; i.e. educational standardization and exchange programmes and common European institutions for policing and border control. Such co-operation is necessary in order to deal with open frontiers, but it also relates to the development of a common enforcement structure in the EU. The political economy of the Euro underlines the far reaching effects of this reform for the tempo and scope of future integration.

The present volume has emphasized the Europeanization of the EU as a system of supranational authority and policy-making. Our approach to Europeanization differs, however, from the international relations tradition and formal legal perspectives in emphasizing the totality of the EU-level institutions and the national political systems. Over the last decade the tendency to view national political systems as relatively closed has been less pronounced. The supranational dimension has to some degree been incorporated into studies involving actors operating across national boundaries. Still it is not uncommon to find studies of policy-making that focus on national systems as the unit of analysis, even if national systems are frequently compared.

Even in a confederal model, the EU represents a new form of supranational system, and the link to the EU which stems from each of the member states is already much more than the mere extension of foreign policy. This creates new challenges and new solutions, in a situation where the logic of economic and political integration demonstrates the need for tighter political unity in the EU system. There is a need for an open-system approach that also takes into account the complex multilevel institutional context of the EU that interacts with strong national traditions (Hix 1999, Wallace and Wallace 2000).

Our discussion of Europeanization has dealt with two major aspects. First, we have introduced a conceptual model that describes the EU as a new type of political system. A fundamental aspect of this is the tension that exists between the member states and the emerging supranational authority at the EC level. A peculiar element of the new EC system is that institutional elaboration at the central level lacks the key dimensions that are normally found when studying the formation of national European political systems. As Hix (1998) has pointed out, the dominant political cleavages in all the member states, the left–right dimension, is not represented in the central EU institutions. Also there are no European parties that can aggregate various interests across various European countries. The EU lacks a common polity, too. Even if the EU is not a state, it has increasingly acquired a number of state-like characteristics (Schmitter 1996, Olsen 1997).

There exists more supranational authority at the central EC decision-making and legislative levels, than there does at the corresponding implementation and law enforcement stages. Formulations of legally binding intentions or objectives may follow procedures for supranational decision-making. However, there is almost no unified EU administrative structure or cohesive force that can reach into member countries. Consequently, national courts will, in the future, have to rule in accordance with the extensive body of EU law and also take on the bulk of law enforcement in EU countries. As a result, the growth of the EU as a supranational system is characterized, at least in the short run, by a certain degree of 'statelessness' when compared with member countries.

Formal institutions and legislation provide a framework for policy-making, but there is considerable room for different outcomes. All formal systems have some degree of freedom in this sense. However, it seems that the loose structure combined with complexity and heterogeneity provides more room for process in determining outcomes than in national political systems. Actors bring to bear their own national styles, strategies and tactics. Consequently, we place emphasis on the different actor strategies, coalitions and dependencies; in short, on the complexity of policy-making and lobbying.

This kind of open-ended policy context can sometimes lead to processes of a confusing nature. Definitions of issues, their relationship to formal procedures and the coalitions that stand behind them, are often complex and shifting. As a result, some of these processes may lend themselves to 'garbage can' interpretations (Cohen et al. 1972, Olsen 1978). In fact Richardson (1996) characterizes the EU as 'an emerging garbage can'. However, the fact that processes may seem to be of this nature, does not mean that outcomes are equally open. On the contrary, institutional features frame and limit the search for possible outcomes. In this sense, there are strong pressures stemming from the norms of rationality in the decision-points, as well as from the more general framework of EU legislation and co-operation (Andersen and Burns 1992). This is also, as pointed out in the introductory chapter, a recurrent theme in the sectoral studies. The institutional structure of the EU provides a general direction of policy formulation, although not determining the specific outcomes.

When looking at specific policy-making areas, it is important to keep in mind the following questions:

What are the factors stimulating or blocking Europeanization? At what level do we find the driving forces? Is it a bottom-up process driven by initiatives and alliances formed at the national level? Is it a top-down process reflecting central EU initiatives, perhaps supported by fundamental changes at the global level? To what extent is policy development driven by the need to relate to other political areas?

The Europeanization of EU policy-making has three aspects:

1 the policy context
2 the policy-making processes
3 the policy output.

Let us briefly look at how the empirical studies vary with respect to these three aspects of Europeanization.

Policy Context, Process and Output

If we look at the *policy context*, we can examine the degree to which policies are institutionalized at the EU level. Is the policy area based on the EC Treaty and, if so, when was it introduced? Has a strong EU policy actually been developed in this area and, if this is the case, what is the relationship to national policies?

Some areas are defined within the Treaty of Rome and so have been established for a long time. Transport was part of the original treaty, but it is only recently that EU policy has succeeded in breaking down resistance to supranational intervention in national infrastructure development. Education, on the other hand, was only mentioned in the Treaty of Rome with regards to vocational training. Other higher educational issues were gradually institutionalized at the EC level during the 1980s, but this policy area was not defined as an EU core policy sector before the Maastricht Treaty. At the turn of the century higher education is one of the key areas of EU policy-making. Telecommunications policy was introduced in the Single European Act as an important aspect of internal market legislation. Within these areas, the member countries have increasingly supported the EU prerogative.

Policy sectors like energy and policing have up until recently mainly been based at the national level. Foreign and security policy was mainly managed within the context of NATO co-operation. Attempts to integrate such policies at the EU level have been met with strong resistance from member states and affected interests. Europeanization of energy policy has been attempted through links to internal market, environmental policy and, to some extent, foreign and security policy. Such attempts have not always been successful. Police co-operation is, even after the Amsterdam Treaty-revision, regarded as an intergovern-mental activity, even if an increased European co-ordination of national efforts was introduced. The inclusion of this sector into the first pillar represents a radical change towards supranational authority. The introduction of the Euro represents both the logical completion of the internal market and a substantial step in the European integration. The EMU is part of the first pillar, but the important decisions in this area (interest rates, money supply) are not dealt with by the traditional EU institutions. This competence is vested in the new European Central Bank. Even after the Amsterdam Treaty the CFSP functioned basically as intergovernmental co-operation. Presently, there are signs of an emerging common defence identity, but so far without any formal institutional changes.

These observations concerning the Europeanization of the policy context demonstrate the ambiguity surrounding future developments in several policy areas. It is important to see sectoral and functional policy development in relation to the overall EU institutional dynamics, but not in a neo-functionalistic sense. One should not rule out a spillover effect, but this should be regarded as something which requires special explanation and not as the driving force of the system. However, there is no doubt that there is a general interaction between economic development and belief in the need for the further progress of the EU on the one hand and the success of specific policy initiatives on the other hand. Still, in the final analysis, such convictions must be based on a minimum of democratic support for these institutions. This involves not only the ability to deliver better solutions than those offered at the national level, but also the ability to respect the principles of democratic process and subsidiarity.

What characterizes the policy-making *process* in different sectors? To what extent can we identify conflicts reflecting different interests among the member countries, or between the member countries and the central EU institutions? To what extent are interests overlapping or complementary? What kinds of alliances are possible, and through which political channels are they expressed?

Telecommunications policy enjoys a high degree of agreement among member countries regarding such issues as standardization but suffers from stiff competition concerning the national industries with regard to key projects and the future structure of this industry in Europe. From 1 January 1998 this sector was fully liberalized in all but a couple of member countries.

The police service is at the core of national state sovereignty. In accordance with this there was, until recently, a widespread agreement that the development towards EC involvement should be very gradual in this area. In the Amsterdam Treaty everybody agreed that it was impossible to run this kind of activity without a supranational structure in place.

Education represents a policy area where, at the outset, a high degree of conflict existed between the EU Commission and the member countries over the extent of EU involvement. After Amsterdam the educational sector has formally been established as an important EU policy area within the first pillar. Energy is one of the areas where there has been a strong polarization between central EU policy initiatives, on the one hand, and national interests unwilling to accept supranational authority, on the other hand. To some extent, one can say that the transport sector represents the same mercantilistic tradition as in the energy sector. The member countries have challenged the free-market ideology of the Commission. Nevertheless, in both sectors, common liberalistic EU policies have been substantially strengthened during the late 1990s.

With regard to CFSP policy, the national states have retained control over the decision-making process. As a result, there are conflicts between attempts to formulate common EU interests and more national perspectives. In recent years efforts have been made to locate more of this policy within the EU decision-making structure. Still, most key decisions in this area are left to intergovernmental decision-making mechanisms. When it comes to the Euro, most of the important decisions are made by the new European Central Bank. However, such decisions are, to a large extent, conditioned by policies made both in traditional central EU institutions and the member states. This raises two questions. One is whether the European Central Bank will be allowed such a degree of autonomy in the future. The second, which is related to this, is whether such a high degree of economic integration is sustainable without a higher degree of political integration.

What are the *policy outputs*; i.e. the kind of policies produced? To what extent do we find Europeanization in different areas? This question is perhaps the one that is most comprehensively addressed in the various chapters on policy areas.

Telecommunications is a good example of how a well-developed policy-making process is about to create a high degree of European liberalization and standardization on products and procedures in that industry. On the other hand, transport demonstrates that well-established supranational competence and decision mechanisms do not necessarily lead to a standardized output. Areas where there are difficulties in establishing a supranational policy mechanism will also have the most problems in creating European-wide results.

A variation of this is also found in the energy sector. Certain aspects of energy policy relating to increased efficiency and reduced imports of oil were carried out by all the member countries in a remarkably similar way during the 1970s and early 1980s, despite the lack of a common policy framework. For a long time attempts to link the broader issue area with a well-established internal market procedure, got stuck in the quagmire of strong and well-organized national interests. However, since the early 1990s the impact of institutionalized policies in areas like the internal market, and to some extent environmental and foreign policy, have created a push towards common policies also in the energy area.

Within the field of education, we also find during the 1990s an increased Europeanification in terms of more common policies, more European-wide educational programmes, and further standardization of curricula, degrees and diplomas. This is particularly the case in relation to higher education. In the areas of justice and police co-operation, there was until the mid-1990s very little common policy, but a gradual increase in the co-ordination of national administrative and operational activities is occurring. After the implementation of the

Amsterdam Treaty, however, a common EU policy is emerging in this area, and justice, asylum and immigration policy became first-pillar issues.

Policy areas vary with respect to Europeanization. However, this process not only leads to new types of political institutions and to the transfer of authority from the national to the supranational level, it also brings increased complexity into the relationship between the EU and its member states, and we may distinguish between three aspects of this.

One aspect of complexity concerns the linking of national traditions through a system of supranational policy-making. This widens the scope of the national policy-making process, and increases the number and types of actors to be taken into consideration. A key dimension is the relation between the national and supranational levels of authority. National traditions may vary a lot in terms of the order and predictability of the policy-making process, but at least they represent familiar settings for the actors.

The second aspect has to do with the fact that the EU is not only supra-national, but also represents new and changing forms of supranational authority. It experiments with new kinds of political authority and new ways of regulating the economy and society. Harmonization and the principle of subsidiarity, for example, open up a number of possibilities which, to a large extent, have to be clarified through international market and political processes, respectively.

The third aspect of complexity stems from the broadening of the EU. For a long time, EU policy was restricted to a few specific areas of economic and social life. The Single European Act, and in particular the Maastricht Treaty, broadens the scope and variety of policy issues which will come under the influence of the EU. In the future, almost all policy areas will have an EU dimension. This implies wider national differences and more intense conflicts which will have to be dealt with at the EU level.

The result is a new form of European governance that is multi-level, multi-centric, with unclear boundaries between factional spheres and formal institutions, and with considerable room for informal partici-pation and influence. One implication of this is the increased importance of European-wide policy networks. Another implication is the increased impact of lobbying at the central EU level. This challenges traditional mechanisms of policy co-ordination at the national level. Various interests in the member countries will be articulated independently of, and even in conflict with, those of national authorities. It follows that the nature of the EU policy-making processes may vary considerably, from a relatively high degree of order and rationality due to control by member states, to processes that may be quite disorderly. Actors are most likely to pursue rational strategies in areas where there are only a few others with similar attitudes. This normally means that the subject matter limits the decisions that can be made, from detailed questions of distribution to general technical rules. When the number of actors is high and the issue allows for complicated politics, the result may be a lack of an overall perspective and co-ordination.

The Future of European Integration

The focus of this book has been Europeanization, and the empirical studies have demonstrated varying degrees of Europeanization. When looking at specific policy areas, there is still a considerable spread in terms of how far this process has gone and what should be expected for the future. The general experience of EU development, and not least the last decade, illustrates how difficult it is to extrapolate about future developments of European integration. The recent revitalization of EU political and institutional dynamics since the mid-1990s has taken most observers by surprise. There was great uncertainty about the schedule and implementation of the Euro, and very few anticipated the strong determination of key member countries to create a strong institutional base for CFSP. The Amsterdam Treaty also opens the way for a further Europeanization based on increased majority voting and a stronger role for the European Parliament.

Presently, at the turn of the millennium, the EU has identified three major challenges: (1) enlargement, primarily to the east, (2) improvement of the balance between political and economic integration, and (3) the EU's role as a global actor.

The first major challenge concerns the enlargement towards the east and the south. This is now firmly on track, although the exact pathway for the accession process is not laid down in detail. Poland, Hungary, Estonia, Slovenia, the Czech Republic and Cyprus made up the 'first wave' countries negotiating entry. Six other countries – Bulgaria, Latvia, Lithuania, Malta, Romania and Slovakia – have also applied to join the EU. Since the Kosovo war, political pressure has grown for these countries to be admitted to the negotiating process. It now seems likely that all countries will be dealt with as one group, but based on individual merits. The Kosovo war has increased the likelihood that more countries in the Balkan region may be accepted as candidates. The great earthquake in Turkey in 1999 also stimulated the EU countries to reconsider their long-standing rejection of Turkey's candidacy.

The enlargement of the EU to the east represents the inclusion in the Union of a new type of member country. All of them are emerging market economies and democracies, but with somewhat different prospects for success. Their per capita GNPs are lower than any other new members of EU in the past, and there are also vast variations within the group. At the same time their legal and administrative structures will have great problems in handling the hundred thousand pages of EU rules and regulations to be implemented when becoming members of the EU.

The most difficult chapters in accession treaties relate to economic and monetary union, the free movement of capital, agricultural policy, free movement of persons, social and employment policies and energy policy. These issues create not only problems for the new potential member countries, but also for the old members. France will, for example, have problems with the potential free access of agricultural products from the new member countries. Germany fears the competitiveness of its industry compared with certain sectors of east European industry. Denmark worries about the impact of enlargement on the established principles for free movement of persons within the EU, particularly with regard to the large differences in welfare systems.

There are strong possibilities of a Europe composed of two or more divisions in the economic field. For some of the existing members the EMU will represent an opportunity to pursue further economic integration without, in the foreseeable future, including any of the candidate countries. Thus, it will be possible to preserve an inner core moving faster than the other members. Some, like the UK and Denmark, have opted out with regard to the EMU, but they are qualified together with Sweden, which used formal legal excuses for not joining from 1 January 1999. Greece was the only member country that did not qualify at that date. Most, if not all future member countries, will have problems of joining the EMU in the foreseeable future. It is likely that all present members of the EU will join the EMU when notes and coins are introduced on 1 January 2002. Denmark rejected EMU membership in a referendum on 29 September 2000. Due to this result, Sweden has postponed its own referendum regarding the same issue. Britain will probably not join in the forseeable future either.

The candidate countries from eastern and southern Europe need to be given what the present Commission president Romano Prodi has called a 'precise pathway' for the accession process. They have a right to know how long the process would take 'even if we don't go into the details of the dates', he said. Mr Prodi's comments signal a pragmatic approach in his relations with members; he argues that EU enlargement needed 'a political vision, not a technocratic one'. It remains to be seen whether all present member countries accept this attitude. In any case the accession treaties will most certainly contain arrangements for a transition period, which may vary considerably among countries. When the EU starts including new members from the East this may also revitalize the discussion about membership in Switzerland, Norway and Iceland. In terms of economic and political development these countries have for a long time fulfilled all criteria for membership, but for internal political reasons have refused to join.

Already the decision-making system in the EU has been under debate, and attempts to reform it have failed. The enlargement will force the EU to put such issues high on the agenda. It seems impossible that the present system will work with 25 or more member states. The ambition is to try to solve this issue before new member countries are admitted. A new IGC has been called for in the year 2000, but there is no guarantee that it will actually succeed. The three most difficult issues are: (1) the number of commissioners and the relationship between commissioners and member countries, (2) the relative weight of the votes of member countries in majority decisions in the Council, and (3) the selection and role of the EU presidency.

Several proposals to widen the agenda of the IGC have been rejected by EU governments. The issues involved are sensitive and governments are anxious to wrap up the Treaty reform talks by the end of the year 2000. There was little enthusiasm for extending the IGC's agenda on the three issues left from the Amsterdam Treaty talks and other related institutional questions. This means that suggestions to split the treaty into two parts, appoint a European public prosecutor, sign up to the European Convention on Human Rights, give the Union a 'legal personality' and extend the EU's competencies into new areas have effectively been struck off the agenda.

The second major challenge has to do with the balance between the degree of economic and political integration. There are three issues. The first issue has to do with the relationship between the EU as an economic community, on the one hand, and as a political actor, on the other hand. This primarily relates to the formal position and role of the CFSP. The EU has developed into something akin to an economic super-power, but without a comparable high degree of political co-operation and joint action on the international arena. The second issue regards the extent to which successful economic integration can legitimate the EU project. Paradoxically, it may be that economic success and transfer of authority to the central EU level will strengthen the need for alternative discourses on political legitimacy. This involves not only the role of the parliament, but also a strengthening of European polity and the need for a wider mobilization of EU citizens.

The third issue regards the relative autonomy of the Economic and Monetary Union. This has two elements. The first is the degree of independence of the European Central Bank from the central EU institutions. The second is the autonomy of macro-economic policies in member countries within the European Monetary Union in relation to the economic policy criteria of the stability pact. To preserve and adjust these balances are of crucial importance when facing future economic cycles with changing political party composition of national governments.

The third major challenge for the EU has to do with the relationship between the EU as an economic and political actor, and the rest of the world. Over the last decade we have witnessed a substantial economic liberalization inside the EU, but also at the same time a more gradual global liberalization process. The development seems to go in two directions. The first trend is a further global liberalization process, orchestrated through the new WTO round of negotiations that started in 1999. The second trend is liberalization through different types of inter-regional co-operation agreements between the EU and Asian (ASEM), African (LOME II) and Latin-American (EU-MERCOSUR) regional economic organizations, etc. The former Commission president Jacques Delors, inspired by the notion of 'the global village', had a vision of a future 'European village'. The future 'European village' would have both a varied and, at the same time, rapidly changing architectural structure. The main challenge, therefore, is to develop a framework that is capable of including all these variations. Recently, French and German lenders, in contrast, have introduced more coherent visions for greater European integration. This brings back the discussion of grand European archi-tecture involving issues of greater federalism, the need for a European constitution and/or the creation of a 'pioneer' group of states.

These considerations about the EU's challenges reflect current perceptions and agendas. They can be regarded as an extrapolation of what the EU has struggled with during the 1990s. One can not rule out that the EU will face quite different challenges and threats in the relatively near future, moving it further away from being primarily an economic community. Increasingly, citizen rights and shared civic values, in addition to increased co-operation in fields of justice and foreign and security policy, become more important. This may push the EU towards a more balanced economic and political entity. This is consistent with the perspective laid out in this book which has emphasized the complexity and the contingent and open-ended nature of the European integration process. On the other hand, recent events have also emphasized the successful, but continuous institutionalization of new forms of political structures. The EU is, in many ways, an emerging rather than an established political system.

CHRONOLOGY OF EVENTS

1947	March	Belgium, Luxembourg and the Netherlands agree to establish a customs union. An economic union is established in October 1947 and a common customs tariff is introduced in January 1948. France and the United Kingdom sign a military alliance, the Treaty of Dunkirk.
	June	General George Marshall, United States Secretary of State, offers American aid for the economic recovery of Europe.
	September	Sixteen nations join the European Recovery Programme.
1948	March	Brussels Treaty concluded between France, the UK and the Benelux countries. The aim is to promote collective defence and to improve co-operation in the economic, social and cultural fields.
	April	Founding of the Organization for European Economic Co-operation (OEEC) by sixteen states.
	May	A Congress is held in The Hague attended by many leading supporters of European co-operation and integration. It issues a resolution asserting 'that it is the urgent duty of the nation of Europe to create an economic and political union in order to assure security and social progress'.
1949	April	Treaty establishing North Atlantic Treaty Organization (NATO) signed in Washington by twelve states.
	May	Statute of Council of Europe signed in Strasbourg by ten states.
1950	May	Robert Schuman, the French Foreign Minister, puts forward his proposals to place French and German coal and steel under a common authority.
	October	Rene Pleven, the French Prime Minister, proposes a European Defence Community (EDC).
1951	April	European Coal and Steel Community (ECSC) Treaty signed in Paris by six states: Belgium, France, Germany, Italy, Luxembourg and The Netherlands.
1952	May	EDC Treaty signed in Paris by the six ECSC states.
	July	ECSC comes into operation.
1954	August	French National Assembly rejects EDC Treaty.
	October	WEU Treaty signed by the six ECSC states plus the UK.
1955	June	Messina Conference of the Foreign Ministers of the six ECSC states to discuss further European integration. The Spaak Committee established to study ways in which a fresh advance towards the building of Europe could be achieved.
1956	June	Negotiations formally open between the six with a view to creating an Economic Community and an Atomic Energy Community.
1957	**March**	**The Treaties of Rome signed, establishing the European Economic Community and the European Atomic Energy Community (Euratom).**
1958	January	EEC and Euratom come into operation.
1959	January	First EEC tariff cuts and increases in quotas.
1960	January	European Free Trade Association (EFTA) Convention signed at Stockholm by Austria, Denmark, Norway, Portugal, Sweden, Switzerland and the United Kingdom. EFTA comes into force in May 1960.
	December	Organization for Economic Co-operation and Development (OECD)

		Treaty signed in Paris. OECD replaces OEEC and included Canada and the United States.
1961	July	Signing of Association Agreement between Greece and the EEC. Comes into effect in November 1962.
	July–August	Ireland, Denmark and the United Kingdom request membership negotiations with the Community.
1962	January	Basic features of Common Agricultural Policy (CAP) agreed.
	July	Norway requests negotiations on Community membership.
1963	January	General De Gaulle announces his veto on UK membership.
		Signing of Franco-German Treaty of Friendship and Co-operation.
	July	A wide-ranging association agreement is signed between the Community and 18 underdeveloped countries in Africa – the Yaounde Convention. The Convention enters into force in June 1964.
1964	May	The GATT Kennedy Round of international tariff negotiations opens in Geneva. The Community member states participate as a single delegation.
1965	**April**	**Signing of Treaty establishing a Single Council and a single Commission of the European Communities (The Merger Treaty).**
	July	France begins a boycott of Community institutions to register its opposition to various proposed supranational developments.
1966	January	Foreign Ministers agree to the Luxembourg Compromise. Normal Community processes are resumed.
1967	May	Denmark, Ireland and the UK re-apply for Community membership.
	July	1965 Merger Treaty takes effect.
		Norway re-applies for Community membership.
	December	The Council of Ministers fails to reach agreement on the re-opening of membership negotiations with the applicant states because of continued French opposition to the UK membership.
1968	July	The Customs Union is completed. All internal customs duties and quotas are removed and the common external tariff is established.
1969	July	President Pompidou (who succeeded De Gaulle after his resignation in April) announces that he does not oppose UK membership in principle.
		Signing of the second Yaounde Convention. Enters into force in January 1971.
	December	Hague summit agrees on a number of important matters: strengthening the Community institutions; enlargement; establishing an 'economic and monetary union' by 1980; and developing political co-operation (i.e. foreign policy).
1970	April	The financial base of the Community is changed by the Decision of 21 April 1970 on the replacement of financial contributions from member states by the Community's own resources. The Community's budgetary procedures are regularized and the European Parliament's (EP's) budgetary powers are increased by the Treaty amending certain budgetary provisions of the Treaties.
	June	Preferential trade agreement signed between Community and Spain. Comes into effect in October 1970.
		Community opens membership negotiations with Denmark, Ireland, Norway and the United Kingdom.
	October	The six accept the Davignon report on political co-operation. This provides the basis for co-operation on foreign policy matters.
1972	January	Negotiations between Community and the four applicant countries concluded. Signing of Treaties of Accession.
	May	Irish approve Community accession in a referendum.

	July	Conclusion of Special Relations Agreement between Community and EFTA countries.
	September	Majority vote against Community accession in a referendum in Norway.
	October	Danes approve Community accession in a referendum. Paris summit. Heads of Government set guidelines for the future, including a reaffirmation of the goal of achieving an economic and monetary union by 1980.
1973	January	Accession of Denmark, Ireland and the United Kingdom to the Community.
		Preferential trade agreement between Community and most EFTA countries comes into effect. Agreements with other EFTA countries come into force later.
1974	December	Paris summit agrees to the principle of direct elections to the EP and to the details of a European Regional Development Fund (ERDF) (the establishment of which had been agreed at the 1972 Paris and 1973 Copenhagen summits). In addition it is agreed to institutionalize summit meetings by establishing the European Council.
1975	February	Signing of the first Lomé Convention between the Community and 46 underdeveloped countries in Africa, the Caribbean and the Pacific (the ACP countries). The Convention replaces and extends the Yaounde Convention.
	March	First meeting of the European Council at Dublin.
	June	A majority vote in favour of continued Community membership in UK referendum.
	June	Greece applies for Community membership.
	July	Signing of the Treaty amending certain financial provisions of the Treaties. This strengthens the European Parliament's budgetary powers and also establishes the Court of Auditors.
1976	July	Opening of negotiations on Greek accession to the Community.
1977	March	Portugal applies for Community membership.
	July	Spain applies for Community membership.
1978	October	Community opens accession negotiations with Portugal.
1979	February	Community opens accession negotiations with Spain.
	March	European Monetary System (EMS) (which had been the subject of high-level negotiations for over a year) comes into operation.
	May	Signing of Accession Treaty between Community and Greece.
	June	First direct elections to the European Parliament.
	October	Signing of the second Lomé Convention between the Community and 58 ACP countries.
	December	For the first time the EP does not approve the Commmunity budget. As a result the Community has to operate on the basis of 'one twelfths' from 1 January 1980.
1981	January	Accession of Greece to Community.
	October	Community foreign ministers reach agreement on the 'London Report' which strengthens and extends the European Political Co-operation (EPC).
1983	January	A Common Fisheries Policy (CFP) is agreed.
	June	At the Stuttgart European Council meeting approval is given to a 'Solemn Declaration on European Union'.
1984	January	Free trade area between Community and EFTA established.
	February	The EP approves the Draft Treaty establishing the European Union.
	June	Second set of direct elections to the EP.
		Fontainebleau European Council meeting. Agreement to reduce UK

<table>
<tr><td></td><td></td><td>budgetary contributions (which Mrs Thatcher had been demanding since 1979) and agreement also to increase Community resources by raising the VAT percentage from 1 per cent to 1.4 per cent.</td></tr>
<tr><td></td><td>December</td><td>Signing of the third Lomé Convention between the Community and 66 ACP countries.
Dublin European Council meeting agrees budgetary discipline measures.</td></tr>
<tr><td>1985</td><td>June</td><td>Signing of Accession Treaties between the Community and Spain and Portugal.
The Commission publishes its White Paper completing the Internal Market.
Milan European Council meeting approves the Commission's White Paper. It also establishes an Intergovernmental Conference to examine various matters including Treaty reform. The decision to establish the Conference is the first time at a summit meeting a decision is taken by a majority vote.</td></tr>
<tr><td></td><td>December</td><td>Luxembourg European Council meeting agrees the principles of the Single European Act (SEA). Amongst other things the Act incorporates various Treaty revisions – including confirming the objective of completing the internal market by 1992.</td></tr>
<tr><td>1986</td><td>January</td><td>Accession of Spain and Portugal to Community.</td></tr>
<tr><td>1987</td><td>June</td><td>Turkey applies for Community membership.</td></tr>
<tr><td></td><td>July</td><td>After several months delay caused by ratification problems in Ireland the SEA comes into force.</td></tr>
<tr><td>1988</td><td>June</td><td>The Community and Comecon (the East European trading bloc) sign an agreement enabling the two organizations to recognize, for the first time, the authority of the Community to negotiate on behalf of its member states.
Hanover European Council meeting entrusts to a committee chaired by Jacques Delors the task of studying how the Community might progress to Economic and Monetary Union (EMU).</td></tr>
<tr><td>1989</td><td>April</td><td>The Delors Committee presents its report (the 'Delors Report'). It outlines a scheme for a three-stage progression to EMU.</td></tr>
<tr><td></td><td>June</td><td>Third set of direct elections to the EP.
Madrid European Council meeting agrees that Stage 1 of the programme to bring about EMU will begin on 1 July 1990.</td></tr>
<tr><td></td><td>July</td><td>Austria applies for Community membership.</td></tr>
<tr><td></td><td>September–December</td><td>The collapse of Communist governments in eastern Europe. The process begins with the appointment of a non-communist Prime Minister in Poland in September and ends with the overthrow of the Ceausescu regime in Romania in December.
Signing of the fourth Lomé Convention between the Community and 68 ACP countries.
Community and USSR sign a ten-year trade and economic co-operation agreement.
Strasbourg European Council meeting accepts Social charter and agrees to establish an Intergovernmental Conference (IGC) on EMU at the end of 1990. Both decisions taken by eleven votes to one, with the United Kingdom dissenting in each case.</td></tr>
<tr><td>1990</td><td>April</td><td>Special Dublin European Council meeting confirms the Community's commitment to Political Union.</td></tr>
<tr><td></td><td>June</td><td>Dublin European Council meeting formally agrees that an IGC on Political Union will be convened.</td></tr>
<tr><td></td><td>July</td><td>Cyprus and Malta apply for Community membership.</td></tr>
</table>

	October	Unification of Germany. Territory of former East Germany becomes part of the Community.
	October	Special Rome European Council meeting agrees that Stage 1 on EMU will begin on 1 January 1994.
	December	The two IGCs on EMU and on Political Union are opened at the Rome summit.
1991	July	Sweden applies for Community membership.
	August–	Break-up of USSR.
	December	Maastricht European council meeting agrees to the Treaty on European Union (TEU). The Treaty is based on three pillars: the European Communities, a Common Foreign and Security Policy (CFSP), and Co-operation in the Fields of Justice and Home Affairs (JHA). The European Communities pillar includes the strengthening of Community institutions, the extension of the Community's legal policy competence, and a timetable leading to EMU and a single currency.
		Association ('Europe') Agreements signed with Czechoslovakia, Hungary and Poland.
1992	February	Treaty on European Union is formally signed at Maastricht by EC Foreign and Finance Ministers.
	March	Finland applies to join the EU.
	May	After several months delay caused by a Court of Justice ruling, the European Economic Area (EEA) agreement between the EC and EFTA is signed.
		Switzerland applies to join the EU.
	June	In a referendum the Danish people reject the TEU by 50.7 per cent to 49.3 per cent.
	September	Crisis in the ERM. Sterling and the lira suspend their membership.
		In a referendum the French people endorse the TEU by 51 per cent to 49 per cent.
	November	Norway applies to join the EU.
	December	In a referendum the Swiss people vote not to ratify the EEA by 50.3 per cent to 49.7 per cent. Amongst other implications this means that Switzerland's application to join the EU is suspended.
		Edinburgh European Council meeting agrees on several key issues, notably: (1) Danish opt-outs from the TEU and any future common defence policy; (2) a financial perspective for 1993–9; (3) the opening of accession negotiations in early 1993 with Austria, Finland, Sweden and Norway.
1993	February	Accession negotiations open with Austria, Finland and Sweden.
	April	Accession negotiations open with Norway.
	May	In a second referendum the Danish people vote by 56.8 per cent to 43.2 per cent to ratify the TEU.
	August	Following great turbulence in the currency markets, the bands for all currencies in the ERM, apart from the Deutsche mark and the guilder, are increased to 15 per cent.
	October	German Constitutional Court ruling enables Germany to become the last member state to ratify the TEU.
	November	TEU enters into force.
	December	Settlement of the GATT Uruguay Round.
1994	January	Second stage of EMU comes into effect.
		EEA enters into force.
	March	Committee of the Regions meets for the first time.

		Austria, Finland, Sweden and Norway agree accession terms with the EU.
	April	Hungary and Poland apply for membership in the EU.
	June	Fourth set of direct elections to the EP.

Austria, Finland, Sweden and Norway agree accession terms with the EU.

April Hungary and Poland apply for membership in the EU.

June Fourth set of direct elections to the EP.

In a referendum on accession to the EU, Austrian people vote in favour by 66.4 per cent to 33.6 per cent.

Partnership and co-operation agreement between European Union and Ukraine is signed in Luxembourg.

Acts of Accession of Austria, Sweden, Finland and Norway are signed.

July Extraordinary meeting of European Council in Brussels: Jacques Santer, chosen to succeed Jacques Delors as President of Commission.

Free-trade agreements signed with Estonia, Latvia and Lithuania in Brussels.

New European Parliament holds first part-session in Strasbourg. Klaus Hänsch is elected President.

October Co-operation agreement between Community and South Africa is signed. Conference on Security and Co-operation in Europe (CSCE) opens in Budapest.

Finnish referendum approves accession to the European Union.

November Swedish referendum approves accession to European Union.

European Monetary Institute Council meets for the first time in Frankfurt.

Norwegian referendum rejects accession to the European Union.

Parliament, Council and Commission adopt financial perspective 1995–99 adjusted to take account of enlargement.

Council adopts first joint action under Article K.3 of Treaty on European Union in the area of co-operation in the fields of Justice and Home Affairs.

December Council adopts Leonardo da Vinci Programme in vocational training and first resolution under Social Policy Protocol.

Treaty on European Energy Charter signed in Lisbon.

1995 January Austria, Finland and Sweden become members of the European Union.

February The Europe Association Agreements establishing an association between the European Union and Bulgaria, Romania, the Slovak Republic and the Czech Republic enter into force.

G7 ministerial Conference on Information Society meets in Brussels.

March Council and Parliament sign Socrates Programme in the field of education.

Stability Pact signed at final Conference in Paris.

The Schengen Agreement comes into force between Belgium, France, Germany, Luxembourg, the Netherlands, Portugal and Spain.

April Liechtenstein approves the participation in the European Economic Area.

Intergovernmental Conference: Council adopts a report on the functioning of the Treaty on European Union.

Intergovernmental Conference: Committee of Regions adopts an own-initiative opinion on the revision of the Treaty on European Union.

Austria signs the Schengen Treaty.

May Liechtenstein participates in the European Economic Area.

The Commission approves the Info 2000 programme to stimulate the development of a European multimedia content industry in the emerging information society.

	The Commission adopts a Green Paper on the practical arrangements for the introduction of the single currency.
June	The Reflection Group set up to prepare for the 1996 Intergovernmental Conference holds its inaugural meeting.
	Europe Agreements are signed with Estonia, Latvia and Lithuania. Romania and Slovakia present applications to join the European Union.
	The meeting of Heads of State or Government held in Cannes is the first at which all 15 Member States are represented. This European Council confirms transition to a single currency by 1 January 1999.
July	The European Parliament appoints Jacob Söderman as Ombudsman of the European Union.
	The Member States sign the Europol Convention for police co-operation.
October	Latvia presents a formal request for accession to the European Union.
November	A Co-operation Agreement is signed with Nepal. The Euro-Mediterranean Association Agreement is signed with Israel.
	The Euro-Mediterranean Conference is held in Barcelona.
	Estonia applies to join the European Union.
December	Madrid European Council sets 29 March 1996 as starting date for Intergovernmental Conference and confirms the introduction of single currency ('Euro') on 1 January 1999.
	Custom Union between European Community and Turkey enters into force.
1996 January	Italy takes over the Presidency of the Council of the European Union.
	Customs Union between EU and Turkey enters into force.
	The Czech Republic formally applies to join the European Union.
	The Commission adopts a Green Paper on review of Merger Control Regulation.
February	The interim agreements with Russia and Ukraine enter into force.
	A Euro-Mediterranean association agreement is signed with Morocco.
March	The Commission adopts a decision on urgent measures to be taken for protection against BSE (bovine spongiform encephalopathy). It imposes a world-wide export ban on British beef and beef products.
	The opening of the Intergovernmental Conference to revise the Maastricht Treaty is held in Turin, Italy. The European Council defines its agenda.
April	A G7 conference on employment is held in Lille, France.
	A G7+1 meeting on nuclear safety is held in Moscow, Russia.
	The European Union signs partnership and co-operation agreements with Georgia, Armenia and Azerbaijan.
May	The Commission adopts a Green Paper on commercial communications in the single market.
	The European Court of Justice affirms that a member state violating Community law by refusing to issue an export licence to a private individual must pay compensation.
June	The co-operation agreements with Vietnam and Nepal enter into force.
	Slovenia formally applies to join the European Union.
	A tripartite conference on Growth and Employment involving the Community institutions, the member states and the social partners is held in Rome, Italy.
	The co-operation agreements with Uzbekistan and Chile are signed.

		The European Council is held in Florence, Italy.
	July	Ireland takes over the Presidency of the Council of the European Union
	October	The Commission adopts a Green Paper entitled 'Education, training and research: the obstacles to trans-national mobility'.
	November	The Commission adopts three Green Papers on the relations between the European Union and the ACP states, a numbering policy for telecommunication services, and a Community strategy for developing renewable energies.
	December	At the London Conference centred on implementing peace agreements in Former Yugoslavia, a plan to consolidate peace is adopted.
		A European Council is held in Dublin, Ireland. It adopts the Dublin declaration on employment and confirms the timetable for the Intergovernmental Conference (IGC).
		A Transatlantic Summit between the European Union and the USA is held in Washington, USA.
		Denmark, Finland and Sweden sign the Schengen Agreement.
1997	January	The Netherlands takes over the Presidency of the Council of the European Union. The Commission adopts a Green Paper on vertical restraints in the EC competition policy.
	February	An agreement is reached on basic telecommunications services within the World Trade Organization (WTO) framework.
		The Parliament adopts a resolution on results of temporary committee of inquiry into BSE.
	March	The parties involved in the Commercial agreement on information technology products within the WTO framework draw up the definitive list of their commitments.
	April	The Commission adopts the Green Paper titled 'Partnership for a new organization of work'.
	May	The Commission adopts its 1997–98 anti-fraud work programme.
		The Council establishes a convention on the service of judicial and extra-judicial documents in civil or commercial matters. The Council establishes a convention on the fight against corruption involving officials.
	June	The Council adopts a regulation establishing a European Monitoring Centre on Racism and Xenophobia.
		The European Council meets in Amsterdam and reaches a consensus on a draft Treaty. It approves various proposals facilitating the smooth passage to the third phase of the Economic and Monetary Union and adopts a resolution on growth and employment.
	July	Luxembourg takes over the Presidency of the Council of the European Union.
		The Commission presents the 'Agenda 2000 – for a stronger and wider Europe' and its opinions on the applications of 10 central European countries.
		The Western European Union (WEU) Extra-ordinary Council adopts a declaration, to be annexed to the final Act of the Amsterdam Treaty, on its role and its relations with the EU and the Atlantic Alliance.
	October	The Ministers for Foreign Affairs of the Member States of the European Union sign the Treaty of Amsterdam.
		The Commission adopts the final report to the Parliament's temporary committee of inquiry monitoring recommendations on BSE.

	December	The Commission adopts a Green Paper on convergence in the communications, media and information technology sectors.
		The Council agrees to ban tobacco advertising.
		An agreement is reached on financial services within the WTO framework.
		The European Council meets in Luxembourg and takes the decisions needed to launch the enlargement process. It also adopts a resolution on economic policy co-ordination.
1998	January	The United Kingdom takes over the Presidency of the Council of the European Union.
		The Co-operation agreement with the Former Yugoslav Republic of Macedonia enters into force.
	February	The Europe Agreements with Estonia, Latvia and Lithuania enter into force.
	March	The Commission adopts the convergence report and recommends that 11 member states adopt the Euro on 1 January 1999.
		A Ministerial meeting launches accession processes for the 10 central and eastern European applicant countries and Cyprus.
	April	The Kyoto Protocol on climate change is signed in New York, USA.
	May	A special Council decides that 11 member states satisfy conditions for adoption of the single currency on 1 January 1999. The Commission and the European Monetary Institute set out conditions for determination of the irrevocable conversion rates for the Euro.
	June	Establishment of the European Central Bank. An agreement amending the fourth Lomé Convention following mid-term review, including new financial protocol and the protocol governing accession of South Africa to the Convention, enters into force.
	July	Austria takes over the Presidency of the Council of the European Union.
	October	The Europol Anti-drugs Convention enters into force.
	November	Ministerial-level meetings of accession conferences with Cyprus, Poland, Estonia, the Czech Republic and Slovenia.
	December	A European Council meeting is held in Vienna, Austria. The Council adopts the employment guidelines for 1999, decides to strengthen the process of convergence of employment policies with a view to a European employment pact, lays down arrangements for external representation of the Euro, approves an action plan for the establishment of an area of freedom, security and justice and agrees on a strategy for Union work in 1999.
		The Council adopts fixed and irrevocable conversion rates between the national currencies of 11 participating Member States and the Euro.
1999	January	Germany takes over the Presidency of the Council of the European Union.
		The Euro is officially launched. Austria, Belgium, Finland, France, Germany, Ireland, Italy, Luxembourg, The Netherlands, Portugal and Spain adopt the Euro as their official currency.
		Jacques Santer, President of the European Commission, calls for Parliament's confidence.
	February	The Agreement between the European Communities and Slovenia enters into force.
	March	The European Commission publishes the codes of conduct for Members of the Commission and the relations between Commissioners and Commission departments.

	Collective resignation of the Commission in wake of the report by the Committee of Independent Experts on the allegations regarding fraud, mismanagement and nepotism in the Commission.
	European Council declaration on the appointment of Mr Romano Prodi, new President of the Commission.
	A special European Council is held in Berlin, Germany. An overall agreement on Agenda 2000 is reached; Mr Prodi is asked to accept the task of being the President of the next European Commission and two statements on Kosovo are adopted.
April	The Council approves a joint action providing support for the reception and voluntary repatriation of refugees, displaced persons and asylum seekers, including those who have fled from Kosovo.
May	The Amsterdam Treaty enters into force.
	The Parliament approves the nomination of Mr Romano Prodi as President of the Commission.
June	The European Council meeting is held in Cologne, Germany. It adopts the first European Union common strategy, which concerns Russia, and declarations on Kosovo and on the strengthening of European common foreign and security policy, and designates Mr Javier Solana Madariaga High Representative for the CFSP and Secretary-General of the Council. It also adopts the European Employment Pact, sets out the brief of the forthcoming intergovernmental conference and decides to lay down an EU Charter of Fundamental Rights.
	The EU–US summit takes place in Bonn, Germany. The EU and the US undertake in a joint statement to strengthen their partnership under the New Transatlantic Agenda and, in particular, to work together to prevent and resolve international crises. They stress the importance of gradually establishing a common European security and defence policy.
July	Finland takes over the Presidency of the Council of the European Union.
	The new European Parliament elects Nicole Fontaine as its President.
September	The European Parliament votes and approves the new Commission.
October	A special European Council is held in Tampere, Finland. An agreement is reached on a number of guidelines and political priorities, in particular relating to the right of asylum, immigration, and access to justice and combating crime.
November	A WTO meeting on the Millennium Round is held in Seattle, USA. Supposed to launch a new round of trade talks, it finishes with the participants unable to reach an agreement.
December	A European Council is held in Helsinki, Finland. It decides to open accession negotiations with Romania, Slovakia, Latvia, Lithuania, Bulgaria and Malta and to recognize Turkey as an applicant country. It agrees to call an Intergovernmental Conference to revise the Treaties in February 2000.

Note

March 1947–June 1994 taken from Neil Nugent, *The Government and Politics of the European Union*, 1994, Macmillan, reproduced with permission of Palgrave.

BIBLIOGRAPHY

Adams, C.F., Jr (1893) *Railroads: Their Origins and Problems*. Revised edition. New York: Putnam.

Agence France Presse (1991) 'French win 5.8 billion dollar contract for high speed train', 29 May.

Ahnfelt, E. and From, J. (1996) *Politisamarbeid og europeisk integrasjon*. Oslo: Ad Notam Gyldendal.

Alesina, A. (1998) *Corriere della Sera*, 24 May.

Alesina, A. and Perotti, R. (1996) *Budget Deficits and Budget Institutions*. NBER Working Paper 5556.

Alexander, E.R. (1989) 'Improbable implementation: the Pressman-Wildavsky paradox revisited', *Journal of Public Policy*, 4: 451–65.

Alexander, V. and Anker, P. (1997) 'Fiscal discipline and the question of convergence of national rates in the European Union', *Open Economies Review*, 2: 335–49.

Allen, D. (1998) 'Who speaks for Europe?: the search for an effective and coherent external policy', in John Peterson and Helene Sjursen (eds), *A Common Foreign Policy for Europe? Competing Visions of the CFSP*. London: Routledge. pp. 41–58.

Allen, D. and Smith, M. (1990) 'Western Europe's presence in the contemporary international arena', *Review of International Studies*, 16 (1): 19–37. Reprinted in Holland, M. (ed.) (1991) *The Future of European Political Cooperation*. London: Macmillan. pp. 95–120.

Andersen, C. (1996) 'European Union policy-making and national institutions – the case of Belgium', in S.S. Andersen and K.A. Eliassen (eds), *The European Union, How Democratic is it?* London: Sage. pp. 83–100.

Andersen, S.S. (1992) 'The power of policy paradigms', Working Paper: Norwegian School of Management, Oslo.

Andersen, S.S. (1993) *The Struggle over North Sea Oil and Gas. Government Strategies in Denmark, Britain and Norway*. Oslo: Scandinavian University Press.

Andersen, S.S. (1995) *Europeisering av politikk. Petroleum, indre marked og miljø*. Oslo: Fagbokforlaget.

Andersen, S.S. (1997a) *Case-studier og generalisering*. Oslo: Fagbokforlaget.

Andersen, S.S. (1997b) 'East of markets – west of states. The negotiations over the Energy Charter Treaty'. Working Paper, Norwegian School of Management.

Andersen, S.S. (1999) 'Hvordan er EU mulig? et ny-insitusjonelt sosiologisk perspektiv'. ARENA Advanced Research on the Europeanization of the Nation State.

Andersen, S.S. and Burns, T.R. (1992) *Societal Decision-Making. Democratic Challenges to State Technocracy*. Aldershot: Dartmouth.

Andersen, S.S. and Burns, T.R. (1996) 'The European Union and the erosion of parliamentary democracy: A study of post-parliamentary governance', in S.S. Andersen and K.A. Eliassen (eds), *European Union: How Democratic is it?* London: Sage. pp. 227–52.

Andersen, S.S. and Eliassen, K.A. (1991) 'European Community lobbying', *European Journal of Political Research*, 20: 173–87.

Andersen, S.S. and Eliassen, K.A. (1992) 'EF lobbying etter Maastricht', *Sosiologi idag* no. 2.

Andersen, S.S. and Eliassen, K.A. (1993a) 'Complex policy-making: lobbying the EC', in S.S. Andersen and K.A. Eliassen (eds), *Making Policy in Europe*. London: Sage. pp. 35–53.

Andersen, S.S. and Eliassen, K.A. (eds) (1993b) *Making Policy in Europe*. London: Sage.

Andersen, S.S. and Eliassen, K.A. (1993c) 'The EU as a new political system', in S.S. Andersen and K.A. Eliassen (eds), *Making Policy in Europe*. London: Sage. pp. 3–18.

Andersen, S.S. and Eliassen, K.A. (1995) 'EU-lobbying – the new research agenda', *European Journal of Political Research*, 27 (4): 427–41.

Andersen, S.S. and Eliassen, K.A. (1996) *The European Union: How Democratic is it?* London: Sage.

Andersen, S.S. and Eliassen, K.A. (1998) 'EU-lobbying – towards political segmentation in the European Union', in P.H. Clayes, C. Gobin, I. Smets and P. Winands (eds), *Lobbying, Pluralism and European Integration*. Brussels: European Interuniversity Press. pp. 167–82.

Andersen, S.S., Eliassen, K.A., Kuvaas, B. and From, J. (1991) 'Norsk implementering av EØS-regler-Hva kan vi lære av Danrnark?', Handelshøyskolen BI. Arbeidsnotat 1991/46. (Rapport 1991–316–12) Senter for Europeiske studier.

Andersen, S.S. and Midttun, A. (1989) *The Articulation of Capital-Interests in Norway: Embeddedness and the Organization of Capital*. Bærum: Norwegian School of Management.

Anderson, B. (1991) *Imagined Communities* (revised edition). London: Verso.

Anderson, C.W. (1977) 'Political design and the representation of interests', *Comparative Political Studies*, 10 (1): 127–51.

Anderson, M. (1989) *Policing the World: Interpol and the Politics of International Police Co-operation*. New York: Oxford University Press.

Anderson, M. (1992) 'The agenda for European police cooperation'. ECPR, Joint Sessions of Workshops, Limerick 30 March–4 April 1992.

Andresen, K. and Sjøvaag, M. (1997) 'Interconnection – an issue on the European Regulatory Agenda. The situation in France, Germany and Britain'. BI Working Paper, Seas: T: 03.97.

Archer, C. and Butler, F. (1992) *The European Community: Structure and Process*. New York: St Martin's Press.

ART (1999) *Rapport public d'activité 1998*. Paris.

Aspinwall, D.M. and Schneider, G. (1998) *The Institutionalist Turn in Political Science and the Study of European Integration*. Unpublished.

Austvik, O.G. (1991) 'Norwegian gas in the new Europe', in O.G. Austvik (ed.), *Norwegian Gas in the New Europe*. Sandvika: Vett og viten. pp. 1–19.

Austvik, O.G. (1996a) 'Pricing of European gas: effects of liberalization and petroleum excise taxes'. Working paper. Lillehammer Høgsholen, Nr 6/1996.

Austvik, O.G. (1996b) Liberalization of the European gas market: the workings of invisible and visible hands. Working paper. Lillehammer, Nr 31/1996.

Austvik, O.G. (1997) 'Petroleum taxation and the prices of oil and gas: perspectives from the supply side'. Working paper. Norwegian School of Management, Nr 4/1997.

Axelrod, R. (1984) *The Evolution of Cooperation*. New York: Basic Books.

Axelrod, R. and Keohane, R. (1985) 'Achieving cooperation under anarchy: strategies and institutions', *World Politics*, V. 38: 226–54.

Azzi, G.C. (1988) 'What is this new research into the implementation of Community legislation bringing us?', in H. Siedentopf and J. Ziller (eds), *Making European Policies Work*. Vol. I: *Comparative Syntheses*. Brussels and London: EIPA/Sage. pp. 190–201.

Babarinde, O.A. (1995) 'The Lomé Convention: an aging dinosaur in the European Union's foreign policy enterprise?', in C. Rhodes and S. Mazey (eds), *The State of the European Union*. Vol. 3: *Building a European policy?* Boulder, CO: Lynne Rienner Publisher. pp. 469–96.

Baldwin, R.E. (1994) *Towards an Integrated Europe*. London: Centre for Economic Policy Research.

Barry, B. (1975) 'Political Accommodation and Consociational Democracy', *British Journal of Political Science*, (5): 477–505.

Bartholomew, M. and Brooks, T. (1989) 'Lobbying Brussels to get what you need for 1992', *Wall Street Journal*, 31 January: 7.

Bartolini, S. (1997) 'Exit options, boundary building, political structuring'. Florence. EUI-Working Paper No x.

Bayoumi, T., Goldstein, M. and Woglom, G. (1995) 'Do credit markets discipline sovereign borrowers? Evidence from U.S. states', *Journal of Money, Credit, and Banking*, 27 (4): 1046–53.

Bayoumi, T., Eichengreen, B. and Von Hagen, J. (1997) 'European monetary unification: implications of research for policy, implications of policy for research', *Open Economies Review*, 8: 71–91.

Beck, U. (1997) 'The reinvention of politics: towards a theory of reflexive modernization', in U. Beck, A. Giddens and S. Lash (eds), *Reflexive Modernization: Politics, Tradition and Aesthetics in the Modern Social Order*. Oxford: Blackwell. pp. 1–56.

Beck, U. (1999) 'To whom belongs Europe', *European Journal of Social Quality*, (1).

Beck, W., van der Maesen, L. and Walker, A. (eds) (1997) *The Social Quality of Europe*. The Hague/Boston: Kluwer Law International. pp. 191–202.

Beer, P. de (1991) 'La visite de M. Michel Rocard en Corse du sud L'incontourriable dossier du TGV', *Le Monde*, 4 May.

Beltran, A. (1993) 'The French National Railways (SNCF) and the development of high speed trains, 1950–1981', in S. Hultén, T. Flink and J. Whitelegg (eds), *High Speed Trains: Fast Tracks to the Future*. London: Leading Edge. pp. 30–8.

Benner, D. and Lenzen, D. (eds) (1996) *Education for the New Europe*. Oxford: Berghan Books.

Benyon, J. (1992) *Police Co-operation in Europe*. University of Leicester: Centre for the Study of Public Order.

Bergesen, H.O. (1991) *Symbol or Substance. The Climate Policy of the European Community*. Oslo: Fridtjof Nansen Institute.

Beukel, E. (1992) *Uddannelsespolitik i EF. Nye mønstre i Europæisk integration*. Odense: Odense Universitetsforlag.

Beukel, E. (1994) 'Reconstructing integration theory: the case of educational policy in the EC', *Cooperation and Conflict*, 29 (1): 33–54.

Bigo, D. (1992) 'The European internal security field'. ECPR Joint Sessions, Limerick.

Birenbaum, P. (1985) 'Political strategies of regulated organizations as functions of context and fear', *Strategic Management Journal*, (4): 135–50.

Bisignano, J. (1996) 'Varieties of monetary policy operating procedures: balancing monetary objectives with market efficiency', July Bank for International Settlements, Basle.

Black, D. (1990) 'European rail renaissance could leave Britain isolated; Government reluctance to help finance a high-speed link to the Channel tunnel may undermine the benefits of the single market', *The Independent*, 13 June: 2.

Black, D. (1991a) 'High-speed rail plan for Europe socially divisive', *The Independent*, 22 November: 8.

Black, D. (1991b) 'Tracks to nowhere: The Government believes that privatisation is the cure for the ills of British Rail. The rest of the world disagrees', *The Independent*, 6 October: 19.

Blackman, C.R. (1998) 'Convergence between telecommunications and other media', *Telecommunications Policy*, 22 (3): 163–70.

Boer, M. den (1991) 'Schengen: intergovernmental scenario for European police cooperation', Working Paper, University of Edinburgh, Department of Politics.

Bohn, H.R. and Inman, R.P. (1996) 'Balanced budget rules and public deficits: evidence from the U.S. states', NBER Working Paper No. 5533. Cambridge, Mass.

Boltanski, L. and Thevenot, L. (1991) *De la Justification: Les Economies de la Grandeur.* Paris: Gallimard.

Boston Globe (1988) 'Florida unveils 4 plans for a high-speed train', 29 March: 38.

Boyer, R. (1996) 'The convergence hypothesis revisited: globalization, but still the century of nations?', in S. Berger and R. Dore (eds), *National Diversity and Global Capitalism.* Ithaca, NY: Cornell University Press.

Bradshaw, J. (1991) 'Institutional reform in the European Community beyond Maastricht', *EIU European Trends*, 4.

Brickman, R., Jasanoff, S. and Ilgen, T. (1985) *Controlling Chemicals. The Politics of Regulation in Europe and the United States.* Ithaca, NY: Cornell University Press.

Broadman, H.G and Balassa, C. (1993) 'Liberalizing international trade in telecommunications services', *The Columbia Journal of World Business*, Winter.

Brociner, A. and Levine, P. (1991) 'Fiscal policy co-ordination and E.M.U., a dynamic game approach'. The Centre for European Economic Studies.

Brociner, A. and Levine, P. (1993) 'EMU: a survey'. The Centre for European Economic Studies.

Brock, C. and Tulasiewicz, W. (eds) (1994) *Education in a Single Europe.* London and New York: Routledge.

Brodeur, J.P. (1983) 'High policing and low policing: remarks about the policing of political activities', *Social Problems*, 30 (5): 507–20.

Bromberg, Elizabeth (1992) 'European Community environmental policy: the role of the European Parliament', Eighth Annual Conference of Europeanists, Chicago.

Brunsson, N. (1989) *The Organization of Hypocrisy: Talk, Decisions and Actions in Organizations.* New York: John Wiley.

Bråten, S. (1971) *Mass-och MissKommunikation: Kontakteu Mellan Mænniskor Och Media.* Stockholm: Beckmans.

Buchanan, J.N., Burton, J. and Wagner, R.E. (1978) *The Consequences of Mr Keynes.* The Institute of Economic Affairs, Hobart Paper, London.

Budd, S. and Jones, A. (1989) *The European Community, A Guide to the Maze.* London: Kogan Page.

Buksti, J.A. (1980) 'Corporate structures in Danish EC policy: patterns or organisational participation and adaptation', *Journal of Common Market Studies*, XIX: 140–59.

Buksti, J.A. and Johansen, L.N. (1979) 'Variations in organizational participation in government: the case of Denmark', *Scandinavian Political Studies*, (2): 197–220.

Buksti, J.A. and Martens, H. (1984) *Interesseorganisationer i EF.* Aarhus: Institut for Statskundskab.

Bull, H. (1982) 'Civilian power Europe: a contradiction in terms?', *Journal of Common Market Studies*, 21 (2–3): 149–70.

Bulmer, S. (1993) 'The governance of the European Union: a new institutionalist approach', *Journal of Public Policy*, 13 (4): 351–80.

Bulmer, S.J. (1998) 'New institutionalism and the governance of the Single European Market', *Journal of European Public Policy*, 5 (3): 365–86.

Buzan, B., Kelstrup, M., Lemaitre, P., Tromer, E. and Wæver, O. (1990) *The European Security Order Recast. Scenarios for the Post-Cold War Era*. London and New York: Frances Pinter.

Cahen, A. (1989) *The Western European Union and NATO*. London: Brassey's (UK).

Calingaert, M. (1993) 'Government business relations in the European Community', *California Management Review*, Winter: 118–33.

Callovi, G. (1992) 'Regulation of immigration in 1993: pieces of the European Community jig-saw puzzle', *International Migration Review*, 26: 353–72.

Cameron, E. (1991) *The European Reformation*. Oxford: Clarendon Press.

Cameron, F. (1998) 'Building a common foreign policy: do institutions matter?', in John Peterson and Helene Sjursen (eds), *A Common Foreign Policy for Europe? Competing Visions of the CFSP*. London: Routledge. pp. 59–76.

Campanella, M.L. (1995) 'Getting the core: a neo-institutionalist approach to EMU', *Government and Opposition*, 30: 347–73.

Campanella, M.L. (1996) 'Central Bank independence and European Central Banking institution-building', *Journal of Public Finance and Public Choice*, 1: 57–97.

Campanella, M.L. (1998) 'EU fiscal discipline after 1999: the Pact of Stability', *ECSA Newsletter*, fall issue, Pittsburgh.

Campbell, J.L. (1994) 'Recent trends in institutional analysis: bringing culture back in'. Working Paper, Harvard University, Department of Sociology.

Campbell, J.L. (1998) 'Institutional analysis and the role of ideas in political economy', *Theory and Society*, 27: 377–409.

Campbell, J.L., Hollingsworth, J.R. and Lindberg, L.N. (eds) (1991) *Governance of the American Economy*. New York: Cambridge University Press.

Capouet, Y. (1992) 'Completion of the internal market for electricity and gas', *Energy in Europe*, 19: 9–13.

Cendrowicz, M. (1991) 'The European Community's relationship with Turkey: looking backwards, looking forwards'. Paper presented at Marmaris Conference, June.

CEPR (1995) 'Flexible integration: towards a more effective and democratic Europe', Monitoring European Integration 6. London: Centre for Economic Policy Research.

CERT (1993) *Proposal on the Commission's Proposal for a Council Directive Concerning Common Rules for the Internal Market in Natural Gas*. European Parliament.

Chandler, A.D., Jr (1977) *The Visible Hand: The Managerial Revolution in American Business*. Cambridge, MA: Harvard University Press.

Checkel, J. (1998) 'Social construction and integration'. University of Oslo: ARENA Working Paper 14/ 1998.

Christiansen, T. (1996) 'A maturing bureaucracy? The role of the Commission in the policy process', in J. Richardson (ed.), *European Union: Power and Policy-Making*. London: Routledge. pp. 77–95.

Chryssochoou, D.N. (1996) 'Europe's could-be demos: recasting the debate', *West European Politics*, 91: 787–801.

Chryssochoou, D.N. (1997) 'New challenges to the study of European integration: implications for theory-building', *Journal of Common Market Studies*, 35 (4): 521–42.

Cini, M. (1996) *The European Commission: Leadership, Organisation and Culture in the EU Administration*. Manchester: Manchester University Press.

Cini M. (1997) 'Administrative culture in the European Commission: the cases of competition and environment', in N. Nugent (ed.), *At the Heart of the Union: Studies of the European Commission*. London: Macmillan.

Claeys, P.-H., Gobin, C., Smets, I. and Winand, P. (eds) (1998) *La Cité Européene No. 16*. Bruxelles: Libre de Bruxelles.

Clements, B. (1998) 'The impact of convergence on regulatory policy in Europe', *Telecommunications Policy*, 22 (3): 197–205.

Close, G. (1978) 'Harmonization of laws: use or abuse of the powers under the EEC Treaty', *European Law Review*, 3: 461–68.

Coen, D. (1998) 'The European business interest and the nation state: large-firm lobbying in the European Union and member states,' *Journal of Public Policy*, 18: 75–100.

Coffey, P. (1990) *Main Economic Policy Areas of the ECC toward 1992: The Challenge to the Community's Economic Policies when the 'Real' Common Market is Created by the End of 1992*. Dørdrecht: Kluwer Academic Press.

Cohen, M.D., March, L.G. and Olsen, L.P. (1972) 'A garbage-can model of organizational choice', *Administrative Science Quarterly*, 17: 1–25.

Colchester, N. and Buchan, D. (1990) *Europe Relaunched – Truths and Illusions on the Way to 1992*. London: Hutchinson/Economist Books.

COM (88) 174: *Review of Member States' Energy Policies*.

COM (92) 226: *Proposed EC Directive on Taxation of CO_2 Emissions and Energy*.

Comité des Regions (1997) *Final Declaration of the European Summit of the Regions and Cities in Amsterdam, May 1997*. Brussels: Comité des Regions.

Commissariat Général du Plan (1999) *L'élargissement de l'Union européenne à l'est de l'Europe: des gains à escompter à l'Est et à l'Ouest*. Paris: La Documentation Française.

The Commission (1990) *Environmental Policy in the European Community*. Brussels: The European Community.

Committee for the Study of Economic and Monetary Union (1989) *Report on Economic and Monetary Union in the European Community*. Luxembourg: Office for Official Publications of the EC.

Conference Européenne des Ministres des Transports (CEMT) (1990) 'Investissements Publics et Privés dans le Secteur des Transports: Table Ronde 81'. Paris: OCDE.

Conference Européenne des Ministres des Transports (CEMT) (1992) 'Trains à Grande Vitesse: Table Ronde 87'. Paris: OCDE.

Conference of the Representatives of the Member States (1997) *Consolidated Version of the Treaty on European Union*. Contents, CONF 4007/97 ADD 1, Brussels, 6 October 1997.

Conference on Security and Co-operation in Europe (1991) 'Charter of Paris for a New Europe and Supplementary Document to give effect to certain provisions of the Charter', *International Legal Materials*, 30 (January): 190–228.

Cordaro, G. (1990) 'Towards 1992: the European Community telecommunications policy', *Telecommunications*, (January): 33–5.

Cornish, P. (1996) 'European security: the end of architecture and the new NATO', *International Affairs*, 72 (4): 751–69.

Corsetti, G. and Roubini, N. (1993) 'Political biases in fiscal policy: reconsidering the case for the Maastricht fiscal criteria', in B. Eichengreen, J. Frieden and J. Von Hagen (eds), *Monetary and Fiscal Policy in an Integrated Europe*. Berlin: Springer. pp. 118–37.

Council of the European Communities (1988) *European Educational Policy Statements*, third edition, June 1987. Brussels and Luxembourg: General Secretariat.

Council of the European Communities (1990) *European Educational Policy Statements*, Supplement to the third edition (December 1989). Brussels and Luxembourg: General Secretariat.

Cram, L. (1994) 'The European Commission as a multi-organization: social policy and IT policy in the EU', *Journal of European Public Policy*, 1 (2): 195–217.

Crawford, M. (1996) *One Money for Europe? The Economics and Politics of EMU*. New York: St Martin's Press.

Curtin, D. (1995) 'The shaping of a European constitution and the 1996 IGC: 'flexbility' as a key paradigm?', *Aussenwirtschaft*, 50 (1): 237–52.

Curwen, P. (1997) *Restructuring Telecommunications. A Study of Europe in a Global Context*. London: Macmillan.

Curwen, P. (1998) 'Education, vocational training, and youth policy', in D. Dinan (ed.), *op. cit.*, pp. 159–61.

Dahl, R.A. (1963) *Modern Political Analysis*. Englewood Cliffs, NJ: Prentice-Hall.

Damgaard, E. and Eliassen, K.A. (1978) 'Corporate pluralism in Danish law making', *Scandinavian Political Studies*, 1 (4): 285–313.

Dang-Nguyen, G. (1986) 'A European telecommunications policy. Which instruments for which prospects?'. Unpublished manuscript. Brest: ENST.

Dang-Nguyen, G. (1988) 'Telecommunications in France', in J. Foreman-Peck and P. Muller (eds), *European Telecommunications Organizations*. Baden-Baden: Nomos.

De Groof, J. and Friess, B. (1997) 'Opportunities and limitations for a European education policy', *European Journal for Education Law and Policy*, 1 (1–2): 9–17.

Dehousse, R. (1992) 'Integration v regulation? On the dynamics of regulation in the European Community', *Journal of Common Market Studies*, 30 (4): 383–402.

Dehousse, R. (1995) 'Constitutional reform in the European Community: are there alternatives to the Majoritarian avenue?' in J.E.S. Hayward (ed.), *Crisis of Representation in Europe*. London: Frank Cass.

Dehousse, R. and Weiler, J.H.H. (1990) 'The legal dimension', in W. Wallace (ed.), *The Dynamics of European Integration*. London and New York: Frances Pinter. pp. 242–60.

De la Serre, Françoise. (1991) 'The integration dilemma: enlarging and/or deepening the Community', *Futures*, 23 (7): 739–46.

Delcourt, B. (1991) 'EC decisions and directives on information technology and telecommunications', *Telecommunications Policy*, 15: 15–21.

Delors, J. (1989) 'The broad lines of Commission policy', *Agence Europe*. Documents No 1542/1543 (26 January).

Denmark, Ministry of Economics (1996) *EU's Udvidelse mød øst: Økonomiske perspektiver*. Copenhagen: J.H. Schultz Information A/S.

De Witte, B. (ed.) (1989a) *European Community Law of Education*. Baden-Baden: Nomos Verlagsgesellschaft.

De Witte, B. (1992) 'The influence of European Community law on national systems of higher education', in J. Pertek (ed.), *General Recognition of Diplomas and Free Movement of Professionals, Seminar Proceedings*. Maastricht: European Institute of Public Administration. pp. 73–89.

Diehl, J. (1988) 'Choking on their own development', *Washington Post*, National Weekly Edition, 4 June: 9.

DiMaggio, P.L and Powell, W.W. (1983) 'The iron cage revisited: institutionalized isomorphism and collective rationality in organizational fields', *American Sociological Review*, 48: 147–60.

Dinan, Desmond (1998) *Encyclopedia Of the European Union*. London: Macmillan.

Dobbin, F. (1993a) 'The social construction of the great depression: industrial policy during the 1930s in the United States, Britain, and France', *Theory and Society*, 22: 1–56.

Dobbin, F. (1993b) 'Public policy and the development of high speed trains in France and the United States', in John Whitelegg, Staffan Hultén and Torbjörn Flink (eds), *High Speed Trains*. London: Leading Edge. pp. 124–44.

Dobbin, F. (1994) *Forging Industrial Policy. The United States, Britain and France in the Railway Age*. New York: Cambridge University Press.

Dobbin, F. (Forthcoming) *States and Industrial Cultures*. New York: Cambridge University Press.

Docksey, C. and Williams, K. (1997) 'The European Commission and the execution of Community policy', in G. Edwards and D. Spence (eds), *The European Commission*, second edition. London: Catermill.

Dogan, R. (1997) 'Comitology: little procedures with big implications', *West European Politics*, 20 (3): 31–60.

Donnelly, J. (1986) 'International human rights: a regime analysis', *International Organization*, 40: 559–642.

Dordick, H.S. (1990) 'The origins of universal service. History as a determinant of tele-communications policy', *Telecommunications Policy*, 14: 223–31.

Dore, J. and De Bauw, R. (1995) *The Energy Charter Treaty*. London: The Royal Institute of International Affairs.

Douglas, M. (1986) *How Institutions Think*. Syracuse, NY: Syracuse University Press.

Doukas, K.A. (1945) *The French Railroads and the State*. New York: Columbia University Press.

Drucker, P.F. (1989) *The New Realities. In Government and Politics/In Economics and Business/In Society and World View*. New York: Harper & Row.

Duchene, F. (1972) 'Europe's role in world peace', in Richard Mayne (ed.), *Europe Tomorrow*. London: Fontana.

Duff, A., Pinder, J. and Pryce, R. (1994) *Maastricht and Beyond. Building the European Union*. London: Routledge.

Duke, S. (1996) 'The second death (or the second coming?) of the WEU', *Journal of Common Market Studies*, 34 (2): 167–90.

Dunham, A.L. (1941) 'How the first French railways were planned', *Journal of Economic History*, 14: 12–25.

Dyson, K. (1983) 'The cultural, ideological and structural context', in K. Dyson and S. Wilks (eds), *Industrial Crisis: A Comparative Study of the State and Industry*. Oxford: Martin Robertson. pp. 22–66.

Dyson, K. (1986) 'West European states and the communications revolution', *West European Politics*, 9 (4): 10–55.

Dølvig, J.E. (1999) 'The global challenge: convergence or divergence of national labour market institutions?', ARENA paper, unpublished.

Ebel, R.E. (1994) *Energy Choices in Russia*. Washington: Center for Strategic and International Studies.

EC (1989) 'Commission opinion on Turkey's request for accession to the Community', SEC(89) 2290 final, Brussels, 18 December.

EC (1990) *Environmental Policy in the European Community*, fourth edition. Luxembourg: Office of Official Publications on the European Communities.

EC (1991) 'A strategy for enlargement. Preliminary report of the SG Study Group on Enlargement'. Brussels: Commission of the European Communities, 14 November.

EC (1992) 'Europe and the challenge of enlargement', *Europe Documents* No. 1790, 3 July.

EC (1993) 'Presidency Conclusions, The European Council, Copenhagen, 21–22 June', *EC Bulletin*, No 6.

EC (1994) 'Report from the Council to the Essen European Council on a strategy to prepare for accession of the associated CEEC', *Europe Documents* No. 1916, 14 December.

ECB Monthly Bulletin (2000) January.

Economic and Social Committee (1980) *European Interest Groups and Their Relationships with the Economic and Social Committee*. Farnborough: Saxon House.

Economist (1983) 'Faster trains, bigger losses', 19 November: 76.

Economist (1984) 'On a rail and a prayer', 6 September: 49.

Economist (1985a) 'Return train', 24 August: 53–60.

Economist (1985b) 'The world and its railways: redefining their role', 31 August: 25–32.

Economist (1985c) 'The world and its railways: higher speeds and lower costs', 7 September: 33–8.

Economist (1985d) 'The world and its railways: the fast track', 14 September: 25–8.

Economist (1988) 'A faster route to Europe', 16 July: 53–4.

Economist (1989) 'Faster and still faster', 18 September: 52.

Economist (1989) 'Freedom to be "Cleaner than the rest"', 14 October: 21–4.

Economist (1991a) 'A wall of waste', 30 November: 73.

Economist (1991b) 'Dirty dozen', 20 July: 52.

Economist (1991c) 'Free trade's Green Hurdle', 15 June: 61.

Economist (1991d) 'The other fortress Europe', 1 June.

Economist (1992) 'Europe's immigrants: strangers inside the gates', 15 February.

Economist (1994) 'Europe's railways: light at the end of the tunnel', 29 October: 23.

Economist (1996) 'Transport and infrastructure: Europe's new model railways', 28 September: 73.

Economist (1999) 'The rail billionaires: the privatisation of British Rail has proved a disastrous failure', 3 July: 57–60.

Edwards, G. (1996) 'National sovereignty vs integration? The Council of Ministers', in J. Richardson (ed.), *European Union: Power and Policy-Making*. London: Routledge.

Edwards, G. and Nuttall, S. (1994) 'Common foreign and security policy', in A. Duff, J. Pinder and R. Pryce (eds), *Maastricht and Beyond: Building the European Union*. London: Routledge. pp. 84–103.

Egeberg, M. (1996) 'Organization and nationality in the European Commission services', *Public Administration*, 74 (4): 721–35.

Egeberg, M., Olsen, J.P. and Saetren, H. (1978) 'Organisasjonssamfunnet og den segmenterte stat', in J.P. Olsen (ed.), *Politisk Organisering*. Oslo: Universitetsforlaget. pp. 115–84.

Eichengreen, B. and Von Hagen, J. (1996) 'Fiscal restrictions and monetary union: rationales, repercussions, reforms', *Empirica*, 232: 23.

Eichengreen, B. and Wyplosz, C. (1998) 'Stability pact. More than a minor nuisance?', *Economic Policy*, (April): 67–112.

Eisenstadt, S.X. (1972) 'Social Institutions', in D.L. Sills (ed.), *International Encyclopedia of the Social Sciences*, Vol. 13: 409–29.

Eldevik, F. (1999) *Liberalisering av gassmarkedet i europa. EUs gassdirektiv av 1998*. ARENA-report 4/1999.

Eliassen, K.A. (1995) 'Legitimacy, effectiveness and the europeification of national policy-making', in M. Telò (ed.), *Démocratie Européene*. Brussels: Institut d'Etudes Européennes.

Eliassen, K.A. (1998) 'Introduction: the new European foreign and security policy agenda', in K.A. Eliassen (ed.), *Foreign and Security Policy in the European Union*. London: Sage. pp. 1–8.

Eliassen, K.A. and Mydske, K.K. (1991) 'EF og Norsk Utdanning i 90-Årene'. Arbeidsnotat 1991/28. Oslo: Senter for europeiske studier.

Eliassen, K.A. and Sjøvaag, M. (1999) *European Telecommunications Liberalisation*. London: Routledge.

Engineering News Record (1985) 'High speed rail line feasible', 31 October: 14.

Engineering News Record (1986) 'High-speed rail network under study in Europe', 6 March: 16.

Engineering News Record (1998) 'German high-speed rail crash hasn't derailed expansion', 15 June: 16–18

Englund, C. (1999) 'The global mobile market and regulatory aspects', in K.A. Eliassen and M. Sjøvaag (eds), *European Telecommunications Liberalisation*. London: Routledge.

Ensminger, J. (1998) 'Anthropology and the new institutionalism', *Journal of Institutional and Theoretical Economics*, 154 (4): 774–89.

Epstein, E. (1969) *The Corporation in American Politics*. Englewood Cliffs, NJ: Prentice Hall.

Eriksen, E.O., Føllesdal, A. and Malnes, R. (1995) 'Europeanisation and Normative Political theory', ARENA working paper.

Europe Agreements (1992) 'Establishing an Association between the European Communities and their Member States, of the one Part and Czech and Slovak Federal Republic, of the other Part'. Mimeo.

Europe Documents (1991a) No. 1683, 15 January.

Europe Documents (1991b) No. 1712, 22 May.

Europe Documents (1992) No. 1790, 3 July.

Europe Documents (1996) 'State of progress in preparing for EU enlargement: Commission Information Memo. No 2000, 9 August.

EU (1994) 'Report from the Council to the Essen European Council on a strategy to prepare for accession of the associated CEEC', *Europe Documents* No. 1916, 14 December.

EU (1995a) 'White Paper: Preparation of the Associated Countries of Central and Eastern Europe for Integration into the Internal Market of the Union (presented by the Commission)', COM(95) 163 final, Brussels, 03.05.1995, annex 10.05.1995.

EU (1995b) 'Presidency Conclusions, Madrid Summit', *Europe*, No 6629, 17 December.

EU (1997a) 'Agenda 2000: For a stronger and wider Union. Document drawn up on the basis of COM(97) 2000 final', *Bulletin of the European Union*. Supplement 5/97.

EU (1997b) Presidency Conclusions, Luxembourg European Council, 12–12–1997 (available on the Internet: *www.europa.eu.int* under Council of the European Union, Press Release Library).

EU (1998a) Presidency Conclusions, Cardiff European Council, 15 and 16 June 1998 (available on the Internet: *www.europa.eu.int* under European Council).

EU (1998b) Composite Paper: Reports on Progress towards accession by each of the candidate countries (available on Internet: *www.europa.eu.int* under Commission – policies – enlargement).

EU (1998c) Presidency Conclusions, Vienna European Council, 11 and 12 December 1998.

EU (1999a) Council – Agriculture (22/02 – 11/03), Press Release No. 6124/99.

EU (1999b) Presidency Conclusions, Berlin European Council, 24 and 25 March 1999.

EU (1999c) Presidency Conclusions, Cologne European Council, 3 and 4 June 1999.

European Central Bank (2000) *Monthly Bulletin*, January.

European Communities, Commission (1988) *Energy in Europe: Energy Policies and Trends in the European Community*. Brussels.

European Communities, Commission (1989) 'Avis de la Commission sur la demande d'adhesion de la Turquie à la Communauté', SEC(89) 2290 final, Brussels, 18 December.

European Communities, Commission (1990a) 'Communication from the Commission to the Council and the Parliament. Association agreements with the countries of central and eastern Europe: a general outline' COM(90) 398 final, Brussels, 27 August.

European Communities, Commission (1990b) Directorate-General Information, Communication, Culture, 'The European Community and Cyprus', April.

European Communities, Commission (1991) Secretariat General, 'A Strategy for Enlargement: Preliminary Report of the SG Study Group on Enlargement', Brussels, 14 November.

European Communities, Council and Commission (1992) *Treaty on European Union*. Luxembourg: Office for Official Publications of the European Communities.

European Communities, Court of Justice (1991) 'Opinion of the Court 14 December 1991'. Opinion 1/91.

European Communities, Court of Justice (1992) 'Opinion of the Court 10 April 1992'. Opinion 1/92.

European Community Education Cooperation (1986) *The First Decade: The Education Information Network in the European Community*. Brussels: Eurydice.

European Conference of Ministers of Transport (1986) *European Dimension and Future Prospects of the Railways*. Paris: OECD.

European Council (1992) 'European Council in Edinburgh – 11–12 December 1992 – Conclusions of the Presidency', *Agence Europe*, 13 December.

European Educational Policy Statements (1988) third edition, June 1987. Brussels and Luxembourg: Council of the European Communities. General Secretariat.

European Educational Policy Statements (1990) supplement to the third edition, December 1989. Brussels and Luxembourg: Council of the European Communities. General Secretariat.

EUROSTAT (1996) 'European Union (EU) Trade with Central and Eastern European Countries: Results for 1995', *Statistics in Focus: External Trade*, No 7.

EUROSTAT (1997) 'EU applicants' trade and growth take off, but living stands 70% below EU', Memo 13/97, 12 December.

Evans, H.E. (1998) 'EU energy and environmental policy: putting the case for a merger', *Energy Economist*, June 1998.

Falk, R. (1997) 'State of siege: will globalization win out?', *International Affairs*, 73: 123–36.

Fangmann, H. (1990) 'Die Europåisierung des Femmeldewesens. Ohne demokratische Legitimation', *Gewerkschaftliche Praxis*, 35(1): 22–8.

Faujas, A. (1991a) 'Un programme de 210 milliards de francs Le schema directeur TGV prevoit la construction de seize lignes ferroviaires à grande vitesse', *Le Monde*, 16 May.

Faujas, A. (1991b) 'Le preferant a son concurrent allemand Le Texas a choisi le TGV français', *Le Monde*, 30 May.

Faujas, A. (1991c) 'Le ministre de l'equipement partisan d'un 'vaste debat' sur les projets d'infrastructures', *Le Monde*, 13 September.

Faujas, A. (1991d) 'Il y a dix ans Le TGV Paris–Lyon sauve le chemin de fer', *Le Monde*, 23 September.

Faujas, A. (1991e) 'Ameliorations, innovations La SNCF developpe des liaisons TGV de province a province', *Le Monde*, 30 September.

Fijnaut, C. (1991) 'Police co-operation in Europe', in F. Heidensohn and M. Farrell (eds), *Crime in Europe*. London: Routledge. pp. 103–20.

Fijnaut, C. (1992) 'Policing Western Europe: Interpol, Trevi and Europol', *Police Studies*, 15 (3): 101–106.

Financial Times (1992) 'Railway finance', 1 May: 14.

Finnemore, M. (1990) 'International organizations as teachers of norms: UNESCO and science policy'. Department of Political Science, Stanford University.

Finnemore, M. (1996) 'Norms, culture and world politics: insights from sociology's institutionalism', *International Organization*, 50 (2): 325–47.

Finnish Presidency (1999) 'The prevention and control strategy for the beginning of the new millenium' (to Multidisciplinary Working Group on Organized Crime MDG).

Fischer, W. and Lundgreen, P. (1975) 'The recruitment and training of administrative personnel', in C. Tilly (ed.), *The Formation of National States in Western Europe*. Princeton, NJ: Princeton University Press.

Fjeldstad, Ø. (1999) 'The value system in telecommunications', in K.A. Eliassen and M. Sjøvaag (eds), *European Telecommunications Liberalisation*. London: Routledge.

Fligstein, N. (1996) 'Markets as politics: a political-cultural approach to market institutions', *American Sociological Review*, 61: 656–74.

Fligstein, N. (1999) *Stability and Change in the Europeanization of Firms*. ARENA presentation, June.

Fligstein, N. and Brantley, P. (1992) 'The 1992 Single Market programme and the interests of business'. Mimeo, Department of Sociology, University of California at Berkeley.

Fligstein, N. and Byrkjeflot, H. (1996) 'The logic of employment systems', in J.N. Baron, D. Grusky and D. Treiman (eds), *Social Differentiation and Social Inequality*. Boulder, CO: Westview. pp. 11–36.

Fligstein, N. and Freeland, R. (1995) 'Theoretical and comparative perspectives on corporate organization', *Annual Review of Sociology*, 21: 21–43.

Fligstein, N. and Mara-Drita, I. (1996) 'How to make a market: reflections on the attempt to create a single market in the European Union', *American Journal of Sociology*, 102: 1–33.

Flink, T. (1991) 'The economic and technical effects of an extended lead-time in R&D projects – the case of the Swedish high speed trains'. Mimeo, Stockholm School of Economics.

Flink, T. (1992) 'On the revitalisation of mature industries: the case of high speed trains in Italy'. Mimeo, Stockholm School of Economics.

Flynn, G. (1991) 'The CSCE and the new European order', in M. Wyatt (ed.), *CSCE and the New Blueprint for Europe*. Washington, DC: Institute for the Study of Diplomacy, Georgetown University. pp. 23–33.

Forster, A. (1998) 'Britain and the negotiations of the Maastricht Treaty. A critique of intergovernmentalism', *Journal of Common Market Studies*, 36 (3): 347–68.

Forster, A. and Wallace, W. (1996) 'Common Foreign and Security Policy', in H. Wallace and W. Wallace (eds), *Policy-making in the European Union*. Oxford: Oxford University Press. pp. 411–35.

Fredebeul-Krein, M. and Freytag, A. (1997) 'Telecommunications and WTO discipline', *Telecommunications Policy*, 21 (6): 477–91.

Freeman, L. (1991) 'Foreign trains could run on BR tracks', *Press Association Newsfile*, 11 July.

Freestone, D. (1991) 'European Community environmental policy and law', *Journal of Law and Society*, 18: 135–54.

Friedman, M. (1995) 'Balanced budget: amendment must put limit on taxes', *Wall Street Journal*, 4: A12.

From, J. (1998) *The role of the EU Competition Directorate General (DG IV) in implementing EU competition policy*. Doctoral Dissertation, Sussex European Institute.

Funfter Gesamtbericht Uber die Tatigheit der Gemeinschaften (1971) Brussels.

Føllesdal, A. (1997) 'Democracy and federalism in the European Union' ARENA working paper 5/1997.

Gabel, M.J. (1998) 'The endurance of supranational governance: a consociational interpretation of the European Union', *Comparative Politics*, (July): 463–75.

Gable, R.M. (1953) 'NAM: influential lobby or kiss of death?', *Journal of Politics*, 254–73.

Garfinkel, L. (1994) 'The transition to competition in telecommunications services', *Telecommunications Policy*, 18: 427–31.

Garrett, G. (1992a) 'International cooperation and institutional choice', *International Organization*, 46: 533–60.

Garrett, G. (1992b) 'Intergovernmental bargaining and European integration', paper presented at the International Conference of Europeanists, Chicago.

General Report On The Activities Of The European Communities. Brussels (published annually).

George, S. (1985) *Politics and Policy in the European Community*. Oxford: Oxford University Press.

George, S. (1991) *Politics and Policy in the European Community*. Oxford: Oxford University Press.

George, S. (1996) *Politics and Policy in the European Union*. Oxford: Oxford University Press.

Gerbet, P. (1983) *La construction de l'Europe*. Paris: Imprimerie nationale.

Ghebali, V.Y. (1992) 'La CSCE à la recherche de son rôle dans la nouvelle Europe', in M. Telo (ed.), *Vers une nouvelle Europe?* Brussels: Editions de Université de Bruxelles. pp. 49–79.

Ginsberg, R.H. (1989) 'US–EC relations', in J. Lodge (ed.), *The European Community and the Challenge of the Future*. London: Frances Pinter. pp. 256–78.

Giovannini, A. and Spaventa, L. (1990) 'Fiscal rules in the European Monetary Union: a no-entry clause', CEPR Working Paper, No 516, Brussels.

Gomien, D., Harris, D. and Zwaak, L. (1996) *Law and Practice of the European Convention on Human Rights and the European Social Charter*. Strasbourg: Council of Europe Publishing.

Gosh, A.R. and Masson, P.R. (1994) *Economic Cooperation in an Uncertain World*. Oxford: Blackwell.

Gowan, P. and Anderson, P. (1997) *The Question of Europe*. London: Verso.

Granovetter, M. (1985) 'Economic action and social structure: the problem of embeddedness', *American Journal of Sociology*, 91: 481–510.

Grant, C. (1994) *Jacques Delors: The House that Jacques Built*. London: Nicholas Brearley.

Grant, W. (ed.) (1985) *The Political Economy of Corporatism*. London: Macmillan.

Greenwood, J. (1997) *Representing Interests in the European Union*. London: Macmillan.

Greenwood, J. and Aspinwall, M. (eds) (1998) *Collective Action in the European Union*. London: Routledge.

Greenwood, L, Grote, J.R. and Ronit, K. (eds) (1992) *Organized Interests and the European Community*. London: Sage.

Gregory, F. and Collier, A. (1992) 'Cross frontier crime and international crime problems, achievements and prospects with reference to European police cooperation', in M. Anderson and M. den Boer (eds) *European Police Co-operation*. Proceedings of a Seminar, University of Edinburgh, Department of Politics, pp. 71–92.

Gretschman, K. (1997) 'Vision or revision. Managing Europe's way to EMU', *EIPASCOPE*, (1–2): 16–19.

Gros, D. (1995) *Towards a Credible Excessive Deficits Procedure*. CEPS Working Document No 95, Center for European Policy Studies.

Gros, D. and Thygesen, N. (1998) *European Monetary Integration*. Essex: Longman.

Grote, J.R. (1990) 'Steuerungsprobleme in transnationalen Beratungsgremien: Uber soziale Kosten unkoordinierter Regulierung in der EG', in T. Eilwein, J.J. Hesse, R. Mayntz and FM. Scharpf (eds), *Jahrbuch zur Staats-und Verwaitungswissenschaft*, Vol. 4. Baden-Baden: Nomos. pp. 227–54.

Grupp, H. and Schnöring, T. (1992) 'Research and development in telecommunications', *Telecommunications Policy*, 16: 839–52.

Gustavsson, S. (1999) 'Myntunion utan fiskal union – det politiske hållbarhetsproblemet'. Unpublished paper. Uppsala: Statsvetenskapliga Institutionen.

Haar, J.H. (1991) *European Integration and Interventionist Political Forces in Britain and Denmark*. Aarhus: Institut for Statskundskab.

Haas, E.B. (1964) *Beyond the Nation State. Functionalism and International Organization*. Stanford, CA: Stanford University Press.

Haas, E.B. (1968) *The Uniting of Europe. Political, Social, And Economic Forces 1950–57*. Stanford, CA: Stanford University Press (first published 1958).

Haas, E.B. (1990) *When Knowledge Is Power. Three Models of Change in International Organizations*. Berkeley: University of California Press.

Habermas, J. (1962) *Borgerlig offentlighet – dens framvekst og forfall*. Oslo: Gyldendal norsk forlag (1971).

Habermas, J. (1997) 'Reply to Grimm', in P. Gowan and P. Anderson (eds) *The Question of Europe*. London: Verso. pp. 259–64.

Haigh, N. (1989) *EEC Environmental Policy and Britain*, second edition. Harlow: Longman.

Haigh, N. and Baldock, D. (1989) 'Environmental Policy and 1992', London: Institute for European Environmental Policy.

Hall, P. (1986) *Governing the Economy: The Politics of State Intervention in Britain and France*. New York: Oxford University Press.

Hall, P. (1992) 'The movement from Keynesianism to monetarism: institutional analysis and British economic policy in the 1970s', in S. Steinmo, K. Thelen and F. Longstreth (eds), *Historical Institutionalism in Comparative Politics: State, Society, and Economy*. New York: Cambridge University Press.

Hall, P.A. (1993) 'Policy paradigms, social learning and the state: the case of economic policy making in Britain', *Comparative Politics*, 25: 275–96.

Hall, P.A. and Taylor, Rosemary C.R. (1996) 'Political science and the three new institutionalisms', *Political Studies*, 44: 936–58.

Hallstein, W., Goetz, H. and Narjes, K.H. (1969) *Der unvollendete Bundesstaat. Europdische Erfahrungen und Erkenntnisse*. Düsseldorf: Econ.

Halpern, S.M. (1986) 'The disorderly universe of consociational democracy', *West European Politics*, 9 (2): 181–97.

Hamel, J., Dufour, S. and Fortin, D. (1993) 'Case-study methods', *Qualitative Research Methods Series*, 32. London: Sage.

Hancher, L. (1998) *EU energy policy*. Norwegian School of Management: Report 4/1998.

Harrison, M. (1991) 'BR train delay could boost tunnel costs', *The Independent*, 12 November: 23.

Hart, T. (1998) 'A dynamic universal service for a heterogenerous European Union', *Telecommunications Policy*, 22 (10): 839–52.

Hayes, M.T. (1981) *Lobbyists and Legislators*. New Brunswick, NJ: Rutgers University Press.

Hayes-Renshaw, F. and Wallace, H. (1997) *The Council of Ministers*. New York: St Martin's Press.

Hayward, J. (1974) *The One and Indivisible French Republic*. New York: Norton.

Heisier, M.O. (1979) 'Corporate pluralism revisited: where is theory?', *Scandinavian Political Studies*, 2(3): 277–98.

Held, D. (1993) 'Democracy: from city-states to a cosmopolitan order?', in D. Held (ed.), *Prospects for Democracy. North, South, East, West*. Oxford: Polity Press. pp. 13–52.

Held, D. (1995) *Democracy and the Global Order: From the Modern State to Cosmopolitical Governance*. Cambridge: Polity Press.

Helenions, R. (1994) 'From protecting of rights to negotiating reforms'. Paper presented at Logic Group Membership in the New Europe, Madrid.

Henning, R.C. (1995) 'System, power, and European monetary integration'. Unpublished paper.

Herman, R. (1988) 'An ecological epiphany', *Washington Post National Weekly Edition*, 5–11 December: 19.

Hermans, S. (1997) 'The Socrates programme: from negotiations to implementation', *European Journal for Education Law and Policy*, 1 (1–2): 19–39.

Hill, C. (1992) 'EPC's performance in crises', in Reinhardt Rummel (ed.), *Toward Political Union: Planning a Common Foreign and Security Policy in the European Community'*. Boulder, CO: Westview Press. pp. 135–46.

Hill, C. (1993) 'The capabilities expectations gap, or conceptualising Europe's global role', *Journal of Common Market Studies*, 31 (3): 305–28. Reprinted in S. Bulmer and D. Scott (eds) (1994) *Economic and Political Integration in Europe: Internal Dynamics and Global Context*. Oxford: Blackwell. pp. 103–26.

Hill, C. (1996) 'United Kingdom: sharpening contradictions', in C. Hill (ed.), *The Actors in Europe's Foreign Policy*. London: Routledge. pp. 68–89.

Hill, C. (1998) 'Closing the capabilities-expectations gap?', in J. Peterson and H. Sjursen (eds), *A Common Foreign Policy for Europe? Competing Visions of the CFSP*. London: Routledge. pp. 18–38.

Hill, C. and Wallace, W. (1996) 'Introduction: actors and actions', in C. Hill (ed.), *The Actors in Europe's Foreign Policy*. London: Routledge. pp. 1–16.

Hills, J. (1986) *Deregulating Telecoms: Competition and Control in the United States, Japan and Britain*. London: Pinter.

Hix, S. (1998) 'The study of the European Union II: the new "governance" agenda and its rival', *Journal of European Public Policy*, 5(1): 38–65.

Hix, S. (1999) *The Political System of the European Union*. London: Macmillan.

Hix, S. and Lord, C. (1996) 'The making of a president: the European Parliament and the confirmation of Jacques Santer as President of the Commission', *Government and Opposition*, 31 (1): 62–76.

Höerth, M. (1999) 'No way out for the beast? The unsolved legitimacy problem of European governance', *Journal of European Public Policy*, 6 (2): 249–68.

Hoffmann, S. (1965) 'The European process at Atlantic cross purposes', *Journal of Common Market Studies*, 3(2): 85–101.

Hoffmann, S. (1982) 'Reflections on the nation state in Western Europe today', *Journal of Common Market Studies*, 21: 21–37.

Hoffmann, S. (1992) 'Balance, concert, anarchy, or none of the above', in G.F. Treverton (ed.), *The Shape of the New Europe*. New York: Council of Foreign Relations Press. pp. 194–20.

Holmes, P. and McGowan, F. (1997) 'The changing dynamic of EU–industry relations: lessons from the liberalization of European car and airline markets', in H. Wallace and A.R. Young (eds), *Participation and Policy-making in the European Union*. Oxford: Clarendon Press.

Hooghe, L. (1999) 'Images of Europe: orientations to European integration among senior officials in the Commission', *British Journal of Political Science*, 29: 345–67.

Hoop, J.J. van der (1991) 'Europe: is rail the way; the railroad industry situation', *Information Access*, October: 80.

Howlett, M. and Ramesh, M. (1995) *Studying Public Policy. Policy Cycles and Policy Subsystems*. Oxford: Oxford University Press.

Huefner, K., Nauman, J. and Meyer, J.W. (1987) 'Comparative educational policy research: a world society perspective,' in M. Direkes, H. Weiler and A. Antal (eds), *Comparative Policy Research*. Aldershot: Gower. pp. 188–243.

Hultén, S. and Flink, T. (1993) 'The Swedish high speed train project', in J. Whitelegg, S. Hultén and T. Flink (eds), *High Speed Trains: fast tracks to the future*. London: Leading Edge. pp. 89–103.

Hurwitz, L. and Lequesne, C. (eds) (1991) *The State Of The European Community*. Boulder, CO: Lynne Rienner Publishers.

Hyde-Price, A. (1991) *European Security beyond the Cold War: Four Scenarios for the Year 2010*. London: Sage.

Ifestos, P. (1987) *European Political Cooperation*. Aldershot: Averbury.

Inman, R.P. (1996) *Do Balanced Budget Rules Work? U.S. Experience and Possible Lessons for the EMU*. National Bureau of Economic Research. NBER Working Paper, No 5838 Cambridge, MA.

International Railway Journal (1990) 'SNCF takes Initiative on HS network', June: 10.

Issing, Otmar (1996) *Europe: Political Union through Common Money?* London: The Institute of Economic Affairs.

Iversen, A.W (1992) 'EFs Miljøpolitikk', in S.S. Andersen and K.A. Eliassen (eds), *Det nye Europa*. Oslo: Tano. pp. 108–22.

Jachtenfuchs, M. (1995) 'Theoretical perspectives on European governance', *European Law Journal*, 1 (2): 115–33.

Jachtenfuchs, M. and Kohler-Koch, B. (1996) 'Regieren im dynamischen Mehrebensystem', in M. Jachtenfuchs and B. Kohler-Koch (eds), *Europäische Integration*. Opladen: Leske and Budrich. pp. 15–47.

Jachtenfuchs, M., Diez, M. and Jung, S. (1998) 'Ideas and integration: conflicting models of a legitimate European political order'. Paper presented at Fifth Biennial Conference of the European Community Studies Association, 29 May–1 June 1997. Published in *European International Relations*, 4 (4): 409–45.

Jacobs, F., Corbett, R. and Shackleton, M. (1992) *The European Parliament*, second edition. Harlow: Longman.

Jacquemin, A. and Sapir, A. (1996) 'Is a European hard core credible? A statistical analysis', *Kyklos*, 49 (2): 105–17.

Jakobsen, M. (1992) 'Europe in the 1990s: the stability in sight'. Occasional Paper No 37. Geneva: EFTA.

Jaks, J. (1992) 'Challenges and paradoxes on the way to a united democratic Europe', in A. Cleese and R. Tokes (eds), *The Economic and Social Imperatives of the Future Europe*. Baden-Baden: Nomos.

Jepperson, R.L. and Meyer, J.W (1991) 'The public order and the construction of formal organizations', in P.J. DiMaggio and W.W. Powell (eds), *The New Institutionalism in Organizational Analysis*. Chicago: University of Chicago Press. pp. 204–31.

Johansen, L.X. and Kristensen, O.P. (1982) 'Corporatist traits in Denmark 1946–1976', in Lernbruch and P.C. Schmitter (eds), *Patterns of Corporatism in Policy-Making*. Beverly Hills: Sage.

Jordan, G. and McLaughlin, A. (1991) *The Rationality of Lobbying in Europe: Why are Euro Groups so Numerous and so Weak?* Oxford: Centre for European Studies Discussion.

Kaiser, K. (1972) 'Transnational relations as a threat to the democratic process', in R.O. Keohane and J.S. Nye (eds), *Transnational Relations and World Politics*. Cambridge, MA: Harvard University Press. pp. 356–70.

Kenis, P. and Schneider, V. (1987) 'The EC as an international corporate actor: two case studies in economic diplomacy', *European Journal of Political Research*, 15: 437–57.

Keohane, R.O. (1988) 'International institutions: two approaches', *International Studies Quarterly*, 32: 379–96.

Keohane, R.O. and Hoffmann, S. (1990) 'Conclusions: community politics and institutional change', in W. Wallace (ed.), *The Dynamics of European Integration*. London: Frances Pinter. pp. 276–300.

Keohane, R.O. and Hoffmann, S. (1991) *The New European Community*. Oxford: Westview Press.

Keohane, R.O. and Nye, J.S. (1974) 'Transgovernmental relations and international organizations', *World Politics*, 27: 39–62.

Keohane, R.O. and Nye, J.S. (1977) *Power and Interdependence: World Politics in Transition*. Boston: Little, Brown and Company.

Kierzkowski, H. (1996) 'Central Europe looks west', in S. Arndt and C. Milner (eds), *The World Economy: Global Trade Policy 1996*. Oxford: Blackwell. pp. 29–44.

Kinnock, N. (1998) 'Using public–private partnerships to develop transport infrastructure', *RAPID*, 14 February Speech 98/37 (Commission of the European Communities).

Kintis, A.G. (1997) 'The EU's foreign policy and the war in former Yugoslavia', in M. Holland (ed.), *Common Foreign and Security Policy: the Record and Reforms*. London: Pinter. pp. 148–73.

Kirchner, E.J. (1981) *The Role of Interest Groups in the European Community*. Aldershot: Gower.

Kirchner, E.J. (1992) *Decision Making in the European Community: The Council Presidency and European Integration*. Manchester: Manchester University Press.

Kirchner, E.J. (1994) 'The European Community: a transnational democracy?', in I. Budge and D. McKay (eds), *Developing Democracy*. London: Sage. pp. 253–66.

Kirkland, R. (1988) 'Environmental anxiety goes global', *Fortune*, 21 November: 118.

Knill, C. (1998) 'European policies: the impact of national administrative traditions', *Journal of Public Policy*, 18: 1–18.

Kohler-Koch, B. (1991) 'Inselillusion und Interdependenz: Nationales Regieren unter den Bedingungen von "international governance"', in B. Blanke and H. Wollmann (eds), *Die alte Bundesrepublik. Kontinuität und Wandel*. Opladen: Westdeutscher Verlag. pp. 4–7. (Leviathan, Sonderheft 12/1991).

Kohler-Koch, B. (1996) 'Catching up with change. The transformation of Governance in the European Union', *Journal of European Public Policy*, 3: 359–80.

Kohler-Koch, B. and Eising, R. (eds) (1999) *The Transformation of Governance in the European Union.* London: Routledge.

Kolankiewicz, G. (1994) 'Consensus and competition in the eastern enlargement of the European Union,' *International Affairs,* 70 (3): 477–95.

Kolte, L. (1989) 'Beslutningsprocessen i EF 1985–89', *Politica,* 4: 376–95.

Koordinatorgruppen Fri Bevegelighet for Personer (1989) *Rapport til Det Europæiske råd, Palma de Mallorca.* CIRC 3624/89, 9 June 1989.

Kramer, L. (1987) 'The Single European Act and environmental protection: reflections on several new provisions in Community law', *Common Market Law Review,* 24: 659–88.

Krasner, S.D. (1983) 'Structural causes and regime consequences: regimes as intervening variables', in S.D. Krasner (ed.), *International Regimes.* Ithaca, NY: Cornell University Press.

Kuvaas, B. (1992) 'Maastrichtavtalen', in S.S. Andersen and K.A. Eliassen (eds), *Det nye Europa.* Oslo: Tano. pp. 38–53.

Labarrére, C. (1985) *L'Europe des postes et des télécommunications.* Paris: Masson.

Laffan, B. (1996) 'The politics of identity and political order in Europe', *Journal of Common Market Studies,* 34 (1): 81–101.

Laffan, B. (1998) 'The European Union: a distinctive model of internationalization', *Journal of European Public Policy,* 5 (2): 235–53.

Laffan, B., O'Donnel, R. and Smith, M. (1999) *Europe's Experimental Union.* London: Routledge.

Lamers, Karl (1994) *A German Agenda for the European Union.* London: Federal Trust and Konrad Adenauer Stiftung.

Lane, J.E. and Ersson, S. (1994) *Comparative Politics.* Cambridge: Polity Press.

Lange, P. (1993) 'Maastricht and the Social Protocol: why did they do it?', *Politics and Society,* 21 (1): 5–36.

Lasswell, H.D. (1956) *The Decision Process. Seven Categories of Functional Analysis.* University of Maryland.

Laurent, P-H. and Maresceau, M. (1998) *The State of the European Union.* Vol. 4: *Deepening and Widening.* London: Rienner.

Laursen, F. (1990a) 'Explaining the EC's New Momentum', in F. Laursen (ed.), *EFTA and the EC: Implications of 1992.* Maastricht: European Institute of Public Administration. pp. 33–52.

Laursen, F. (1990b) 'The Community's policy towards EFTA: regime formation in the European Economic Space (EES)', *Journal of Common Market Studies,* 28 (June): 303–25.

Laursen, F. (1991a) 'Comparative regional economic integration: the European and other processes', *International Review of Administrative Sciences,* 57 (4): 515–26.

Laursen, F. (1991b) 'EFTA countries as actors in European integration: the emergence of the European Economic Area (EEA)', *International Review of Administrative Sciences,* 57 (December): 543–55.

Laursen, F. (1991–92) 'The EC and its European neighbours: special partnerships or widened membership?', *International Journal,* 47 (Winter): 29–63.

Laursen, F. (1994) 'The not-so-permissive consensus: thoughts on the Maastricht Treaty and the future of European integration,' in F. Laursen and S. Vanhoonacker (eds), *The Ratification of the Maastricht Treaty: Issues, Debates and Future Implications.* Dordrecht: Martinus Nijhoff and Maastricht: European Institute of Public Administration. pp. 295–317.

Laursen, F. (1996) 'Relations between the EU and the Central and Eastern European countries since 1989: an overview', in F. Laursen and S. Riishøj (eds), *The EU and Central Europe: Status and Prospects*. Esbjerg: South Jutland University Press. pp. 3–28.

Laursen, F. (1997) 'Towards an Eastern European enlargement of the European Union', *Journal of International Political Economy* (Tsukuba, Japan), 1 (2): 61–82.

Laursen, F. (1998) 'The Central and Eastern European countries in the new Europe: the pre-accession strategy', *TKI Working Papers on European Integration and Regime Formation* 15/98. Esbjerg: South Jutland University Press.

Laursen, F. and Vanhoonacher, S. (eds) (1992) *The Intergovernmental Conference on Political Union: Institutional Reforms, New Policies and International Identity of the European Community*. Maastricht: European Institute of Public Administration.

Lehning, P.B. (1993) 'Citizenship, democracy and justice in the new Europe', in L.J.G. Van der Maesen and W. Beck (eds), *Social Inequalities, Social Policy and Older people in the European Union: The Report of the Second Expert-meeting on Older People and Social Policy, 26–27 November 1993*. Amsterdam: SISWO. pp. 195–208.

Lenaerts, Koen (1994) 'Subsidiarity and Community competence in the field of education', *The Columbia Journal of European Law*, 1 (fall): 1–28.

Lenzen, Dieter (1996) 'Education and training for Europe?', in D. Benner and D. Lenzen, (eds) *Education for the New Europe*. Oxford: Bergham Books. pp. 7–28.

Lepsius, M.R. (1990) *Interessen, Indeen und Institutionen*. Opladen: Westdeutscher Verlag.

Lepsius, M.R. (1997) 'Deinstitutionalisierung von Rationalitätskriterien', in Göhler, G. (ed.), *Institutionenwandel*. Opladen: Westdeutscher Verlag. pp. 57–70.

Levitt, B. and March, J. (1988) 'Organizational learning', *Annual Review of Sociology*, 14: 319–40.

Levy, David A.L. (1997) 'Regulating digital broadcasting in Europe: the limits of policy convergence', *West European Politics*, 20 (4): 24–42.

Lewis, Arnold (1997) '"Fed up" in Europe: regional airlines battle the bias toward rail', *Business and Commercial Aviation*, 80: 86.

Lewis, J. (1998) ' Is the "hard bargaining" image of the Council misleading? The Committee of Permanent Representatives and the Local Elections Directive', *Journal of Common Market Studies*, 37 (4): 479–504.

Liberatore, A. (1991) 'Problems of transnational policymaking: environmental problems in the European Community', *European Journal of Political Research*, 19: 281–305.

Lijphart, A. (1969) 'Consociational democracy', *World Politics*, 31 (2): 207–25.

Lijphart, A. (1977) *Democracy in Plural Societies: A Comparative Exploration*. New Haven, CT: Yale University Press.

Lindberg, L.N. (1971a) 'Political integration as a multidimensional phenomenon requiring multivariate measurement', in L.N. Lindberg and S.A. Scheingold (eds), *Regional Integration. Theory and Research*. Cambridge, MA: Harvard University Press. pp. 45–127.

Lindberg, L.N. and Scheingold, S.A. (1970) *Europe's Would-Be Polity: Patterns of Change in the European Community*. Englewood Cliffs, NJ: Prentice-Hall.

Linklater, Andrew (1995) 'Neo-realism in theory and practice', in K. Booth and S. Smith (eds), *International Relations Theory Today*. Cambridge: Polity Press. pp. 241–62.

Lipset, S.M. (1990) *Continental Divide: The Values and Institutions of the United States and Canada*. New York: Routledge.

Lodge, J. (ed.) (1989) *The European Community and the Challenge of the Future*. London: Frances Pinter.

Lodge, J. (1992) 'The European Community Foreign and Security Policy after Maastricht. New problems and dynamics', in M. Teib (ed.), *Vers une nouvelle Europe*. Brussels: Editions de l'Université de Bruxelles. pp. 111–32.

Lodge, M. (2000) 'Isomorphism of national policies? The "Europeanisation" of German competition and public procurement law', *West European Politics*, forthcoming.

Lonbay, J. (1989) 'Education and law: the Community context', *European Law Review*, 14 (6): 363–87.

Lord, E. (1997) 'Commentary: EU energy policy', *European Policy Analyst*, London, second quarter.

Louis, L.V. (1990) *The Community Legal Order*, second edition. Luxembourg: Office for Official Publications of the European Communities.

Lucron, C.P. (1992) 'Contenu et portée des accords entre la Communauté et la Hongrie, la Polande et la Tchécoslovaquie', *Revue du Marché commun*, 357 (April): 293–9.

Ludlow, P. (1991a) 'Europe's Institutions: Europe's Politics', in G.F. Treverton (ed.), *The Shape of the New Europe*. New York: Council on Foreign Relations Press. pp. 59–91.

Ludlow, P. (1991b) 'The European Commission', in R.O. Keohane and S. Hoffmann (eds), *The New European Community*. Boulder, CO: Westview Press. pp. 85–132.

Ludlow, Peter, et al. (1995) *Preparing for 1996 and a Larger European Union: Principles and Priorities*. CEPS Special Report No 6. Brussels: Centre for European Policy Studies.

Lynn-Jones, S.M. (1991) *The Cold War and After: Prospects for Peace*. Cambridge, MA: The MIT Press.

Lyons, P.K. (1990) *The New Energy Markets of the Soviet Union and East Europe*. London: Financial Times Business Information.

Lyons, P.K. (1992) *EC Energy Policy. A detailed Guide to the Community's Impact on the Sector*. London: Financial Times Management Report.

Lyons, P.K. (1994) *Energy Policies of the European Union*. London: EC Inform.

Macdonald, A. (1991) 'French railway courts investors at high speed'. *The Reuter Library Report*, October 10.

Maesen, L.J.G. and Beck, W. (1993) *Social Inequalities, Social Policy and Older People in the European Union: The Report of the Second Expert-meeting on Older People and Social Policy, 26–27 November 1993*. Amsterdam: SISWO.

Maillet, Pierre (1996) 'La cohérence des politiques économiques dans une Europe différenciée: Une exigence pour les nouvelles institutions,' *Revue du Marché commun et de l'Union européenne*, No 399 (June): 422–37.

Majone, G. (1988) 'Policy analysis and public deliberation', in R.B. Reich (ed.), *The Power of Public Ideas*. Cambridge, MA: Harvard University Press. pp. 157–78.

Majone, G. (1991) 'Cross-national sources of regulatory policymaking in Europe and the United States', *Journal of Public Policy*, 11: 79–106.

Malta (1990) *Report by the EC Directorate to the Prime Minister and Minister of Foreign Affairs regarding Malta's Membership of the European Community*. Valetta: Department of Information.

Mansbach, R.W. (1996) 'Neo-this and neo-that: or, Play it Sam (again and again)', *Mershon International Studies Review*, 40: 90–5.

March, J.G. and Olsen, J.P. (1984) 'The new institutionalism: organizational factors in political life', *American Political Science Review*, 78: 734–49.

March, J.G. and Olsen, J.P. (1989) *Rediscovering Institutions. The Organizational Basis of Politics*. New York and London: The Free Press.

March, J.G. and Olsen, J.P. (1995) *Democratic Governance*. New York: Free Press.

March, J.G. and Olsen, J.P. (1998). 'The institutional dynamics of international political orders', *International Organization*, 52 (4): 943–69.

Maresceau, M. (1992) 'The European Community and Eastern Europe and the USSR', in J. Redmond (ed.), *The External Relations of the EC: The International Response in 1992*. London: Macmillan.

Maresceau, M. (1993) '"Europe Agreements": a new form of cooperation between the European Community and Hungary, Poland and the Czech and Slovak Republic', in Müller-Graff (ed.), *Legal Adaptation to the Marker Economy of the EC*. Baden-Baden: Nomos.

Maresceau, M. (ed.) (1997) *Enlarging the European Union: Relations between the EU and Central and Eastern Europe*. London: Longman.

Marin, B. and Mayntz, R. (eds) (1991) *Policy Networks. Empirical Evidence and Theoretical Considerations*. Frankfurt A.M.: Campus.

Marks, G. (1992) 'Structural policy in the European Community', in A. Sbragia (ed.), *Euro-Politics*. Washington, DC: The Brookings Institution.

Marks, G. (1993) 'Structural policy and multi-level governance in the EC', in A. Cafruney and G. Rosenthal (eds), *The State of the EC*, Vol. 2. London: Longman. pp. 391–410.

Marks, G. and McAdam, D. (1996) 'Social movements and the changing structure of political opportunity in the European Union', *West European Politics*, 19: 249–78.

Marks, G., Hooghe, L. and Blank, K. (1996) 'European integration from the 1980's: state-centric v. multi-level governance', *Journal of Common Market Studies*, 34 (3): 341–77.

Marsh, D. (1991) 'Privatization under Mrs Thatcher: a review of the literature', *Public Administration*, 69: 459–80.

Martin, P.L., Honekopp, E. and Ullmann, H. (1991) 'Conference report: Europe 1992, Effects on Labour Migration', *International Migration Review*, 24: 591–603.

Mathijsen, P.S.R.F. (1990) *A Guide to European Community Law*, fifth edition. London: Sweet & Maxwell.

Matlary, J.H. (1991) *From the Internal Energy Market to a Community Energy Policy?* Oslo: Fridtjof Nansen Institute.

Matlary, J.H. (1997a) *Energy Policy in the European Union*. London: Macmillan Press.

Matlary, J.H. (1997b) 'Epilogue: new bottles for new wine', in K.E. Jørgensen (ed.), *Reflective Approaches to European Governance*. London: Macmillan. pp. 201–13.

May, K. (1992) 'Politics derailing high-speed train', *Ottawa Citizen*, 26 March: D13.

Mayntz, R. (1983) 'The conditions of effective public policy: a new challenge for policy analysis', *Policy and Politics*, 2: 123–43.

Mazey, S. and Richardson, J. (eds) (1993) *Lobbying in the European Community*. Oxford: Oxford University Press.

Mazey, S. and Richardson, J. (1996) 'The logic of organisation: interest groups', in J. Richardson (ed.), *European Union: Power and Policy-Making*. London: Routledge. pp. 200–15.

Mazey, S. and Richardson, J. (ed.) (1999) *Interest Intermediation in the EU: Filling the Hollow Core?* London: Routledge.

McAuley, M. (1984) 'Political culture and Communist politics: one step forward, two steps back', in A. Brown (ed.), *Political Culture and Communist Studies*. Basingstoke: Macmillan in association with St Anthony's College, Oxford.

McGowan, L. and Wilks, S. (1995) 'The first supranational policy in the European Union: competition policy', *European Journal of Political Research*, (28): 141–69.

McKinnon, R.I. (1996) 'Monetary regimes, government borrowing constraints, and market-preserving federalism: implications for EMU'. Paper presented at the conference 'The Nation State in a Global/Information Era: Policy Changes', Queen's University, Kingston, Ontario, 13–15 November (unpublished).

McLaughlin, A.M. and Maloney, W.A. (1999) *The European Automobile Industry: Multi-Level Governance, Policy and Politics*. New York: Routledge.

Melody, W.H. (ed.) (1997) *Telecom Reform. Principles, Policies and Regulatory Practices*. Lyngby: Den Private Ingeniørfond.

Menanteau, J. (1991) 'Les grands contrats du TGV. Avec les marchés à l'étranger, GEC-Alsthom découvre de nouveaux metiers', *Le Monde*, 26 June.

Meny, Y., Muller, P. and Quermonne, J.L. (eds) (1996) *Adjusting to Europe: The Impact of the European Union on National Institutions and Policies*. London: Routledge.

Meyer, J.W. (1980) 'The world polity and authority of the nation state system', in A. Bergesen (ed.), *Studies of the Modern World-System*. New York: Academic Press. Reprinted in Thomas, G.M. (1987) 'Ontology and rationalization in the Western cultural account', in G.M. Thomas, J.W. Meyer, F.O. Ramirex and J. Boli, *Constituting State, Society and the Individual*. Newbury Park, CA: Sage. pp. 41–70.

Meyer, J.W. and Jepperson, R.L. (1997) 'The "actors" of modern society: The cultural construction of agency'. Unpublished. Department of Sociology, Stanford University.

Meyer, J.W. and Rowan B. (1977) 'Institutionalized organizations: formal organization as myth and ceremony'. *American Journal of Sociology*, 83 (2): 340–63.

Meyer, J.W. and Scott, R.W. (1983) *Organizational Environments. Ritual and Rationality*. London: Sage.

Meyer, J.W., Boli, J. and Thomas, G.M. (1987) 'Ontology and rationalization in the Western cultural account', in G.M. Thomas, J.W. Meyer, F.O. Ramirez and J. Boli (eds), *Constituting State, Society, and the Individual*. Newbury Park, CA: Sage. pp. 12–38.

Meyer, J.W., Boli, J., Thomas, G.M. and Ramirez, F.O. (1997) 'World society and the nation-state', *American Journal of Sociology*, 103 (1): 144–81.

Middlemas, K. (1995) *Orchestrating Europe: The Informal Politics of European Union 1973–1995*. London: Fontana.

Miller, A.C. (1989) 'Panel to consider ambitious plan for network of high-speed trains', *Los Angeles Times*, 18 October: A24.

Miller, W.G. (1989) 'Europe high-speed rail network closer as three nations agree on a new link', *Boston Globe*, 14 August: 12.

Milward, A. (1992) *The European Rescue of the Nation State*. London: Routledge.

Moe, A. (1988) 'The outlook for Soviet gas exports to Western Europe: a country by country analysis'. Paper Presented at the 10th Annual Conference of the International Association of Energy Economists, Luxembourg, 4–7 July 1988.

Molle, W. (1994) *The Economics of European Integration*. Watertown, MA: Dartmouth Publishing.

Monford, A.C. (1994) 'Plastics: shaping a single vision of Europe'. Paper presented at the Logic of Group Membership in the New Europe, Madrid.

Moravcsik, A. (1991) 'Negotiating the Single European Act', in R. Keohane and S. Hoffmann (eds), *The New European Community*. Boulder, CO: Westview Press.

Moravcsik, A. (1993) 'Preference and power in the European Community: a liberal inter-governmentalist approach', *Journal of Common Market Studies*, 31 (4): 473–524.

Moravcsik, A. (1996) 'Studying Europe after the Cold War: a perspective from international relations', *TKI Working Papers on European Integration and Regime Formation z/ab.* Esbjerg: Sough Jutland University Press.

Moravcsik, A. (ed.) (1998a) *Centralization or Fragmentation? Europe Facing the Challenge of Deepening, Diversity, and Democracy.* New York: Council on Foreign Relations.

Moravcsik, A. (1998b) *The Choice for Europe: Social Purpose and State Power from Messina to Maastricht.* London: UCL Press.

Moravcsik, A. (1999) 'A new statecraft? Supranational entrepreneurs and international cooperation', *International Organisation,* 53 (2): 267–85.

Moravcsik, A. and Nicolaidis, K. (1999) 'Explaining the Treaty of Amsterdam: interests, influences, institutions', *Journal of Common Market Studies,* 37 (1): 59–85.

Morén, K. (1991) *Deneuropeiskefestning-asylpolitikk og politisamarbeid mot 1992, avhandling kriminologi mellomfag h.91.* Universitetet i Oslo: Institutt for kriminologi.

Morgan, Kevin and Webber, Douglas (1986) 'Divergent paths: political strategies for telecommunications in Britain, France and West Germany', *West European Politics,* 9 (4): 56–79.

Morgenthau, H. (1946) *Politics Among Nations: The Struggle for Power and Peace.* New York: Knopf.

Morgenthau, H.J., Michelson, A.A. and Davis, Leonard (1973) *Politics among Nations: The Struggle for Power and Peace.* New York: Knopf.

Morris, B., Bochm, K. and Vileinskas, M. (1986) *The European Community: A Practical Directory and Guide for Business, Industry and Trade.* London: Macmillan.

Mueller, M. (1993) 'Universal service in telephone history', *Telecommunications Policy,* 17 (3): 352–69.

Mundell, R. (1961) 'A theory of optimum currency areas', *American Economic Review,* 51: 657–75.

Muscatelli, A.V. (1997) 'International macroeconomic policy co-ordination', in V.A. Muscatelli (ed.), *Economic and Political Institutions in Economic Policy.* Manchester: Manchester University Press. pp. 98–133.

Nadelmann, E.A. (1990) 'Global prohibition regimes: the evolution of norms in international society', *International Organization,* 44: 479–526.

Nash, C. (1993) 'High speed rail services: British experience', in S. Hultén and T. Flink (eds), *High Speed Trains: Entrepreneurship and Society.* London: Leading Edge. pp. 78–88.

Neave, G. (1984) *The EEC and Education.* Stoke-on-Trent: Trentham Books.

Nee, V. and Strang, D. (1998) 'The emergence and diffusion of institutional forms', *Journal of Institutional and Theoretical Economics,* 154 (4): 706–15.

Neher, J. (1989) 'French hope U.S. hears high-speed train whistle', *Chicago Tribune,* 25 September.

Neilson, F. and Salk, J. (1998) 'The ecology of collective action and regional representation in the European Union', *European Sociological Review,* 14: 231–54.

Nentwich, M. and Falkner, G. (1997) 'The Treaty of Amsterdam: towards a new institutional balance', *European Integration Online Papers* (EioP), 1 (15) (http://eiop.or.at/eiop/texte/1997–015a.htm).

Newman, D. (1990) 'Lobbying in the EC', *Business Journal,* February.

Nice, D.C. (1989) 'Consideration of high-speed rail service in the United States', *Transportation Research,* 23A: 359–65.

Nora, S. and Minc, A. (1978) *L'Informatisation de la société.* Paris: La Documentation française.

Nordic Council (1991) *Energy for Europe: Resources, Economy, Cooperation.* Report from a Nordic Council Seminar at Holmenkollen, Oslo, Norway, 14–15 October 1991. Copenhagen: Nordisk Ministerråd.

Noreng, Ø. (1994) *Liberalisering av det europeiske gassmarkedet.* Report to the Norwegian Ministry of Energy and Industry.

Noreng, Ø., Andersen, S.S. and Nilsen, P.A. (1998) *Klima for alle pengene. Klimapolitikk – økonomisk risiko for Norge?* Oslo: Universitetsforlaget.

Norris, P. (1997) 'Representation and the democratic deficit', *European Journal of Political Research*, 32 (2): 273–82.

North, D. (1981) *Structure and Change in Economic History.* New York: Norton.

North, D. (1990) *Institutions, Institutional Change and Economic Performance.* New York: Cambridge University Press.

Notermans, T. (1998) 'Policy continuity, policy change and the political power of economic ideas'. ARENA Working Paper 1998.

Nugent, N. (1991) *The Government and Politics of the European Community.* London: Macmillan.

Nugent, N. (1994) *The Politics and Government of the European Union*, third edition. London: Macmillan.

Nugent, N. (1997) 'At the heart of the Union', in N. Nugent (ed.), *At the Heart of the Union: Studies of the European Commission.* London: Macmillan. pp. 1–26.

Nugent, N. (1999a) 'Decision-making', in L. Cram, D. Dinan and N. Nugent (eds), *Developments in the European Union.* Basingstoke: Macmillan.

Nugent, N. (1999b) *The Politics and Government of the European Union*, fourth edition. London: Macmillan.

Nuttall, S. (1992) *European Political Cooperation.* Oxford: Clarendon Press.

Nuttall, S. (1996) 'The Commission: the struggle for legitimacy', in Christopher Hill (ed.), *The Actors in Europe's Foreign Policy.* London: Routledge. pp. 130–47.

Nye, J.S. (1968) 'Comparative regional integration: concepts and measurement', *International Organization*, 22: 855–80.

Nye, J.S. (1971) 'Comparing common markets: a revised neofunctionalist model', in L.N. Lindberg and S.A. Scheingold (eds), *Regional Integration. Theory and Research.* Cambridge, MA: Harvard University Press. pp. 192–231.

Nye, J.S. and Keohane, R.O. (1973) *Transnational Relations and World Politics.* Cambridge, MA: Harvard University Press.

Nye, J.S. and Keohane, R.O. (1975) 'International interdependence and integration', in F.I. Greenstein and N.W. Polsby (eds), *Handbook of Political Science.* Reading, MA: Addison-Wesley.

Nylander, J. (1998) 'First movers, insider groups and the role of the Commission: the liberalisation of the European electricity market'. Department of Sociology. Working paper presented at the Uppsala Theory Circle meeting, 15 June 1998.

OECD Working Papers No 79 (1995) 'The changing role of telecommunications in the economy: Globalisation and its impact on national telecommunication policy'.

Ohmae, K. (1991) *The Borderless World: Power and Strategy in the Interlinked Economy.* New York: Harper Perennial.

Ojeda, A.A. (1997) *Legal Problems of the European Model of Social Quality: Comments on its Reform.* Seville: University of Seville.

Olsen, J.P. (1978) *Politisk Organisering: Organisasjonsteoretiske synspunkt på folkestyre og politisk ulikhet.* Bergen: Universitetsforlaget.

Olsen, J.P. (1992) *Analysing Institutional Dynamics.* Bergen: LOS-sentret, notat 92/14.

Olsen, J.P. (1997) *The Changing Political Organisation of Europe: An Institutional Perspective on the Role of Comprehensive Reform Efforts*. Oslo: Arena.

Olsen, J.P. (1998) 'The new European experiment in political organization'. Paper presented at the conference 'Samples of the future', Scancor, Stanford University, 20–22 September 1998.

Orloff, Ann Shola and Skocpol, Theda (1984) 'Why not equal protection? Explaining the politics of public social spending in Britain, 1900–1911, and the United States, 1880s–1920', *American Sociological Review*, 49: 726–50.

Ottawa Citizen (1999) 'Florida derails $6.3B train project: Bombardier loses deal to build bullet train', *The Ottawa Citizen*, 15 January: D3.

Padgett, S. (1992) 'The Single European Market: the politics of realization', *Journal of Common Market Studies*, 30 (1): 53–75.

Pappalardo, A. (1981) 'The conditions for consociational democracy: a logical and empirical critique', *European Journal of Political Research*, (9): 365–90.

Patel, P. and Pavitt, K. (1989) 'European technological performance: results and prospects', *European Affairs*, 2/89: 56–63.

Pedersen, T. (1992) 'Political change in the European Community. The Single European Act as a case of system transformation', *Cooperation and Conflict*, 27 (1): 7–44.

Pelkmans, J. (1987) 'The new approach to technical harmonization and standardization', *Journal of Common Market Studies*, 25 (3): 249–69.

Pelkmans, J. and Young, D. (1998) *Telecoms 98*. Brussels: Center for European Policy Studies.

Perotti, R. (1996) 'Fiscal consolidation in Europe: composition matters', *AEA Papers and Proceedings*, 105–10.

Perrin-Pelletier, F. (1985) 'The European automobile industry in the context of 1992', *European Affairs*, (1): 85–95.

Persson, T. and Tabellini, G. (1995) 'Double-edged incentives: institutions and policy co-ordination'. CEPR Discussion Paper No 1141.

Pertek, J. (ed.) (1992a) 'General Recognition of Diplomas and Free Movement of Professionals, Seminar Proceedings'. Maastricht: European Institute of Public Administration.

Pertek, J. (1992b) 'L'Europe des universités', in J. Pertek and M. Soveroski (eds), *EC Competences and Programmes within the Field of Education*. Maastricht: European Institute of Public Administration. pp. 21–42.

Pertek, J. (1992c) 'TEMPUS: L'enseignement supérieur, point de rencontre priviliégié entre la Communauté et l'Europe centrale et orientale', in J. Pertek and M. Soveroski (eds), *EC Competences and Programmes within the Field of Education*. Maastricht: European Institute of Public Administration. pp. 49–62.

Pertek, J. and Soveroski, M. (eds) (1992) *EC Competences and Programmes within the Field of Education*. Maastricht: European Institute of Public Administration.

Peters, B.G. (1992) 'Bureaucratic politics and the institutions of the European Community', in A.M. Sbragia (ed.), *Europolitics: Institutions and Policy making in the 'New' European Community*. Washington, DC: Brookings. pp. 75–123.

Peters, B.G. (1996) 'Agenda-setting in the European Union', in J. Richardson (ed.), *European Union: Power and Policy-Making*. London: Routledge. pp. 61–76.

Peters, B.G. (1997) 'Escaping the joint-decision trap: repetition and sectoral politics in the European Union', *West European Politics*, 20 (2): 22–36.

Peters, B.G. (1999) *Institutional Theory in Political Science. The 'New Institutionalism'*. London: Pinter.

Petersen, J.H. and Nedergaard, P. (1992) *Det nye EF. Traktaten om den europmiske union*. Copenhagen: CO Metal, Industriens Arbejdsgivere; Den danske Europabevegelse.

Peterson, J. (1992) 'The European technology community: policy networks in a supranational setting', in D. Marsh and R. Rhodes (eds), *Policy Networks in British Government*. Oxford: Oxford University Press.

Peterson, J. (1995) 'Decision-making in the European Union: towards a framework for analysis', *Journal of European Public Policy*, 2 (1): 69–93.

Peterson, J. (1997) 'States, societies and the European Union', *West European Politics*, 20: 1–23.

Peterson, J. (1999) 'The Santer era: the European Commission in normative, historical and theoretical perspective', *Journal of European Public Policy*, 6 (1): 46–65.

Peterson, J. and Bomberg, E. (1999) *Decision-making in the European Union*. Basingstoke: Macmillan.

Peterson, J. and Sjursen, H. (eds) (1998) *A Common Foreign Policy for Europe?* London: Routledge.

Philip, A.B. (1983) 'Pressure groups in the European Community', in A.B. Philip (ed.) *Institutions and Politics of the European Community*. London: Frances Pinter.

Philip, A.B. (1987) 'Pressure groups in the European Community and informal institutional arrangements', in R. Beuter and P. Taskaloyannis (eds), *Experiences in Regional Co-operation*. Maastricht: European Institute of Public Administration.

Pierson, P. (1996) 'The path to European integration: a historical institutionalist analysis', in W. Sandholz and A.S. Sweet (eds), *European Integration and Supranational Governnance*. Oxford: Oxford University Press. pp. 27–58.

Pierson, P. and Leibfried, S. (1995) 'Multitiered institutions and the making of social policy', in S. Leibfried and P. Pierson (eds), *European Social Policy: Between Fragmentation and Integration*. Washington, DC: The Brookings Institution. pp. 1–40.

Pijpers, A. (1991) 'European political cooperation and the realist paradigm', in Martin Holland (ed.), *The Future of European Political Cooperation*. London: Macmillan. pp. 8–35.

Pijpers, A. (1996) 'The Netherlands: the weakening pull of Atlanticism', in C. Hill (ed.), *The Actors in Europe's Foreign Policy*. London: Routledge. pp. 247–67.

Pinder, A. (1991) *The European Community and Eastern Europe*. London: Chatam House Papers.

Pisani-Ferry, Jean (1995) 'L'Europe à géometrie variable: une analyse économique', *Politique Étrangère*, pp. 447–65.

Polino, M.N. (1993) 'The French TGV since 1976', in J. Whitelegg, S. Hultén and T. Flink (eds), *High Speed Trains: Fast Tracks to the Future*. London: Leading Edge. pp. 38–47.

Pollack, M.A (1996) 'The new institutionalism and EC governance: the promise and limits of institutional analysis', Governance. London: Macmillan.

Pollack, M.A. (1997) 'The Commission as an agent', in N. Nugent (ed.), *At the Heart of the Union: Studies of the European Commission*. London: Macmillan.

Pollack, M.A. (1999) 'Delegation, agency and agenda setting in the Treaty of Amsterdam', European Integration online Papers (EioP) 3 (6) (http:eiop.or.at/eiop/texte/1999–006a.htm).

Potter, S. (1989) 'High-speed rail technology in the UK, France and Japan', *Technology Analysis and Strategic Management*, 1: 99–121.

Potter, S. (1993) 'Managing high speed train projects', in J. Whitelegg, S. Hultén and T. Flink (eds), *High Speed Trains: Fast Tracks to the Future*. London: Leading Edge. pp. 145–61.

Pressman, J.L. and Wildavsky, A. (1984) *Implementation*, third edition. Berkeley, CA: University of California Press.

Preston, C.r (1997) *Enlargement and Integration in the European Union*. London: Routledge.

Prévot, H. (1989) *Rapport de Synthèse a l'issue du debate public sur l'avenir du service public de la Poste et des Telecommunications*. Paris: Le Debat Public.

Puchala, D.J. (1972) 'Of blind men, elephants and international integration', *Journal of Common Market Studies*, 10: 267–84.

Putnam, R.D. (1988) 'Diplomacy and domestic politics: the logic of two-level garnes', *International Organization*, 42: 427–60.

Putnam, R. and Bayne, N. (1987) *Hanging Together*. Cambridge, MA: Harvard University Press.

Railway Age (1989) 'Florida: one contender left', December: 42–3.

Rasmussen, H. (1988) 'The implementation of directives', in H. Siedentopf and J. Ziller (eds), *Making European Policies Work*, Vol. II: National Reports. Brussels and London: EIPA/Sage.

Rawls, J. (1971) *A Theory of Justice*. Cambridge, MA: Harvard University Press.

Rawls, J. (1996) *Political Liberalism*. New York: Columbia University Press.

Razzolini, L. and Shugart, W.F. II (1997) 'On the (relative) unimportance of a balanced budget', *Public Choice*, 90: 215–33.

Reddy, W.M. (1984) *The Rise of Market Culture: The Textile Trade and French Society, 1750–1900*. Cambridge: Cambridge University Press.

Regelsberger, E. and Wessels, W. (1996) 'The CFSP institutions and procedures: a third way for the second pillar', *European Foreign Affairs Review*, 1 (1): 29–54.

Rein, M and Schon, D. (1991) 'Frame-reflective policy discourse', in P. Wagner, C.H. Weiss, B. Wittroch and H. Wollman (eds), *Social Sciences and Modern States. National Experiences and Theoretical Cross-roads*. Cambridge: Cambridge University Press.

Republic of Cyprus (1991) *Cyprus: The Way to Full EC Membership*. Press and Information Office.

Rhodes, C. and Mazey, S. (eds) (1995) *Building a European Polity?* Boulder, CO: Lynne Rienner.

Rhodes, R.A.M. (1986) *European Policy-Making, Implementation and Subcentral Governments: A Survey*. Maastricht: European Institute of Public Administration.

Rhodes, R.A.M. and Marsh, D. (1992) 'New directions in the study of policy networks', *European Journal of Political Research*, 21: 181–205.

Richardson, J. (1996) 'Policy-making in the EU: interests, ideas and garbage cans of primeval soup', in Richardson, J. (ed.), *European Union: Power and Policy-making*. London: Routledge. pp. 2–23.

Richardson, J. and Jordan, G. (1979) *Governing under Press: The Policy Process in a Post Parliamentary Democracy*. Oxford: Martin Robertson.

Risse-Kappen, T. (1995) *Co-operation Among Democracies*. Princeton, NJ: Princeton University Press.

Roche, M. (1991) 'Retour au rail à Londres', *Le Monde*, 30 May.

Rokkan, S. (1966) 'Norway: numerical democracy and corporate pluralism', in R.A. Dahl (ed.), *Political Oppositions in Western Democracies*. New Haven, CT: Yale University Press. pp. 70–115.

Rometsch, D. and Wessels, W. (eds) (1996) *The European Union and Member States. Towards Institutional Fusion?* Manchester: Manchester University Press.

Rometsch, D. and Wessels, W. (1997) 'The Commission and the Council of the Union', in G. Edwards and D. Spence (eds), *The European Commission*, second edition. London: Catermill.

Roney, A. (1995) *EC/EU Fact Book – a Complete Question and Answer Guide*. London Chamber of Commerce and Industry.

Rosecrance, R. (ed.) (1976) *America as an Ordinary Country*. Ithaca, NY: Cornell University Press.

Rosenthal, G. (1991) 'Education and training policy', in L. Hurwitz and C. Lequesne (eds), *The State Of The European Community*. Boulder, CO: Lynne Rienner. pp. 273–83.

Ross, G. (1995) *Jacques Delors and European Integration*. Cambridge: Polity Press.

Rotfeid, A.D. (1992) 'European security structures in transition', in SIPRI *Yearbook 1992: World Armaments and Disarmament*. Oxford: Oxford University Press. pp. 563–82.

Ruggie, G.R. (1975) 'International responses to technology: concepts and trends', *International Organization*, 29: 557–83.

Rummel, R. (1996) 'Germany's role in the CFSP: "Normalitat" or "Sonderweg"?' in C. Hill (ed.), *The Actors in Europe's Foreign Policy*. London: Routledge. pp. 40–67.

Ryba, R. (1995) 'Unity in diversity: the enigma of the European dimension in education', *Oxford Review of Education*, 21 (1): 25–36.

Røvik, K.A. (1998) *Moderne organisasjoner. Trender i organisasjonstenkningen ved årtusenskiftet*. Oslo: Fagbokforlaget.

Sandholz, W. and Zysman, J. (1989) '1992: Recasting the European Bargain', *World Politics*, XLII (1): 95–128.

Sandholz, W. (1993) 'Institutions and collective action: the new telecommunications in Western Europe', *World Politics*, (45): 242–70.

Sargent, L.A. (1985) 'Corporatism and the European Community', in W. Grant (ed.), *The Political Economy of Corporatism*. London: Macmillan. pp. 229–53.

Sargent, T. and Wallace, N. (1981) 'Some unpleasant monetarist arithmetic', *Quarterly Review*, Federal Reserve Bank of Minneapolis, (fall): 1–17.

Sbragia, A. (1991) 'Environmental policy in the political economy of the European Community', prepared for Workshop of The Consortium for 1992, May 1992, Stanford, California.

Sbragia, A.M. (ed.) (1992a) *Euro-Politics: Institutions and Policymaking in the 'New European Community'*. Washington, DC: The Brookings Institution.

Sbragia, A.M. (1992b) 'Thinking about the European future: the uses of comparison', in A.M. Sbragia (ed.), *Euro-politics: Institutions and Policymaking in the 'New European Community'*. Washington, DC: The Brookings Institution. pp. 257–92.

Sbragia, A. (1996) *Debt Wish. Entreprenerial Cities, U.S. Federalism, and Economic Development*. Pittsburgh, PA: University of Pittsburgh Press.

Scharpf, F.M. (1988) 'The joint-decision trap: lessons from German federalism and European integration', *Public Administration*, 66 (3): 239–78.

Scharpf, F.W. (1994) *Optionen des Föderalismus in Deutschland und Europa*. Frankfurt: Campus Verlag.

Scharpf, F.W. (1996) 'Politische Optionen im vollendeten Binnenmarkt', in M. Jachtenfuchs and B. Kohler-Koch (eds), *Europäische Integration*. Opladen: Leske and Budrich. pp. 109–41.

Scharpf, F. (1999) *Governing in Europe. Effective and Democratic?* Oxford: Oxford University Press.

Schengen Convention Border Controls (1990) *Commercial Laws of Europe*, Vol. 14, February 1991, Part 2.

Scherer, J. (1990) 'Regulatory instruments and EEC powers to regulate telecommunications services in Europe', in D. Elixmann and K.-H. Neumann (eds), *Communications in Europe*. Berlin: Springer. pp. 235–56.

Scherer, J. (ed.) (1998) *Telecommunications Law in Europe*, fourth edition. London: Butterworths.

Schimmelfennig, F. (1999) 'The double puzzle of EU enlargement. Liberal norms, rhetorical action and the decision to expand to the East'. ARENA-paper 15.

Schmeltzer, J. (1992) 'A speeding bullet seeing economic benefits, Texas takes lead as high-speed train projects gather steam in U.S.', *Chicago Tribune*, 12 January: 1.

Schmidt, S. (1991) 'Taking the long road to liberalization', *Telecommunications Policy*, 15: 209–22.

Schmidt, S.K. (1997) 'Sterile debates and dubious generalizations', Journal of Public Policy, 16 (3): 233–71.

Schmitter, P.C. (1974) 'Still the century of corporatism', Review of Politics, 1: 85–131.

Schmitter, P.C. (1977) 'Modes of interest intermediation and modes of societal change in Western Europe', Comparative Political Studies, 10: 7–38.

Schmitter, P.C. (1992) Interests, Powers, and Functions: Emergent Properties and Unintended Consequences in the European Polity. Department of Political Science, Stanford University.

Schmitter, P.C. (1996) 'Imagining the future of the Euro-polity with the help of new concepts', in G. Marks, F. Scharpf, P.C. Schmitter and W. Streeck (eds), Governance in the European Union. London: Sage. pp. 121–50.

Schmitter, P.C. and Streeck, W. (1990) Organized Interests and the Europe of 1992. Washington, DC: American Enterprise Institute.

Schmitter, P.C. and Streeck, W. (1992) 'Organized interests and the Europe of 1992', in N.J. Ornstein and M. Perlman (eds), Political Power and Social Change. The United States Faces a United Europe. Washington, DC: American Enterprise Institute.

Schneider, V. and Werle, R. (1990) 'International regime or corporate actor? The European Community in telecommunications policy', in K. Dyson and P. Humphreys (eds), The Political Economy of Communications. International and European Dimensions. London and New York: Routledge. pp. 77–106.

Schneider, V. and Werle, R. (1991) 'Policy networks in the German telecommunications domain', in B. Marin and R. Mayntz (eds), Policy Networks. Empirical Evidence and Theoretical Considerations. Frankfurt a.M.: Campus. pp. 97–136.

Scholten, L. (1987) Political Stability and Neo-Corporatism: Corporatist Integration and Societal Cleavages in Western Europe. London: Sage.

Schulte, B. (1997) 'Juridical instruments of the European Union and the European Communities', in W. Beck, L.J.G. Van der Maesen and A.C. Walker (eds), The Social Quality of Europe. The Hague/Boston: Kluwer Law International. pp. 45–66.

Schutte, J.J.E. (1991) 'Schengen: its meaning for the free movement of persons in Europe', Common Market Law Review, 28: 855–75.

Schwarze, J. and Schermers, H.G. (eds) (1988) Structure and Dimensions of European Community Policy. Baden-Baden: Nomos.

Scott, R.W. (1981) Organizations. Rational, Natural and Open Systems. Englewood Cliffs, NJ: Prentice-Hall.

Scott, R.W. (1991) 'Unpacking institutional arguments', in P.J. DiMaggio and W.W. Powell (ed.), The New Institutionalism. Chicago: University of Chicago Press.

Shapiro, M. (1992) 'The European Court of Justice', in A.M. Sbragia, (ed.) Euro-politics: Institutions and Policymaking in the 'New European Community'. Washington, DC: The Brookings Institution. pp. 123–56.

Shonfield, A. (1972) Europe: Journey to an Unknown Destination. London: Penguin Books.

Showstack, S.A. (1997) 'Political participation, political rights and the politics of daily life', in W. Beck, L.J.G. Van der Maesen and A.C. Walker (eds), The Social Quality of Europe. The Hague/Boston: Kluwer Law International. pp. 191–202.

Sidjanski, D. (1982) 'Les groupes de pression dans la Communauté européenne', Il politico, 3: 559–60.

Siedentopf, H. and Ziller, J. (eds) (1988a) Making European Policies Work, Vol. I: Comparative Syntheses. Brussels and London: EIPA/Sage.

Siedentopf, H. and Ziller, J. (eds) (1988b) *Making European Policies Work*, Vol. II: *National Reports*. Brussels and London: EIPA/Sage.

Silis, D.L. (ed.) (1972) *International Encyclopedia of the Social Sciences*, Vol. 13. New York: Macmillan.

Simon, S. and Duhot, M. (1994) *Environment and Europe*. Deventer: Kluwer Press.

Sjursen, H. (1997) *Western Policy-making in the Polish Crisis (1980–83): The Problem of Co-ordination*. PhD thesis, London School of Economics.

Sjursen, H. (1998) 'Missed opportunity or eternal fantasy? The idea of a European security and defence policy', in J. Peterson and H. Sjursen (ed.), *A Common Foreign Policy for Europe? Competing Visions of the CFSP*. London: Routledge. pp. 95–112.

Sjøstedt, G. (1977) *The External Role of the European Community*. Farnborough: Saxon House.

Skogerbø, E. and Storsul, T. (1998) 'National compromises and transnational alliances: the battle of universal service regulations in Europe', Arena Working Paper, University of Olso, No.11.

Slot, T. and Vershuren, P. (1990) 'Decision making speed in the European Community', *Journal of Common Market Studies*, XXXIX (1): 75–85.

Smith, K. (1995) *The Making of EU Foreign Policy: The Case of Eastern Europe*. PhD thesis, London School of Economics.

Smyrl, M. (1998) 'When and (how) do the Commission's preferences matter?', *Journal of Common Market Studies*, 36 (1): 79–99.

SOPEMI (1992) Continuous Reporting System on Migration. Paris: OECD.

SPRU-report (1989) *A Single European Market*. University of Sussex, Science Policy Research Unit.

Starr, P. (1989) 'The meaning of privatization', in S. Kamerman and A. Khan (eds), *Privatization and the Welfare State*. Princeton, NJ: Princeton University Press.

Stavridis, S. and Hill, C. (eds) (1996) *Domestic Sources of Foreign Policy: West European Reactions to the Falklands Conflict*. Washington, DC: Berg.

Stein, A.A. (1982) 'Coordination and collaboration: regimes in an anarchic world', *International Organization*, 36: 299–324.

Stern, J. (1990) *European Gas Markets. Challenges and Opportunities*. London: Royal Institute of International Affairs.

Stern, J. (1992) *Third Party Access in European Gas Industries. Regulation Driven or Market Led?* London: Royal Institute of International Affairs.

Stern, J.P. (1998) *Competition and Liberalization in the European Gas Market. A Diversity Model*. London: The Royal Institute of International Affairs.

Steunenberg, B. and Dimitrova, A. (1999) 'The search for convergence of national policies in the European Union: an impossible quest?': ARENA-paper 16.

Stinchecombe, A.L. (1997) 'On the virtues of the old institutionalism', *Annual Review of Sociology*, 23: 1–18.

Strang, D. and Meyer, J.W. (1993) 'Institutional conditions for diffusion', *Theory and Society*, 22: 487–511.

Streeck, W. (1999) 'Negotiating markets: rethinking the European social model'. Presidential Address, Society for the Advancement of Socio-Economics, Madison, Wisconsin, July.

Streeck, W. and Schmitter, P.C. (1991) 'From national corporatism to transnational pluralism: organized interests in the single market', *Politics and Society*, 2.

Subcommittee on High-Speed Rail Systems (1985) 'High-speed rail systems in the United States', *Journal of Transportation Engineering*, 2: 79–94.

Surel, Y. (1998) 'The role of cognitive and normative frames in policy-making', Florence: EUI-working paper 4.

Susskind, L.E. (1994) *Environmental Policy. Negotiating more Effective International Regimes*. Oxford: Oxford University Press.

Sverdrup, U. (1998) *Europesisering av budsjettsystemer*. Prosjektnotat ARENA.

Sweden, Utrikesdepartementets Handelsavdeling (1992) *Agreement on the European Economic Area*. 2 Vols. Stockholm, February.

Sweet, A.S. and Sandholtz, W. (1998) 'Integration, supranational governance, and the institutionalization of the European polity', in W. Sandholtz and A.S. Sweet (eds), *European Integration and Supranational Governance*. Oxford: Oxford University Press.

Taylor, P. (1991) 'The European Community and the state: assumptions, theories and propositions', *Review of International Studies*, (17): 109–25.

Taylor, P. (1996) *The European Union in the 1990s*. Oxford: Oxford University Press.

Teichler, U. (1996) 'Student mobility in the framework of ERASMUS: findings of an evaluation study', *European Journal of Education*, 31 (2): 153–80.

Telò, M. (ed.) (1994) *L'Union européenne et les défis de l'élargissement*. Brussels: Editions de l'Université de Bruxelles.

Teubner, G. (1992) 'Die vielkdpfige Hydra: Netzwerke als kollektive Akteure hoherer Ordnung', in W. Krohn and G. Kilppers (eds), *Emergenzund Selbstorganisation*. Frankfurt: Suhrkamp. pp. 189–216.

Thatcher, M. (1994) 'Regulatory reform in Britain and France: organizational structure and the extension of competition', *Journal of European Public Policy*, 1 (3): 441–64.

Thatcher, M. (1999) 'Liberalisation in Britain: from monopoly to regulation of competition', in K.A. Eliassen and M. Sjøvaag (eds), *European Telecommunications Liberalisation*. London: Routledge.

Thelen, K. (1999) 'Historical institutionalism in comparative politics', *Annual Review of Political Science*, 2: 369–404.

Thelen, K. and Steinmo, S. (1992) 'Historical institutionalism in comparative politics', in S. Steinmo, K. Thelen and F. Longstreth (eds), *Structuring Politics: Historical Institutionalism in Comparative Analysis*. Cambridge: Cambridge University Press.

Therborn, G. (1995) *European Modernity and Beyond. The Trajectory of European Societies 1945–2000*. London: Sage.

Therborn, G. (1997) *On Politics and Policy of Social Quality*. Uppsala: SCASS.

Thomson, D.F. (1987) *Political Ethics and Public Office*. Cambridge, MA: Harvard University Press.

Thornhill, J. (1991) 'Repackaged, recycled, restricted', *Financial Times*, 6 December: 17.

Toffler, A. (1990) *Power Shift. Knowledge, Wealth, and Violence at the Edge of the 21st Century*. New York: Bantam Books.

Tonra, Ben (1997) 'The impact of political cooperation', in Knud Erik Jørgensen (ed.), *Reflective Approaches to European Governance*. London: Macmillan. pp. 181–98.

Transport Europe (1995) 'High-speed rail networks: EU ministers ask how fast is a "high-speed Train"?', *Transport Europe*, (49), 23 March.

Travel Trade Gazette (1997) 'Eurostar derails Paris air traffic', 14 May: 37.

Travel Trade Gazette (1998) 'Rail links get up a head of steam', 15 July: 39.

Travel Trade Gazette Europa (1997) 'Common approach to fast-track Europe urged', 3 April: 9.

Treaty on European Union (1992) *Europe Documents*, No 1759/60, 7 February.

Tsebelis, G. (1994) 'The power of the European Parliament as an agenda setter', *American Political Science Review*, (88): 128–42.

Tulasiewicz, W. and Brock, C. (1994) 'Introduction', in C. Brock and W. Tulasiewicz (eds), *Education in a Single Europe*. London and New York: Routledge. pp. 1–20.

Tulder, R. van, and Junne, G. (1988) *European Multinationals in Core Technologies*. Chichester: Wiley.

Tunnels and Tunnelling (1997a) 'Europe's rail tunnels face budget constraints', May: 13.

Tunnels and Tunnelling (1997b) 'Italy's commitment to high speed rail links', April: 31.

Ulrich, S. (1994) 'Internationalt politisamarbeid', *Nordisk Tidsskrift for Kriminalvidenskap*.

Ungerer, H. (1989) *Telecommunications in Europe*. Luxembourg: Office for Publications of the EC.

Ungerer, H., Berben, C. and Costello, N.P. (eds) (1989) *Telecommunications for Europe 1992. The CEC Sources*. Amsterdam: IOS.

Ungerer, W. (1990) 'The development of the EC and its relationship to central and eastern Europe', *Aussenpolitik*, 41 (3): 229–30.

Union Internationale des Chemins de Fer (1989) *Proposal for a European High-speed Network*. Paris: UIC.

Usherwood, S. (1998) 'Energy policy', in G. Glöcker, L. Junius, S. Usherwood and J. Vassallo, *Guide to EU Policies*. London: Blackstone Press. pp. 120–31.

Van Craeyenest, F. (1989) 'La Nature jurisdique des résolutions sur la coopération en matiére d'éducation', in B. De Witt (ed.), *European Community Law of Education*. Baden-Baden: Nomos. pp. 127–33.

Van der Klugt, A. (1992) 'EC action in the field of education and Central and Eastern Europe', in J. Pertek (ed.), *General Recognition of Diplomas and Free Movement of Professionals, Seminar Proceedings*. Maastricht: European Institute of Public Administration. pp. 93–102.

Vandermeersch, D. (1987) 'The Single European Act and the environmental policy of the European Community', *European Law Review*, 12: 407–29.

Van Dijck, J. (1989) 'Towards transnationalization of economic and social life in Europe', *European Affairs*, 1.

Van Schendelen, M.P.C.M. (ed.) (1993) *National Public and Private EC Lobbying*. Aldershot: Dartmouth.

Vaubel, R. (1985) 'International collusion or competition for macroeconomic policy coordination?: a restatement', *Recherches Économiques de Louvain*, 51: 223–40.

Vaubel, R. (1998) Personal communication.

Verbruggen, M. (1997) 'The Commissions's Green Paper "Education, training, research: the obstacles to transnational mobility": content and comment', *European Journal for Education Law and Policy*, 1 (1–2): 41–8.

Verheijen, T. (1992) 'The PHARE programme', in J. Pertek (ed.), *General Recognition of Diplomas and Free Movement of Professionals, Seminar Proceedings*. Maastricht: European Institute of Public Administration. pp. 43–8.

Verhoest, P. (1995) 'Regionalism and telecommunications infrastructure competition', *Telecommunications Policy*, 19 (8): 637–45.

Vervaele, L.A.E. (1992) *Fraud against the Community – The Need for European Fraud Legislation*. Deventer and Boston: Kluwer Law and Taxation Publisher.

Vipond, P. (1995) 'European banking and insurance: business alliances and corporate strategies', in J. Greenwood (ed.), *European Casebook on Business Alliances*. Hemel Hempstead: Prentice-Hall.

Vogel, D. (1986) *National Styles of Regulation*. Ithaca, NY: Cornell University Press.

Von Hagen, J. (1993) 'The role of budgeting procedures for improving the fiscal performance of the member states of the EC', in A. Wildawsky and E. Zapico-Goni (eds), *National Budgeting for Economic and Monetary Union*. Dordrecht: Martinus Nijhoff.

Von Hagen, J. and Eichengreen, B. (1996) 'Federalism, Fiscal Restraints, and European Monetary Union', *AEA Papers and Proceedings*, 134–38.

Von Molthe, G. (1992) 'NATO takes up its new agenda', *NATO Review*, 40 (1): 3–7.

Wagerbaum, Rolf (1990) 'The European Community's policies on implementation of environmental directives', *Fordham International Law Journal*, 14: 455–77.

Walker, N. (1991) 'The United Kingdom police and European co-operation'. Working Paper, University of Edinburgh, Department of Politics.

Wallace, H. (1984) 'Implementation across national boundaries', in D. Lewis and H. Wallace (eds), *Policies into Practice: National and International Case Studies in Implementation*. London: Heineman Educational Books.

Wallace, Helen (1989) 'Widening and deepening: the European Community and the new European agenda'. *RIIA Discussion Paper* No 23. London: The Royal Institute of International Affairs.

Wallace, H. (1990) 'Making multilateral negotiations work', in Wallace, W. (ed.), *Dynamics of European Integration*. London: The Royal Institute of Internation Affairs. pp. 213–28.

Wallace, H. (1996a) 'The institutions of the EU: experience and experiments', in H. Wallace and W. Wallace (eds), *Policy-making in the European Union*. London: Oxford University Press.

Wallace, H. (1996b) 'Politics and policy in the European Union', in H. Wallace and W. Wallace (eds), *Policy-making in the European Union*. London: Oxford University Press. pp. 3–36.

Wallace, H. (1999) *European policies and polities*. 'Think piece' presented at Workshop on Governance and Citizenship, organized by DGXII, Brussels, 8–9 September 1999.

Wallace, H. and Wallace, W. (1996) *Policy-making in the European Union*. Oxford: Clarendon Press.

Wallace, H. and Wallace, W. (2000) *Policy Making in the European Union*. Oxford University Press. Oxford.

Wallace, W. (1983) 'Less than a federation, more than a regime: the Community as a political system', in H. Wallace, W. Wallace and C. Webb (eds), *Policy Making in the European Community*, second edition. Chichester: Wiley. pp. 403–36.

Waltz, K.N. (1979) *Theory of International Politics*. New York: McGraw-Hill.

Weale, Albert (1997) 'Democratic theory and the constitutional politics of the European Union', *Journal of European Public Policy*, 4: 665–9.

Weaver, R.K. and Rockman, B.A. (eds) (1993) *Do Institutions Matter? Government Capabilities in the United States and Abroad*. Washington, DC: The Brookings Institution.

Webber, D. (1998) 'High midnight in Brussels: an analysis of the September 1993 Council meeting on the GATT Uruguay Round', *Journal of European Public Policy*, 5 (4): 578–94.

Weber, M. (1993) *The Sociology of Religion*. Boston: Beacon Press.

Weiler, J.H.H. (1991) 'The Transformation of Europe', *The Yale Law Journal*, 100: 2403–83.

Weiler, J.H.H. (1997) 'Demos, telos, ethos and the Maastricht Decision', in P. Gowan and P. Anderson (eds), *The Question of Europe*. London: Verso. pp. 265–97.

Weiler, J.H.H., Haltern, U.R and Mayer, F.Z. (1995) *European Democracy and its Critique*, in J. Hayward (ed.), *The Crisis of Representation in Europe*. London: Frank Cass.

Weir, Margaret and Skocpol, Theda (1985) 'State structures and the possibilities for "Keynesian" responses to the Great Depression in Sweden, Britain, and the United States', in Peter Evans,

Dietrich Rueschemeyer and Theda Skocpol (eds), *Bringing the State Back In*. New York: Cambridge University Press. pp. 107–63.

Weitz, R. (1992a) 'The CSCE and the Yugoslav Conflict', *RFE/RL Research Report*, 1 (5): 24–6.

Weitz, R. (1992b) 'The CSCE's New Look', *RFE/RL Research Report*, 1 (6): 27–31.

Werle, R. (1990) *Telekommunikation in der Bundesrepublik. Expansion, Differenzierung, Transformation*. Frankfurt a.M.: Campus.

Werle, Raymund (1999) 'Liberalisation of telecommunications in Germany', in K.A. Eliassen and M. Sjøvaag (eds), *European Telecommunications Liberalisation*. London: Routledge.

Wessels, W. (1990) 'Administrative interaction', in W. Wallace (ed.), *The Dynamics of European Integration*. London: Frances Pinter. pp. 229–41.

Wessels, W. (1992) 'The EC and the new European architecture: the European Union as trustee for a (pan) European weal', in M. Telà (ed.), *Vers une nouvelle Europe?* Brussels: Editions de l'Université de Bruxelles. pp. 35–48.

Wessels, Wolfgang (1996) 'Evolutions possibles de l'Union européenne. Scénarios et stratégies pour sortir d'un cercle vicieux', *Politique Étrangère*, 61 (1): 139–50.

Wessels, W. (1997) 'An ever closer fusion? A dynamic macropolitical view on integration processes', *Journal of Common Market Studies*, 35 (2): 267–99.

Weyman-Jones, T.G. (1986) *Energy in Europe: Issues and Policies*. London: Methuen.

White, H. (1988) 'Varieties of markets', in B. Wellman and S.D. Berkowitz (eds), *Social Structures: A Network Approach*. New York: Cambridge University Press. pp. 226–60.

Wilks, S. (1992) 'The metamorphosis of European competition policy', Department of Politics Working Paper, Exeter, RUSEL Working Paper.

Wilks, S. (1996) 'Regulatory compliance and capitalist diversity in Europe', *Journal of European Public Policy*, 3 (4): 536–59.

Williamson, Oliver E. (1975) *Markets and Hierarchies: Analysis and Antitrust Implications*. New York: Free Press.

Williamson, Oliver E. (1985) *The Economic Institutions of Capitalism*. New York: Free Press.

Williamson, P.J. (1989) *Corporatism in Perspective: An Introductory Guide to Corporatist Theory*. London: Sage.

Wincott, D. (1996) 'The Court of Justice and the European policy process', in J. Richardson (ed.), *European Union: Power and Policy-making*. London: Routledge.

Wind, M. (1997) 'Rediscovering institutions: Allmenn reflectivist critique of rational institutionalism', in K.E. Jørgensen (ed.), *Reflective Approaches to European Integration*. New York: St Martin's Press.

Witte, E. (ed.) (1988) *Restructuring of the Telecommunications System. Report of the Government Commission for Telecommunications*. Heidelberg: R.v. Decker's.

Wyatt, D. and Dashwood, A. (1987) *The Substantive Law of the EEC*, second edition. London: Sweet & Maxwell.

Wæver, Ole (1996) 'European security identities', *Journal of Common Market Studies*, 34 (1): 103–32.

Zagorin, R. (1989) 'An expanding game', *Time Magazine*, 29 May.

Zelizer, V.A. (1988) 'Beyond the polemics on the Market: establishing a theoretical and empirical agenda', *Sociological Forum*, 4: 614–34.

Zysman, John (1983) *Governments, Markets, and Growth: Financial Systems and the Politics of Industrial Change*. Ithaca, NY: Cornell University Press.

Ørstrøm Møller, L. (1990) *Det Internationale Samfund*. Copenhagen: Akademisk Forlag.

INDEX